# HAND OF FIRE

"Few know Kirby's name but everyone is familiar with the characters he co-created: Captain America, the Hulk, the Fantastic Four, Thor and countless others. Kirby was the throbbing heart and soul of the American comic book industry and a crucial figure in global popular culture. Charles Hatfield's erudite and enthusiastic survey of Kirby's career is among the very best studies ever devoted to a cartoonist, a major work of scholarship that does justice to the creator's protean and influential life's work."

—**JEET HEER**, coeditor of the *Walt and Skeezix* books

"With judicious intelligence and infectious enthusiasm, Charles Hatfield takes on the daunting task of understanding the titanic career and accomplishments of Jack Kirby, emphasizing the crackling excitement of what he compellingly refers to as Kirby's 'delirious graphiation.' Focusing on two of the peak periods of Jack Kirby's long history of innovation—his years as Marvel's founding conceptualist and the self-edited/written/drawn Fourth World saga of the 1970s—*Hand of Fire* explores the specificity of Kirby's achievement without ignoring the very real commercial constraints on his practice and demonstrates the far-reaching legacy of his prodigious output. Hatfield helps us understand how Kirby's art works specifically as *narrative drawing* and explores its profound connection to the aesthetics of the sublime. His discussion of comic art in relation to sign theory represents an exciting contribution to comics studies."

—**SCOTT BUKATMAN**, author of *Matters of Gravity: Special Effects and Supermen in the 20th Century*

**GREAT COMICS ARTISTS SERIES**
M. Thomas Inge, General Editor

# HAND OF FIRE

## The Comics Art of Jack Kirby

## CHARLES HATFIELD

UNIVERSITY PRESS OF MISSISSIPPI • JACKSON

www.upress.state.ms.us

Designed by Peter D. Halverson

The University Press of Mississippi is a member of the Association of American
University Presses.

Publication of the book was made possible, in part, by a subvention from the
College of Humanities, California State University, Northridge.

First printing 2012

∞

Library of Congress Cataloging-in-Publication Data

Hatfield, Charles, 1965–
Hand of fire : the comics art of Jack Kirby / Charles Hatfield.
p. cm. — (Great comics artists series)
Includes bibliographical references and index.
ISBN 978-1-61703-177-9 (hardback) — ISBN 978-1-61703-178-6 (paper) —
ISBN 978-1-61703-179-3 (ebook)  1. Kirby, Jack—Criticism and interpretation.
2. Cartoonists—United States.  I. Title.
PN6727.K57Z69 2012
741.5'973—dc23                                          2011026939

British Library Cataloging-in-Publication Data available

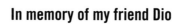

In memory of my friend Dio

# CONTENTS

# ACKNOWLEDGMENTS

This one's been a long time coming: not just the handful of years I've spent pushing and pulling at the book's text, not just the seventeen-plus years since my first professionally published article on Jack Kirby—my first professional publication, period—but much longer, so long, in fact, that the roots of the business are beyond the reach of my memory. I became an active collector of Kirby when I was ten (with *Kamandi* #32, dated August 1975) but I'm positive I knew his style well before that. It's as if Kirby has always been with me. As I said, a long time.

I'm glad, though, that I took my time getting to this. As much as this book is the result of a childhood fascination, it is also the result of work done and bridges crossed over the past several years. I couldn't have done what I've done here even a handful of years ago. I definitely could not have done without the friends and colleagues I've lucked into over the past fifteen years or so as I've pursued writing about comics.

I can't name everyone who has helped me get to this point; I can't remember them all. For that I'm sorry. But I thank the following for lending information, support, and images, and in some cases a critical eye, in recent times: Tim Bavlnka, Bart Beaty, Steve Bissette, Isaac Cates, Michael T. Gilbert, Gene Kannenberg, Marc Kardell, Mike Rhode, Mark Rogers, Ben Saunders, Marc Singer, Rusty Witek, and Kent Worcester. I also want to thank John Morrow and Jon B. Cooke for past and present help, and for boosting my understanding of Kirby and of comics. Many thanks as well to Tom Roberts for helping me get in the game, and Tom Inge for opening the window of opportunity for this project.

Emphatic thanks are due to Craig Fischer and Jarret Keene, who generously reviewed the manuscript in beta and whose feedback made a world of difference; Ian Gordon and Jeet Heer, who, crucially, did the same at the next phase; and Scott Bukatman and Paul Gravett, who read and cheered as the book hurtled over the finish line. Special thanks, doubly underlined, go to my editor Walter Biggins, whose tireless eyes and ears and great patience enabled me to get there. Finally, thanks to Pete Halverson for elegant design and Geoff Grogan for the beautiful cover.

Some raw materials for what follows appeared in *The Comics Journal*'s Kirby memorial issue of April 1994 (#167), my aforesaid "first," and in scattered issues of *The Jack Kirby Collector* between 1995 and 2002. I thank both magazines for being crucial parts of my writing and reading life. Also, some elements appeared in the catalog for the exhibition *Faster than a Speeding Bullet: The Art of the Superhero*, which ran at the University of Oregon's Jordan Schnitzer Museum of Art in fall 2009. In addition, portions were presented to the Comic Arts Conference (2003 and 2008), the Glasscock Center for Humanities Research (2006), the American Literature Association (2007), the Museum of Comic and Cartoon Art Festival (2009), and the *Understanding Superheroes* conference that accompanied the Schnitzer exhibition (2009). Finally, I thank California State University, Northridge for facilitating my research via the Jerome Richfield Memorial Scholarship (2005–06) and two Research, Scholarship and Creative Activity Awards (2005–06 and 2007–08), and the CSUN College of Humanities in particular for providing a subvention to help support the book's production.

As always, a shout-out to my brother Scott (Free), whose homemade comics are the first I can remember, and to my entire extended family. Most particular thanks—fervent, babbling thanks, with a Kirbyesque shower of exclamation points—to my own Forever People, the ones who make it all worthwhile, Michele, Coleman, and Nick. TAARU!!!

And thank you to Jack Kirby, though much too late, for a lifetime of reading, gazing, and sheer slack-jawed delight—a dream from which I have yet to wake.

I dedicate this one to the memory of Dionisio (Dio) Sanchez (1965–2010), fellow fan and writer, who mastered the art of friendship.

# HAND OF FIRE

Fig. 1. The burning hand. Jack Kirby, with Mike Royer (inks and lettering), "The Pact." *The New Gods* #7 (Feb.–Mar. 1972), page 20, panel 5. © DC Comics.

# INTRODUCTION

And across the wall a hand of flame . . .
— *The New Gods* #7 (1972)

A wall of white stone stands alone in a barren, wind-whipped field. Rugged yet ageless—unadorned, enigmatic, and still—the wall is a slab higher than any man is tall. A silent sentinel, this slab stands as if waiting. For what?

A man approaches, in the aspect of a pilgrim: frayed, war-weary, staff in hand, and stripped to the waist. He stops before the wall. Inside himself this man is bearing a heavy weight.

The wall stands as if in expectation, as if waiting for the man to reach out, to speak out. The man suddenly shouts, shaking his staff toward the wall, flinging his name and his terrible burden outward as if in challenge. Abruptly the wall answers with a deafening WABOOOMM!!—and a hand of fire sweeps across the slab, writing on its obdurate white surface, in flaming characters, a message of grace, inspiration, and counsel.

Across the wall, the pyrographic hand inscribes its meaning, transforming blank whiteness into a signifying surface (fig. 1). Its index finger—pointing, writing—is a stylus of fire. The message is so much cosmic calligraphy.

Or cartooning.

Here, faced by this synthetic, hand-me-down image—an echo of the prophetic writing on the wall that appears in the Book of Daniel, also of the inscribed tablets of Exodus, perhaps too a reminder of Michelangelo's hand of god, finger pointing toward creation—we are in the graphic world of Jack Kirby, cartoonist. The image hails from a late-career work by Kirby, the comic book *The New Gods* #7, which he wrote and drew in 1971, said to be one of his favorites. If Kirby's pilgrim—Izaya—is obviously confronting God, it takes but a little critical nerve to see the wall's provoking whiteness as also the (to a cartoonist) ever-challenging white blankness of the uninscribed page.

Characteristically, Kirby sees the Absolute—he calls it the Source—as an inscribing hand, and its message as an act of divine graphiation. Yet the text on this page tells us that it is not the wall so much as the pilgrim who must "communicate"; it is the man who must put the question to the Source Wall and provoke its answer. The question is born of desperation, out of a life of violence, struggle, and confusion. The answer is delivered in typically robust Kirby fashion: an explosion and a vision. This is the kind of delirious mythmaking that Jack Kirby brought to comics.

Kirby (1917–1994) was an American cartoonist and writer embedded in comics, a field he entered while still in his teens. For more than forty years, Kirby worked steadily at comics, including both newspaper comic strips and periodical comic books, but he spent most of his time on the latter: the roughly half-tabloid-size, newsstand-ready comic book, or magazine, as it developed from the mid-thirties. That format, the "comic book" so beloved of collectors, still represents for many the kernel identity of American comics, and it was in said format that Jack Kirby excelled. With his dynamic, eccentric style, Kirby left a deep and unmistakable handprint on both the comic book and the industry that grew up around it. That his work has been so widely imitated, to the point of becoming an industry standard in the 1960s, does not lessen its eccentricity—its peculiar charm and energy—but has made it more difficult to appreciate his genuine impact. Influence, when widespread enough, camouflages itself.

"Kirby" became, over forty-plus years of almost uninterrupted comic book production, part of the very atmosphere breathed by comic artists and fans, indeed an enveloping constant of comics culture. "Kirbyesque" is a familiar adjective to comic book enthusiasts, and "doing Kirby" is something many, many comic artists have attempted, some repeatedly and even obsessively. In short, Jack Kirby is one of the premier visual stylists and storytellers—for some readers *the* premier artist, in American comic book history.

Starting in the late thirties and persisting to the late seventies, Kirby produced comic book work on a monthly basis, with but one significant interruption: his time as an infantryman during World War II. He was to carry this war experience around with him for the rest of his life, often telling war stories full of odd, unassuming details and spiced with a generous sense of the absurd. He was, by most accounts, a voluble yarn-spinner, particularly where the war was concerned: he had a fund of battlefield stories, tales so tall that listeners sometimes wondered about their truthfulness but that he told with absolute conviction. These stories were to inform his work and his life, as indeed nightmares about the war are said to have dogged his sleep for the rest of his days (Evanier, *King* 69).

Kirby's sense of life was, by all evidences, conflictual; for him the idea that stories are based in conflict was not a learned abstraction but a gut-level understanding, a basic intuition stemming, it seems, from his violence-fraught childhood in the claustral tenements of New York's fabled Lower East Side. Born Jacob or "Jakie" Kurtzberg, the first son of Austrian Jewish immigrants, Kirby would characterize his early days as nail-tough, hardscrabble, full of street fights and physical threats. A kid interested in reading and drawing might have had a crushingly hard time in such an environment, but Kirby, described over and over as a scrapper, learned to weather the violence of what he later called the "street code" and, boxer-like, carried with him forever after a mix of seething anger, brash, almost pugnacious self-sufficiency, and gentlemanly kindness, the latter fondly remembered by his colleagues and fans. In-depth descriptions of Kirby—there have been many—unfailingly reveal a generosity of spirit and gentleness with family and friends that belie the brawling ferocity, the sheer kinetic oomph, and the tamped-down, rechanneled anger that characterize his best-known comics work.

Fighting for space in the teeming density of the Lower East Side, and spurred by economic desperation, Kirby learned to be an illustrator and cartoonist (he is said to have drawn on whatever was available, including the floor of his tenement) as well as a devoted moviegoer and reader. He became a fan of fantastic literature, mythology, pulps, and the early, embryonic science fiction of his day, and this heady jumble of classics, classics-in-the-making, and unembarrassed junk stocked his imagination, giving him characters, stories, and tropes he would continually recycle—reinvent—in the years ahead. Yet his early experiences in the Lower East Side, which in later life he described as a multiethnic battleground, never left him. Life in the tenements as an adolescent led him to a benevolent youth organization called the Boys Brotherhood Republic, which, following scholar Kenneth Kidd (*Making American Boys*), we might describe as a "boy work" institution dedicated to channeling boyhood ferociousness toward mutually supportive, prosocial ends.

Here, as well as on the streets, Kirby developed the attitudes toward rough-and-tumble boyhood he would draw from in his later work. Crucially, the BBR gave him an understanding of male camaraderie that suggested a way out of the goading poverty, endemic social misery, and rooftop battles—in sum, the astringent toughness—of tenement life. He brought his BBR experience to a comic book genre that, along with longtime partner Joe Simon, he founded—the kid gang, a chip off Hollywood's then-popular *Dead End* or "East Side Kids" film formula (launched in 1937), but imbued with Kirby's firsthand knowledge. Kirby helped launch quite a few of these "gangs": *The Young Allies, The Newsboy Legion, The Boy Commandoes, Boy Explorers, Boys' Ranch*, and, in later, post-Simon comics, the mutant *X-Men*, the godlike *Forever People*, and the unsung *Dingbats of Danger Street*. He would also draw from the kid gang formula to create or co-create such adult superhero teams as the *Challengers of the Unknown* and *The Fantastic Four*, and even knock out war stories about gangs of battle-hardened soldiers such as *Sgt. Fury*'s "Howling Commandos" and "The Losers."

For Kirby, life was defined by conflict and, paradoxically, camaraderie. His work, in whatever genre, embodied terrible urgency and, at its most optimistic, a countervailing sense of brotherly connection. Tenement life squeezed him out, the Boys Brotherhood Republic shaped him, and WWII (by which time he was already a committed comics professional) intensified his brisk, action-filled, conflictual style, above all his agonistic sense of what it was to be alive and to tell stories. Everything he did as a narrative artist—everything recognizably "Kirby"—was informed by this sense of life as a battle, even the quiet stillnesses that paced and prepared for the action. While he picked up his narrative rhythms and the rudiments of style from such obvious sources as Milton Caniff's masterful adventure strips and of course the popular films of the day, the restive, explosive qualities of his work were authentically Kirby and bred in the bone.

Kirby's work manifested other qualities: romance, for example, sentimentality, a certain loopy sense of humor, and, visually, the lilting, balletic grace often exhibited by his figures. Yet what defined him as a comic artist was, above all, violent action and the potential for action—and a vaulting determination to overcome constraints. Oddly enough, his most commercially potent work carried these qualities into two genres that, in terms of audience and outlook, appear categorically opposed: the costumed superhero genre, which he jolted to life early on with his headlong, violent approach to action—and the romance genre, launched by Simon and Kirby after the model of women's pulp magazines and usually tightly constrained in contrast to the hurtling eagerness of the superhero.

These two genres, considered opposites in terms of (gendered) audience address and style, were Kirby's bread-and-butter mainstays for large chunks of his career. Romance demanded a lot of Kirby's time in the 1940s and '50s. While more famous by far for his superheroes, he produced, co-produced, and oversaw the production of scads of now-neglected romance comics, and, despite a professed impatience with the genre, contributed some of its most dramatically charged work.

In fact, Kirby, over forty-plus years, tried his hand at just about every genre then popular in comic books: superheroes, romance, crime, horror, westerns, war, science fiction, globetrotting adventure, and even (briefly) funny animals,

*Archie*-style teen humor, and *Classics Illustrated*. Kirby's oeuvre extends from *Captain America Comics* to *Young Romance*, from *Black Magic* to *Police Trap*, from *Western Love* to *Foxhole* to the *Strange World of Your Dreams*—and all these in only the first half of his career. His diversity and the sheer daunting volume of his output (roughly estimated at 21,000 pages) are matters of pride among fans. Though Kirby was said not to be the fastest comic book artist of his day, nor the most technically gifted, he was the *best* of the fastest, and the most imaginatively driven, and so produced a near-suffocating quantity of work at a high standard. Admittedly, much of Kirby's work was of assembly-line nature and thus only glancingly touched by him; many comics bearing his telltale hand appear diffuse, uneven, and hardly Kirbyesque. Even much of the work solely attributable to Kirby is compromised; comparatively few of his comics achieved the gemlike formal consistency and precision more often reached by such peers as Will Eisner or Harvey Kurtzman. Yet much of Kirby's work is highly accomplished, and many of his comics are fierce and memorable. The best are stunningly conceived and rendered, crackling with his full imaginative commitment to the work and boasting a resistless narrative pulse and ineffable graphic genius. Given his backbreaking output, Kirby's work should be judged by these high points—though the drastic inconsistency and hasty, often faddish and opportunistic nature of his work should also be borne in mind.

Kirby's prolificacy points to a basic problem in the reception of comics as they enter critical acceptance and academic study: until recently, few American comic book artists had the time or freedom for rumination, refinement, or revision, and the breakneck periodical scheduling of their work practically ensured that some rough or ill-finished work would be made public. For most comic book artists of Kirby's generation, the ratio of unpublished to published work, that is, rough drafts to finished work, was small; sketching and drafting were unthinkable luxuries. Pages were composed, not at leisure, but against tight deadlines. The nature of the comic book industry made near-impossible the deliberate cultivation of style and the advantages of conscious artistic self-discovery. The medium's production rhythm, as Jean-Paul Gabilliet has put it, "compromised the research necessary for innovation" (130).

Artists in the field had to grow up and make their mistakes in public. What's more, they had to start work that other people finished, and finish work others started. Finally, comic book artists of Kirby's era typically received no royalties, meaning no incentives for outstanding or very popular work. No fan culture yet existed to sustain and glorify them, and no star system to highlight and capitalize on their names. Hence they were forced to produce new pages, day in, day out, at flat rates, as if fused to their drawing tables, with little opportunity to step away from the work or consider new approaches to suit new projects. Kirby's default approach, so well adapted to this peculiar business environment, kept him working at a constant pitch for decades; the relentless pace of his working life determined the breathless narrative pacing of the comics themselves.

As much as any artist, Kirby embodied what was necessary to survive in the comic book industry—the unflagging speed, energy, and eagerness to please that were part of the toolkit of the early comic book artist—even as, over the long haul, he and his family suffered from the instability bred by industry conditions and practices. He was perhaps uniquely adapted to an industry that nonetheless treated him poorly, and, ironically, his drive to survive such treatment, to prosper under such conditions, is the very thing that led him to become the master of impatient, explosive, hyperkinetic action comics. Eventually he became so well conditioned that he could work only at full tilt. The circumstances that demanded constant output from Kirby, and thus made his work so uneven, also shaped his signature style; his powers as an artist are inseparable from the working conditions that, over the years, caused him so much grief. That is why latter-day readings of Kirby as simply a victim or martyr to industry conditions cannot help but be ironic.

Kirby galvanized many comic book genres and had an extensive, mazy, bemusingly complex career, so it seems strange he should publicly be known mainly as the superhero artist *par excellence*. Yet he is linked to superheroes as John Ford is to westerns: he excelled at them, and something of his personal outlook or sensibility inheres in them. The recognition of Kirby's superhero work, particularly his comics of the 1960s, is what has positioned him critically and drives the continuing interest in his art. Though he seemed at home in many genres, none were more hospitable to him than superheroes, which, increasingly over the course of the sixties, enabled him to access different issues, themes, and characters; to crystallize and grow into his trademark late style; to attempt stories of apocalyptic scope, which gave his graphic imagination freer play and greater challenges; and, in sum, to raise the stakes of the newsstand comic book. During the sixties this new infusion of Kirby's graphic energy, high-concept bravura, and mythopoeic grandeur practically transformed superheroes into a new genre, one that has sustained the comic book specialty market and fandom for decades and that now hails us, with bemusing frequency, from multiplex, television, and videogame screens.

We can and should be more precise about why Kirby is indelibly linked to superheroes. Many reasons come to mind. For one, the genre perfectly fit his violent, conflictual understanding of story and his gut impulses as a storyteller. For another, Kirby contributed novel and exciting work to the genre at two different stages of his career, both during the formative age (in fan parlance, the Golden Age) of comic books in the 1940s and during the transformative (or Silver) age of the sixties.[1] Thirdly, through superheroes Kirby stretched as a cartoonist, graphically and thematically, nudging the genre in the direction of epic fantasy and science fiction. This trend, beginning at Marvel Comics in the sixties, climaxed in the early seventies with a grandly conceived but abortive experiment at rival publisher DC Comics. This experiment, the so-called Fourth World, is of great importance to the following study. It included several different but interrelated series that launched simultaneously, a new and risky strategy for expanding the scope of superhero comics. This "stretching" of the genre enabled much that has occurred in comic books since, enlarging the thematic horizons of the field in such a way that the grand structural ambitions of the Fourth World are now commonplace.

Fourthly, Kirby's work on the Marvel superheroes of the sixties, in particular *Thor* (1962–1970) and most particularly *The Fantastic Four* (1961–1970), established the definitive and oft-imitated late-Kirby style: the visual template from which much subsequent superhero work has derived, and which indeed Marvel embraced as a house style. Through these books, Kirby became the "Kirby" known to most present-day comic book fans, and the default stylist for superheroes. Finally, and most famously, Kirby created or co-created, designed and co-designed, much of the so-called Marvel Universe of characters and concepts, establishing the brand now owned by the publicly traded corporation Marvel Entertainment (or rather, by its owner as of this writing, The Walt Disney Company), and in recent years assiduously adapted to film, electronic gaming, toys, apparel, and other merchandising.[2] Kirby, in collaboration with Marvel's then-leading scriptwriter and editor-in-chief Stan Lee, co-created such properties as the Fantastic Four, the Hulk, the X-Men, the Avengers, the Silver Surfer, and the Black Panther, often providing the initial spark of inspiration and almost always serving as the characters' first designer.

What *co-created* really means varies from example to example, but it is clear that Kirby was much more than an illustrator: he was designer, development artist—co writer at the least—and, always, graphic storyteller. In most cases, as will be argued in what follows, he independently plotted the stories on which he worked; in many cases he in effect wrote the first drafts of these stories under Lee's editorship. The stories were typically generated *graphically* (a major theme of what follows). Exactly how Kirby did this and under what circumstances, and what the nature of his contribution to Marvel was, may become better understood—and certainly will be more often debated—as a result of pending litigation, for suits and countersuits over copyright are now in progress between Kirby's heirs and Marvel.[3]

Legal controversy aside, the Marvel period of the sixties was the dazzling second act of Kirby's already-remarkable career. It was a needed shot in the arm for, on the long term perhaps the salvation of, New York's beleaguered comic book industry. It was also the period of Kirby's maturation as a cartoonist and the crystallizing of his style and sensibility. That is why this study takes the sixties period as its conceptual center. Kirby's grand-scale mythic take on the superhero helped revitalize the periodical comic book, then already a marginal and declining medium, by inspiring an ongoing act of creation: the continual building and rebuilding of a fictive universe shared by scores of creators and hundreds of thousands of devout readers. Once that universe was established, however, Kirby chafed. He felt himself sidelined by Stan Lee's growing public presence, frustrated by Lee's exclusive editorial control over their co-created properties, undervalued and denied due financial assurances by the company's owners, and denied the freedom to take comics to what was, for him, the logical next step. During the late sixties, he delayed taking that step while dreaming up a battery of new characters and concepts that, uncharacteristically, he withheld from Marvel, in hopes either of moving to a new publisher or, perhaps, improving his bargaining position with Marvel—if and when the time came.

Late in 1970 Kirby launched these new properties at Marvel's competitor, DC Comics (then still officially a part of National Periodical Publications), in a suite of interrelated comic books that came to be known, first among fans and later officially, as The Fourth World. This project, launched, oddly enough, with a run (1970–71) on the long-lived Superman spin-off series *Superman's Pal, Jimmy Olsen*, revolved around *The New Gods* (1971–72) and included sister titles *The Forever People* (1971–72) and *Mister Miracle* (1971–74). All these series shared a common conflict and villain, the über-fascist Darkseid, whose plans to enslave all life were opposed by a motley group of demigods and heroes. The Fourth World was to be Kirby's magnum opus: a coordinated, orchestrated project of unprecedented scope, a multi-pronged epic that did all that Marvel's *Fantastic Four* and *Thor* had done, but without Stan Lee's intervening, diluting, and (to Kirby) now-intolerable presence.

The Fourth World *was* all this, but, in addition, it was a work of reckless, careening improvisation. It was also, admittedly, a relative commercial failure— or at least not a glorious, Marvel-toppling success—prompting DC suddenly to cancel *The New Gods* and *The Forever People* late in 1972. This wrenching disappointment came as a breakpoint for Kirby, nearly killing his already-wounded faith in the viability of the comic book industry. Though *Mister Miracle* continued for a while (a limping shadow of its old self) and Kirby went on to produce other lively work for DC, the company's abandonment of the Fourth

World stunned him. His remaining years in the industry would be colored by this setback. It was here, at DC in the early seventies, that Kirby first became known among fans as both an auteur and a sacrificial figure.

Kirby the Auteur was at times controversial, for his untrammeled eccentricity alienated as many readers as it enthralled. After the Fourth World, his devoted fans increasingly found themselves playing the role of apologists for the oddness of his work, and in truth his career entered a downward slide. Yet this late-period Kirby, post 1970, whether commercially successful during its original publication or not, is what enables us to read his total output retrospectively and tease out themes and preoccupations that are distinctly his. The "Jack Kirby" of the seventies, though wounded and by some measures stumbling, at last moved out of the shadows of other creators and was fully recognized as a writer as well as cartoonist. Granted, his writing is often described as an acquired taste; his cadences are sometimes frantic, his captions wildly emphatic. There is at times a stilted, or alternately a hysterical, quality about his way with words. At other times, however, there is a savage eloquence and an underrated narrative and thematic shrewdness. His strongest texts possess a hallucinatory quality by turns giddy and terrifying. In any case, despite initial skepticism, Kirby's experiments brought a sense of cosmic scale to fantasy and adventure comics that the industry has sought to inhabit ever since. The Fourth World has proved the most influential failed series in the history of the superhero.

Kirby's leap to DC in 1970 gave him an opportunity to stake a name for himself as the credited writer and editor—in a word, author—as well as illustrator of his own tales. "Edited, written and drawn by Jack Kirby," or some variation thereof, was his most typical byline in the DC comics of the early seventies, the Fourth World and all the rest. Kirby was to claim similar credit for his creations throughout the rest of his career, a final period that established him as the rash, impatient mind behind some quirky and, commercially speaking, only fitfully successful comics—almost all of which, ironically, would later be revived by a comics industry anxiously seeking new concepts to colonize. Some of Kirby's late productivity would inspire endless tinkering and revamping (The Fourth World, *The Demon*, *The Eternals*); some would be selectively strip-mined for serviceable concepts (e.g., *OMAC*, *Machine Man*); some would be willfully ignored or criticized for playing hob with established comic book continuity and neglecting the significant tonal shifts in mainstream comics (his late runs on *Black Panther* and *Captain America*). At least one beloved series would resist significant revamping and enjoy no major relaunch to date despite scattered attempts: *Kamandi, the Last Boy on Earth*. All of these properties were recognized as Kirby's brainchildren, and, in their original versions, peculiar to his sensibility. To the extent that they made that sensibility distinct, that is, to the extent they delivered undiluted Kirby, all these late works would influence subsequent attempts to parse out Kirby's and Stan Lee's respective contributions to Marvel and determine their respective shares of creative "credit" for the Marvel Universe.

In short, it was in the seventies that Kirby ostensibly freed himself from editorial interference and finally became identified as an independent creator: not half of Simon & Kirby, not half of Lee & Kirby. He emerged as an auteur with a voice, preoccupations, and tics of his own. Solo Kirby, without the benefit of Lee's active editorship, found fans and detractors; no longer would the artist's name be greeted uniformly with adulation. Frankly, the new work was strange, and, by contrast to the capering effervescence of vintage Lee, sometimes distant. The scripting could be prolix. Often it was bizarrely inflected, with a thumping earnestness and showering of exclamation points that made Lee's hyperbole seem, if not understated, then at least controlled. Yet Kirby's writing could also be weirdly powerful. It is Kirby's work of the seventies, after the Lee/Kirby explosion yet prior to his strained post-retirement comics in the mid-eighties, which most fully reveals his talent for broad-strokes mythopoesis, his apocalyptic imagination, and the tameless ferocity of his graphic sense. If the Marvel of the sixties was the pivot of his career, the work Kirby produced from 1970 through 1978 is that which most effectively expresses his personal sensibilities.

Kirby's oh-so-promising, then brutally disappointing, period at DC spurred his final, last-ditch return to Marvel (1976–78), still nominally editing his own books but never free from editorial muzzling. At Marvel in the mid-seventies, he would produce works of increasingly frenzied storytelling and continued graphic brilliance, notwithstanding the company's inferior production standards. His work was no longer very popular; in fact many regarded this last stay at Marvel as a disaster. Even as Kirby redirected old characters—Captain American, The Black Panther—in controversial ways, he created several new, and to many fans, perplexing, properties, the most ambitious of which was the apocalyptic science fantasy series *The Eternals*. This final run at Marvel constitutes the end of Kirby's sustained relationship with mainstream comics, the breakpoint beyond which he would retire, at least in name, from the comic book business, and, from this reader's point of view, the last extended run of consistently readable Kirby. Afterwards Kirby went to work in the animation field, to his great satisfaction but with little impact, then produced a brief spate of comic book work for independent publishers (1981–84) in which his editorship at last went unchallenged but his narrative eccentricities had fossilized into a repertoire of odd and distracting mannerisms. These very late stories were at times nearly incoherent in their frothing, emphatic tone. A brief, post-retirement foray at DC yielded only reminders of Kirby's glory days, despite an ill-starred attempt to finish the Fourth World (1984–85) as well as a lamentable toy-merchandising series featuring DC and Fourth World characters (*Super Powers*, 1984–85). The latter was drawn but not scripted by Kirby, now physically debilitated and clearly unable to conjure his accustomed powers. It is known that in later years he suffered from a palsied hand (the result of a stroke) and faltering eyesight, and these troubles, over time, sadly reduced his drawing to a crabbed and shaky memory of what it had been (Evanier, *King* 138, 208–09). This was the autumnal period for Kirby, after which he effectively retired for good, approaching age seventy.

The years from 1970 to 1985 define solo "Kirby" in all its frantic, outward-thrusting, undomesticated strangeness. From 1977 or early 1978 onward, the work becomes so narratively convulsive, so visually uneven (with a style in obvious decline), and so dependent on overworked concepts as to drive off all but loyalists. Even here there are bursts of goosepimply excitement—for instance, the early issues (1981–82) of *Captain Victory and the Galactic Rangers* are positively febrile—but at this point considerations of narrative and craft frankly take second place to wallowing in the fervidly Kirbyesque for its own sake (something I confess to enjoying, but, then, I'm afflicted with the special helplessness of the fan). For this reason it is Kirby's work from 1970 through the late mid-seventies that best represents Kirby the Auteur, one with a style and outlook that render him distinctive and, though often imitated, truly inimitable. The Kirby of the seventies casts a light backward to the fevered inventiveness of Marvel in the sixties (still tethered by Stan Lee's editorial savvy) and forward to the spectacularly declining though obviously personal work of the eighties.

With that in mind, the present study favors mid to late Kirby: from the sixties at Marvel through the early seventies at DC, and then again to the mid-seventies at Marvel, with 1978 as an endpoint. Kirby's work from these periods animates current discussion of his career, and is that which is most avidly replayed, repackaged, and exploited in today's comics and other media. Therefore it is my focus. Implicitly, then, this book is structured by sizeable absences and in effect downplays or merely synopsizes much of Kirby's long career—an unavoidable move, in my view, since that career encompasses so many book-length studies' worth of material. Readers will, I hope, grant the impossibility of treating all of Kirby directly and deeply in one volume, and focus less on what I have omitted than on what I am able to accomplish.

I have set out to offer neither a full biography of the man—biographical resources are listed in our Appendix—nor a thorough bibliography, but rather a critical point of entry and a reexamination, one that aims to help uninitiated readers and Kirby fans alike to appreciate and place in context his most celebrated works. What biographical information I have given is for the sake of explaining Kirby's working life: its busyness and rhythms, its gains and reversals, and its creative satisfactions and frustrations, as I understand them. I should add that, though this is not a history of the comic book industry, it does describe some of the environments in which Kirby worked, most notably Marvel in the sixties, because those environments shaped and motivated his art. I have emphasized the work and Kirby's investment in it, avoiding biographical speculation that could not be corroborated. What follows, then, is a critical study and appreciation, with emphases formal and thematic. My goals are to highlight the works for which Kirby is best known, explore those works thematically and as expressions of his authorial sensibility, and encourage a deeper appreciation of the mature Kirby as both cartoonist and storyteller. Other critical and biographical studies will, I expect, extend and deepen what I do here. Fan studies of Kirby are plentiful—again, see our Appendix—and further academic studies will surely follow.

That said, I think it important to sketch in the contours of Kirby's career at the outset, if only to acknowledge its breadth and for the sake of directing the possibly disoriented reader. Thus Chapter 0 (if I may) offers a brief overview of Kirby's working life. This synopsis will hopefully remind readers of the full extent of Kirby's work—including those aspects I must leave unexamined—while providing reference points necessary to navigate through the rest of the book.

Of course, other important navigational aids would be examples of Kirby's work itself. Those wanting a relevant sample of Kirby to consult alongside this book are referred to the now in-print compilations of his sixties and seventies work at Marvel and DC, with the proviso that reading said work in reprints is a different experience than reading it in its original, now hard-to-find comic book editions. In fact few of the reprints—reproductions, rather—come close to capturing the original experience. Marvel reproductions in particular, given the apparent lack of available original art or first-generation film for some of the comics in question, have been faulted for their variable quality, and in some cases may have entailed undocumented touchup work, or even tracing or redrawing, resulting in subtle changes to linework. That said, for convenience's sake I refer readers to: the Marvel Masterworks or lower-cost Marvel Essentials editions of the series *Fantastic Four*, *Thor*, *Uncanny X-Men*, and the sixties' *Captain America* (the number of volumes per series varies depending on edition); DC's recent Omnibus editions of Kirby's seventies work, in particular the *Fourth World* (four volumes) and *The Demon* (one volume); and Marvel's trade paperback reprinting of *The Eternals* (two volumes). In addition, Titan Books' recent *The Best of Simon and Kirby* and the DC Show-case Presents edition of *Challengers of the Unknown*, Vol. 1, would be helpful. These titles, of course, represent only the iceberg's tip—and it is certain that the amount and formatting of Kirby in print will have changed by the time this book goes to press. For further information on Kirby and Kirbyana in print as of this writing, see the Appendix.[4]

While Chapter 0 signposts the phases of Kirby's career, Chapter 1 seeks to establish a background of a different kind by analyzing some of the formal dimensions of Kirby's art. Diverting from historical to aesthetic questions, I focus on a core issue, Kirby's *narrative drawing*, in particular the hallmarks and gradual distillation of his graphic style. This chapter describes more precisely qualities of Kirby's work that are usually described impressionistically: its liveliness, forcefulness, and idiosyncrasy. Admittedly, the chapter is in part a study in the impossibility of (if also the inevitable critical impulse toward) rendering comic art into words. After all, pictures, as James Elkins says in *On Pictures and the Words That Fail Them*, are irreducibly complex, at once "inside" and "outside" linguistic, semiotic, and logical "structures of meaning" (xii); indeed they are, in Elkin's phrase, "irrecoverably *incoherent*," resisting our attempts to say just what they mean and how they mean (47). Nonetheless I see some value in making the effort, since comic art typically is (a point I'll return to) an art bent on maximum legibility and rhetorical efficiency even as it evokes the expressionistic and unexplainable.

The book's remaining chapters proceed in rough chronological fashion, delving more deeply into periods, creative projects, and issues sketched in at the start. Chapter 2 reopens the contentious historical (and once again timely) question of Kirby's creative input at Marvel, examining the nature and extent of his contribution to that company's vaunted rebirth in the sixties. This vexed issue, only vaguely understood outside of dedicated fandom, shaped the remainder of Kirby's career as well as the stories that fans, comics professionals, and scholars tend to tell about him to this day. Because opinions about Kirby's relationship to Marvel inform the way his career both before and after Marvel is recounted, Chapter 2 addresses the question from a comprehensive critical perspective, explaining how Kirby came to be at Marvel in the sixties, how he worked for and helped transform the company over the decade, and how his disappointments there goaded what came later.

Chapter 3 comes at Marvel from a different angle, re-examining what the company accomplished—and what it emboldened Kirby to accomplish later on his own—from the perspective of the superhero as a genre. Sketching the historical development of the genre, this chapter argues that Kirby, Marvel, and their readers changed the superhero fundamentally.

Chapter 4 tacks in another thematic direction, contextualizing Kirby's signature work on Marvel's *Fantastic Four* and *Thor*, with their expansive cosmic vistas and mind-boggling high concepts, in terms of his obsessive interest in the technological sublime. Said interest animates much of Kirby's work, in particular the apocalyptic grandstanding of his solo output, and so this chapter links the celebrated work of the sixties to later, less celebrated, but equally revealing comics. Thus Chapter 4 explores the way Kirby yokes together the beautiful and the terrifying, the magical and the technological. Along the way, it underlines Kirby's love of science fiction and suggests why Kirby's late work kicks and shoves against the narrow limits of the superhero genre as he found it.

Kirby sought to drastically expand those limits in his short-lived Fourth World, which, as our next two chapters explain, combined old notions, a new scope, and, for costumed adventure comics, an unparalleled conceptual richness. As Kirby's most obviously personal project and the context of some of his most personal stories, the Fourth World merits extended treatment, which Chapters 5 and 6 give from multiple perspectives, including those of genre, theme, and graphic style, thus expanding on issues laid out in earlier chapters. Together these two chapters focus on Kirby at the zenith of his ambition, with Chapter 5 establishing the contours and importance of the Fourth World and Chapter 6 performing close readings and interpretations of two stories in particular.

With its outsized approach to superheroes, the Fourth World gave free reign to Kirby's apocalyptic leanings.[5] Here I have in mind two meanings of *apocalypse*. First is the original sense of the word derived from the Greek *apokalypsis* (revelation), meaning an act of revealing or uncovering. Second is the more popular sense—though a misnomer—meaning a cataclysm, more specifically the end of the world, that is, an eschatological vision of the end of history. The idea of an apocalyptic "vision" or mode is often loosely applied to American literature and culture, at times so loosely as to dilute the word's meaning, so it may help to revisit briefly the roots of the apocalypse as genre.

I take my cue from John J. Collins's *The Apocalyptic Imagination*, which, drawing on scholars in Biblical literature, establishes the genre's contours. Collins identifies the apocalypse as a subgenre of revelatory literature within "a narrative framework" in which "a revelation is mediated by an otherworldly being to a human recipient, disclosing a transcendent reality which is both temporal, insofar as it envisages eschatological salvation, and spatial insofar as it involves another, supernatural world" (5). By this definition, an apocalypse is a story that ties together origins and endings: it reveals a supernatural world to a human subject or subjects and prophesies a future history ending in an ultimate undoing or re-creation. The former sense, apocalypse as revelation, applies to Kirby's Fourth World saga from the outset, with its faux-scriptural evocation of a personal cosmology and mythic pantheon. It applies also to the trope of secret history seen repeatedly in Kirby, most obviously in *The Eternals*, which rewrites history, recontextualizes scripture, posits a new genealogy for the human species, and indulges Kirby's trademark love of mingling the archaic-historical and the science-fictional. The latter sense, apocalypse as ending, looms threateningly in *Thor*, the Fourth World (as signaled by Kirby's punning use of the name "Apokolips" to represent the forces of evil), and *The Eternals*, among many other Kirby comics. It is the very pretext of the post-apocalyptic *Kamandi, The Last Boy on Earth* (1972–1978), a postmodern farrago of received tropes, themes, and genres that became Kirby's longest-running solo creation of the seventies. In essence, *Kamandi* is an outlandish road trip through an upside-down world ironically akin to our own, one in which boyhood heroism, half-civilized, half-savage, is the only bulwark against humanity's complete ruin. That series is sadly beyond our present scope, though its mash-up of technology and savagery may be regarded as the logical fulfillment of *Thor*'s mythology-cum-science fiction and an anticipation of *The Eternals'* SF-cum-mythology.

Chapter 7, our last, considers Kirby's apocalyptic bent as it examines the factors that compromised and finally scuttled *The Eternals*, a project reminiscent of the Fourth World but hobbled by Kirby's increasing inability to channel his work into the straits of Marvel continuity he had helped establish. Placing *The Eternals* in the context of Marvel and Marvel fandom in the mid-seventies, this final chapter shows how uncomfortably Kirby's work fit into said context, and how changes in his work and in prevailing tastes shunted Kirby out of the very world he had designed a decade earlier. We end on *The Eternals* because the problems it raises show where Kirby was and what he was up against professionally just before his aggrieved retirement from mainstream comics. The original premise of *The Eternals*, which has subsequently been tinkered with, rationalized, and diminished by various post-Kirby revivals, fundamentally posed trouble for Marvel fandom: on the one hand, its core concept was *too* apocalyptic, too encompassing; on the other, its blunt style and zigzagging narrative were widely considered childish throwbacks to an earlier time. For a fanbase ever more self-conscious and eager to find maturity in comics, these were signs of Kirby's obsolescence. Patchy in execution, *The Eternals* would prove to be Kirby's last great high-concept series, after which, angry and battle-worn, he would soon retire from the monthly business of comic book production.

Since that time Kirby has become a hero, a martyr, and the center of a thousand arguments. A well-loved figure among fans and professionals who otherwise don't agree much about anything, Kirby is subject to countless proprietary claims and critical positions. Talking seriously about him amounts to taking positions about many topics: comic books, cartooning, superheroes, the study of popular culture, and where they all fit within the larger culture artistically, economically, and ideologically. I don't expect, then, that everyone will be satisfied with the vision of Kirby that emerges in what follows. I believe Kirby warrants full and unrestrained critical treatment, and so that is the approach I have taken.

Of course, that amounts to writing criticism about a kind of work never intended to attract criticism and that hardly ever had the luxury of either foresight or hindsight: work for hire, so called, commercial in spirit and produced under the unrelenting pressure of serial freelancing. Those were the overriding realities of Kirby's career. I have borne them in mind throughout, but Kirby's work, I believe, exceeds those realities and holds up well. I have tried to take his work seriously without stuffiness.

Kirby's comics represent populist myth-making of a dizzyingly inventive kind. His work is a fund of readily exploitable characters and concepts that can be and have been adapted and remade across the mediasphere. But this study also, and more importantly, focuses on Kirby as a graphic storyteller, meaning that it treats his work first and foremost as narrative drawing. The guiding idea behind *Hand of Fire* is that Kirby's drawing is storytelling, and that, conversely, his storytelling almost always used drawing, not scriptwriting, as its vehicle; the narrative and the drawing were coextensive, mutually animating and reinforcing, and inseparable. Kirby was a *cartoonist* (a word whose glory we have sacrificed in our haste to give respect to "comics creators" and "graphic novelists"). At the same time, he was a writer through and through. Cartooning, as I define it, is emphatically not the same as illustrating a prior text; Kirby *generated* stories through drawing. His stories and characters were affordances to his graphic sense; vice versa, his graphics were inspired by imagined narratives. It is my contention that *story* and *discourse*, in the narratological sense, are not separable in comics, and certainly not in Kirby's comics, but rather part of a unified autopoietic process. I hope that, as readers delve further into this book, they constantly envision that image of the artist's hand scrawling and sketching across the inviting blankness of the page, calling images and stories simultaneously into being.

If narrative drawing is the heart of this study, I admit to making sorties into many other areas: from semiotics, through genre theory, to studies of influence and fandom. Literary explication and analysis play a role as well. In other words, the book moves around pretty freely. Its methodological diversity owes to the sheer volume, diversity, and density of Kirby's work, the complexity of his working arrangements, and the necessity of charting his influence on present-day comics. Kirby is a big fish, so one has to use all kinds of nets.

Thematically, this book forms part of a dialogue with my first, *Alternative Comics* (2005). That book, though it frames comics as a literary form, insists on the form's specificity: its distinct semiotic and aesthetic properties, its generic and socio-economic peculiarities, and its "populist, industrial, and frankly mercenary origins" (ix). In it I argue against assimilating comics into existing canons of literariness without regard to "their special formal characteristics and the special circumstances of their making" (162). It occurs to me that the territory staked out by the present study is defined precisely by those populist origins and circumstances. Whereas my first book only briefly acknowledges the imaginative gusto of mainstream comic books at their commercial peak—that period of frenetic, market-driven playfulness fans mythologized as a Golden Age—the present one takes up the mainstream, specifically the generative work of Kirby, the special, often difficult circumstances under which he worked, and the impact he had on comics—superhero comics in particular.

Kirby is a major figure for not only mainstream but also alternative comics, his work as essential to understanding the comic book medium as the grand populist work of Griffith, Chaplin, Disney, or Ford is to understanding American cinema. His work bubbles under the literary comic and graphic novel in the same way that vividly remembered children's texts so often inform writing for adults. Indeed Kirby is frequently evoked by alternative and avant-garde cartoonists who, in the face of the literary graphic novel's putative new realism, seek to recuperate and celebrate the fantastic and dreamlike qualities of comics. Alternative readings of Kirby are a lively part of the discourse of comics creators and fans, even those averse to the very mainstream comics Kirby helped establish. Moreover, Kirby, beyond being a totemic figure in comic book culture, is a crucial figure in American visual culture in general, an abiding influence on visual storytellers in all media, an under-acknowledged major contributor to children's culture, and even an inspiring subliminal presence in literary fiction (where he has recently been invoked by Michael Chabon, Jonathan Lethem, and Junot Díaz). His traces are everywhere. With this in mind, *Hand of Fire* aims to show what made—what makes—Jack Kirby a singular narrative artist: a cartoonist and writer of ineffable power, endearing eccentricity, and lasting influence.

# 0

# KIRBY'S IMPROBABLE CAREER

Jack Kirby's career succeeded by accidents both happy and unhappy, and was scarred here and there by unfortunate or ill-timed decisions and plain hard luck. Biographical accounts paint him—despite his commercial successes, artistic clout, and widespread influence—as a man little used to taking care of his own business dealings. One has a sense of Kirby being shepherded through the business by colleagues and family, and often in particular by his wife Rosalind, or Roz. In any case, though Kirby's was a name to conjure with among comic book fans, his relative fame did not translate dependably, much less automatically, into financial security and comfort. When not part of the Simon and Kirby partnership, he most often lived the emblematic life of the comic book freelancer, dependent on publishers' whims. Even Simon & Kirby often had their backs to the wall.

Frankly, Kirby's career path looks like a series of patch jobs. It is difficult to outline and synopsize. Because of his freelance jobbing and the variousness of his undertakings and associations, his working life does not sort into neat patterns. In this Kirby is much like most comic book freelancers: his career seems to have been jerry-built, a hodgepodge determined by (often unanticipated) needs and opportunities and thus marked by both sudden hairpin turns and gradual attritions. Although comics was his vocation, Kirby did not, could not, shape his career with anything like professional foresight, and many career moves that would turn out to be momentous for him over the long haul were made without forethought or grand ambition. He did try, in the late fifties, to secure a newspaper comic strip, a more lucrative and respected job that could have lifted him out of the life of a comic book journeyman—but those attempts were short-lived. Until the late sixties, he seemingly had no inward sense of his own resources and potential as a solo act, nor any propensity for long-term planning. Despite the occasional commercial ambitiousness of the Simon & Kirby shop—the two tried self-publishing in 1954—it was not until the launch of the Fourth World in 1970 that Kirby undertook a solo project with a firm publication plan and long-range structural ambitions (short-circuited when the Fourth World was preemptively scrapped).

Still, it's tempting to divide Kirby's working life into a series of distinct phases, if only to appreciate the vast, sprawling scope of his career. Of course these putative phases cannot be firmly separated, for in most cases Kirby was not conscious of starting a new phase, and, again in most cases, each new phase overlapped with the previous, sometimes for months, sometimes for years, due to the vagaries of freelance work and in some instances to time lags between the creation and publication of the work. The discreteness of these phases, then, is no more than a useful fiction: a mere piton for the sake of the climb. With that caveat in mind, we can break Kirby's career down roughly into six sometimes-overlapping periods, the better to show what he accomplished and under what circumstances:

**1. Early Kirby, prior to 1941:** This phase includes Kirby's juvenilia and first few years of professional work, initially as an animator's assistant at the Fleischer Brothers studio (1935–c. 1937) and then as a comic strip and comic book artist working for various syndicates and shops: Lincoln Features (1936–39), the Eisner-Iger shop and its Universal Phoenix Syndicate (1938), Associated Features (1938–39), and Fox (1940). During this period Kirby apprenticed in various genres—fact-based cartoon panels, humor, westerns, science fiction, historical adventure—attempting different styles and imitating various then-popular newspaper strip cartoonists (notably Milton Caniff, creator of the very popular *Terry and the Pirates*). This formative period bleeds into the next:

**2. Simon & Kirby:** This is the phase—the long and life-changing period, rather—of Kirby's business and creative partnership with fellow cartoonist Joe Simon, from 1940 to roughly the mid-fifties. Kirby's professional successes, early and late, would have been impossible without the relative stability provided by this partnership, and indeed the Simon & Kirby team, one of the most successful of the comic book's formative era, warrants its own study.

For present purposes, the Simon & Kirby period may be roughly divided into prewar, wartime, and postwar subperiods. The two artists' association began with their meeting at Fox in 1940 and continued through a tentative phase of freelance jobbing as a duo (1940–41) to the point where their partnership became formal and solidified at Martin Goodman's comic book company, generally referred to as Timely, early in 1941. *Captain America Comics*, published by Timely, was Simon and Kirby's prewar triumph, and generated a kind of graphic excitement that galvanized the then-new superhero genre.

Simon and Kirby then enjoyed a string of hits, most notably *The Boy Commandos*, for rival publisher DC, starting in 1942 as America lurched into WWII. By this point "Simon & Kirby" had become a studio—a place where other professionals could find work—and a recognized brand name. During wartime Simon and Kirby were both called into military service, and Kirby saw heavy combat in the European theater, eventually returning with a medical discharge in 1945. In the interim, the "Simon & Kirby" byline continued to appear on features they had launched for DC. Postwar S&K begins in 1946 with failed projects—said to be casualties of a market glut—for publisher Alfred Harvey, followed by a spate of crime comics, notably *Headline* for publisher Crestwood and *Real Clue Crime Stories* for Hillman, as well as various odd jobs. Then, in 1947, S&K introduced a hugely popular new genre, romance comics, which they went on to exploit at Crestwood (*Young Romance, Young Love*) for years, helping to set a style that became, via Roy Lichtenstein and Pop Art, a familiar, often-parodied aspect of American pop culture.

Romance comics are the open secret in Kirby's career: a genre obstinately neglected by today's collectors and fans. This neglect, dictated by investment in superhero and adventure comics, gives a distorted sense of Kirby's career. Make no mistake: to S&K, the romance genre was a godsend, and a major, in fact *the* major, source of their productivity and earnings from the late forties to the late fifties. Harry Mendryk's blog series "Art of Romance" (from his *Simon and Kirby* blog, 2008–2010), which is the most complete study to date of S&K's work in the genre, makes the point that romance was quite lucrative, that in fact it kept the studio going for years. Mendryk shows that Kirby's artistic output in romance between 1947 and 1959 exceeded that of all other genres; indeed, in Kirby's work for the S&K shop, romance outnumbered all other genres *combined* ("A Final Transition"). Romance was not simply a trend for S&K to follow, it was a foundation; as Jean-Paul Gabilliet notes, the genre accounted for as much as a quarter of the market by the end of the forties (33). S&K had brought this wildfire to comic books, and fanned it effectively for quite some time.

For superhero fans this ought to be more than a matter of mere archaeology, for what Kirby learned from romance comics—and what Stan Lee learned as well—shaped the celebrated superhero narratives that followed, with their soap opera-like emphasis on love, loss, and anguish. Kirby never abandoned a genre, but rather reworked earlier genre conventions in new forms, splicing and adapting. His superhero comics are especially notable for this restless, poaching instinct; he understood that superheroes could be a mega-genre drawing from many other sources (as we'll see in Chapter 1's opening example). Arguably, romance, after the fifties, became part of the basic makeup of superheroes, a lasting and important substrate. In any case, romance sustained S&K and is a vital, under-examined part of Kirby's career.

Romance and crime (*Justice Traps the Guilty*) were S&K's bread and butter by the late forties, followed by horror (*Black Magic*) in 1950. Crestwood, under the Prize imprint, was their main publisher. In 1954, pricked by entrepreneurial ambition—specifically by overtures from a printer—Simon and Kirby established their own comic book publishing house, Mainline (Simon, *Makers* 137; Beerbohm 89–90). Unfortunately, this move came at exactly the wrong moment, the industry's near-collapse, a crisis from which, arguably, the comic book has never fully recovered. It was triggered by a perfect storm of factors: not only a censorious public campaign against comic books, which resulted in attempts at legal repression and eventually in the industry's defensive adoption of the Comics Code in late 1954, but also by broad social and economic changes. Among these were the rise of television, declining public interest in comics, and seismic shakeups in the business of magazine distribution (regarding this well-covered period, see Nyberg, Hajdu, Beaty, and particularly Gabilliet 44–49). Mainline bottomed out, and Simon and Kirby were forced to gut it—this not long after a legal dustup with Crestwood had soured their relationship with that company. This bruising period may also have strained Simon and Kirby's relationship with each other (Ro 56), though that point remains speculative and Simon has denied it ("Average" 48). The S&K partnership gradually melted away, as the two men sought jobs individually where they could.

There is a great story—not just a summary, as above—in Simon & Kirby. Indeed the early history of comic books, to 1955, might well be told through both Simon's and Kirby's intertwining histories. Besides the popular characters and titles they created, the studio and brand name they maintained for so long served as a de facto signpost of the industry's health as well as a source of work, and sometimes a place of learning, for many other artists. Some were not merely invisible assistants, but crucial contributors to the shop's style and reputation. A few cartoonists worked with S&K for a long time—prominent names include Bill Draut, Mort Meskin, and John Prentice—and others for shorter but intensive spells—for instance, Bruno Premiani, John Severin, or Leonard Starr—while still others passed through only briefly, among them such now-celebrated names as Steve Ditko, Carmine Infantino, and Bernard Krigstein (readers are again referred to Mendryk's excellent *Simon and Kirby* blog to learn more). To an extent these cartoonists were encouraged to showcase their own styles, and they sometimes signed their work; many inked their own pencils. On the other hand, the S&K studio's output had a distinctive "look," typified by the use of startling opening splashes, a kinetic inking style that was at once brusque and atmospheric, and, in their early work, an ornate and dynamic approach to page layout, characterized by bullseye (round) panels, fractured or zigzagging panels, and overlapping elements such as bodies hurtling over panel borders (see fig. 6).

Simon had a penchant for elaborate, sometimes even gimmicky, layouts that Kirby admired and absorbed early on (Simon, "Says" 15). Together they became popularizers of what Joseph Witek has termed the "high baroque" approach to page design that marks so many Golden Age comic books ("Arrow" 154). As early as the end of 1940, Simon & Kirby experimented with treating the page as a single design in which the constituent panels were sutured together by overlapping figures. Simon's layout sense and Kirby's ferocious, wildly exaggerated figure work spurred each other, with panels stretching to frame and accommodate the figures and the figures stretching to fill and over-fill the panels. At a time when comic books were still in thrall to their origins as reprinted newspaper dailies, stacked row upon row in mechanical, predictable order on the page, S&K made a terrific impact, well evoked by historian Gerard Jones: "The stories didn't matter, so much drama did [Kirby's] anger bring to the figures bursting out of panels, the bodies hurtling through space as fists and feet drove into them, the faces contorted in passion, the camera angles swinging wildly and the panels stretched and bent by the needs of the action [. . .]. Suddenly every young artist was drawing action like Jack Kirby" (200–201). In other words, S&K helped explode the comic book panel and redesign the comic book page.

If, as Thierry Groensteen has observed, the comics panel typically functions as a habitat for characters (an idea we'll revisit in Chapter 1), then S&K's panel layouts and characters were in thrilling counterpoise: a tense graphic tug-of-war where each goaded the other. Characters violating panel borders soon became a S&K trademark, spurred in part by the splayed, distended figures and acute foreshortening of their admired contemporary Lou Fine, who was likewise driven to open up his layouts to make room for heroic anatomy (on Fine's influence at this crucial early stage, see Burroughs, "Fine Development"; Amash, "Influence"; Theakston, *1940–1941*, pages 119–120; Simon, *Makers* 34 and "Says" 14). As veteran comic book artist Murphy Anderson, another Fine fan, put it, Kirby went the extra mile, "jumping the borders all the time and throwing things right out at the reader." Not only was there "more action" on Kirby's pages than anyone else's, but there was "more action in just the layout" (Anderson 18). Anderson and other cartoonists who grew up watching Kirby learned that adventure comics could break the rules and sacrifice "good drawing" and decorum for effect. Heroic anatomy and baroque layout leapfrogged forward together, opening up the comics page to more rhetorically expressive and even outlandish decorative effects (regarding these layout concepts, see Peeters). Along with their contemporary Will Eisner (Kirby and Fine's one-time boss), S&K took the lead in showing what a comic book page could be: not just stacked tiers of panels imitating a newspaper comics page, but a whole canvas. Though they later retreated from the use of grandstanding decorative layouts, they remained masters of rhetorical page design.

In short, Kirby had a stunning impact on comics even during the early years with Simon, and S&K fast became a name to be reckoned with. Despite this, however, the two were never guaranteed success and comfort, and indeed sometimes traveled a hard road together. Notwithstanding their great successes during the forties and early fifties, they were vulnerable to the exigencies and hazards of the market. The S&K partnership, from its founding as a fugitive, moonlight gig in 1940, through their abrupt firing from Timely in late 1941, to their failed postwar projects at Harvey, often fell prey to publisher caprice or unanticipated marketplace hiccups. Their first bona fide hit, *Captain America Comics*, was summarily wrested from them by Timely publisher Goodman. Some of their most fondly remembered titles, such as *Stuntman* and *Boy Explorers* (both Harvey, 1946), *Boys' Ranch* (Harvey, 1950–51), and *Fighting American* (Crestwood/Prize, 1954–55), were actually very short-lived. Business arrangements sometimes went south: with Goodman, of course, but also later with Crestwood. Things went doubly sour when Mainline, disastrously mistimed, fell prey to the aforementioned industry implosion of the mid-fifties.

Until the shocks of the Mainline period, S&K had been one of the most successful creative and business partnerships in comic books, establishing a name brand and packaging hit titles for many publishers. For this, they are now recognized as pillars of the comic book's mythical Golden Age. Yet S&K were hardly immune to the vagaries of the business, as they were often reminded. What's more, in testimony to the unpredictability of the industry, the quality of their studio's output varied drastically. Kirby's own artistic contribution to the work seesawed in terms of quantity and finesse, becoming a veritable graph of trends, opportunities, and reversals: the ins and outs of work, the comings and goings of other artists at the studio, and sudden spikes or plunges in production. Sheer volume of output often trumped quality of finish. The inconsistency of the studio's work has prompted this stinging assessment from Gabilliet: "If [C. C.] Beck, Eisner, and [Jack] Cole produced work at a high standard by working exclusively on a single title, Simon and Kirby, whose range was much wider and whose production was more voluminous, were, at the end of the day, the most competent of the hacks" (122). Though this judgment is too harsh, it must be admitted that Simon and Kirby were creatures of the market: quintessential comic book packagers determined to exploit and ride out the market's volatility, willing to produce the most ephemeral and formulaic of material if necessary, ready to imitate, to swipe or recycle their own work when needed, and to fish for trends. If figures like Eisner and Cole have often been portrayed as exceptions for the personal nature of their best-loved work, Simon and Kirby were archetypal commercial jobbers. Their studio's output suffered for it, sometimes the two men suffered personally as well.

Mainline was simply the last and bitterest blow. The problem in 1955 was that the entire business climate around comic books had grown so hostile as to make impossible any sudden recovery or entrepreneurial jujitsu. Mainline's fall therefore brought S&K's fabled partnership to a calamitous dead end. Reportedly Simon and Kirby had pumped their royalty earnings—boosted by their long and very successful run with Crestwood—into Mainline, but the company never got a chance to perform. Though it had launched confidently enough in 1954 by riding a handful of popular trends, Mainline had no time to build a following; the company abruptly lost newsstand access when its distributor Leader News—who had also distributed EC Comics' popular, controversial, and suddenly canceled line of horror and suspense titles—collapsed (Beerbohm 94–95). Sandbagged, Simon and Kirby were at a loss and all but exhausted. They sold the Mainline titles, perforce, to another publisher—the larger, more secure, but undeniably third-rate Charlton—and moved on. The partnership had not exactly dissolved but both were forced to prospect for work. Kirby cast around for freelance jobs, while Simon transitioned into advertising. At some point the S&K studio was shuttered, and they no longer shared a workspace (see Mendryk, "Now For . . ."). Simon later masterminded two short-lived comics lines on which Kirby worked (Harvey, 1957–58, and Archie Publications, 1959), then created the long-lived *Mad* imitation *Sick* (1960). The S&K partnership that had weathered so much since 1940 sputtered and gradually died in the late mid-fifties while Kirby kept soldiering on as a comic book freelancer (as well as occasionally angling for newspaper strips).

**3. The 1950s "gap":** Again, one period bleeds into the next: after 1955, from the de facto dissolution of S&K to the end of the decade, Kirby scrounged work through various avenues. During this phase he produced minor features such as *Yellow Claw* for Atlas (formerly Timely) in 1956–57, then "Green Arrow" for DC in 1958–59. These read, in hindsight, like holding actions.

Other ventures, however, were more auspicious. For one, Kirby did secure a newspaper strip, the now little-known science-fiction continuity *Sky Masters of the Space Force* (1958–61), scripted by brothers Dick and Dave Wood and inked, for a time, by celebrated EC veteran Wallace Wood (no relation). This was to be Kirby's one sustained, mature effort at a newspaper strip, though, as it happened, not sustained long enough to make a mark. Distributed by a minor syndicate, the George Matthew Adams Service, at its peak *Sky Masters* ran in well over 300 newspapers nationwide, yet it was to last just over two years (its separate Sunday continuity lasted about one year). Around the same time, Kirby produced a new comic book series now loved among fans, *Challengers of the Unknown*, launched for DC in 1957. Though this feature was born in the S&K shop toward the end of their full-time partnership (reportedly, Simon was the one who brought *Challengers* to DC), it was not billed as a S&K feature, and Kirby ended up running with the idea without his former partner (Evanier, *King* 101; Simon, "Average" 48).

Initially scripted by Dave Wood, and later by Kirby and Ed Herron, *Challengers* was a smart, original comic about a group of men who together survive a plane crash and so decide to dedicate themselves to exploration and adventure: the genesis of a formula later applied to *The Fantastic Four*. But both *Challengers* and *Sky Masters* were scuttled by, oddly, a poisoned business deal with an editor named Jack Schiff, who, apart from working with Kirby at DC, had brokered the *Sky Masters* deal and thus helped Kirby secure the newspaper gig and who demanded ongoing payment for same. Kirby refused, legal proceedings ensued, and, in 1959, the court found against Kirby (Cooke, "Sky Masters" 24). Having thus lost, in Schiff, an important ally at the otherwise inhospitable DC, Kirby was unable or unwilling to do further work for the company, one of the most successful and most reputable (or least disreputable) in the comic book business. This cost him a critical source of freelance work. Perhaps partly as a result of this dust-up, Kirby eventually discontinued the ailing *Sky Masters* and never again drew a newspaper strip full-time.

These disastrous reversals pitched Kirby into renewed uncertainty and his family into financial crisis. By the late fifties, Jack and Roz had three children—the fourth would arrive by late 1960—and providing for the family informed everything he did. This crisis precipitated his unexpected return, circa 1958–1959, to freelancing for Martin Goodman, whose firm, formerly Timely, formerly Atlas, was then without a name, without a brand. It would be rechristened Marvel.[1]

**4. The Marvel Sixties:** Once again, the transition from period to period is vague. Having done a trickle of freelancing for Atlas in the mid-fifties, Kirby resumed jobbing for the company, or what was left of it, around late 1958, becoming, by decade's end, its prize artist. While drawing a motley bunch of romance, western, and monster comics for the former Atlas, he continued freelancing for other publishers such as Archie Publications and Gilberton (publishers of *Classics Illustrated*) until 1961.

That year, spurred by the success of rival DC, Kirby and Stan Lee, his editor and collaborator under Goodman, galvanized the then-current superhero revival with a peculiar variation on the genre, *The Fantastic Four* (cover-dated November 1961). Thus was seeded, in fact if not yet in official name, the new Marvel Comics, which set the foundation for the Marvel Universe: a group creation built up over time, by Kirby, Lee, and many others. This was, as I will discuss in Chapter 2, an insanely busy and productive period for Kirby. Lee and Marvel worked him very hard. High points included his long runs with Lee on *The Fantastic Four* (to 1970), whose definitive look was partly set by inker Joe Sinnott, and *Thor* (1962–70), mainly inked, in a contrasting style, by Vince Colletta. This period proved to be a godsend for the industry. Until 1970 Kirby worked as Marvel's powerhouse cartoonist, character designer, and de facto layout tutor, reestablishing the superhero as the mainstream comic book's most innovative genre and generating many if not most of the concepts that Marvel would exploit from that point forward.

This period, central to the present study, is now Kirby's most popular, during which a generation of fans who knew little or nothing of S&K learned to love "Jolly Jack" Kirby for their own reasons. Of all the properties Kirby had a hand in creating, those from Marvel in the sixties have generated the most subsequent work by other comics creators, been most often adapted into other media, and seeped most thoroughly into popular consciousness. Yet Kirby never worked for Marvel (as opposed to Timely) as anything other than a freelancer. He never held a salaried position with the company.

When Marvel's ownership changed in 1968 his relationship to the company became even more precarious. Founder Goodman had sold the company to the Perfect Film and Chemical Corporation, a change that benefited Lee, who got a three-year contract, but left Kirby, whose last contract with Goodman had already expired, in a vague, untenable position. This ultimately propelled him out of the company, though Kirby delayed his move until 1970 (Raphael and Spurgeon 127–28; Ro 124–25; Evanier, *King* 150–57). His Marvel period ended acrimoniously, as Kirby—unable to negotiate a contract with Perfect Film, convinced he had been cheated by Goodman of a promised financial stake in the company, and overshadowed by Lee—resented his sacrifices to Marvel and so struck a new contract with DC. Since then the exact nature of his working relationship with Lee has been the subject of interminable speculation and controversy among fans (a subject I'll examine in, again, Chapter 2).

**5. The Seventies: first at DC, then again at Marvel:** Finally, a sudden, decisive break. Flush from his near-decade-long run on Marvel superheroes, and animated by the comparatively grand scope of his mid-decade creations, Kirby returned to DC (then still officially part of National Periodical Publications)[2] in 1970 bearing a raft of concepts for what was to become the Fourth World and nursing visions of establishing his own West Coast comic book production outfit. At this point Kirby's work became known for its eccentricity as well as its grandeur, and indeed infamous for its outrageousness, both visually and conceptually. During this tenure at DC, Kirby found a new degree of autonomy, in keeping with the company's then-spirit of editorial loosening and experimentation. In fact DC in the late sixties and early seventies was a company in transition: anxious to compete with Marvel, the once-staid house of Superman and Batman was trying out blatantly topical content and a greater diversity of styles. By 1970 National/DC had become part of Kinney National Services, Inc., later to become Time Warner, and a general spirit of change was in the air.

Kirby had been wooed to DC by Carmine Infantino, himself an accomplished comics artist, who had advanced from years of freelancing for DC to becoming the company's art director, then editorial director (and ultimately publisher, during Kirby's tenure). Infantino brought a new dispensation to DC, taking the then-unusual step of hiring artists, rather than sometime pulp writers, as editors—and it was against some resistance that Infantino brought Kirby on board (Infantino, "Comments" 9). With Infantino's intercession, Kirby acted, at least nominally, as his own editor, managing his own small, de facto shop.

Reveling in these new conditions, Kirby went for broke, pouring out work at a breathtaking pace and solidifying his odd, late-period style in which the tics of his Marvel work were magnified and his distinct graphic shorthand fine-tuned into a trademark repertoire of visual symbols and gimmicks. His newly commissioned inker, Mike Royer, proved to be the most faithful finisher of Kirby's artwork to date—in sharp contrast to the inconsistent, often shoddy Colletta, whom he replaced—and Royer's bold brush technique occasioned the final shift toward late Kirby style: a roughhewn, craggy, titanic style more in step with Kirby's original renderings than with the softened appearance of most of his Marvel art to that point. Kirby would seek to maintain this look in all his subsequent work. He also hired two young part-time assistants, Mark Evanier (now Kirby's authorized biographer) and Steve Sherman, to help handle the everyday logistics of finishing and packaging the books. Through such measures he exerted a new degree of control over the finished product. More importantly, he dreamed of establishing his own bullpen of artist collaborators—Wallace Wood, say, or Dan Spiegle—to fill out his line of books. This never came to fruition, however, as DC preferred to have Kirby drawing Kirby, and brushed off his various ideas for new publishing initiatives and formats (Evanier, *King* 165 and "Unknown Kirby" 7–10).

Kirby's grand project for DC, the Fourth World, began coyly via his unexpected revamping of the long-lived yet inauspicious *Superman's Pal, Jimmy Olsen* (a spin-off dating back to 1954). Hijacked for Kirby's purposes, *Jimmy Olsen* suddenly became a spewing fount of new concepts, dizzying in their profuseness. Superman's sidekick Jimmy, along with Superman himself and a revival of Simon & Kirby's forties-era kid gang, the Newsboy Legion, were drawn into a hectic, multifaceted storyline inspired equally by science-fiction dreams of genetic engineering and by the then-timely counterculture of "hippies" and "dropouts." Here Kirby soon introduced a threatening new face, that of the villain Darkseid, first shown slyly in miniature on a TV monitor.

*Jimmy Olsen* proved to be only the narrow end of the wedge, the deceptive starting point for something bigger: *The Forever People, The New Gods,* and *Mister Miracle*. These titles together were the Fourth World. The cycle began promisingly, a mythopoeic riff on "superhero comics" that departed from traditional costume fare and offered instead an operatic spectacle of otherworldly demigods and creatures, all locked in a struggle with the fate of humanity hanging in the balance. While breaking new ground, the cycle enabled Kirby to revive some old, familiar notions from his Golden Age work with Joe Simon, including not only the kid gang (both the Newsboy Legion and the super-powered Forever People) but also the acrobat hero à la Sandman or Stuntman (now reimagined as the near-godlike escape artist, Mister Miracle, a kind of costumed super-Houdini).

The Fourth World, as I'll argue in Chapters 5 and 6, suggested a new, mythically imposing way of doing superheroes. If it sometimes allowed Kirby to revisit familiar turf, its scope and complexity were ahead of its time. When the project was suddenly axed in 1972, Kirby's dreams of transforming comic books were smashed. Angry and diminished, he was put to work on various other comics for DC; nominal self-editorship aside, he was reduced to filling out the terms of his contract, a deal which now seemed onerous. Still, Kirby produced memorable work under this burden, his most successful series being the post-apocalyptic *Kamandi* (which he wrote and drew from 1972–75, and continued drawing for other writers to early 1976). His remaining DC projects were fitfully inspired and often bizarre: the horror-cum-superhero series *The Demon* (1972–74); the disturbing superheroics of *OMAC* (1974–75), set in a chilly futuristic dystopia; a revamped *Sandman,* the first issue of which was, improbably enough, Kirby's last full-length collaboration with Joe Simon (1974); and an unexpected sojourn on an old-fashioned WWII series, "The Losers," in the comic book *Our Fighting Forces* (1974–75), which boasted startling, in some cases cruelly grim, stories. By 1975, though, Kirby was clearly marking time, as shown by a scattering of miscellaneous, contract-fulfilling one-shots and filler issues.

Kirby's final return to Marvel, from 1976 to 1978, was regarded at the time as ruinous. The company, in the wake of Stan Lee's retirement as editorial director, was tattered and ill-organized, its offices broken down into a cluster of editorial camps barely held together by Marvel continuity, its creators and fans anxiously conserving said continuity and thinking in directions inimical to Kirby's footloose imagination. Starting with a controversial run on his old standby *Captain America*, then officially titled *Captain America and the Falcon* (1976–77), Kirby ran smack into changing tastes, alienating fans of the more recent, updated and socially relevant versions of Marvel characters such as "Cap" and the *Black Panther* (1977–78). This awkward period was crowned by two offbeat series that gave vent to Kirby's penchant for the technological sublime: an ongoing adaptation of/sequel to the film *2001: A Space Odyssey* (1976–77), which was a stuttering series of repetitive, self-contained tales lacking a strict continuity, and the inconsistent yet conceptually daring fantasy epic *The Eternals* (1976–78), a property that would later, after Kirby, become subject to much revision and editorial fidgeting. Despite the ravishing visuals in such comics, Kirby's work of the period was rejected by much of Marvel fandom as either too far out or too childish in tone. Near the end, this final run at Marvel was diluted by backward-looking concepts such as *Machine Man* (a robot), *Devil Dinosaur*, and, surprisingly, a *Silver Surfer* graphic novel co-created with Stan Lee, all in 1978. To be fair, the familiar premises of these books were often enlivened by staggering, nightmarishly intense drawing.

Then, at last, dismayed by the reception of his latest work and stung by the sense that comic books had all but thrown him away, Kirby parachuted out of the comics business. He began working again in animation (circa 1977–78), and eventually got steady, secure, and gratifying work as a nominal producer and conceptual artist doing behind-the-scenes development work for animated television series, most of which would go unproduced. This was an inglorious, fading period for Saturday morning children's television, pre-cable, and a low point for TV animation generally, a state of affairs that Kirby's involvement, though fondly recalled by fans, did nothing to change.

**6. The direct market era, from 1981 onward:** A few years post-retirement, Kirby did return to comics, this time working with small, independent publishers who targeted the so-called direct market, that is, comic book shops, where hobbyists gathered. In this period Kirby emphatically distilled, intensified, and made even more grotesque his trademark style, crossing the line into work that seems of interest mainly to devotees. Notably, he volunteered his time to draw writer Steve Gerber's satirical series *Destroyer Duck* (1982–83), an outgrowth of and benefit for Gerber's lawsuit against Marvel over ownership of his signature character, Howard the Duck. Marked by Gerber's barbed, unsettling humor, *Destroyer Duck* revolved around a two-fisted funny animal's fight against the monolithic "Godcorp"—surely a thinly veiled dig at Marvel—whose corporate motto, *Grab it all, own it all, drain it all*, was thought up by Kirby (Gerber 39). *Destroyer Duck* was generally read as a revenge fantasy, and Kirby's participation in it as a symptom of his bitterness toward Marvel.

Around this time Kirby also created two science-fiction-cum-superhero series born out of unrealized movie and television projects: *Captain Victory and the Galactic Rangers* (1981–84), a militaristic and paranoiac tale of alien invasions and world-shattering violence, and *Silver Star* (1983–84), a revisiting of evolutionary themes previously tackled in such comics as *X-Men*, though here presented breathlessly as if radically new. These comics are perhaps most notable as signal contributions to the then-fledgling independent comics publishing movement: *Captain Victory* was the first title published by upstart Pacific Comics, a company that set out to compete with Marvel and DC by offering identically formatted four-color comic books whose creators would retain their copyrights and earn royalties, a critical, precedent-setting move. In that sense *Captain Victory* was important: it sold well and made waves. But, from this reader's perspective, after the first few issues the series becomes a tough slog. Some fans consider it a coded sequel to *The New Gods* (see, for example, Morrow, "Connection"); however, tonally and artistically it is no match. These late comics are marked by odd verbal cadences, pounding earnestness, increasing loss of technical control, and further stylization, to the point of gross distortion: the final, inimitable eruption of Kirby's always-volatile artistic sensibility, now heightened to the point of self-parody.

In spite of growing physical hardship and a debilitating public fight with Marvel management (see Chapter 2), Kirby rounded off this last active period with an anticlimactic return to his Fourth World properties at DC and some pained, obviously hobbled penciling for DC's toy-related *Super Powers* (two miniseries, 1984–85). A late, ill-considered coda to *The New Gods*, comprised of a reprint series with some new material and, finally, a self-styled graphic novel titled *The Hunger Dogs* (1985), did nothing to salve the aggrieved memories of those who had longed for a proper conclusion consistent with the original series. By 1985 Kirby's drawing looked painfully diminished. After this final spell at DC (1984–86), he effectively retired altogether. Subsequent Kirby creations, so called, including the Secret City Saga or "Kirbyverse" (for Topps Comics) in 1993 and *Phantom Force* (for Image Comics, then Genesis West) in 1993–94, were, with the exception of a few inventory pages by Kirby, essentially developed by other artists and writers working with castoff Kirby concepts from years before (one suspects that Kirby had, figuratively, drawers full of such concepts). These efforts were outgrowths of the early mid-nineties boom in comic book collecting and speculation with nominal ties to Kirby: tributes, in essence, rather than new Kirby productions. Kirby died in 1994 on the heels of these short-lived pastiches (others would follow).

The above outline can only suggest the tremendous variety of Kirby's work over his forty-plus years in comics, and perhaps fictionalizes his career insofar as it puts a neat shape on what was really a mazy, unpredictable route marked by overlaps, reversals, and retrenchments. What's notable about this route is how often necessity mothered invention—how an impasse brought Kirby a renewed sense of urgency and success on new terms. For example, in the immediate postwar period S&K launched but then quickly abandoned new titles, apparently due to an oversaturated market; they had to weather a painful period of adjustment. Yet out of that period came the birth of romance comics in 1947 and thus firm financial footing for Simon and Kirby in the late forties and early fifties. After the shelving of "Simon & Kirby" as an ongoing partnership in the late fifties, Kirby's promising new projects (*Sky Masters* and *Challengers*) were effectively scotched by legal and professional battles; as a result, he shifted to Goodman's former Atlas and editor Stan Lee, where sheer need eventually drove him to infuse the line with his trademark energy and style and to design an entire menagerie of bankable characters. That was Marvel Comics. Toward the end of the sixties, anxiety and frustration over his treatment at Marvel led Kirby to design and hoard a fund of new concepts (a rare withholding for him) and then launch, in a wild, creative rush, the DC titles of the early seventies, which, if not entirely successful, served to redefine him. In all these cases, Kirby put pencil to paper to sell comic books, revive his career, and nudge the field toward another breakthrough.

Kirby's best work always came out of hardship and reflected a kind of desperate, spontaneous energy (even the long-simmering Fourth World, as finally published, included quite a bit of frantic improvisation). After all, Kirby's job, as he saw it, was to sell comics. That driving sense of economic necessity, testimony to his Depression-era upbringing and the relentless nature of the comic book business, underlies his whole career. It helps explain why that career is such a scattering of publishers, partners, genres, and titles, nearly impossible to summarize. The truth is that economic anxiety, along with Kirby's in-grained self-image as a provider, so shaped and determined his outlook that the idea of total artistic autonomy in comics, aloof to commercial consider-ations, would have been nonsensical to him. As I've noted, the nature of the business in his day did not generally allow for that kind of self-regard and self-cultivation.

The greater, underlying truth is that the determinant of Kirby's working life and artistic style was social class. Historian Jeet Heer, speaking of Kirby's disputes with Lee and Marvel, has remarked, "If you don't understand how social class works in America, you can't understand [his] anger," and that is something we should not forget in our eagerness to gentrify comics ("Class and Comics" n. pag.). Throughout much of his career, Kirby and his fam-ily negotiated the rigors of class and the threat of poverty, hovering uncer-tainly around middle-class status, fighting to stay solvent and secure, and, no doubt, always conscious of the arc that had led Kirby from the tenements to the fickle and yet promising field of comic books—a then young, dynamic field open to innovation and responsive to his talents, but also risky and demanding. The Kirbys lived and struggled according to the rhythms of this field, with the memory of poverty always behind them. Kirby always re-membered his origins. For example, in a 1982 interview with his former boss Will Eisner, he spoke of his art in ways that implicitly link his violent style of narrative drawing, his class origins, and his fight for survival, noting that he "tore [his] characters out of the panels [and] made them jump all over the page [. . . in] the service of trying to get a real fight." Says Kirby, "I was in that fight, in that situation. [. . .] I was trying to get at the guy who was trying to get at me" (Eisner, *Shop Talk* 211–12). This was why, he explained, he had to draw in an "extreme" manner: "I wanted to transmit the power of people in the ring." When asked about his kid gang comics, he mused about his origins:

> I began to remember people from my own background, and I began to subtly realize they were important and that I wasn't ashamed of them. I was no longer ashamed of myself, and I began to see them as I should have seen them from the beginning [. . .].
>
> [This] was far from Long Island. I was still trying to get into Brook-lyn. (212)

Armed with that determination, Kirby fought with and shaped the comics field for decades, leaving behind a bemusing legacy, a scurrying, crazy path of jobs, periods, and creations, all a testament to his need as well as his talent.

Granted, Kirby's present fame stems largely from the Marvel of the sixties, yet he did so much more that singling out any one aspect of his work at the expense of others feels like a sin of omission. The scope of his career has bred subspecialties among collectors: Golden Age devotees treasure the seminal S&K comics; Silver Age fans favor his fifties and sixties work; a few collectors, diehard Kirby fans, lovingly extol his eccentric solo comics of the eighties. In short, Kirby created enough work to sustain fans from many angles. Had he abandoned comics in 1955, Kirby would still be considered one of the major artists in the medium's history, for he was an indefatigable workhorse, a distinctive stylist, and a formative influence on the design of the comic book page as both narrative and graphic unit. By his mid-twenties he was an artist other artists followed, and his output was prolific and, genre-wise, diverse. What drives the present study is the conviction that, notwithstanding Kirby's diffuse, decades-long productivity, certain works stand out as vividly stamped with his sensibility. These are my core interest. To better situate those works, and to encourage appreciation of both Kirby in particular and cartooning in general, the next chapter explores the question of Kirby's drawing as narrative art: what it does, how it works, and why it looks the way it does.

# 1

# KIRBY'S NARRATIVE ART

Style is a result of our failure to achieve perfection.
— A favorite saying of Will Eisner[1]

The style not as the inscription of imagination, but as imagination's vehicle,
the conductor of its convulsion . . .
— DONALD PHELPS, *Reading the Funnies* (38)

BAAAAAM!! Kirby's graphic ferocity, the sheer, brawling kineticism of his style, calls to mind combat: the slugfest, the siege, the riot, in sum the carnal indulgence of raw physicality and untamed rage. Take for example the opening two-page spread, pages 2 and 3, from the first issue of *The Demon* (DC Comics, Aug.–Sept. 1972), written and penciled by Kirby and inked and lettered by the redoubtable Mike Royer (see plate 1). In this scene, prologue to a tale of demonic possession and warring supernatural powers, the army of the sorceress Morgaine le Fey storms the walls of Camelot. This opening spread, in its scale, intensity, and seething violence, showcases Kirby's cartooning at its peak.

Beyond bringing to life a dramatic scene, though, what exactly is Kirby doing in this drawing? How does this image work, if we may speak of it as doing work? To what extent is it realistic, or abstract? To what extent is this image open to analysis? Finally, beyond the usual documentary evidence of its provenance, how can we tell, or why do we *think* we can tell, that this page was drawn by Jack Kirby? All these are questions of style, something as difficult to analyze but as necessary to appreciate as breathing.

## WHAT WE TALK ABOUT WHEN WE TALK ABOUT STYLE

Kirby's style, universally recognized among American comic book fans, has been and continues to be invoked, mimicked, and parodied in countless comics, both mainstream and alternative, yet remains hard to discuss except as a grab-bag of mannerisms or tricks. In general, the problem of style has proven a hard nut for analysis; many comics scholars have despaired of getting a handle on it. For example, R. C. Harvey has said that style, "the mark of the maker," is too personal for analysis: too peculiar to the individual practitioner and too subtle in its effects. Criticism based on style, he argues, comes down to mere "question[s] of personal taste" (*Funnies* 16–17; *Comic Book* 10). Until Scott McCloud's popular study *Understanding Comics* (2003), fans lacked even the rudiments of a toolbox that would help them speak analytically about differences among comic art styles.

McCloud helped introduce into the context of comics a wider theoretical discussion of drawing. I propose to extend that discussion here, with two emphases. First, I'll invoke semiotics, the study of signs and sign processes, in an effort to better understand the kinds of "signs" that Kirby's cartooning creates. Semiotic analysis of comics has a long lineage, particularly in European scholarship, and has been the subject of much debate and reappraisal; in fact it is taken for granted within continental studies (see, for example, Fresnault-Deruelle, "Semiotic Approaches"; Groensteen, *System*). However, it remains under-applied to artists like Kirby and to American comic books in general. Second, taking my cue from Thierry Groensteen's observations about narrative drawing, I'll examine what it is that makes cartooning, and Kirby's in particular, so unlike illustration. In the end, I'll argue that Kirby's narrative drawing oversteps any neat classification of signs, exceeds illustration, outruns the conventions of realism, and, in sum, constantly redraws relationships among the various functions of drawing and between naturalism and cartoon stylization. I aim to show that Kirby's style—that every accomplished cartoonist's style—is the result of tension and struggle.

To begin with, let's re-approach the question *How does this image work?* That invites thinking about what drawings are and how they may communicate. Charles Peirce's doctrine of signs, which he called *semeiotic*, offers a tempting way of addressing the issue.

The usual way of staging a meeting between a "theorist" like Peirce and an artist like Kirby is to "apply" the theorist to the artist: typically, we read the artist through the lens of the theory without necessarily reflecting on the efficacy or limits of the theory as such. I don't intend to do that here. Rather, I mean to stage a confrontation that will allow us to read the theorist through the artist; that is, one that will redound on the theory itself and enable us to consider the theory's potential limitations or difficulties. My line of inquiry, in other words, isn't merely "What can Peirce reveal about Kirby?" but also includes "What can Kirby reveal about the usefulness and limits of Peirce's semeiotic?" The answers to these questions have a larger bearing on comic art in general.

My goal, mind you, is not to debunk semiotics; I don't see how that would be useful or possible. Nor do I presume to discover difficulties Peirceans have not already discussed. I mean only to stage a dialogue through which we can see the challenges that comics and cartooning pose to sign theory. There is something unavoidably ambiguous, mysterious even, about the everyday art of cartooning, and wrestling with the theory should help bring that to the fore. Kirby's cartooning in particular poses a tough case for analysis because of its all-encompassing influence, its unmistakable quirkiness, and the sheer difficulty of talking about it on any other terms besides those of personal taste, emotional payoff, or nostalgia. I contend that Kirby's narrative drawing represents a complex fusing of mimetic, symbolic, and graphic qualities, a fusing that may be partly explained with the help of Peirce's doctrine.

We can start by unpacking one of Peirce's triads, or so-called trichotomies, of signs, with a tip of the hat to graphic design theorist Clive Ashwin (whose application of Peirce to the art of drawing, published in 1989, sparked my own). If we define a sign, in semiotic fashion, as anything taken to refer to, or stand for, something else, then the drawings and panels and other symbols that comprise comics are clearly signs.[2] Peirce posited several different ways of classifying signs, but the most influential of his classifications, and the one I have in mind, rests on three different kinds of relationships he saw between signs and their referents.[3] These relationships may be roughly outlined as follows:

1. A sign may be taken as an *icon*, meaning a semblance or likeness; that is, it may be regarded as resembling its referent (take, for example, a portrait).
2. A sign may be taken as a *symbol*; that is, it may be understood as bearing an entirely artificial, or conventional, relationship to its referent (a word, for example, or alphanumeric symbol).
3. A sign may be taken as an *index*; that is, it may be understood as caused or produced by its referent, or as being in a direct physical or demonstrative relation to its referent: a pointer, in other words, rather like a demonstrative pronoun (for instance, a fingerprint or bullet hole taken as evidence, or, as Peirce said, a weathervane spinning in the wind or the sound of a knock at the door).

In practice, applying these terms can be an abstruse and frustrating exercise (the more so when one considers that, for Peirce, these are but part of a more complex and never completed system). When teaching I gloss these three relationships, icon, symbol, and index, by asking students to consider how they interact in a commonplace object such as a dollar bill. The U.S. one-dollar bill bears what we agree is a semblance, which is to say an icon, of George Washington; it also bears signs that symbolize "the United States" or aspects thereof in an abstract, obviously conventional way, such as the Great Seal with its familiar eye-in-the-pyramid (a combination of iconic forms that serves a symbolic function). Finally, the dollar bill bears marks, or indices, that advert to its physical origins: marks that guarantee each bill's authenticity and uniqueness, such as the U.S. Treasury's bright green seal. Such marks are understood to be tokens of presence, or a past presence. As such, they connote genuineness and responsibility.

Though temptingly neat in examples like these, the concepts of icon, symbol, and index tend to blur and complicate in practice, and Peirce's own explanations of the categories are difficult to grasp. What, for example, should we make of the various signs that comprise an algebraic equation, the many variables, superscripts, and operational symbols? Peirce wrestled with myriad such examples, in the process subverting the discreteness and ease of his own terms. In fact he developed other triads to describe the nature of signs and how they relate to the grounds of interpretation, and, over time, sought to build all these into a fine-toothed system of classification.[4] Despite all this, it is the categories of icon, symbol, and index that remain most attractive, because they correspond to intuitive ideas about how signs work. Signs can resemble, signs can symbolize, signs can point to a relationship or mark a physical trace. What could be clearer? As Ashwin has established, these categories can be used as a tool for understanding the art of drawing. Their interaction helps explain the varied levels of specificity and the many different purposes of drawing: representational, emotive, persuasive, social, poetic, metatextual (202–03).

Peirce's triad of relationships recalls another way of talking about drawing, one better known among comics fans, namely McCloud's much-discussed "Big Triangle" of style (*Understanding Comics* 52–53; an interactive version can be found at scottmccloud.com). The Triangle offers a way of grounding the usual impressionistic judgments about differences in style, for example "cartoony" versus "realistic" (fig. 2). Like Peirce's trichotomy, McCloud's Triangle, with its three vertices of literal resemblance, symbolic "meaning," and pure pictorial abstraction, constitutes a triadic theory of signs. In effect McCloud builds on Peirce's three relationships, even though he seems unfamiliar with Peirce (confusingly, *Understanding Comics* assigns the word "icon" a different

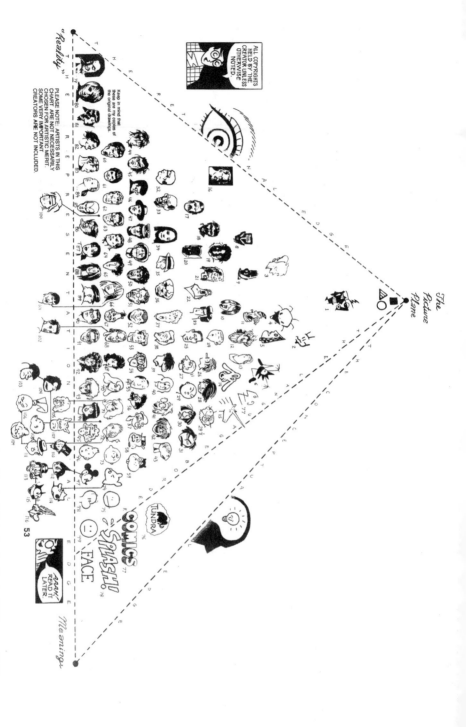

Fig. 2. What McCloud calls The Big Triangle: a tool for understanding comic art style. Scott McCloud, "The Vocabulary of Comics." *Understanding Comics* (1993), pages 52–53.

meaning than Peirce does). The base of McCloud's Triangle (its x-axis) describes a shift from photorealism to cartooniness, that is, symbolic abstraction: as the reader's eye sweeps from left to right, McCloud's sample images become less and less "realistic," in the accustomed sense, and more and more simplified and schematic. This move could also be described as the shift from, in Roland Barthes' grand phrase, the "analogical plenitude" of the photograph (Barthes 18), toward more obviously coded images or ideograms (and, finally, to words). In Peircean terms, the Triangle's base describes the move from icon to symbol.

The Triangle's height (its y-axis) describes the movement toward what McCloud calls "the picture plane," meaning toward absolute pictorial abstraction, or appreciation of the formal aspects of the picture as such. Another way to put this is that, as our eyes lift from bottom to top, we move toward the realm of pure *mark-making* (what one might be tempted to call the non-semiotic, though, as we'll see, this isn't quite right). This movement tends to make us more conscious of the artist's hand, that is, of style as the result of physical handiwork. Near the top of the Triangle, then, we find roughly sketched or boldly stylized images that barely, or don't quite, cohere as intelligible representations but do serve as obvious graphic reminders or traces—that is, indices—of the artist's activity. Such radical mark-making foregrounds the telltale signs of presumed individuality that are always potentially available in handcrafted artwork, such as brushstrokes. The masterworks of modern art offer a wealth of obvious examples, from the drip-paintings of Pollock to the graffiti-like scribbles of Cy Twombly: champions of the spatter, the freed and looping line, the smudge. So too do alternative comics, with, for example, the postpunk gestural school epitomized by Kirby devotee Gary Panter, who, while often working in a cartoony register, is typically less concerned with delimiting forms clearly and more with giving vent to an anxious, hyper-energetic expressionism (Hatfield, *Alternative* 61). Among cartoonists, Panter is known for liberating the graphic mark.

McCloud places Kirby about dead center in the Triangle, which seems about right. Yet, as elegant and instructive as this tool is, it runs into trouble along its edges. In particular, trouble looms on the Triangle's left side, what McCloud calls the "retinal edge," which denotes the furthest extreme of analogical plenitude, as in a photograph. Here McCloud courts trouble by deferring to "reality," that is, toward real things in the real world. Oops: invoking real life to describe a created image is bound to become, indeed has been for some time, a point of controversy. This is the very source of that long-seething argument between, philosophically speaking, naturalists and conventionalists.[5]

Naturalists, meaning proponents of resemblance theory, argue that the rules of pictorial realism are based on the real, on what Ernst Gombrich called "real visual resemblance" ("Image and Code" 21) or Peirce called "topological similarity." Conventionalists, on the other hand, argue that the rules of pictorial realism, no less than of abstract art, are based on arbitrary, culturally determined conventions that must be learned. The naturalist position assumes that resemblances between images are grounded in universal experience and objective fact; in contrast, the conventionalist position argues that the rules of "resemblance" are grounded in codes and customs that are culturally constructed and changeable. "Realism," by this argument, is not a privileged doorway to transcendent truth but simply another historically contingent artistic idiom, no more intrinsically trustworthy or real than any other. What is at stake in this unending, probably unendable, debate is whether we should base theories of imaging strictly on the idea of mimesis in the most literal sense, that is, imitation. This debate has already bedeviled McCloud: see, for instance, a scuffle between McCloud and scholar Jeff Miller in the pages of *The Comics Journal* some years ago (Miller, "Hardly Bullshit"; McCloud, "I Didn't Say That").

Peirce's terms *icon* and *symbol* might seem to offer a way out of this impasse without forcing us to go McCloud's route—in other words, without forcing us to invoke the disputed authority of the real. With Peirce's help, we might simply say, without invoking art's relationship to "reality," that the left side of McCloud's Triangle tends toward the iconic and the right toward the symbolic. But this doesn't help very much, of course, for it just defers the debate to another level, since the very category of the "iconic" still assumes an intuitive sense of likeness, or topological similarity, which brings us right back to the initial problem. The idea of real visual resemblance undergirds the idea of iconicity, therefore the Peircean iconic sign still runs afoul of that basic question, or buzzing cloud of questions rather, raised by McCloud's retinal edge: in what sense can iconic images be said truly to "resemble" their objects? Do realistic images, as opposed to abstract or cartoony ones, genuinely shade over into reality, or do they represent merely a different, equally artificial set of conventions? Is the gap between images and reality insuperable? Can any image truly be called closer to reality than another? This is the problem of the iconic or so-called natural sign, a devilish one that, as W. J. T. Mitchell reminds us, has long plagued semiotics, and that, once recognized, threatens to collapse the neat systems semiologists like Peirce have constructed (*Iconology* 56–59). Said problem is basic and yet intractable.

We could dodge this obstinate question by allowing that Peirce's three sign categories are not mutually exclusive—a given sign may function as icon and index and symbol all at once—and that Peirce's triad aims not to reify sign "types" so much as to distinguish between the different ways we, as readers or interpreters, may *understand* signs. By this logic, signs are not icons or indices or symbols because of some inherent essence but only insofar as they evoke a certain response from the sign reader (you, me, us). The reader's knowledge, mind-set, and purposes are paramount. For Peirce, in fact, signs are to be understood not solely in relation to objective reality but also in terms of the different understandings readers implicitly bring to bear when reading them. Taking a cue from Rudolf Arnheim's *Visual Thinking*, we may distinguish between, not different "types" of signs, but the different yet often overlapping *functions* of signs, with the understanding that (and this is certainly relevant to Kirby) one sign often can serve more than one function (136). As Arnheim says, images "can dwell at the most varied levels of abstractness," simultaneously referring to things at "a lower level of abstractness" and things at "a higher level of abstractness" than themselves (137–38). For instance, the image of the eagle on the dollar bill may refer both to an actual eagle (that is, to a lower level of abstractness) and to an idea about national identity or destiny (a higher level of abstractness). As Peirce himself advises, the relationship between sign and object is not given but rather created or inferred in the mind of the observer, on the grounds of what the observer *takes* to be the sign's evident relation to its object. This inference, in Peirce's term the *interpretant*, is the very basis of semiosis, without which we have no meaningful sign, only mere signal. The quality or qualities of each sign, then, is/are determined by the reader.

With this in mind, perhaps we could use Peirce's three relationship terms under erasure, so to speak. Each term could be defined not as an objective entity but rather as a way of *reading*, a way that privileges a certain assumption on the reader's part. An iconic reading privileges assumptions of likeness; a symbolic reading privileges assumed codes or conventions; an indexical reading privileges assumptions of presence, past presence, or direct connection. In other words, when we read or pick out icons as such, we assume resemblance; when we pick out symbols, we assume (consciously or not) a stable code that renders the symbol meaningful; when we pick out indices, we infer that the signs are pointers, testifying to (in the case of artwork) the past presence of the artist. The categories *icon, symbol*, and *index*, then, without conferring absolute authority to the "realistic" or iconic, can stand in shorthand fashion for common assumptions about likeness, symbolism, and presence or cause.

That may be the best we can do with these terms: find a way to better articulate common assumptions about how signs work. For this purpose, Peirce's terms retain their value, provided we take care not to allow them to become reified or absolute. Leaving aside the continual debate over the terms, we may use them to designate three different ideas about the way artistic images, including Kirby's, function. Admittedly, this is not a wholly satisfactory solution either; any attempt to rescue Peirce's terms is likely to rest on some kind of metaphysics (as does McCloud's Triangle, along its edges). Suffice to say that Peirce's trichotomy of relationships, or some cognate set of terms, can provide us with a toolbox to describe more precisely the functions of a drawing as commonly understood: drawings may be seen as *pictures* (this is what Arnheim calls images that aim for likeness), or as abstract symbols, or as demonstrative evidences of a real cause, in our case of an artist's handiwork. How then might we apply these tools, or attempt to apply them, to Kirby's narrative drawing?

First off, we should recognize that the idea of the icon—the recognizable likeness—is at the heart of narrative drawing but is not nearly enough to explain it. The effort to create pictures that are true or at least legible likenesses, what I call the mimetic impulse, is essential to but not enough to account for artistic style. The late Will Eisner often remarked that style results from failure and frustration, from grappling with one's own weaknesses as an artist and turning them to advantage (what once were vices are now habits, so to speak). Indeed, as artists grow they seem to become more fully themselves, i.e., more fully at home in an idiolect all their own, in which their departures from textbook anatomy and technical draftsmanship no longer matter. Witness Eisner's own, wonderfully rumpled work, which, over time, became more fully Eisnerish, or Kirby's, which, with the passing years, became ever more Kirbyesque.

Arguably, this process of development takes place as the cartoonist struggles with him/herself to reconcile the several functions of drawing: the iconic, the symbolic, and the indexical. By *indexical* in this context I mean the individual graphic signature of the work, meaning its personal, handmade quality, what I call the idiographic. Though iconic drawing may be the goal or motive for many, at least initially, the eventual outcome is inevitably some mixture of qualities we read as iconic, symbolic, and personal. In the case of very successful cartoonists like Kirby, the audience becomes intimately involved in this growth process as it learns to accept, even expect, an artist's tics and tricks: the kinds of symbolic shorthand and the idiographic uniqueness that inevitably mark the artist's handiwork. At a certain point, at least for the very popular cartoonist, the personal language of style trumps mimetic considerations: idiolect matters over resemblance. In the case of Kirby, realism comes second to Kirbyism.

Thinking about "Kirby's style" leads us back to a core problem in Peirce's semeiotic, namely that *all* signs, on some level, function for us as symbols, because our understanding of them must to some degree be based on association, convention, and code, i.e., on the way we have learned to think rather than simply on the givens of likeness or presence. Many argue that our reading of icons and indices, no less than of symbols, is based on custom (this would be the extreme conventionalist position). Indeed Peirce himself recognized that, though sign-reading inevitably involves a mix of likenesses, indices, and symbols, "the complex whole [of semiosis] may be called a *symbol*; for its symbolic, living character is the prevailing one" (*Essential* Vol. 2, 10, emphasis in original). By this light, the symbol is, as Floyd Merrell says, "the only sign in the full sense of the term," i.e., the purest and most encompassing type of sign (*Semiosis* 100). Kirby's style, recognized as such, forcefully demonstrates this problem in a way that illuminates both sign theory and the question of style at once—for thinking about *any* recognizable style partakes of the symbolic as well as the indexical. Kirby's style is always *symbolic of Kirby* and of the constellation of ideas associated with him. This admission, in essence that all signs are symbolic, threatens to collapse our trichotomy, but we can learn from the collapse: we can learn about Kirby, and we can learn about the limitations of the theory in such a way as to boost our appreciation of comic art in all its dynamism and protean-ness, its profound slipperiness.

Kirby's pictures of course tilt toward the symbolic. Reading them requires grounding in certain peculiar conventions. For example, his dynamic and contorted figures, while recognizable as such to the initiated reader, may be less so to the uninitiated. This question becomes more acute as we move toward late-period Kirby, with its trademark squiggles, slashes, and geometric, block-like forms, as opposed to more traditionally rendered human figures. Also, Kirby's shorthand efforts to render motion in a static medium force his artwork toward a distinctive symbolism. As McCloud has observed (*Understanding* 111), and as Mark Alexander has shown in *The Jack Kirby Collector*, Kirby's motion and explosion lines have their own palpable life, especially in his mid- to late-sixties and subsequent work. As Alexander says of the Kirby-burst, his renderings of crackling, flaring, or radiating energy, "these abstract diagrammatic lines become so dynamic and stylized, that they [take] on a physical presence all their own" (70). Conversely, "physical" bodies in Kirby shade toward the abstract and diagrammatic: under the pressure of storytelling, Kirby draws characters with their legs splayed five feet apart, not because this is how these characters are supposed to look at rest but because, clearly, they are *not* at rest. Kirby is not about rest. He treats bodies as bodies in *time* or vectors of *force*, as well as abstract design elements.

In other words, Kirby's handling of movement and action continually urges his iconic renderings of form toward the symbolic. Though often described as cinematic by admirers, in a sense his style represents a distinctly *un*cinematic approach to evoking movement in static form, a way that recalls, as I've noted elsewhere, Futurism in its decomposition of movement and Cubism in its all-at-once depiction of different perspectives (*Alternative* 54). Though Kirby's drawings may seem to represent discrete and explosive instants of action, in fact they capture extended spans of action in synoptic tableaus. His drastic foreshortening, anatomical distortions, and slashing diagonals help to freeze time on the page.

Returning to the opening double-spread from *The Demon* #1 (again, see plate 1), we can see how Kirby's cartooning activates a tension between iconic reading, based on assumptions of likeness, and symbolic reading, based on knowledge of Kirby's distinctive conventions and codes. Here figures crowd the extreme foreground and middle distance, while isolated figures appear in the deep background as well. The foregrounded characters loom into view, affronting the borders of the image (a Kirby trademark). Motion lines and clusters of dots (another Kirby trademark) give palpable presence to fleeting temporal phenomena such as the catapulting of flaming missiles, the roiling of smoke, and a battering ram hammering its target. Meanwhile, the posing of most of the figures suggests a determined rush toward the left-hand margin. Figures assault the reader in extreme close-up and recede "backwards," "into" the depths of the image, along a pronounced diagonal. At the same time, the reading order of the text, *contrary to the direction of the attackers*, guides the eye from left to right. The resultant tension between word and image contributes to our sense of opposition and conflict.

The foregrounded heads in the bottom corners effectively frame the receding diagonal of the battering ram, while, above, shapes suspended in midair (as if falling) suggest the tumult and danger of the siege. The characters exhibit an angular or geometric quality that approaches abstraction (see, for instance, the archer's hand on the far right), yet also suggests directionality, purpose, and fierce, frenetic activity. Via the composition of the entire spread, Kirby captures successive moments simultaneously, giving us the whole arduous siege as a single, synoptic image. To those readers who used to complain, as some did, that Kirby's huge splash pages were self-indulgent and hindered the development of his (then typically seventeen to twenty-two page) stories, I would have to say, no, quite the opposite: in their quick conjuring of scene and situation, the best of them are wonders of narrative efficiency and compression.

This spread from *The Demon* #1, in sum, is not a snapshot in the strict sense but a montage. Here is a bald-faced violation of that dictum most famously handed down by Lessing in his seminal *Laocöon* (1766) and since reinforced *ad infinitum*: that, whereas writing and storytelling are arts of time, unfolding in sequence, painting and drawing are arts of space, to be apprehended all at once and thus necessarily separate from writing. Kirby always ignored this distinction. That's what comics artists do, and Kirby did it especially well. The power of drawings like this one from *The Demon* stems from the tension between reading the image as a single moment and reading it as a synchronous compressing of an extended length of time—in short, a tug-of-war between an iconic reading, assuming semblance, and a symbolic one based on convention. Such tension is intrinsic to Kirby, for his style, as Christopher Brayshaw has observed, pits three-dimensional "figuration" and two-dimensional "design" against each other, enacting a fierce dialectic (56). That tension is animated by two things: Kirby's approach to movement in a static medium and the improvised unfolding of his art as pure design.

In sum, Kirby's iconic drawings, goaded by story, drift toward the symbolic and the purely graphic, devolving to abstract ideograms of force, movement, and power (as in, for example, the impact of that battering ram). His renderings are more suggestive than literal.

If this is so, if Kirby's iconic drawings shade into the symbolic, then his indexical qualities—his idiographic fingerprints, so to speak—are also in effect symbolic. For one thing, most readers encounter these qualities through reproduction rather than Kirby's originals, since comics typically, and Kirby's comics certainly, are a mass-reproduced art. To speak of his *presence* or touch on the page, or on the board, is ipso facto to indulge in metaphor. The images most of us know are copies, offset-printed, most often mediated by other artistic hands and processes far removed from Kirby's drawing board (coloring, for example, which in Kirby's day usually proceeded from preliminary color guides to anonymously hand-cut color separations). Also, for initiated readers, Kirby's mannerisms—his geometric forms, slashing lines, squiggles, dots, bursts, and so on—become symbolic of the artist himself and his legacy, and may be so even when used by another cartoonist. Kirbyism can be aped; indeed these mannerisms are often used by others to invoke the very idea of Kirby.

Witness for example the Kirby pastiche from Matt Madden's book of Oulipian comics exercises, *99 Ways to Tell a Story* (2005), or the sustained mimicry of Tom Scioli in the series *Gødland* (2005–). In each case the stylistic pastiche is slavish, going beyond bedrock matters of composition and staging to minute tics of Kirby's rendering, and in each case the idea of "Kirby" himself is intended to pop up in the reader's mind. Such stylistic homage to Kirby is so common as to constitute a code in its own right: for fans, a ritual invocation of the King. In *Gødland*, the constant stylistic mimicry serves to invoke Kirby's reputation for overflowing narrative invention and plain bizarreness (qualities eagerly sought by Scioli and *Gødland*'s scriptwriter, Joe Casey). In Madden, the homage invokes the idea of stepping between worlds: the mundane opening of a refrigerator, part of the basic scenario behind all the exercises in *99 Ways*, becomes the opening of a threshold to another, stranger place. Because we read Kirby's mannerisms—even seemingly "nonsemiotic" ones—as just that, *his*, they exceed the indexical and take on symbolic value.

Comics readers become adept at recognizing and reading signature styles. Disruptions in a style, if they are not rationalized on a narrative level—as, say, a flashback, frame narrative, or other-dimensional sequence—can be disturbing. As a young reader, I was often thrown by stylistic inconsistencies in comic books, such as telltale changes in the inking and lettering of a single story. Glitches like this are common, given the hurried production and assembly-line nature of most comics. The distinctive marks left by different artists within a single comic often clash, detracting from that interdependence and interplay of images that Groensteen refers to as *iconic solidarity* (*System* 17–18). What happens is that the reader becomes distracted by apparent shifts in the indexical qualities of the drawing. The effects of this are not trivial, for they work against the reader's assumption of a singular, in Philipe Marion's phrase, *graphiateur*, that is, implied graphic author or enunciator (see Marion's *Traces en cases*; Baetens). Suddenly one can no longer believe that the work before one's eyes is the result of a unified personal effort. Often readers can be persuaded that such an effort took place even when it didn't (as in fact is usually the case with Kirby, who was typically inked by other artists), but shifts in the visual texture of the work in mid-episode tend to undermine this willed belief. In other words, the idiographic handiwork of the artist or art team, by its very constancy, lends a semblance of consistency and "presence" to the finished work. This can be so even when the seeming indices of the artist's presence can be "faked" by technical means, as is the case with cartoonists who use custom-made computer fonts to mimic their own handwriting, as in Alison Bechdel's *Fun Home* or much of Jeff Smith's *Bone* (regarding which topic, see Kannenberg, "Graphic Text"). Readers invest in the handcrafted mannerisms of favorite cartoonists.

By now Kirby's mannerisms have been so widely studied and copped by other cartoonists that they have ceased to be anything like a guarantee of Kirby's presence and have instead become part of a visual language shared among artists and fans. As with Eisner, Wallace Wood, R. Crumb, and other revered stylists, one continually sees new students of Kirby who have internalized, or sought to internalize, both his underlying structural qualities and his surface mannerisms. In the above cases, the putative indices of Kirby—that is, certain types of signs originally attributed to his direct presence at the drawing board—have become *symbols* of Kirby, adverting to him even when Kirby himself was not involved. This tendency becomes clearer as fans study the mannerisms of Kirby ever more self-consciously, as in many issues of *The Jack Kirby Collector*, which offer detailed taxonomies of Kirby's technique.[6]

More broadly, indexical qualities in a drawing that point to the artist's identity—say, the telltale differences between Kirby's renderings of Thor and Walt Simonson's—become symbolic of that artist, his work, his career, and his reputation. What's more, any slavish imitation of an artist's style, once recognized as such, takes on a certain ideological value as a perceived rip-off, homage, or parody. Such imitation is, if you think about it, an odd thing: the result of an artist apprenticing his own eye and hand to another artist's peculiar and hard-won style, a style born of personal experience and struggle. In this way Kirby's own artistic life has dominated others, something he reportedly never wanted, indeed is said to have discouraged. At this point the telltale signs of his handiwork have become invested with tremendous symbolic heft, and thus copied over and over; we are surrounded with many ersatz Kirbys, which, like ersatz Picassos or Van Goghs, force us to fall back on a metaphysics of historical presence to prove which is the "real" and which the fake. Thus even the indexical trace, the physical, idiographic marker of the artist's presence, becomes in the end a symbol of something greater: a history, a legacy, an artist-myth. As symbols, such signs are conventional and can be faked, giving the lie to the metaphysics of presence. The artist's trace always carries with it a seed of doubt. I'm reminded of Jacques Derrida's rather different use of the word *trace*: not a guarantor of presence but rather a marker of absence: "The trace is not a presence but is rather the simulacrum of a presence that dislocates, displaces, and refers beyond itself" ("Differance" 156).

We have a come a long way from the pristine separateness of sign "types." If Peirce's trichotomy serves to tease out our assumptions about the ways drawings can work—as icons, as symbols, as indices—it also obviously has its limitations. When dealing with a popular cartoonist like Kirby, whose work has been widely reproduced, disseminated, and imitated, it is the collapse or limitations of Peirce's terms that are most instructive. In fact Kirby's mature style acts out a powerful confusion of, or tension among, the iconic, the symbolic, and the idiographic. I would argue more generally that, to a degree, all comic art is semiotically ambiguous this way, organically and inconsistently straddling the presumed divisions between sign "types." Cartooning derives much of its power from this very indeterminacy.

Suffice to say that comic art is rife with contradiction. It is a rhetorical art that at once privileges narrative meaning, inviting paraphrase, transcription, and glossing, and yet evokes the pleasures of pure graphiation, of lively mark-making. Comics, especially Kirby's, are often filled with delirious mark-making—idiosyncratic doodling, frankly—yet their narrative frameworks can render even the seemingly random mark meaningful, as a symbol of energy or movement or as a means of world-building or emotional coloring—even ideological positioning. Granted, these things are true of drawings in general, but the narrative function of comics practically begs the reader to make these associations. By way of story, comics invite especially intense participation in meaning-making; they invite us to interrogate and make sense of their graphic marks. As minutely readable narrative texts, comics invite study, and so it is that comics fans become remarkably attuned to the idiographic peculiarities of their favorite artists. Narrative cartooning, in sum, destabilizes any distinction between meaningful and meaningless, in Mieke Bal's phrase "subsemiotic," marks (see Bal 400–401 and Elkins, *Pictures* 3–6). Everything counts.

## KIRBY'S NARRATIVE ART IN ACTION: AN EXAMPLE

The greatest thing I learned from Jack Kirby is not to fear a *blank* sheet of paper.
— MIKE ROYER, interviewed by John Morrow (Part 2, 104)

Returning again to *The Demon*'s opening sequence, we find a late-period distillation of Kirby's narrative art. The scene-setting two-page spread, in its depth and complexity, shows off his skill with forced perspective, foreground framing, and receding diagonals. The severe close-ups in the foreground demonstrate Kirby's yen for recreating what psychologists call *visual looming*—the sense of things coming at you—which he accomplishes by sizing and rudely cropping the foreground figures to suggest they are pushing toward the reader, assaulting the hyper-frame of the page as if to break through its membrane. Here the very "board" of the page becomes one of the constraints that, characteristically, Kirby attempts to tear open. The violence implicit in this approach is reinforced by Kirby's graphic inscription of movement: the motion and impact lines, the arcs of flame, the multiply-reinforced vectors of action. The sequential written text—the element that most obviously submits the reader's gaze to a precise order and a sense of timing—at once arrests and reinforces the sense of urgency evoked by the whole scene. The characters' actions are implied in the grotesque stylization of their figures: despite the obdurate, geometric solidity of the close-up hands and faces, these are characters rendered as, essentially, the clash and bare containment of terrible forces. A world defined by mounting cataclysmic violence is conjured in a single image: "a time when great powers clashed on Earth and beyond—!"

The first six pages of *The Demon* #1, the sequence in which this spread appears, are Kirby in microcosm. The story is archaic in its trappings but unrooted in the niceties of history and breathlessly contemporary in idiom: an unwitting mockery, perhaps, of the Arthurian ethos evoked by Harold Foster in the classic *Prince Valiant*, an episode of which from 1937 inspired the design of Kirby's demon. The tale's opening splash page (page 1, just before our spread) shows the siege from the besieged's point of view, depicting Camelot as a flaming, smoking deathtrap. Merlin the magician looks out from a single window, tightly clutching his "Eternity Book," anticipating the castle's fiery end. Turning the page, we find our scene-setting spread (on pages 2 and 3), an anachronistic riot of fanciful architecture, weaponry, and costume. The text is apocalyptic and, typical of Kirby, fiercely punctuated: "*The Fates were bringing an age to a close!!!*" Turning the page again, to page 4, we find it divided into three panels, one above and two beneath (fig. 3). The first depicts a terrific explosion—BAAAAAM!!—rendered as dots, tendrils of energy, and a radial image of hurtling masonry, metal, and impact lines. The image inclines to the abstract, although the narration and our unfolding sense of story may make us feel otherwise; again, Kirby's style enacts that tension between the iconic, symbolic, and idiographic.

This is a scene of war—well-trod territory for Kirby. Though the plot is comprised of hand-me-down Arthurian and Gothic elements, the text is contemporary in its frame of reference (atypically, the narration is in the past tense, though it will later revert to comics' conventional present tense). A fallen fighter blurts out exposition that, but for a reference to magic, could be at home in any war comic: "*Fall back!* We *can't* hold against such spells!" The caption warns us of "forces in play," forces still called "magic" by frightened men, but there is a suggestion here of the late Arthur C. Clarke's "law": that a technology advanced enough will, to the uninitiated, be indistinguishable from magic (*Profiles of the Future* 36). The narrator speaks as someone from a later age recalling a distant legend, with a poetic touch of uncertainty that is belied by the visuals ("It is said . . . ," "Legend would say . . .").

A bemusing sense of timelessness is introduced via the villainess, Morgaine le Fay, who is introduced in the first of two panels below (panel two). She is an otherworldly sight, and would be equally at home in one of Kirby's SF comics. In the next image (panel 3), her pointed finger and commanding words make her objective clear: "Now *find* Merlin! I want him taken *alive!!*" The atmosphere is less that of Arthurian epic than some strange pottage of Kirby's own.

Morgaine's features are abstract, unknowable, and forbidding, a metallic mask topped with curling, serpentine horns. The elaborateness of her headgear recalls Kirby's Galactus (from Marvel's *Fantastic Four*) or his version of Hela, Goddess of Death (from Marvel's *Thor*); more particularly, it brings to mind characters from Kirby's then very recent Fourth World, such as Mantis

Fig. 3. The blurring of ancient and modern idioms: magic and science. "Unleash the One Who Waits," page 4.

of Apokolips (introduced in *Forever People* #2) and the "Bugs" of New Genesis (*New Gods* #9). This peculiar design sense is characteristic: a face that is abstract, mask-like, but graphically exciting, topped by branching or snaking lines and conflating organic and inorganic forms. Such faces are targets for the eye, and, for Kirby, typically signs of inhuman or otherworldly origin. Smoke issues from Morgaine's outstretched fingers when she first appears, an index of her power (presumably, the explosion of the preceding panel issued from her hand).

The facing page (5) divides, classically, into three tiers and five panels, and the action accelerates (fig. 4). The first tier introduces the titular demon, Etrigan, whose appearance is partly obscured (in the original comic, we get a full, unobstructed look only at the end of the issue; the Omnibus reprint of 2008, however, inserts a page of Etrigan originally cut from the comic). In a page-wide shot, Etrigan is seen—half-seen rather, smashing through Morgaine's "shock troops" and scattering them. Again, as on the preceding page, force radiates outward from a central point (Etrigan) and the action is framed so as to hurtle toward the reader. The two tiers below consist of an even four-square grid. First, we get a canted close-up of Etrigan, in which the debris flying around him, the rough lines of his cloak, and the image's oddly tilted angle all coincide to reinforce our sense of suspended action (panel two). Then the remaining panels—three, four, and five—recede to long shots as Etrigan answers the summons of his master, Merlin. Panel three effects this transition effortlessly, using Etrigan's figure as a foreground framing element to stress the distance between the demon and his master (*"Up here, Etrigan!"*). In the succeeding panels, stylized flames and smoke—piles of dots and a few squiggly lines—threaten to overwhelm the small figures, even as the wizard summarily explains the story's premise: that the demon's "destiny" is to await a new summoning, perhaps long hence, on Earth. The iconic quality of these drawings is almost smothered by Kirby's graphic shorthand.

The final page of this opening chapter (page 6) will slow the action and deliver us to the series' point of departure. Turning the page, we see another three-tiered layout, this time with six panels (fig. 5). The panel layout is characteristically conservative: two panels, then one, then a tight grouping of three. More important is what happens *in* each panel, and from what perspective. In panel one, fire and smoke swallow the receding figure of the demon, as Merlin's hand (foregrounded like Morgaine's on page 4) reaches toward him, another visual pointer (note how Kirby steers our eyes around the page). In panel two, reversing panel one, Merlin prophesies in fiery close-up, again holding the Book. It almost seems as if he is on fire, though calm. The next tier, panel three, delivers a climax, as the explosive end of Camelot—a great,

Fig. 4. Accelerating action: Kirby's breakdowns at work. "Unleash the One Who Waits," page 5.

tilting vector to the right—takes up a single page-wide oblong. The running figures are dwarfed and flattened by a surge of impact lines and foregrounded debris: a near-abstraction. Then the bottom tier divides into an even triptych—a classic Kirby tactic—in which Etrigan transforms into a man, in the process losing his memory (a transformation that will be replayed in reverse, again in a triptych, at the climax of this issue). The emphatic narration slows the story's pace even as it glosses the character's metamorphosis; the images, though, are discreet long shots, hiding Etrigan's visage from the reader in anticipation of the story to come. The final panel is the least dynamic of the sequence, its purpose to effect a transition and pose an enigma, a "hook." Kirby's trademark effusiveness is banked, his telltale shorthand reined in. The hero walks away from us, reversing the logic of his entrance, leaving the reader grasping after his secret. There is a stillness here—a breather—yet a provocation as well.

The rest of *The Demon* series spins out from this transformation. What is Etrigan, after all, but a demonic superhero, his identity hidden behind that of a mortal man and only revealed in times of crisis? Character-wise, we are in classic Kirby territory, a conflation of the superheroic and the monstrous, much like the Thing, the Hulk, or Orion of the *New Gods*. The character's form-fitting costume is, arguably, a dead giveaway: standard superhero stuff enlivened by a few medievalizing details. Likewise the story's divided geographic loyalties: in the chapters to come, the plot will shuttle back and forth from the Gothic, quasi-medieval settings of a vintage monster movie to a "Gotham City" locale typical of superhero-dom. Yet throughout there is an ambient sense of ruin and decay in the images, leaning to the Gothic and folkloric: ancient, time-battered *Mitteleuropean* settings, monolithic castles and nightmarish crypts, frayed and flaking stone. Kirby's design chops, so often unleashed on high-tech, futuristic settings, are here set to work on a Central European atmosphere that seems equally hospitable to his pen, conjuring memories of S&K's moodily evocative *Black Magic* (1950–54) or perhaps the pseudo-Slavic neverland of Dr. Doom's "Latveria" in Marvel's *Fantastic Four*. The end result? A farrago of generic elements—horror, medieval fantasy, superhero—energized and sold by Kirby's graphic performance.

Everything about the foregoing six-page sequence is trademark Kirby, and everything contributes to its total effect: the brusque rendering, index and artifact of both Kirby's handiwork and Mike Royer's painstaking fidelity to same; the ahistorical and eclectic settings, the abstract design elements such as Morgaine's mask, and the habitual forms of symbolic shorthand (smoke, fire, impact, *power*); the classical, conservative, and yet dynamic layouts, the taut pacing achieved through those layouts (note the increasing number of panels

Fig. 5. A climax, then a slowing down, via a Kirby triptych. "Unleash the One Who Waits," page 6.

per page), and the seemingly effortless iconic drawing, which shifts viewpoints and distances with ease; the emphatic, quirkily written narration, always in tandem with and punctuating the visuals ("wondrous Camelet thundered, trembled, and *departed* from the pages of history!!"); and, saturating all, the apocalyptic urgency of the story, the sense that the "Fates" are fully engaged and that everything depends on the battle's outcome. It will be clear by now, I hope, that in this performance text and image are inseparable, succeeding or failing together, each keyed and responsive to the rhythms of the other. Though isolated spreads by Kirby may make a feast for the eyes, his art is inescapably narrative art.

The thing to remember about *The Demon* #1 is that the essence of the story came about through a spontaneous process that started with daydreaming and then, sans script, leapt straight to the drawing board. Like so many of Kirby's concepts, *The Demon* began as an unwritten notion brainstormed via conversation (Kirby's ability to dream up plots while socializing being legendary) and then quickly came to life at his drawing table as a series of sketches. His then-assistant and now-biographer Mark Evanier describes the process, which began with DC's request that Kirby craft a proposal for a supernatural-themed horror or "monster" comic: "[Jack] had that discussion with [DC] on a Friday, and, apart from the name, didn't give it a lick of thought while he focused on an issue of *The Forever People* that needed to be finished." That Sunday, Evanier, along with fellow assistant Steve Sherman, happened to go out to dinner with Kirby and his family: "After we'd all ordered, Jack got strangely quiet. He just sat there as we talked, saying nothing, retreating (or more accurately, advancing) into some other world. It may even have occurred to me to think, 'Hey, Jack's writing something.'" Once the food came, Kirby "softly and without preamble" began to reel off a story. "It was the complete plot of the first story of *The Demon*, including the basic premise and characters and setup. . . . Between the time he'd ordered a burger and the arrival of that burger, [he] had created a new comic book" (Introduction 4). Then, right after getting home from dinner according to Evanier, Kirby found the gist of his final character design in a collection of *Prince Valiant*—a sign, perhaps, that Kirby meant to comb through his beloved Foster for historical reference, or, as Evanier suggests, that he remembered exactly what he wanted and went looking for it. The letter column in *The Demon* #6 (Feb. 1973) tells the story differently, saying that Kirby's initial design, worked out through "a few sketches," looked like something else and that the Foster homage came about almost by accident (in contrast, Evanier says the final version of the character was "almost identical" to Kirby's first drawing).

In any case, soon after Kirby set to work, he had "enough sketches and a few paragraphs" to form his proposal to DC (Evanier). The final design of the character, and possibly supporting characters, would have come through those early conceptual drawings—a handful, maybe—as images and ideas gathered in Kirby's mind, delivered by the momentum of his thinking and penciling. Once DC greenlit the proposal and asked for *The Demon* #1, Kirby would, as was his wont, have gone straight to penciling the comic, with few additional written notes. At that point the story would have been elaborated, particularized, gridded, and paced via the drawing itself. This is the point when, plotwise, happenings would have become *sequences*, synopsis would have become action, and clashing forces would have been made vivid and concrete. Kirby's penciling played an essential generative role in both the initial pitch and the process of crafting the full story. The drawings gave life to Kirby's internal imaginings, without reference to a detailed prior script.

This point is critical. We know that Kirby's preferred approach to writing, laying out, and drawing a comic was simply to attack the pages, writing and drawing on the art boards without preliminary page roughs or scripts. He would inscribe both pictures and words as he dreamed them up (photocopies of Kirby's pencils for *The Demon* provide evidence of the process: see for example *The Collected Jack Kirby Collector*, Vol. 3, and *The Jack Kirby Collector* #44). In fact Kirby created many enduring comic book properties simply by penciling stories from next to nothing. Certainly he disliked being constrained by the demands of an outside scripter; his days at S&K had made him impatient with anything other than a direct, hands-on approach (Evanier, *King* 100). His process was, as Evanier has often remarked, fast and instinctual.

Other artists who observed Kirby at work were often dumbfounded by his confidence and unflagging energy: Carmine Infantino, for instance, said of Kirby in the forties, "What he would do [is] he never laid anything out. He'd start at the top of the panel and just draw. [. . .] It was incredible" ("Incredible" 16). Gil Kane, who worked for S&K in the early forties, remembered Kirby as working nonstop, grinding down one pencil after another all day long, and chatting as he drew, with casual fluency (Interview with Cooke, 41). Even Joe Simon has said that "there was something very mysterious about the way [Kirby] drew" ("Says" 14). Kirby admirer Jim Steranko has described Kirby's process as "elemental": "He would compose the action of a scene in his mind, then, almost as if it were projected onto the page by a telepathic device, he would render it, as one would trace over a drawing. He almost never erased" ("Man" 166). This description, oft repeated in Kirby lore, is invoked by Michael Chabon in his novel *The Amazing Adventures of Kavalier & Clay*

(2000), in which the Kirby-like cartoonist hero Joe Kavalier works the same way, "as if some invisible force beam from his eyes were dragging the tip of the pencil across the page," sans any guidance other than "faint, cryptic guidelines" on the page (82).

Leaving aside the perhaps inevitable elements of exaggeration and mythology in accounts such as these, the overwhelming evidence shows that Kirby wrote and drew many of his stories directly to the boards. So storytelling, composition, and rendering, and in many cases the brainstorming and development of ideas as well, were part of a seamless graphic process: *narrative drawing*. Kirby's juggling of drawing and of signs, of mimetic, symbolic, and idiographic functions, was one long reckless improvisation.

## KIRBY VERSUS REALISM

> The comics image, more than being an utterable, a descriptible,
> and an interpretable, is also an appreciable.
> — THIERRY GROENSTEEN, *The System of Comics* (161)

One result of that improvisation on display in *The Demon*, and yet so obvious as to go unremarked by experienced readers, is the sheer grotesque exaggeration of the imagery. Not everyone responds well to this quality. Some comics readers, even some who are immersed in contemporary superheroes and therefore hugely, if sometimes unconsciously, in Kirby's debt, find his narrative art powerfully off-putting. "God, I hate his stuff," is a sentiment I've heard many times from diehard comics readers—that or "I hate his *later* stuff." Granted, late-period Kirby is exceedingly cartoony by the standards of today's best-selling superhero comics; it is goofy and savage. Obviously it is not photorealistic. If, as Eisner remarked, style is a result of and consolation for failure, then perhaps the defining failure of Kirby is his failure, always but particularly in his later, more eccentric work, to uphold the standards of realism or classicism epitomized by the illustrators he admired as a boy.

Of course this is not to imply that pictorial realism represents a privileged, natural, accurate, or (here's that word again) iconic standard from which cartoon art unfortunately strays, or that Kirby *should* somehow have upheld the standards of realism. Realism here is not to be confused with the Real or the serious or the emotionally compelling, much less the necessary. Rather, I mean to suggest that pictorial realism was a dominant style that informed Kirby's influences and to which he aspired in his youth. His formative influences as a comics artist, after all, included the celebrated adventure strip artists of the Depression era, and notable among these were a handful praised for helping to bring the canons of pictorial realism to the comics page.

Kirby idolized three in particular: Milton Caniff, whose late-colonial adventure series *Terry and the Pirates*, a cracking blend of rugged chiaroscuro drawing, cinematic storytelling, rounded characterization, enticing sensuality, and far-flung, pulpy exoticism, did more than any other strip to inspire comic book adventure; Foster, whose *Tarzan* and especially *Prince Valiant* introduced an imposing historical sweep and grand illustrative Romanticism to newspaper strips, fresh out of the Golden Age of book illustration; and Alex Raymond, whose space opera *Flash Gordon* trumped Foster's high Romanticism with a florid, baroque, and languidly erotic manner that channeled equally Old Master painting and contemporary commercial illustration. Caniff, for his part, brought compellingly complex characters and a new degree of scenic realism to the adventure continuity genre pioneered by Roy Crane in the late 1920s (*Wash Tubbs*); like Crane he retained a sense of humor and an openness to broad, cartoony figures, but he couched these in a more realistic setting. Foster and Raymond, on the other hand, were celebrated for infusing adventure comics with an unparalleled beauty, sensuousness, and painterly sense of scale, so much so that many fans would be reluctant to call them "cartoonists." Together, these three rather different artists, Caniff, Foster, and Raymond, but especially the latter two, became the taproot of a long and living tradition: a lavish illustrative approach to comic book drawing. That Kirby admired yet could not cleave to their standard is one of the most revealing things about his narrative art.

Kirby was an avid student of these artists. Caniff, who had a coarser, high-contrast style (adapted from his esteemed colleague Noel Sickles), was the most economical storyteller of the bunch, indeed a master yarnspinner. Graphically, he was less beholden to nineteenth-century academicism and Romanticism, favoring a kind of rough-hewn impressionism that offset the conventionally realistic against the expressively cartoonish, evoking cinematic realism without requiring him to smother his drawings, and his readers, in incidental detail. This style of drawing proved seminal; in fact Caniff's *Terry and the Pirates* supplied a graphic idiom for generations of adventure strip cartoonists both in the United States and abroad, and became a template for "Golden Age" comic books. Caniff's direct influence on Kirby, as on fellow comic book pioneer Will Eisner, is obvious. Foster and Raymond influenced Kirby too, but, in contrast to Caniff, they favored detail and extravagance, leaning hard on the fantastical, visionary, and archaic-historical (medieval, Gothic, baroque, et cetera). In them the spirit of Romantic revivalism that suffused late-colonial adventure fiction was most blatant, and sumptuous.

Kirby often named Caniff, Foster, and Raymond as inspirations, and they came early enough to hit him hard. Another who seemingly influenced him, though not so often remarked, was Burne Hogarth, an artist who arrived slightly later. Hogarth succeeded Foster on *Tarzan* in 1937 and brought the strip to new extremes of kineticism and graphic tension. Though he began by emulating Foster, whom he greatly admired, Hogarth gradually elaborated and intensified his style; believing Foster's approach "too relaxed," he determined to seek greater energy and tension. Kirby pushed this way as well. As Hogarth would recount decades later, "I was aiming not only for grace, but for the internal sense of [the figure's] kinetics and dynamics, that it had to exude a sense of sustained inner power. You can feel it in a cat walking. You can feel that the muscles are all there, a stalking, intent quality [. . .]. This was like the freeing of an internal tightly-wound clock; it'll unwind slowly, but there's potential powerful, life-force energy in every simple act" (Interview 77). Hogarth's figures were tensely articulated, invested with energy as if spring-loaded, and hyper-dynamic, founded on what he himself called "highly exaggerated contrasts." He studied the Renaissance masters—Michelangelo was a favored point of reference—and sought to bring similar figure attitudes to the comics, while exploring an overall sense of page design that was distinctly modern and native to the comics page. *Dynamic tension* or *dynamic opposition*—again, these are phrases he used—informed his figures, and this approach, as he well knew, saturated the comic books, so that, looking back late in life, he saw his own influence working through Kirby and others (Interview 99). A voluble commentator on art and comics, Hogarth would reflect that, along with Foster and Raymond, he had been engaged in "developing a whole *new syntax* of the figure," a taxonomy of movement in which classicism and the mythic, gravity-defying spirit of the hero were blended (76). He sought to teach this "syntax" to others through *Dynamic Anatomy* (1958) and subsequent textbooks and by co-founding what would become the School of Visual Arts. While Kirby never studied art with such formality, his ferocious, bounding, and grotesquely articulated figures seem directly descended from Hogarth's dynamically contorted forms.

Certainly comic book artists working in the 1940s in the mega-genre of heroic fiction, including superheroes and globe-trotting adventure, picked up on Hogarth. Comic books were indebted from the start to Caniff, Foster, and Raymond, in particular their work during the middle of the thirties, what historian Ron Goulart has christened "the adventurous decade." Kirby, growing up with such work—eleven years old when Foster's *Tarzan* began (1929); sixteen when Raymond appeared with the triple threat of *Flash Gordon*, *Jungle Jim*, and *Secret Agent X-9* (early 1934); just over seventeen when Caniff departed the tentative *Dickie Dare* and launched *Terry and the Pirates* (late 1934); and not quite twenty though already a professional cartoonist when *Prince Valiant* debuted—was in their debt. By the time Hogarth took over *Tarzan* from Foster, these artists had built a pictorial vocabulary for adventure strips, one that Kirby studied fervently. Caniff, Foster, Raymond, and later Hogarth helped establish in comics an aesthetic of exoticism and pictorial lushness, at once enabled by and tensely counter-posed to a comparative realism. Said aesthetic shaped and continues to shape the repertoire of comics, particularly mainstream comic books.

Kirby's work, however, as it evolves through its major identifiable stages— the obvious signposts being S&K, then the early sixties at Marvel, then the latter sixties and on into the seventies (*The Demon*, etc.)—does not exhibit the degree of realism associated with his influences. In Kirby the balance between realism and rude expressiveness, between naturalism and exaggeration, is drawn differently. The result, by the early seventies, was a style that eventually polarized comics readers: a graphic approach notable for, as we've seen, its assertive stylization, brash, explosive manner, and continual tilting toward spatial and temporal abstraction. It's as if Kirby mis-learned the lessons of his influences, so that, as his career hurtled onward, his work came to resemble theirs less and less. Late Kirby style, the style instantly recognizable to parodists and fans, is far removed from Caniff or, especially, the lingering, sensual appeal of Foster and Raymond. The dynamic Hogarthian posing of contorted figures in space is still there, but without the appeal to beauty and idealized anatomy; something punchier and more assaultive has taken over. One has the sense of the artist growing more fully into himself, developing, without plan or self-consciousness, that graphic idiolect we know as his. In its unaccommodating weirdness, late Kirby is a hell-bent smashup between the grand and the grotesque—and, in every Kirby comic that clearly bears his creative stamp, one can't help but see this "late Kirby" threatening to emerge, behind the varied and often softening influence of his many different collaborators and finishers.

Because the identity of "Kirby" is partly in the very telltale strokes of his pencil—those indexical marks that Royer sought to reproduce so faithfully— our appreciation of his style has had to change even in the years since his passing, as the fan press, most particularly *The Jack Kirby Collector*, has made abundantly available reproductions of Kirby's uninked, unfinished pencils. Fans can now revel, by facsimile, in traces of his raw, spontaneous delivery. Thierry Groensteen reminds us that comics drawing, besides essentially serving narrative and structural purposes, represents a graphic performance, one that is not wholly reducible to a verbal utterance (a paraphrase) but rather is "delectable" on its own terms, in all its graphic materiality (*System* 126, 161). The telltale stylization of Kirby's drawings, though, has everything to do with their narrative purposes, their containment in and contributions to a gridded comics narrative that attempts to move, or rather, asks the reader to move, at a breakneck pace. *Pacing*, both the nonstop demands of Kirby's working pace and the frenetic would-be pacing of the comics themselves, is the overriding reality that determined Kirby's style, his characteristic distortions of and departures from the canons of realistic drawing.

Among those who hold to the Foster/Raymond tradition of Romantic illustration, a certain misconception about comic art has proved particularly unhelpful to understanding Kirby's work. That is the misconception that eloquence in comics will be best achieved by pairing eloquence of written language with classical elegance of drawing. An entire tradition in superhero comics depends on this misapprehension: that superheroes stories are best realized with a high degree of realism—not sordid realism, of course, but an idealized, selective realism—and that therefore the litmus test of comic book art is its treatment of the realistically proportioned, classically formed, beautifully posed human figure. Admittedly, calling this a *mis*apprehension amounts to dismissing an entire aesthetic approach to the genre—guilty as charged—and comic book production is increasingly dominated by said approach, typified by the photorealist paintings of Alex Ross and the hyper-detailed line art of pencilers like Bryan Hitch, John Cassaday, and Steve McNiven. Such artists often wed photorealism to Kirbyesque dynamics, in a cinematic style referred to by fans as "widescreen." Not coincidentally, these styles have emerged in tandem with a prolonged and anxious bid to elevate the stature of superhero comics, in parallel with and capitalizing on the literary graphic novel movement. These are "serious" styles.

The rationale behind this aesthetic was perhaps best expressed, albeit inadvertently, by the aforementioned Gil Kane (1926–2000). A one-time assistant to, later a colleague, admirer, and in sense rival to Kirby, Kane developed a reputation in the latter half of his career for both artistic experimentation and, like his close friend Hogarth, a penetrating insightfulness as a practitioner-critic. These qualities were evidenced in his pioneering experiments with the graphic novel form (*His Name is . . . Savage!*, *Blackmark*) and in his frequent commentary on other artists in the field. Though Kane's career was forged in mainstream, work-for-hire comic book production, in his interviews one detects his impatience with the constraints of the comics field as he came to know it—and a profound disconnect between the genre-bound, mostly superhero, material from which he earned his living and his own devotion to intellectual self-cultivation. At the same time, though, Kane remained steeped in

the heroic ideal of Foster, Raymond, and Hogarth. While articulate in his cri-
tiques of comic art—his comments about Kirby and other contemporaries are
instructive—Kane remained bound, more self-consciously than Kirby, more
self-consciously than most, to an aesthetic rooted in the inheritance of Romanticism and fantasy, an aesthetic that his most personal works, such as the
novel-cum-comic book *Blackmark* (1971), attempted to dignify. His preferred
strategy was the juxtaposition of elegant drawing with extensive, novelistic
text, as he explained in later years through a variety of metaphors:

> [. . .] I also wanted to intersperse prose. [. . .] I was experimenting with
> the whole idea of getting a richer mix. And I was less concerned with
> content than I was with the texture of the material. [. . .] I wanted more
> of a *read* . . . ("Reflections" 85)

> I've never felt that [comics] is a purely visual medium that depends on a
> kind of elaborate pantomime in order to go through with the gags. Text
> is like sound in a sound film. It is not possible in my mind for the draw-
> ing to convey all the information. [. . .] I depend heavily on the written
> material. (Interview by Eisner 185)

> [A] movie did it all: [. . .] it gave you the moment, and guaranteed the
> moment, by not merely taking the physical action, but by doing every-
> thing humanly possible with sound effects and music, to point out what
> was happening. So I wanted to do that in comics. I wanted to use text
> in that way. ("Reflections" 86)

> I tried specifically to create an extra dimension in the use of prose [. . .]
> to orchestrate an unbroken picture continuity with an ongoing prose
> obligato. ("Kane on Savage" 53)

Despite these efforts, Kane's reputation rests largely on his pictures: the intelligence and drive of his panel compositions and the grace and beauty of his
figure work. The latter, à la Hogarth and Kirby, was dynamic and contorted
while aiming for a balletic classicism (see Harvey, *Comic Book*, Chapter 5).
Kane's ideal, at work in comics-for-hire like *Captain Action* (1968–69) but
most obviously sought after in his later graphic novels, was to join such expressive drawings with a heated, articulate text, pseudo-literary in form and
yet colorful, insistent, and often brutal in the manner of the pulps.

Kane's graphic novels, in other words, combined heroically posed figures
(within or without the standard comics grid) with large blocks of text. He

took pride in the rhythmic organization of the two ("Reflections" 88–89). Unfortunately, the resulting works have a stuttering, overdetermined quality, the result of the momentum of the drawings colliding with the different momentum of the script. The illustrations are often uneasily partnered with the verbose narration, pulling the reading in opposing directions at once. In short, these books exaggerate comics' fundamental tension between text and image. This was, for Kane, some version of Literature and Art getting it together—but this quest to elevate comics led him, arguably, to an impasse.

McCloud argues the futility of this approach in *Understanding Comics* by depicting the would-be poet and the would-be painter working at cross purposes to one another, eventually finding that their different standards and ambitions have opened up an insuperable gap between them (48). Such ambition often results in work that, viewed as comics, is painstaking yet lifeless (notwithstanding the great skill of artists like Kane). As Groensteen points out, comic art does not necessarily answer to the canons of realism or illustrative classicism, but is fueled essentially by its narrative purpose. It is narrative drawing, in contradistinction to illustrative drawing, which, as Groensteen argues, relates differently to written text, leans more heavily toward the decorative, and, by virtue of its separateness from the text, typically elicits "a more contemplative reading" (163). By contrast, the comics drawing of Kirby is, always, narrative.

Narrative drawing is in some senses a self-deprecating or self-evading art. There is a fundamental tension in such drawing between the very *picture-ness* of the pictures and their compelling narrative function. Picture-ness is hard to describe, for, as James Elkins argues, pictures "are always partly nonsemiotic," that is, outside or in excess of narrative and linguistic structures. Indeed the pleasure and provocation they offer reside in precisely that. "To see what a picture is, is to see what about it cannot be described," its inenarrable, untellable, and so-called subsemiotic qualities (47). To ignore such qualities is to ignore pictures: "Parts of pictures are disorderly, unpredictably irrational, inconsistently inconsistent, and ill suited to stories of symbols or visual narratives; we tend to ignore those aspects in favor of readily retrievable meanings. But those abandoned elements are *what pictures are* [. . .]" (xviii, his emphasis). Yet Groensteen cautions us, rightly I think, that to read a comic is to anticipate a narrative structure, to prioritize "the dynamic of the story." On first reading, therefore, the comics image "is apprehended principally in its enunciable quality, as an utterable," a statement with a specific transcribable meaning ("A Few Words . . ." 91). By this logic, even the disorderly, unnarratable, and "purely" visual aspects of a comic drawing are subsumed to its narrative purpose. This tension is, depending on one's viewpoint, either eased or heightened in comics that favor a traditional illustrative manner, place the text outside of the image, and encourage the reader to linger in a contemplative mood, such as in Foster or much of Raymond, with their luscious, Old Master-like tableaus. In Kirby there is no question of lingering.

Kirby's art leans continually on what Groensteen identifies as the five undergirding principles, or tendencies, in narrative drawing: *anthropocentrism*, meaning a tendency to privilege characters in action and to treat each comics panel as, primarily, a habitat for characters[7]; *synecdochic simplification*, meaning the drawing's tendency to excise elements unnecessary to the understanding of the narrative, in effect paring away redundancies and representing the whole of the situation through selected parts; *typification*, meaning the graphic simplification of characters down to a handful of identifiable features (the modus operandi of caricature and, of course, an invitation to the evils of stereotyping); *expressivity*, meaning the evocativeness—the dramatic and emotional loading or intensification—of each stand-alone image, in terms of gesture, expression, and the semblance of movement; and, finally, *rhetorical convergence*, a term more difficult to gloss but conveying, in essence, the way the comics image strives after maximum legibility via the concurrence of all its various graphic elements, from paneling to composition to rendering, et cetera (161–62). In short, narrative drawing tends to be action- and character-oriented, streamlined, dependent on typing, and expressive, and it obeys above all a rhetorical function. Kirby's art certainly is and does all of these things.

Suspended between these five principles is the cartoonist's art: a field of tensions created by opposing demands. The principle of expressivity, for example, may flout the demands for simplification and typification, for expressivity is as much graphic as narrative, realized through singular, vivid, at times "disorderly" images that are not just narratively functional but packed with emotional intensity and the seeming potential for movement. Since expressive drawing is gestural and personal, the demand for expressivity may at times run counter to simplification and typing. This is another way of saying that narrative drawing, despite its often schematic nature, is not reducible to stagnant clip art but instead constitutes, as Groensteen puts it, "a singular graphical writing," as in handwriting, one that impresses us with its energy and personal flair (*System* 125). As Harry Morgan reminds us, comic art is typically *autographic*, testifying to the liveliness and quirkiness of drawing-by-hand even as it aims for streamlining and simplification ("Graphic Shorthand" 24–28).

Other tensions are in play as well. For instance, the need for expressivity of "movement" places great demands on the artist, involving him/her in a play of tensions between the drawing and its framing, that is, the panel. Likewise, the inevitably rhetorical function of the drawings may work both with and against the demand for graphic expressivity, since the requirement of legibility may clash with a gestural spontaneity in style. The tensions at play among anthropocentrism, simplification, expressivity, and the drive for legibility may determine the extent to which the drawings surround characters with, or isolate them from, settings—that is, the extent to which characters interact with the *mise en scène* and the drawings strive to evoke a sense of place (all within the narrow, bounded space of the panel). When does establishing a character's environment become more important? When does following through on a character's actions become more important? How does the character interact with, or crash into, its environment, and how can all that crashing be bounded within the panel? Out of such tensions comes artwork that is, in fact, radically inconsistent and fairly crackles with the ingenuity of continual, desperate problem-solving. This tense quality is particularly obvious in action-adventure comics, with their privileging of movement, in sharp distinction to the aesthetic of "pictorial stillness" (I borrow the phrase from Daniel Clowes' *Modern Cartoonist*) that, flouting conventions established by Kirby, characterizes so many contemporary alternative comics.

This dialectic between (seeming) movement and (seeming) stillness serves to highlight the overriding quality of Kirby's drawing: its breathless, bounding quality, that is, its obedience to a nonstop narrative momentum. The *imperative* element in Kirby's art is the semblance of movement, which, by contrast, invests his rare stillnesses with terrific emotional impact (as in the conclusion of our *Demon* example). All the parameters of his art—such as composition, framing, and rendering—can be defined by their observance of this principle. If the work of Milton Caniff epitomizes the tendencies of narrative drawing, then Kirby's work, at first derivative but later tumbling in its own eccentric orbit, distorts and twists within the Caniff tradition, favoring an exaggerated expressivity of movement. Kirby sacrificed, or drastically redefined, grace and proportion in keeping with his impatient, almost frantic narrative vision. Underlying this vision is a hovering sense of threat—an apocalyptic imagination excited by the prospect of disaster. As Kane once remarked, with Kirby it's always a "nuclear situation," on every page ("Gil Kane" 4a).

If, following Groensteen, we regard cartooning as narrative drawing that obeys the five demands of anthropocentrism, simplification, typification, expressivity, and maximum readability, we can add here several new considerations:

First (and I believe this is implicit in Groensteen), a cartoonist's skill in narrative drawing develops in tandem, and in tension, with her/his developing mastery of the architectonic aspects of the comics page, by which I mean the interrelated aspects of narrative breakdown, gridding (or paneling), and page layout. In this connection, consider that Kirby's drawing thrives as he experiments with, but then moves away from, the high baroque or decorative sense of page design that characterizes his early work with Joe Simon.

Second, a cartoonist may and probably will learn to balance the five demands in trademark, idiosyncratic ways, what I have elsewhere called protocols, or formal habits (*Alternative* 71–72). The word *habit* probably gets closer to what I mean. These habits will shape her/his distinctive "style" or idiolect. For example, in Kirby synecdochic simplification and the drive for expressivity take extreme forms, leading to such protocols as, say, the close cropping of figures so that only parts of face (typically the eyes) can be seen. This is a punctuating and intensifying habit that often occurs in Kirby's breakdowns. Similarly, Kirby's drive for expressivity, or intensification, results in other habits such as the drastic use of motion lines or foreshortening, which serve to enable his highly compressed breakdowns of violent action.

Third, and finally, negotiating the five demands determines how a cartoonist arrives at her/his peculiar balancing of what I've called here the iconic, the symbolic, and the physically indexical or idiographic. Demands for simplification, typification, and expressivity are likely to pitch us toward the symbolic register, rather than the straightforwardly iconic; at the same time, demands for expressivity often encourage the kind of graphic excess we identify as idiographic: the expressive hallmarks, the handwriting if you will, of the individual cartoonist. And yet the idiographic qualities of the artist's handiwork are constrained by, and are usually supposed to subserve, the principle of maximum readability. By this light, cartooning becomes, consciously or not, a tense balancing act. If we cannot in the end establish an ironclad division of sign types, if our semiotic classifications remain slippery, we can at least define a field of tensions in which likeness, symbolism, and graphic expressivity are counterpoised. Peirce's triad serves to delimit that field of contrary impulses and helps explain why (though not exhaustively *how*) cartooning, while commonplace, is such a mysterious activity.

## THE DEVELOPMENT OF KIRBY'S STYLE

How Kirby learned to negotiate these tensions can be seen by contrasting his mature work at Marvel with his early work in collaboration with Simon. Witness, for example, a late-sixties page in which Kirby revisits a Golden Age S&K property but in a new register (see plate 2). In *Captain America* #109 (Jan. 1969), Kirby, along with scripter Stan Lee, retells the origin of the super-patriot: how frail Steve Rogers, an army reject, is transformed by the

"Super-Soldier" project—essentially a scientific miracle—into the superhumanly powerful "Cap." Here Kirby, as was his wont, not only drew this story but almost certainly conceived and certainly "gridded out" its plot; that is, he made the crucial decisions about how the story should be broken down and the page laid out, decisions that served to pace and stage the action. All this he accomplished by composing the pencil under-drawings that lay beneath inker Syd Shores's brushwork. Kirby's pencils would have been tight and specific, and his intentions clarified by his handwritten plot notes in the margins (which are just visible in our reproduction of the original art). Out of, or over, Kirby's detailed pencils and notes, Lee crafted the final script. This distribution of workload, as I will discuss in our next chapter, came to be known as the Marvel method or Marvel "style." The resultant odd chemistry—Kirby's momentum and sizzle, Lee's anchoring verbiage—owes as much to Kirby's designing intelligence as to Lee's. What Kirby is doing here, in essence, is re-inhabiting an old story that by 1969 was already very much a part of his own career story, and bringing to it the benefit of all his years in comics. Note that, though the drawings on this page are not in the least bit vague or elusive, they are highly abstract.

This version contrasts sharply with S&K's original telling of the tale from *Captain America Comics* #1 (March 1941), likewise penciled by Kirby and (according to Simon, *Makers* 44) inked by Al Liederman (fig. 6). The later Kirby has, in essence, assembled a vocabulary of distinctive graphic mannerisms that not only announce the work as *his* but also redraw the balance between the iconic and the symbolic, between the mimetic and the idiographic. In the revised version, the sequence of Steve Rogers's metamorphosis is both more prolonged and more intensely focused on Steve's figure itself, to the exclusion of background elements. Kirby, updating the mechanics of Cap's origin by emphasizing the idea of radiation or "vita-rays" (his marginal notes use the words *radiation* and *radiates*), transforms the sequence into a play of abstract graphic elements, all of which serve to guide the eye around the page: fanciful high-tech gear, radiating lines, and of course coruscating mark or dot patterns, what fans often call "Kirby krackle," which by 1969 had become his trademark method of portraying sizzling energy. The later version of the tale is a longer version, so it accommodates a longer, more visually indulgent metamorphosis; it is also more insistently focused on Steve himself: his form, his sensations, and his emotional reactions (fitting, as the later version is framed as a personal recounting of, or flashback to, his origin). Above all, the new version is more graphically oriented.

This is not to say that the earlier version is unexciting. The two versions seek to create excitement and tension in different ways. The earlier one, typical

Fig. 6. Cap's origin as originally told. Joe Simon and Jack Kirby, with Al Liederman (inks), "Meet Captain America." *Captain America Comics* #1 (Mar. 1941), page 5. As reprinted in *Captain America: The Classic Years* (Marvel, 1998). © Marvel.

of S&K's early Golden Age output, leans toward Witek's high baroque, in that certain panels overlap and impose on others, violating borderlines as if the action they depict is impossible to contain. Specifically, S&K use Steve's figure to invigorate the page: Steve repeatedly breaks through panel borders as if to emphasize his growth and transformation. Simon describes the collaborative process behind this page, and this story, thusly:

> I wrote the first issue of *Captain America Comics* with penciled lettering right on the drawing boards, with very rough sketches for figures and background. Kirby did his thing, building the muscular anatomy, adding ideas and pepping up the action as only he could.
>
> Then he tightened up the penciled drawings, adding detailed backgrounds, faces and figures. (*Makers* 43–44)

The basic panel layout, presumably, came from Simon's roughs, though the breaking of the panel borders may have come from Simon and Kirby together, inasmuch as Kirby filled out the roughs with heroic figures and extra details (as noted in Chapter 0, baroque layout and heroic anatomy often push and pull against each other). In any case, the seven panels here are united graphically by the changing figure of Steve, which, appearing three times in medium shot, overlaps and joins successive panels and in effect creates a descending column down the middle of the page. The approach is less keyed to Steve's own sensations, since the character does not speak at all; as a result, the sequence seems to be about the professor glorying in his success.

By contrast, the later version (perhaps partly due to Lee's input?) punctuates the professor's monologue with Steve's own dialogue, which affirms his self-awareness; moreover, the later Kirby draws Steve as undergoing a staggering physical transformation, preparing for his triumphant emergence in the last panel. The whole sequence is more abstract yet also more emotionally intense: not merely glowing with energy, the later version of the character is seen, first, being bombarded by rays, then staggering in a cloud of fizzing Kirby krackle. In fact the third panel decomposes Steve's figure itself into a dot pattern—a recurrent visual trope in late Kirby—prolonging and partly obscuring, for suspense's sake, his transformation. In the last panel, Steve fully emerges from this bath of energy, becoming a T-shaped locus of tension as he leans against background machinery as if for support (or, conversely, in a Samson-like show of strength). Essentially, the page prepares for Steve's final, triumphant declaration by wreaking havoc with his form. So, in sum, the later version allows for greater graphic excitement in the successive images, due to its simpler, more conventional, and less crowded layout—a retreat from the high baroque—and its determined focus on Steve's body as seen from a consistent angle. Thus it reinforces the idea that Steve's metamorphosis is a kind of galvanizing birth trauma. When Cap emerges from those crackling dots, he does not, as in the earlier version, dispassionately look at himself as if in self-appraisal, but instead seems both exultant and stunned.

Two important things are happening in this retelling. First off, Kirby and Lee are approaching the old S&K character as if his importance were already established and his origin had already taken on mythic status (as indeed had already happened by the Silver, or revivalist, Age of the superhero). The retelling represents a chance to get inside the old story and redramatize it, elaborating, filling in, and improvising over its basic structure. Such revisiting and revision of the past was a staple of Silver Age superhero comics, adverting to their historical awareness and self-consciousness as inheritors of the preceding Golden Age. The architects of the Silver Age, at both Marvel and DC, already knew they were working with mythic materials. Secondly, Kirby's visual elaborations here show his greater command of cartooning as a balance of mimetic, symbolic, and graphic purposes. What he had achieved by this point was a redrawing of the genre's balance between pictorial realism and cartoon stylization.

From his earliest work, through his peak collaborations with Simon, to his mature work in the 1960s, Kirby continually renegotiated that balance, discovering, solidifying, and amplifying his personal style. His first, self-inked stories designed specifically for comic books—typified by science fiction tales like "Solar Legion" and "Comet Pierce" (both 1940), which came just before and at the start of his work with Simon—show him rendering in a Raymond-esque way, imitating *Flash Gordon*, with a slick inking style that favors deep black-spotting, tight feathering, and occasional drybrush (see Theakston, *1917–1940*, page 89). With a likely nod to former Eisner-Iger stablemate Lou Fine, early Kirby aims for sensuousness of line, but his blacks are heavier and his overall look denser, with figures sometimes defined via large feathered swaths of black. Many of the figures seem to have been polished to a shine. Soon after, Kirby's work coarsened considerably, as he and Simon and company began cranking out a great deal of work (for example, *Captain America Comics*) at a breathless pace. At this point, in the early forties, the S&K style blossomed, as their trademark antic layouts and frenzied fight scenes helped make up for the rushed, often slapdash quality of the drawing. Feathering and such took second place to sheer bounding energy: Kirby picked up Simon's design sense and mostly lost the Fine-like elegance and slick inking sheen.

His mature work in the S&K studio, a step beyond, came around the late forties to early fifties, and often featured his own inking (or touching-up of other artists' inks), the result being the quintessential S&K style, with its kinetic black-spotting, quick dashing or blotting strokes, and what Harry Mendryk has called "picket-fence" crosshatching, that is, the practice of intersecting a pair of long lines with a series of short, quick, "picket"-like strokes, often used to create clothing folds ("Glossary"). In this way even static scenes of dialogue and exposition crackle with a barely repressed energy. Kirby popularized this technique and took it far, creating a vigorous, rough-hewn surface that became his idiographic fingerprint. Steranko explains: "The idiosyncratic element in [Kirby's] approach . . . was in his *application of blacks*—bold, slashing strokes at regular intervals that allowed chips of the background board to show through, creating rich textures, powerful silhouettes, and defining shadow areas (rather than turning edges like traditional feathering)" ("Inking" 79, his emphasis). Kirby typically treated shadows as masses of brushstrokes rather than uniform pools of darkness, and he got into the habit of defining shapes by the buildup of flecks of black. The results are well displayed in a turbulent page from "The Girl Who Tempted Me" (*Young Romance* #17, Crestwood/Prize, Jan. 1950), in which, true to S&K's romance aesthetic, the layout is a stable, fairly conventional six-panel grid but the drawings aim for a sense of emotional violence (fig. 7). Here even the simple draping of clothing on a body is invested with breathtaking force. This technique was certainly influenced by Caniff's chiaroscuro approach, but also, as Steranko points out in the above source, by the brushwork of J. C. Leyendecker, one of the reigning commercial illustrators of the early twentieth century, whose kinetic strokes, as if aiming for an unfinished look, allowed the underpainting to show through as highlights even in areas of deep shadow (Eisner too absorbed this technique, and, again, clothing folds are often the giveaway).

By the time Kirby hit his mid-sixties peak at Marvel, though, he had gone further still into energetic abstraction to such a degree that even his figure work was affected: gone were the lithe, graceful figures of his early work, now replaced by knobby, roughly sculpted forms boasting an angular modernist severity bordering on the grotesque. He was far from the understated elegance of Foster, even from the sleekly burnished dynamism of Hogarth. He had abandoned any Leyendecker or Raymond or Fine-like pretensions to beauty and adopted an approach to form and shading that was almost brutally stylized, exaggerating the forcefulness of his earlier drawing style and turning the tics of his rendering into a codified vocabulary of graphic symbolism. At the same time, he came to favor regular, conventional layouts that lacked the flash of early S&K but allowed him to focus all his energies on composition and narrative flow. In short, Kirby had come to inhabit an even more obvious idiographic shorthand, a distinct and mannered style that Marvel sought to

Fig. 7. Vintage S&K: kinetic inking lends emotional turbulence. Joe Simon and Jack Kirby, "The Girl Who Tempted Me." *Young Romance* #17 (Jan. 1950), page 9. As reprinted in Richard Howell, ed., *Real Love* (Eclipse, 1988). © Joseph H. Simon and the Estate of Jack Kirby.

reproduce as a house look—and which is distilled in our later *Captain America* example.

Kirby's mannered style supplied the very blueprint for superhero fantasy in the late sixties. That style, it should be clear, is at odds with the illustrative tradition deriving from Raymond, Foster, and Caniff, certainly with the Raymond/Foster ideal of beauty, academicism, and verisimilitude. It exceeds even Hogarth's tensely exaggerated figure work. If Kirby started out wanting to draw like these artists, he failed. The creative yield of that failure, though, was a stylized and evocative pseudo-realism at once bombastic, eye-catchingly graphic, and unique to his sensibility. By the latter sixties Kirby had developed (and he would continue to develop) a very personal and distinctive way of reconciling cartooning's mimetic impulse—its never-ending striving toward realism and pictorial fullness—with its symbolic and indexical, hand-crafted qualities. In the process he sacrificed loveliness and naturalism and went for sheer vaulting energy; as Kane once noted, he went from figures to "just the idea of a figure," in the process becoming more abstract and more immersed in his own mannerisms, his own hieroglyphics ("Gil Kane on Jack Kirby," page 40). What he forfeited in realism and grace he gained in intensity.

In light of all this, is it too great a leap to describe the work of the comic artist as a struggle? It should be evident by now that Kirby's style represents an especially tense and fiercely, brilliantly, elaborated version of that struggle. Perhaps this is why Kirby was, for so long, the superhero artist par excellence: his style constitutes an unresolved yet generative compromise between realism and symbol, naturalism and fantasy. The failure of Kirby's pictorial realism—better yet, the fact that he ended up outflying realism's gravitational pull—highlights tensions basic to the superhero genre, not only graphic but also thematic tensions. Superheroes, after all, are a genre in which writers and artists repeatedly have sought to recuperate the fantastic by recourse to doses of realism: psychological, social, and pictorial. As critic Tom Crippen suggests, realism provides a spice of difference, an "other" side, to superhero comics, not fundamentally setting their horizons but giving their fantasies, by weight of contrast, some ballast, some sense of solidity and grandeur. Realism and superhero fantasy "slide against each other" in a kind of tectonic action (134). This is why new developments in superhero comics—from the Marvel of the early sixties, through the self-consciously "relevant," politically tinged superheroes of the early seventies and the revamped *X-Men* of the late seventies and early eighties, to the various revisionist and revivalist superheroes of the eighties and nineties—have so often been described in terms of their putative realism, despite their ever-obvious fantastic and wish-fulfilling character. The narrative art of Kirby, though grossly unrealistic compared to that of many of his peers (consider for example the figure work of Alex Toth or Carmine Infantino or many of the EC artists), brought a sense of solidness and scope to the most outrageous of fantasies, and so enabled Marvel's sense of irony and vaunted "realism" during the sixties. Today's fashionable superhero artists, though working in an idiom defined by Kirby's narrative momentum, design sense, and conceptual chutzpah, have sought to resolve the tension between realism and fantasy in favor of a meticulous hyper-realism (a fussiness reliant on digital production and improved printing). In fact the history of superhero comics post-Marvel, beginning with Neal Adams in the late sixties, is a series of reactions, whether direct or deferred, to/against the Kirby aesthetic.

By the time of *The Demon* (1972–74), Kirby's eccentricities had become pronounced enough to repel many fans. Marvel artists like John Buscema had, in a few years, domesticated the Kirby style, smoothing down its rough edges with a touch of classicism, while Kirby himself had blossomed into further weirdness. But cartoonists just then arriving to comic books, such as Walter Simonson and John Byrne, would continue to turn to Kirby as the sustaining inspiration of their superhero work, filtering his breathless dynamism through the more ornate graphic design sensibilities of Adams and his successors, negotiating their own graphically exciting compromises between realism and fantasy, and struggling for their own personal "styles." Kirby and Adams are, in this sense, the artists whose influence bridges the late newsstand period and the early direct market period of comic book sales. Kirby, in hindsight, is the more cartoony, while Adams represents a compromise between Kirby, the old Foster/Raymond illustrative standard, and (in this sense like Raymond) slick, photorealistic advertising graphics. Today's superhero comics, in their continual Kirby-inspired effort to fashion modern *mythoi* from the old ingredients of genre, are superficially more serious; graphically, they tend to steer closer to the photorealistic and finely rendered work of Adams, or, more nearly, the latter-day painted efforts of the Loomis and Rockwell-inspired Alex Ross. But the worlds they inhabit, and the character designs they have inherited, are still Kirbyesque in conception and scope. Each subsequent revitalizing of superhero style, Ross's for example, takes as its repertoire of images the fantastical visions of Kirby. The irony of this is that, among current superhero fans, appreciation of Kirby-as-cartoonist seems to have languished, as if his narrative drawing is seen only in terms of the superhero's narrow lineage and in contrast to the genre's current so-called realism, rather than in the context of cartooning more broadly understood. It is as if Kirby's style is simply something to be outgrown, even as his concepts are ransacked *ad infinitum*.

To find appreciations of Kirby's art that go beyond the orbit of the Marvel/DC superhero, one has to look to the alternative comics culture—Panter for instance—or to the rare critical intervention from a fine-arts perspective, for example the placing of Kirby among the *Masters of American Comics* assembled for John Carlin and Brian Walker's controversial museum exhibition in 2005–07 (see Carlin et al.). In some circles, Kirby has at least taken on the role of outsider artist: an intuitive and obsessive primitivist with a Wölfli-like *horror vacui* and a yen for bizarre, Darger-esque mythopoesis. Jonathan Lethem's critical characterization of him—admiring, bemused, a bit embarrassed—epitomizes this view, labeling Kirby an "autistic" genius whose work "spun off into abstraction," an obsessive and "disastrous genius uncontainable in the form he himself had innovated." To Lethem, this makes Kirby "great/awful" (8). Yet in the superhero culture Kirby remains not so well understood, or so frankly, so critically, confronted. He is half-hidden by the very properties he created and the continuing exploitation and revision of same. Sure, many fans can spot Kirby or a Kirby imitation from a mile away, but appreciation of his narrative drawing as such tends to lag behind love of the characters he designed. Ironically, the long-term consequences of Kirby's success, among them a specious realism in superhero comics, have rendered his own distinctive achievement as a narrative artist harder to see.

## 2

# KIRBY, STAN LEE, AND THE CREATION OF MARVEL COMICS

In 1985 one of the beloved, sustaining myths of comic book culture came hurtling down: that of the Marvel Bullpen. According to this long-savored myth, the Marvel Comics of the sixties—in the eddies of which the comic book industry still spun, and still spins to this day—was a bastion of collegiality and capering fraternal humor, a "bullpen" of close, like-minded eccentrics who turned Marvel's editorial offices into a friendly, comfortable, freewheeling shambles. At the center of this happy madness were the comically self-aggrandizing figures of Marvel's editor-in-chief Stan Lee—more familiarly, Smilin' Stan or Stan the Man—and his signature artists, none more prolific or popular, and none more important to the myth, than the compact, cigar-chewing, childishly eager persona of "Jolly Jack" Kirby. They sometimes appeared as characters in the comics themselves. For readers versed in the Marvel comics of the sixties—but unversed in the contentious, demythologizing coverage of the industry that had arisen in the eighties—the nominal team of "Stan and Jack" was something to prick up the antennae, something to conjure with: a nostalgic beacon.

What finally happened to topple this myth in the mid-eighties is that Jack Kirby, who by then was years removed from day-to-day business with Marvel, found himself singled out and, as he saw it, punished for his indispensable contributions to the company. Marvel, in defiance of what had by then become standard industry practice, refused to return to Kirby his original artwork unless he signed a statement explicitly disavowing any creative credit for, or stake in, the Marvel characters for which he was famous (see "Held Hostage"; Dean, "Kirby and Goliath"; Morrow, "Art vs. Commerce"). When this became known—well, to say that it stirred up controversy in comic book fandom would be coy. Championed by many in the industry, particularly by *The Comics Journal*, the pugnacious trade magazine that broke the story, Kirby became, after Jerry Siegel and Joe Shuster of *Superman* fame, the archetype of the classic comic book creator denied credit and fair compensation for his work by the corporate rights-holders who now profited from that work. The *Journal* circulated a petition among professionals and devoted considerable space and rhetorical fire to rallying readers around Kirby, in the process attacking if not upending the long-held idealization of Marvel as an Edenic clubhouse (Dean 95; see also "Held Hostage" 60–61). Those who had followed industry coverage presumably already knew better, but, still, many fans were shocked, enough so that Marvel became a byword for corporate cupidity and ingratitude. Some fans (ahem, I'll raise my own hand here) even boycotted Marvel publications as a result.

In 1987, a legal settlement was reached, its terms confidential, under which Kirby at last received a reported 1,900 (or, per Evanier, 2,100) of the more than 8,000 original pages he had created for Marvel, much of his artwork having already been lost to shoddy warehousing or stolen outright (see Heintjes 20; Morrow, "Commerce" 31; Evanier, *King* 205). The ripples of this struggle, though, did not end with the settlement: eventually, in a sometimes-volcanic interview given to *The Comics Journal* in 1989, Kirby made plain his bitterness over Marvel's official disregard, what he saw as their pusillanimous, impersonal treatment of him and his family, and even the happy-go-lucky myth of jollity and artistic solidarity fostered so fervently by Stan Lee. Moreover, Kirby disputed Lee's share of creative contribution to the early Marvels, claiming sole authorship: "Stan Lee and I never collaborated on anything!" It turned out that Kirby worked at home—no hectic bullpen for him—and he preferred it that way, outside of Lee's orbit. "I used to write the stories just like I always did," he said. Lee, in his view, was simply "an editor . . . Stan Lee wasn't a guy that read or told stories" (Interview with Groth 37–38).

With that, the cherished dream of the Marvel Bullpen came crashing, toppling. Whatever the factual accuracy of Kirby's recollections—as we'll see, the issue of how Marvel came to be is considerably more complex—the myth of Marvel as a fraternal clubhouse was definitively smashed, for anyone who cared to pay attention.

The recollections of comic book fans are full of stories about the loss of innocence: about changes or traumas that served to sunder them from their putatively idyllic, untroubled childhoods. I suppose this one is mine—but not mine alone, for a great many comic book fans have read the story of Kirby versus Marvel exactly this way, as a rude slap into awareness. That story is not such a shock now, but neither has it gone away. Granted, the controversy quieted in the nineties and early 2000s, and in those years the landscape has changed: at this writing, Stan Lee is detached from Marvel in all but his honorific status as "Chairman Emeritus" (in fact even in the eighties his involvement with

Marvel's publishing was scant); Marvel itself, a different outfit than it was in 1985, has increasingly granted Kirby auteur status via comic book credits, trade paperback collections of his work, and, especially, costly hardcover collections for Kirby devotees (see our Appendix). Lately, however, the controversy has returned with a vengeance, this time with potentially far-reaching legal consequences for Kirby's estate, which has not profited from most of the Marvel products bearing his work, is now in the process of challenging Marvel's copyrights to various properties he helped create (though how or indeed whether this will come to trial may take a long time to tell).

In any event, fans' concern over creative credit for Kirby, or lack thereof, is now growing, the recent spate of feature films and home video releases produced or co-produced by Marvel Studios being a clear catalyst. For example, Kirby fans anxiously anticipated the on-screen billing and, later, DVD documentary acknowledgment of Kirby as co-creator of the Fantastic Four in the first feature film based on that property, released in 2005 (Morrow, "Kirby on Film"; Will Murray, "Visit"). Between 2005 and 2009, when Kirby's heirs brought their case, interest in Kirby's struggle against the company revived and grew (see for example "2005 Kirby Tribute Panel," 69–72), though not to such a pitch as to rival the interest generated by the news, in August 2009, that Marvel had been bought by Disney. (That acquisition itself has influenced coverage of the Kirby case, of course.) Among many fans there remains a stubborn, nagging sense that Kirby has been under-acknowledged for his creative role, and a desire to see his name officially enshrined as co-creator of some of Marvel's most enduring properties.

So, can we say what really happened at Marvel in the sixties?

## THE TROUBLE WITH AUTHORSHIP

*Marvel Comics*, of course, is more than simply a name. The phrase stands for a whole set of ideas, including the Marvel "style," Marvel's corporate "universe" and its ever-looping continuity, and the drastic changes that Marvel worked on the superhero genre from the sixties onwards. In short, *Marvel* signifies an entire tradition: a distinct aesthetic and editorial approach to making comic books (and, latterly, adaptations of comics books). At the heart of that approach is the legacy of Kirby: his graphic energy, stylized violence, cosmic scope, distinctive design sense, and horde of larger-than-life characters. Marvel in the sixties was the stage for what became Kirby's most famous work—a great leapfrogging advance in his narrative art—and became the grounds of his still-unfolding career-story, his myth. Marvel was the hinge of Kirby's career.

Yet the conditions under which Kirby worked at Marvel—not simply constraints on an otherwise free-spirited artist, but *enabling* conditions that called Kirby's most famous work into being—make impossible any simple assignment of creative credit to Kirby's or anyone else's single authorship. Sure, Kirby's larger body of work, in all its vitality and fluorescent weirdness, argues that he was author and architect of much that we now know as Marvel; yet the circumstances of the company's rise were so complex that the respective contributions of Marvel's core creators are tough to separate out. Kirby's crucial if often remote working relationship with Lee (then Marvel's editor-in-chief and lead writer), his status as a mere freelancer under Lee, and his lack of any acknowledged proprietary claim on the properties he created for the company—all these make it hard to speak of Kirby as the sole force behind Marvel's success, his own late-career claims notwithstanding. What has become clear with some forty years of hindsight is simply this: although Kirby would not have been capable of creating a publishing empire like Marvel on his own, he did serve as the dynamo that powered Marvel and revitalized Lee's then-idling career as a comic book writer. Everything else is a little fuzzy.

"Fuzzy" applies to the entire history of the company, or rather the successive companies, that we now call Marvel. The Marvel Comics line, in the familiar sense, began in 1961 but quickly moved to incorporate characters from comic books published as far back as 1939. Or, to put it another way, Marvel launched in 1939 and again in 1961: the universe of titles and characters that would come to be known as Marvel grew out of Martin Goodman's pulp magazine operation in the late thirties, then survived a winding, sometimes unlucky publishing history under many different aliases before consolidating and, in effect, being reborn in the early sixties.

The company's history is a maze: known among collectors as Timely, then Atlas, this shifting, shifty operation began in 1939 with a single comic book, *Marvel Comics* #1 (retitled *Marvel Mystery Comics* as of #2). The company went on to achieve notoriety with its often crudely rendered, violent, and, after 1941, aggressively warlike line of costumed superhero comics. As noted in our Chapter 0, Kirby was there as early as 1940, partnering with line editor Joe Simon to create a flock of titles, most famously *Captain America Comics* (1941). This "Timely" period included signature super-characters the Human Torch, created by Carl Burgos, the Sub-Mariner, created by Bill Everett, and of course the star-spangled Captain America. After Goodman unceremoniously fired Simon and Kirby late in 1941, young Stan Lee succeeded to the position of editor-in-chief of Timely, which position he held until entering the Army in 1942. After the war, in 1945, Lee returned and resumed the editor's duties, replacing his friend and short-term substitute, cartoonist Vince Fago.

During the postwar falling-off of superheroes, Lee faithfully observed Goodman's policy of strip-mining other popular genres, such as *Archie*-style teen comics, romance, and horror, producing a flood of nakedly imitative material: whatever the market would bear. This period, the late forties to late fifties, was the mostly unloved "Atlas" era, the name owing to Goodman's magazine distribution outfit, Atlas News Co., Inc. (c. 1951–52 to 1956), though the comics themselves bore dozens of different publishers' names in the indicia—a sign of Goodman's financial caginess.[1] Most of the fifties went by at Atlas without a superhero in sight, exceptions being very brief, abortive revivals of Golden Age heroes Marvel Boy (1950, a revival in name only) and later the Human Torch and Captain America (1953–54) and the Sub-Mariner (1954–55). These produced only a handful of issues.

In the late fifties, as recounted in Chapter 0, Kirby was uprooted and lost. Split from his erstwhile partner Simon and badly burned by failed business deals, he sought work at Atlas, or rather the firm formerly branded as Atlas, putting aside the bad blood of past dealings with Goodman to become, gradually, editor Lee's ace in the hole. This process began with a trickle of work circa late 1958, and then accelerated to near-exclusivity by the end of 1959. The former Atlas was in bad shape, having surrendered its name and nearly died following a sudden, ruinous contraction in 1957: Goodman had lost distribution, and for a brief time Lee, on Goodman's order, had essentially frozen operations—that is, he had stopped giving out work (Lammers 49). The company had very nearly shut down. What remained after Goodman secured a last-ditch distribution contract was little more than a small module in his larger firm Magazine Management. (This critical period remains underdocumented, and is only briefly mentioned in most studies [see, for example, Daniels, *Marvel* 80; Raphael and Spurgeon 61; McLaughlin 136]. Tom Lammers has done the best study to date.) Lee was still reeling from that implosion when Kirby came on board. In addition, a favored artist of Lee's, the prolific and highly accomplished Joe Maneely, had died in June 1958, the victim of an accident (Apeldoorn, "When" 8–9; Raphael and Spurgeon 59–60; Vassallo 35). This loss had hit Lee hard. The once-Atlas of that period, then, was only a shadow of its former, market-deluging self. Into this near-vacuum Kirby stepped and quickly set to work, pouring his energy, at first, into a range of generic titles.

Here is how Kirby recalled the turning point at Marvel in the notorious *Comics Journal* interview: "I came in [to the office] and they were moving out the furniture, they were taking desks out—and I needed the work! I had a family and a house, and all of a sudden Marvel is coming apart. Stan Lee is sitting on a chair crying. He didn't know what to do [. . .]. I told him to stop crying. I says, 'Go in to Martin and tell him to stop moving the furniture out, and I'll see that the books make money.' And I came up with a raft of new books and all these books began to make money" (Interview with Groth 38). It's unclear whether Kirby meant for this story to refer to his return in 1958 or to the period just before *The Fantastic Four*'s launch in 1961. In any case the account seems self-mythologizing and is hard to credit. At one point Kirby refers to Lee as being "just still out of his adolescence," which is inaccurate, and characterizes him as helpless and childlike, which is unlikely. Lee explicitly denied all this years later (McLaughlin 137). Gary Groth, who conducted the *Journal* interview in 1989, acknowledged on its reprinting in 2002 that some of Kirby's statements "should be taken with a grain of salt; [. . .] most observers and historians consider Kirby's claims [in the interview] to be excessive" (19). What's clear is that by 1989 Kirby was angry, and determined to undo Lee's version of history.

In any case, it was about three years after Kirby's return to freelancing for Goodman that the new Marvel era began. It started unassumingly enough with the arrival of Lee and Kirby's *Fantastic Four*, a series about a dysfunctional family of misfit superheroes. Unveiled in late 1961, *The Fantastic Four* included Mr. Fantastic, an egghead scientist with Plastic Man-like stretching powers; his love interest the Invisible Girl, capable not only of transparency but also, eventually, of projecting telekinetic force fields (she would later rename herself the Invisible Woman); the Human Torch, a youthful hothead reviving the name and super-power of Burgos' wartime Torch but otherwise unrelated; and, most impressively, the bestial malcontent Ben Grimm, alias the Thing, a hulking, rocky-skinned, super-strong monster with tragic undercurrents—the prototype of Marvel's many alienated, almost unwilling heroes.

With the introduction of this strange, fractious band of characters, Marvel Comics in the modern sense was born. Within months the Fantastic Four had encountered a revamp of Everett's Sub-Mariner. Later Captain America and even Burgos' original Human Torch would be exhumed and reinstated in the ever-unfolding Marvel continuity, so that, by the seventies, all of the major (and many minor) costumed characters from the Timely era had been revived and made, retroactively, part of a putatively continuous history. In other words, the mostly unconnected superhero comics of the forties were retrofitted with the new Marvel continuity. By the mid-sixties Kirby's style had established a new gold standard for superhero comics, and his co-creations, with Lee, were legion: Dr. Doom, the Hulk, Thor, the Avengers, the X-Men, the Silver Surfer, Galactus, the Black Panther, the Inhumans, and many more, a pantheon of bizarre, sometimes pitiable, often incomprehensibly powerful super-freaks, outcasts, gods, and monsters. With these eccentric characters

Marvel rescued, contemporized, and redefined the superhero genre, establishing itself as *the* purveyor of mythic comic book fantasy and one of the most successful brands in the history of American comics.

Exactly how Marvel redefined the superhero is the subject of our next chapter. Suffice to say that the company's surprisingly successful run in the sixties was a pivotal period not only for superhero comics and the comic book industry in general but particularly for Kirby. It is here that late-period Kirby begins. To be more precise, late Kirby looms in 1959–1960 with his entrenchment as a prolific and eventually a nearly exclusive freelancer for Goodman and Lee (for whom he had done brief, tentative freelance work years prior, in 1956–57). More properly, late Kirby might be said to begin with the company's reentry into the superhero genre, with *Fantastic Four* #1 (dated Nov. 1961 but actually released in August). Unobtrusively labeled "MC" on its cover, *FF* #1 came just a few months after Goodman had quietly reintroduced the long-dormant corporate name "Marvel Comics" to the fine print of his publications, in effect reviving a tag that had served him as an on-again, off-again brand since 1939. This new incarnation of Marvel, however, would not be explicitly cover-tagged as the "Marvel Comics Group" until cover-date April to May 1963.

Better still, we could say that late Kirby begins with the gradual extension and enrichment of the Marvel Universe, accomplished through a series of comics from 1962 onward, but especially after 1963. A rereading of Marvel titles from late 1963, such as the first *Fantastic Four* annual or the first installments of the "Tales of Asgard" backup series in *Journey into Mystery* (spun off from *Journey*'s lead feature "Thor"), reveals ever-greater ambition on the part of Kirby and Lee, as elements previously introduced into the Marvel mythos are newly explored or made more prominent, filling in the broad outlines of a fictive world they had only begun to sketch. Notably, the Marvel titles of this period approach mythology (an old and favored subject of Kirby's) more confidently, allowing "Thor," until then largely set in a contemporary urban milieu typical of superheroes, to branch off into the distinctly atypical "Asgard," with its otherworldly settings and fast-and-loose adaptations of Norse myth. This expanded scope becomes most obvious when reading *Thor* (the former *Journey into Mystery*) and *Fantastic Four* in 1966–67. Kirby's growing ambition shows in his narrative drawing, which reaches new heights in terms of graphic design, violent stylization, and conceptual inventiveness. The work he produced in 1966–67 anticipates what he later aimed to create, albeit with greater freedom and ambition, in the grand if ultimately frustrated Fourth World project, produced not for Marvel but for rival publisher DC.

Through the late mid-sixties Kirby "stretched" the superhero genre with work that made familiar his signature late-period style (as seen in Chapter

1): a rough-hewn, intensely geometrical, almost monumental approach that nonetheless conveys immeasurable energy in its looming shapes, extreme fore-shortening, slashing lines, brusque figure work—and telltale graphic short-hand: Kirby's trademark renderings of impact, fire, hurricane winds, sizzling energy, metamorphoses of all kinds, and other temporal phenomena (as in our late-period *Captain America* example, plate 2). In comics such as Mar-vel's *Fantastic Four* and *Thor*, even in the more earthbound *Captain America*, and then in DC's *New Gods*, Kirby pushed these graphic protocols as far as he could, granting them palpable presence and, increasingly, exploiting full-page and double-page spreads to create vast, unearthly vistas. With outsized characters and concepts such as Galactus (in *Fantastic Four*), Ego the Living Planet (in *Thor*), and the Promethean Galaxy (in *New Gods*), Kirby indulged his passion for epic-scale drawing and blurring the boundaries between living and unliving, organic and inorganic, masses. Though all were derived from the traditional superhero comic, these notions were comparatively huge, and, for comic books, dizzying in their originality and unapologetic strangeness. Here Kirby blossomed into his late apocalyptic mode, tilting wildly toward his own quirky vision of the technological sublime (which we'll plumb in Chapter 4). Fired up by a new sense of license, by the expanded vista now open to his high-concept gimmicks and graphic chutzpah, Kirby took his narrative art—in terms of simplification, typification, expressivity, and sheer gutsy distinctiveness—to a mind-boggling new level.

For Kirby, the Marvel of the sixties was the springboard to a grander ap-proach. It was also the period of his most sustained association with a single company, other than his independent partnership with Simon during the for-ties and early fifties. Finally, it became the source of some of Kirby's greatest frustrations and disappointments as an artist—and the inspiration for fan-dom's latter-day re-envisioning of Kirby as a persecuted, underappreciated spiritual godfather. In short, this formative era at Marvel was, again, the hinge of his entire career. The extent to which Marvel's multimedia publicity has recognized or slighted Kirby as co-creator of its "universe" remains a topic of fans' arguments to this day.

It would be an exaggeration to credit Kirby with full authorship of his work at Marvel; the sixties, after all, were a pivotal decade for Stan Lee as well. As editor and chief spokesman for Marvel, Lee's presence was sustaining, generative, and overwhelming: his verbal swagger and editorial cunning were definitive to Marvel, and documentary evidence suggests he was, early on, both Kirby's guide and active collaborator in envisioning such properties as *The Fantastic Four*. At the launch of the *FF* in 1961, Lee was seemingly in the pilot's or co-pilot's seat, dreaming up the book's premise with Kirby at the be-hest of Goodman, who reportedly asked for a new title to compete with DC's then-blooming superhero revival. Lee is known to have created a detailed plot outline for *FF #1*, which has been reprinted several times—in *Fantastic Four #358* (Nov. 1991), in Tom DeFalco's book *Comics Creators on Fantastic Four*, in facsimile in the prozine *Alter Ego*, and elsewhere—although under what circumstances and at precisely what stage remains unclear (see Thomas, "First"). Other plot synopses by Lee from this era have also survived.

Kirby's artistic treatment of said synopses always went well beyond literal fidelity to the text (*FF #1* is a famous case in point), but such documents do testify to Lee's hands-on guidance or at least active editorial oversight of the project. Presumably, Lee continued to play this proactive role for some while. Years later, as his public role grew more prominent and his stumping for Marvel more constant, his contributions to Kirby's comics became less substantial; yet Lee continued to exercise a powerful editorial hand, dialoguing and captioning Kirby's pages in ways that at times shifted the plots—usually subtly but on a few occasions drastically—away from Kirby's original conceptions (for examples, see Gartland, "Failure," Parts One and Four).

By the *FF*'s heyday in 1966–67, Kirby seems to have been plotting the series with minimal consultation from Lee—a point I'll back up later—and was clearly setting the scope and atmosphere of the book. Ditto *Thor*. Yet Lee always had final editorial say and at times altered the books in ways that Kirby, always intent on the next deadline, did not even notice: reportedly Kirby seldom read the printed comics, believing that the crucial creative work was happening solely on his drawing board and mindful, always, of the next project. Lee's contribution, though overstated then and arguably overstated now, had a lot to do with determining the final tone of the Marvel books, their mix of ardent philosophizing, hothouse sentimentality, brazen salesmanship, and rhetorical cheek. Examples are legion, and often playfully intrusive on the action:

Occasionally, a tale needs no introduction! This is such a tale! A rainy night—a strangely forlorn figure—and rare wonderment awaits us—! (*Fantastic Four #51*)

*Confusing* enough for you, faithful one? Well, hold on tight—we've only *begun!!* (*Fantastic Four #56*)

A strange beginning for a *superhero saga*, thou dost think? Ahh, thou suspectest *not* the glory and grandeur awaiting thee within . . . (*Thor #143*)

WARNING! Prepare yourself for the unexpected *shock of a lifetime* which awaits you at the *conclusion* of this cataclysmic chronicle—! ("Captain America," *Tales of Suspense #98*)

Jolly Jack informs us that he has drawn Wyatt driving a *Ferrari Dino V-6 Berlinetta Special*—given to him, no doubt, by an oil-rich grandfather who is definitely with it!—This has nothing to do with our *tale*, but we thought you'd like to know! (*Fantastic Four* #59)

And now, for *bludgeoning BATTLE beyond compare* . . . By the golden gates of Asgard, we most earnestly urge thee, o keeper of the faith . . . *READ ON!* (*Thor* #151)

(This last example, by the way, claims to be "powerfully presented in pulse-pounding Panoramascope.") Lee's stew of verbal bounciness, jokey reflexivity, earnest humanism, cheerful cynicism, and grandstanding, Barnumesque hype established the Marvel ethos—the myth of the happy Bullpen—and, moreover, Lee consciously cultivated the Marvel readership, wooing older and non-traditional fans to comics (or back to comics). Kirby produced what many consider his greatest sustained work within this context, in a collaborative process that was, perhaps, not truly collaborative (in the sense of knowingly sharing work) but that nonetheless served to harness, discipline, and spotlight his strengths. Stan Lee—Kirby's boss in essence, a relationship that may have rankled the older, once-independent Kirby—helped make all of this happen, and was, though not sole architect, conservator and chief promoter of the Marvel mythos.

It would be just as much of an exaggeration to credit, or blame, Lee and Kirby with full responsibility for the state of superhero comics in the late newsstand era, that is, the sixties and seventies, let alone the rise of postmodern superheroes in the direct market as it flourished in the eighties onward. After all, Marvel's popular *Amazing Spider-Man*, though vaguely linked to a mothballed S&K concept (see Theakston, "Birth"; Evanier, *King* 127–28), did not turn out to be a Kirby project. Rather, Spider-Man was definitively developed by artist Steve Ditko in collaboration with Lee. As the company's leading solo hero, Spider-Man became another cornerstone of the Marvel Universe; the character was soon much-imitated and became the very type of the pitiable, self-involved, but still heroic Marvel character, the quintessential adolescent superhero. Kirby, despite his confusing latter-day claims, was not substantially involved in developing this new character.

Following Kirby/Lee and Ditko/Lee came younger creators bent on consolidating and further extending the Marvel Universe, such as scripter Roy Thomas and hyperrealist artist Neal Adams. Such creators shored up Marvel's continuity and more openly essayed progressive and topical themes, reflecting the concerns of youth culture and the gradual shift in social mores. Lee, for his part, was willing enough to embrace these changes, and indeed occasionally used late-sixties Marvel comics to broach social issues such as racism and the antiwar movement (a turnaround from Marvel's nakedly jingoistic comics of the early to mid-Vietnam era). But Lee's successors went further. Thomas and Adams, and after them a generation of writers weaned on fandom, deepened Marvel's fictive continuity and yet at times also tried to use the comics as a means of topical social argument. These efforts prepared the way for the dominant comic book franchises of the eighties, such as the revived *X-Men* (1975–), spearheaded by writers Len Wein and especially Chris Claremont and pencilers Dave Cockrum and John Byrne, and the revamped *Daredevil* (1979–83), darkly reimagined by cartoonist Frank Miller. The former often explicitly confronted intolerance and bigotry; the latter proffered a tense new dialogue about the ethics of vigilantism and the role of violence in superhero comics. These benchmark series harkened back to the unapologetic topicality of the earliest superhero comics, but also enabled an ever more hermetic, inward-turning fascination with continuity. Lee and Kirby, obviously, could not anticipate these departures, nor were they solely responsible for setting up or policing Marvel's increasingly crowded story-world.

That said, Kirby and Lee created the core of the Marvel Universe. Their jointly billed comics supplied more elements of Marvel's subsequent continuity than any other books until the *X-Men* craze of the late seventies and early eighties. Moreover, as conceptual artist, Kirby made a deeper impression on the company than any other. His outpouring of designs and concepts in the sixties established the company's reputation as an uncorked, unstintingly creative, even visionary outfit with a relentless flow of ideas. Indeed Marvel would become known, in both house hype and fan parlance, as the House of Ideas—an implicit tribute to Kirby's profuse imagination. The evidence of Kirby's post-sixties productivity, in contrast to Lee's, argues that, without Kirby, the seminal Marvel characters and concepts would simply not exist. Kirby brought the high concepts, and then Lee—Marvel's executive editor and taskmaster, chief scriptwriter and spokesman—shaped and polished the concepts to deliver them to the stands on a reliable basis. This joint effort, in which each man came to believe he was the principal creative partner, was arguably the professional peak for both, and yet Kirby would continue to conceive new characters and designs well after leaving Marvel. Indeed, as we've established, it was only after Marvel that Kirby became fully known as author, designer, and, finally, editor of his own work. This too was a kind of peak. Lee, in contrast, sought to escape the grind of comics production, and by the mid-seventies had all but retired from comic book scripting. Indeed he had been renegotiating and withdrawing from his role as scenarist (literally, creator of scenarios) throughout the sixties.

The question lingers—just what prompted Kirby to leave Marvel in 1970? As noted, the sale of Marvel to Perfect Film and Chemical in 1968 created terrible uncertainty for Kirby, who, in contrast to Lee, could not secure a contract. The new owners apparently didn't understand Kirby's crucial role at the company, but they understood Lee's (Evanier, *King* 150). In hindsight, it seems Lee worked hard to strengthen his position at Marvel prior to and during that transition, so that he would be seen as indispensable to the company's identity, no matter its owners. Lee's role in what had been Martin Goodman's company grew more central at the expense of Kirby and eventually even Goodman himself, who remained as publisher until 1972, succeeded by Lee, and then went on to found the short-lived Atlas/Seaboard company (wholly unrelated to Marvel, 1974–1975) to compete with Lee. The question of Marvel's authorship is entangled in the question of what Lee—who was, after all, never Marvel's owner—did to shore up his own status at the company. Presumably the owners at Marvel understood what "writer" meant, but did not understand the centrality of narrative drawing. Kirby thus languished while Lee throve.

In the late sixties Kirby had apparently come to believe that his star was in eclipse, overshadowed by Lee's tireless editorial and publicity presence. If so, he wasn't wrong. The voice of Marvel Comics, Lee's, increasingly ventured into the wider world to promote Marvel, attracting journalistic attention that confirmed the widespread view of the company as a kind of hip, hyper-energetic Pop Art. A seamless continuity of script and hype, all composed or tweaked by Lee, created a single, consistent voice: his. This voice also represented Marvel to its owners. After the mid-sixties, Lee's mock-gallant, cheerfully absurd persona became, more and more, the perceived kernel of Marvel, the presumed source of its line identity and imaginative heat. His star rose. By contrast, Kirby chafed under his relative belittlement in the press. He did not have, or did not publicly project, the keen, gregarious personality—the varnish of class and style—Lee had, and, though loyal fans surely knew better, he came off in press accounts, to the extent that he was mentioned at all, as little more than a hired hand in Stan's growing empire.

One notorious example, reportedly a source of great friction between Lee and Kirby, was an article in the *New York Herald Tribune* in January 1966 (Freedland). Said article portrayed Lee as Kirby's mentor and master and characterized Marvel as solely the result of "Lee's vision" (in the years to come more articles would assume the same). The piece, a giddy feature story packed with colorful tidbits, implicitly belittles Kirby, describing him as "a middle-aged man with baggy eyes and a baggy Robert Hall-ish suit" (29) in contrast to Lee's urbanity and "Ivy League wardrobe" (26); in essence, it's a profile of Lee as a New York celebrity. As Jeet Heer points out, the classist overtones of these descriptions are hard to miss: "Lee is a slick suburbanite [while] Kirby by contrast is a lower-middle-class yokel" ("Comics and Class" n. pag.). Lee is spry and vivacious, Kirby lumpen. The article goes so far as to depict an office "plotting" session in which Lee, full of energy, instills the inert Kirby with his ideas and drive. This was galling to the elder Kirby, who, as mentioned, had been art director at Goodman's Timely decades before (and who had regarded the then teenage Lee as a manic young gofer rather than a substantial collaborator). In fact, "galling" is a gross understatement: Kirby and his wife Roz were mortified by the *Herald Tribune* article, and it seriously wounded the two men's relationship (Thomas 18; Ro 104–05).

Speculating about Kirby's shifting mind-set throughout his Marvel years is risky but ever so tempting. Returning circa 1958–59 to freelance for the then thirty-five-ish Lee (by that time editor-in-chief) must have been humbling for Kirby, the more so because Lee's comics line was then skeletal and, as it had been for years, almost entirely undistinguished, a far cry from industry leadership or the kind of visibility and clout that Kirby, with Joe Simon, had once enjoyed. To fall under Stan's shadow in the mid-sixties, even as the freshly recreated Marvel leapt to new prominence, must have been bemusing at the least—to the extent that the dogged, deadline-centric Kirby allowed himself to notice what was transpiring. At first Kirby, it appears, was simply too busy to take note of his changing fortune; he worked tirelessly, and, again, was unskilled at safeguarding his talents against the vicissitudes of the business. His realization of Lee's growing cachet was slow and belated, and only gradually ignited to anger. But the anger did come.

Why is it so hard to understand who did what at Marvel? Kirby's contributions to the company were hidden partly by the very manner in which he worked. The so-called Marvel method or Marvel "style" of production made it difficult to determine individual contributions to the finished comics, creating a situation in which both the scripter (most often Lee, in the early days) and the penciler, or breakdown artist, could claim substantial credit for the undergirding concepts and the page-by-page narrative delivery of the stories. Under the Marvel method, the artist independently created breakdowns, meaning page layouts and drawings—roughs at the least, but often thoroughly detailed drawings—after which the nominal writer would supply dialogue and captions. The "writer" was more accurately an *ex post facto* scripter, or reviser: the dialoguer responsible for placing text on already-determined layouts (said layouts often included rough textual notes as well as images). This process placed cartoonists in the driver's seat narratively, calling on them to break down plots and lay out pages on their own without minute, page-by-page input from another scenarist.

The extent to which Lee, over the years, continued to serve as initial scenarist or co-scenarist, as he seems to have done in Marvel's early days, has been a source of unending controversy and certainly confusion among fans and general readers alike. Evidence attests that by the mid-sixties Lee was not in full control, in some instances may not even have been mindful, of the overall narrative direction in either Kirby's *Fantastic Four* or Steve Ditko's *Amazing Spider-Man*, as the scope of both series expanded toward sustained, multi-issue arcs. Yet Lee continued to be credited as the nominal "writer." Kirby and Ditko, both ambitious narrative artists, chafed under this arrangement, with Ditko eventually demanding and receiving credit as plotter of *Spider-Man* and Kirby finally being billed, ambiguously, as co-creator of *The Fantastic Four*, now usually described simply as "produced by" Stan Lee and Jack Kirby.

In the early sixties Lee served as scenarist or at least active story editor, crafting scenarios or assembling outlines from which artists such as Ditko and Kirby (and none more effectively than Ditko and Kirby) worked. This is how Marvel's seminal properties came to life: through substantial collaboration and with Lee's editorial prompting and shaping. Things changed, however. Though Lee may have been hands-on in the beginning, eventually he came to trust his best artists to deliver the narrative goods, and so began writing, or simply dictating, brief, summative scenarios rather than full, line-by-line, moment-by-moment scripts. This method eventually devolved to mere conversation, or, in some cases, no prior consultation with the artists at all (as we'll see in the key example of *Fantastic Four* #48 in our next chapter).

The Marvel method had its practical advantages, and evolved because of practical reasons. It seems to have arisen unintentionally out of the so-called "mystery" or suspense comics edited by Lee and most often scripted either by Lee or by his brother Larry Lieber in the late fifties to early sixties in titles such as *Strange Tales* and *Journey into Mystery*. These typically featured either atmospheric tales of insinuating dread (most often Ditko) or, more famously, drive-in movie-style tales of rampaging, outsized monsters that, Kong- or Godzilla-like, would run amok and incite panic (most often Kirby). Lee, Kirby, and Ditko produced so many variations on these formulaic comics that they became used to working together, so much so that Lee eased off from writing out full scripts and learned to allow for and give more play to the artists' respective signature styles (McLaughlin 139). The monster stories, for instance, though flatly interchangeable in theme, boasted a dashed-off graphic vitality thanks to Kirby's yen for towering grotesques. Lee, having written full, if formulaic, scripts for many years (at times he supplemented his editor's salary with freelance scriptwriting), eventually backed away from full scripting, increasingly letting the artists enliven what would else have been boilerplate, generic stories. Hence came Marvel's production method, which at its best allowed both cartoonist and scripter wide latitude (a freedom born of mutual neglect) but at its worst could lead to confusion as the cartoonist's envisionment of the action was tweaked and embellished by a script at cross-purposes to the art. Said method, a pragmatic accommodation to unremitting production demand, was initially a departure from business as usual, but Lee came to depend on it.

All this is hazy and hard to document, though many fans have tried (most helpful is Mike Gartland's "A Failure to Communicate," a series of articles in *The Jack Kirby Collector* that analyzes the Kirby/Lee collaboration). On balance, it seems fair to say that in the early sixties Lee and his artists worked more closely together, with Lee drafting the outlines of plots brainstormed during informal conferencing or conversation with the artists. For instance, during the formative period of *The Fantastic Four*, Lee and Kirby seem to have conferred initially about characters and plots, after which Lee prepared treatments or outlines—or gave out guiding concepts at least—that piloted or prompted Kirby, or gave him narrative targets to shoot for as he broke the story down into pages. Afterwards Lee applied the finishing touch of dialogue and captions—crucial for nuance—as well as, on occasion, overseeing small but important editorial changes, such as the retouching of artwork for the sake of visual continuity and perhaps tighter logic, or at least more obvious exposition. Though years later Kirby claimed Lee's creative role was minimal to nonexistent, evidence suggests that Lee was more involved in guiding those early stories than Kirby's memory could allow. This gradually changed, however.

Practically speaking, the Marvel method freed up much of Lee's time, as he was not responsible for making decisions about breakdown or staging at the script phase, and did not have to work through the details of physical actions or confrontations. He left these to the kinetic sensibilities of the cartoonists. For example, see Lee's synopsis of *Fantastic Four* #8 (Nov. 1962), first reproduced in the fanzine *CAPA-alpha* #2 (Nov. 1964) and also excerpted in Gabilliet's *Of Comics and Men*: "In street, Thing suddenly gets into a daze, and heads for Puppet Master's apt., followed by I.G. [Invisible Girl]. Thing, under PM's spell, reveals I.G.'s presence, some interesting scenes showing how PM captures her, and he finally succeeds . . ." (Gabilliet 127). We do not know whether the writing of this synopsis preceded or followed conversation between Lee and Kirby, but what is clear is that Lee did not have to worry about describing every "interesting scene." He also did not have to worry about dialogue until confronting nearly-finished pages, a mercy that allowed him to attack the pages as found objects, with a certain improvisatory élan that helps account for the freshness and jouncing vivacity of his best scripting (as well as the blithe excesses of his worst). He was a willful translator, reinterpreting the artist's sequences and intentions, writing *over* a visual story that already existed in substantially developed form. Sometimes his translations were faithful, sometimes not. His work came most often at the fore end (in initial consultation with the artist) and the aft end (dialoguing and captioning), leaving the middle to the artist. This all-important "middle" included, at the least, layout, pacing, staging, the working-out of transitions and minor plot points, and the choreographing of action: all the ingredients of sequential narrative drawing, all the elements of page design, of *mise en page*, composition, and reader orientation, of dramatic visual emphasis, tonal control, gesture, and expression.

In the case of Kirby and Ditko in the mid-sixties, the middle also included much more: at the least, the occasional creation of major characters out of whole cloth (e.g., the Silver Surfer, as we'll see), the frequent introduction of supporting characters, the interpolation of new and wholly unexpected action sequences, and moments of invention that startled even Lee. What Kirby and Ditko provided to Lee, then, was not illustration but concepts, characterization, plot points, and full-fledged narrative drawing: storytelling via images, with recourse to simplification, typification, graphic expressionism, and all the myriad devices, the visual shorthand, of cartooning. Cartooning is storytelling. So, while the Marvel method lightened Lee's workload, it made greater demands on the artists' time, and so reinforced the artists' sense that they were working on stories over which they could exert significant claims to ownership (creative if not legal).

When Lee's contributions to the initial plotting eased off, freeing him to act as editor, production manager, and promoter of the expanded Marvel line, the synopses became briefer, more informal, or simply nonexistent. Ditko and Kirby grew into their own, supplying not only interesting "scenes" but interesting plots, and eventually stamping their respective books with their design sensibilities, predispositions, even moral outlooks or glimmerings of same— all while Lee remained the nominal writer of the books. In terms of sustained series work, if not individual high points, Ditko and Kirby produced the best, most consistent work of their careers under this odd and finally irksome arrangement.

What all this means is that the notion of *authorship*, in the elevated Romantic sense of undiluted individual creation, is almost impossible to apply to the earliest of the Marvel superhero comics. This does not mean there were no authors, just that authorship was multiple and the traces of individual contributions are so mingled and confused that readers will forever be chasing the question. Lee was Marvel's spokesman, its conductor but not sole motive force; Ditko and Kirby, especially Kirby, were great motivators. In the case of the Kirby and Lee teaming, the Marvel method allowed both men to make vaulting claims to authorship, Lee in his mid-to-late career ascendancy as the feted spokesman and public face of Marvel, and Kirby, whose memory was just as fallible, in late-career backlash mode: the onetime star artist of Marvel, now alienated.

Because Lee brought his editorial presence to Kirby's Marvel work, sanding its rough edges and scoring it with the self-important yet ingratiating cadences of his speech—and because Kirby worked flat-out from deadline to deadline, building pages and often, so the evidence shows, providing his own textual notes for those pages, text Lee would at times ignore—each man could believe himself the creative architect of Marvel's seminal sixties work. Lee adapted Kirby's drawings and textual marginalia to suit his editorial preferences, at times recklessly, while Kirby seldom looked closely at the published results, preferring—or financially driven, rather—to move relentlessly forward. Each was to come away from the classic Marvel period with a different estimation of his own role and a different understanding of their working relationship, hence the controversies that linger to this day. To read Lee's affable, self-serving retellings of Marvel history, starting in the sixties and accelerating through the seventies, alongside Kirby's angry jabs at Lee in the eighties, is to come to a bitter and ironic impasse.

The upshot of this is that mainstream comic books are a poor, or at least a difficult, case for auteur theory. The collaborative process behind the seminal Marvel books was irreducibly complex, unpredictable—and messy. It is also thinly documented. Today fans are encouraged to identify popular creators (scriptwriters, artists, writer-artists) as auteurs with distinct sensibilities even under the strictures of periodical work-for-hire comics, but it was not so in the sixties. While it's tempting to read contemporary comic books through the lens of auteur theory, the nonstop production schedules and inevitable parceling out of the creative work make mainstream comics an intractable limit case—the more so in the newsstand era prior to the development of the star system, when deadlines were unyielding, production far more routinized, and general readers less attentive to the niceties of creative credit. Of course one can, with effort, identify auteurs within such a mechanized framework, but myriad factors impinge on and complicate attempts to assign sole authorship. To treat the torrent of Marvel Comics in the sixties, or any part of that outpouring, as work uniquely, singly attributable to one author takes a great leap of faith.

We could argue, then, no single author of Marvel Comics, nor any single architect of the Marvel Universe, exists. Of course, "Stan Lee" has long served various author-functions for fans, not least the conferral of a single tone or attitude on what is, really, a shapeless amassing of decades' worth of inconsistent, heterogeneous work. But though Lee was Marvel's impresario and publicist *par excellence* in the sixties and early seventies, and though at first he contributed to the comics' content as a scripter, polishing if not steering the work of various narrative artists, he did not solely create any enduring Marvel properties. Nor did he, in fact, serve as scenarist for many of the most celebrated Marvel comics of the mid to late sixties. By the same token, Kirby—though he provided the conceptual material, the character designs, the unmistakable graphic style, the pacing, and, eventually, the plotting and overall direction of the Marvel books with which he was linked—did not *solely* author any of the seminal Marvels of the period. His work was constrained and subliminally altered at the editorial level, with text that reshaped and at times redirected his plots. Furthermore, Lee's vitalizing influence saturated Marvel and determined its editorial ethos. Kirby worked harder but, commercially, Lee *made things happen.*

The classic Marvels were the result of friction across a peculiar interface: that between the obsessive work of individual narrative artists (think of Kirby toiling, week in, week out, at his taboret) and the magazine market they served. Yes, Marvel had personality, quirkiness, individual flair, but the company came out of and exemplified a market-driven approach to comics. Lee understood this. Kirby did too. At bottom, Marvel comics justified their existence and derived their legitimacy from a *heteronomous*—that is, external and market-centered—rather than an *autonomous*, or internal and art-centered, standard of cultural production (I'm using these terms in ways drawn from Pierre Bourdieu, in particular his "The Field of Cultural Production" and *The Rules of Art*). This ought to be a numbing obviousness, since such is the nature of most comics most of the time. Yet, given the myth of Marvel and the seriousness with which fandom regards the Marvel Universe, it bears repeating: Marvel was, fundamentally, a commercial, extrinsically motivated product line driven by the same relentless market imperatives as almost all other comic books up to that point. The Marvel line arose from circumstances that disallowed individual claims to sole creative credit, and in fact the company, in its boom period, thrived on conditions that made individual attributions of credit very, very difficult. The story of Kirby at Marvel, in sum, is that of so many singular artists who toiled in popular media under conditions of heteronomy: artists whose primary job, and goal, was to make sales for the sake of studio, publishing house, or brand. Consider the great filmmakers who worked, often chafed, under the studio system during Hollywood's peak years—or, in comics, the many artists and writers who have bridled against the terms of corporate-owned, work-for-hire production. Attempts to assign authorship of vintage Marvels to a single creator are like auteurist readings of Hollywood studio films, in which ascriptions of creative genius run afoul the more complicated realities of heteronomous, market-driven, assembly-line work.

Marvel's genius was to make that "assembly line" seem personal rather than mechanical. The vividness and singularity of Marvel comics made fans want to ascribe authorship (after all, we wouldn't search for an author if the work weren't so crazily alive). The awkward truth is that Marvel was a hell-for-leather improvisation shaped by the looming reality of deadlines, the vicissitudes of publisher-to-freelancer relations, and informal, ever-shifting, and (in hindsight) ill-documented relationships among various persons. Moreover, the platonic idea of "Marvel" as a collective achievement, a coherent wonderland knowingly shaped by sustained collaboration, is something that came well after Kirby and Lee got the ball rolling, so we ought not to speak of Marvel as something that arrived or was "authored" all at once. To reread early Marvel comics in the context of their original publication, retracing their history month by month through the sixties, is to see just how ad hoc, tentative, and inconsistent the whole enterprise was. In essence, the *idea* of Marvel postdates the seminal comics of that era. So, again, authorship slips beyond our grasp.

Yet tossing out the concept of authorship entirely would be mystification of another kind. Jack Kirby was a singular comic book creator, not an identityless cog in a machine, and he did exert part-authorship over Marvel. His Marvel comics were not simply assembly-line product, in the sense of rationalized factory output; in fact comic book production, despite its frequent reliance on shops in which pages were cranked out in bulk, has generally been closer to small-scale, intimate, artisanal work than to the thrum of the factory floor. The process of physical production that made these comics possible typically began on Kirby's drawing board, and Kirby produced objects—art boards, pages, parcels—that bore stories that guided other artisans in the process, going forward. And so it was that Kirby generated the raw materials of Marvel. His contributions effectively re-formed and revitalized the company, which without him would not have become the Marvel we know. Without him it wouldn't have left the ground. Lee did not have Marvel in mind when he put Kirby to work, but Kirby had the energy to make Lee dream big. All that was wanted was the go-ahead from Goodman (which came in 1961).

What's more, signs of Kirby's authorial influence permeate Marvel's sixties output. This is not to deny Lee's input or underplay the importance of the Lee/Kirby teaming—or the simple fact that Kirby worked at Lee's behest—but to insist on a critical redress. Kirby's role as co-creator of Marvel, as first among its diverse artistic hands, as its first character-builder and designer and the artistic benchmark for most of Marvel's other artists, has until recently been so underplayed or muddled in the journalistic and scholarly treatment of Marvel that, even today, rebalancing is still justified.

Once one reads Kirby's post-sixties output, in particular the comics he created for DC during his wild spell of inspiration after ditching Marvel, the hallmarks of his style and sensibility become more obvious, and these can and should be read back into his collaborative Marvel work. Also, the mounting historical evidence (for example the now-routine publishing of photocopies of Kirby's penciled pages) suggests that Lee and Kirby's nominal collaborations were often not forethought or intentional, but rather the outcome of Lee's verbal elaborations on ideas brought to the boards by Kirby, the final results being artifacts of a merciless production schedule in which any clash of sensibilities was simply and invisibly resolved by editorial fiat. The Lee/Kirby teaming, in any case, was not static, but a slippery process that changed by the mid-sixties, so that Kirby, at times working on his own, ended up providing the lion's share of concepts and character designs in his peak Marvel work, most clearly on *Fantastic Four* and *Thor*. Jack Kirby is the beating heart of those books.

Let's not be desperately Romantic here. Comic book fans often elide the complex realities of the production process when defending the idea of the "creative team": an industry euphemism for an often-circuitous yet almost assembly-line-like process by which the final, published work may end up significantly different from that envisioned by the original plotter (whether scenarist or artist) and in which some nominal "team" members may never even meet (reportedly, inker Joe Sinnott did not even meet Kirby until well after their famed collaboration on *Fantastic Four*). Proponents of the "creative team" often assume that intra-team relations are smooth and that the ostensibly clear-cut, legally binding work-for-hire arrangements in today's publishing industry have always been in place, that their nature has always been well understood and uncontested, even happily accepted, by the creators of the past. In fact, relations between publishers and comic book artists-for-hire were often fuzzy and disputable, and attempts to judge the working arrangements of, say, the forties or sixties by the understandings of today too often serve a dubious, wish-fulfilling revisionism: a desire to believe that comic book professionals are, whatever their occasional spats, one big happy family, and that historical disputes can and should be resolved in such a way as not to threaten the proprietary claims of the corporations that now own most of the recognized comic book properties.

Kirby did not enter into freelance work for Marvel with any such understanding, nor with a desire to rejoin Stan Lee's bullpen or put a brighter face on the sometimes-ugly relationships between publishers and freelance talent.

Nor did his work with Lee constitute a deliberate, self-sacrificing contribution to the greater good of "Marvel." Lee was, at bottom, Kirby's editor and hence the source of his continued work and income, not only the comradely creative partner implied in the early Marvel titles. Yes, Lee and Kirby, as characters, sometimes made self-reflexive cameos in those comics, self-mythologizing guest appearances that implied that Lee and Kirby shared an office space and a collegial, all-for-one-and-one-for-all attitude—but the fact is that Kirby and Lee typically met only briefly, at intervals, with sometimes long stretches between substantial conversations. In fact "creative teams" in mainstream comics have seldom been true teamings, that is, genuine, intentional collaborations involving interplay at all or almost all levels of the creative process. The Lee/Kirby teaming, by the middle sixties, was certainly not such a willed, intensive collaboration. It was a relay, not a duet.

Kirby was, though not *the* author, an essential co-author of vintage Marvel. His creative presence is sometimes severely filtered and mitigated in those comics, but traces survive and reassert themselves upon rereading. Admittedly, his authorial role has been overstated by some of his adherents—there are numerous examples in the Kirby fan press—but beyond said fandom it has generally been understated or ignored, at the cost of historical and critical misunderstanding. Clearly, Kirby warrants recognition as Marvel's signature artist and founding conceptualist. Despite the vague, shifting nature of his teamings with Lee and others, the depersonalizing pressures of market-driven production, and the often volatile, inconsistent nature of the work produced under such conditions—despite these things, Kirby stands as Marvel's *co-founder.* Marvel, unmistakably the pivot, the hinge, of his long career, gave vent to his sensibility, and Marvel's superheroes belong to a larger pattern of interests and themes that recur across his several decades of work. If some zealous fans go too far in ascribing to Kirby an undiluted artistic autonomy, if they downplay the extent to which Kirby's own instincts, like Lee's, were commercial, still their advocacy has done the valuable service of repositioning Kirby, so that we can now understand him not merely as an illustrator of Stan Lee's concepts but as a conceptualist and storyteller in his own right.

## FROM SMALL THINGS: MARVEL'S RAGGED GROWTH

To say that Kirby worked hard for Marvel would be an understatement. He infused Marvel with his energy and style, as if determined to transform the company and thus his circumstances. Frankly, he was working against the odds, for Goodman's outfit by the late fifties had faint prospects, and no history of seeding new, original, trendsetting work. Goodman had always been calculatedly derivative, with a reputation for earmarking trends, riding them into exhaustion, and then prospecting for newer trends. Timely/Atlas had at times been recklessly prolific, but not since its edgy superheroes of the WWII era had the firm been known to offer anything sharp or different or vital; it was, by 1958, a dry husk, a small, starveling publisher with no recent hits, no market clout, nothing to boast of creatively, and a publishing lineup contractually confined to a punitively small scope. Its distributor at this time was Independent News, owned by National Periodical, parent company of DC, who firmly limited the number of comics Goodman could publish— reportedly, just eight per month at the start (Vadeboncoeur 5; Lammers 51; McLaughlin 136, 175; Daniels, *Marvel* 81). Freelancing for Goodman and Lee was, in short, an ignominious gig, one that Kirby, over time, set out to change. Kirby was the pivot point, but *how* exactly did this transformation happen?

Naturally Kirby did not undertake his work for Magazine Management with any degree of foresight or calculation. He did not "plan on" Marvel. In fact Kirby appears seldom to have planned on things or nursed his career carefully. Though over time he developed a sense of his own talent, nonetheless he seemed ill-suited to protect and shepherd that talent through the bewildering harshness of the business. Over his forty-plus years in comics (as noted in Chapter 0) he often let others lead the way in his business dealings. Joe Simon, for example, was a mentor as well as partner, and, by his willingness to take risks, helped Kirby flourish artistically.

By contrast, Kirby on his own, at least the early Kirby, was risk-averse. Simon's memoir *The Comic Book Makers* characterizes the young Jacob Kurtzberg as a diffident, uncertain artist who was at first quite reluctant to give up his salaried job at Fox Features for the greener pastures of working with Simon as a team (40–41). Simon, on the other hand, moved easily from Fox to moonlighting with Kirby to editorship of Goodman's fledgling comics line at Timely, eventually bringing on Kirby to serve as art director. Simon was willing to take on other or "outside" work and to reposition himself constantly, for he knew what he and Kirby were worth and did not scruple at grasping for other opportunities (even while working under contract for publishers like Fox or Goodman). Where Kirby hesitated, Simon jumped.[2]

Though Kirby was gifted, and though his skill and clout had increased over the years with Simon, his solo freelancing in the latter fifties had proven brutal, elbowing him first into the unknown, then back to Goodman—hardly a propitious move for someone who by then had been working in comics for over twenty years. Formerly an art director, the co-director of a busy shop, and even a publisher—in other words, formerly an object of other cartoonists' envy—Kirby had slipped far. Because the mid-fifties had clobbered S&K business-wise, and also because the entire comic book industry had shrunk so traumatically, Kirby had tumbled into a position of great risk—from which he had at first ventured promisingly, but then fallen hard and fast (the Schiff/DC fiasco). By late 1959, the forty-two-year-old Kirby was giving most of his time to the very place out of which he had been shoved at age twenty-four: Martin Goodman's outfit, now miserably shrunken and presided over by someone whom Kirby had never worked for and did not know well, Stan Lee. This was not the result of a plan.

For years the Timely/Atlas line had been baldly stenciled from other, better books by other publishers. Being derivative was how Goodman and Lee worked—derivative *and* fast—so the company's biggest claim to notoriety had been its sheer volume of production. Even this they had sacrificed by the late fifties, due to their abrupt loss of distribution in 1957: the catastrophe that nearly killed the line and impelled Goodman to make his desperate deal with Independent News, a tough, frankly astringent deal that, again, severely limited his output, as if to curb his former newsstand-glutting ways. This was the sharply contracted outfit that Lee managed in the late fifties, a vestige of his earlier, much busier operation. Goodman and Lee's comics were nothing to write home about, and, furthermore, working for Goodman was no affectionate homecoming; S&K had been booted by him some eighteen years before. So it was sheer necessity that drove Kirby to Magazine Management—and necessity that would drive him to revitalize the company's comics line.

On the cusp of the sixties, Kirby worked almost exclusively for Goodman and Lee for the better part of two years without effecting major changes. The only departure was his aforementioned long run of thematically rote but visually funky "mystery" comics, which in Kirby's case meant mostly monster comics: generic, anthology-borne short stories, usually about giant, marauding creatures, conceptually flat but given a vital jab in the ribs by Kirby's outlandish artistry. Here Kirby helped distill the company's take on science fiction, which was grotesque and paranoid. Between 1959 and 1962 Kirby drew a ream of these monster-movie-style SF stories for Marvel, the bulk appearing in the titles *Strange Tales* and *Journey into Mystery* (which had started as pre-Code horror titles) and the new *Tales of Suspense* and *Tales to Astonish*. The stories were typically on the order of cautionary tales, much like films such as *Godzilla* (U.S. version 1956) and *Gorgo* (1961). In general, they featured covers and splash panels depicting towering monsters, beneath which small humans ran, or stood gaping or pointing. Offsetting the formulaic nature of the stories was a dash of invigorating absurdity: the tales had Kirby's energy and, courtesy of Lee, confessional, first-person titles typical of sensation-mongering tabloids and comics, such as, "I Created Sporr, the Thing That Could Not Die!" (*Tales of Suspense*, Sept. 1960). Such comics, in essence, comprised the safe juvenile remnants of the once-controversial (and once-prospering) horror genre, now defused post-Comics Code. They wedded denatured horror to drive-in movie sci-fi. DC had comparable "mystery" titles on which Kirby had also worked for a time, such as *House of Mystery* and *Tales of the Unexpected*, but they lacked the chutzpah of the Marvel books; they had nothing like Kirby's comically grotesque monsters or Lee's daffy way with names: Goom, the Thing from Planet X; Googam, Son of Goom; fan favorite Fin Fang Foom; and so on (many of the names were recycled, sometimes with small changes). Whereas Steve Ditko produced some "mystery" comics for Marvel that were genuinely mysterious, famously in *Amazing Adult Fantasy* (1961–62), which was essentially his vehicle, Kirby dealt mainly in rude spectacle. Ditko had a talent for occultism and the uncanny; Kirby was all in for gigantism (other artists also worked on the Marvel mystery/monster titles, but without distinction). What Kirby's monster stories offered was a chance for him to draw myriad weird creatures in violent action. As science fiction, they weren't much, being brief and obsessively narrow in concept, but they paved the way for *The Fantastic Four* (and thus for Kirby's cartoon sublime, a topic I'll engage in Chapter 4).

*The Fantastic Four*, an edgy, post-nuclear amalgam of superheroes and the monster comics, was the ticket. From then on Marvel—now decisively *Marvel*, not just a nameless appendix within the offices of Goodman's larger Magazine Management—repurposed its artists and fixed its sights on the superhero genre, a process that began slowly but accelerated once the sales figures were in. In 1962 and 1963 Marvel Comics came to life, haltingly, then more confidently, with Kirby supplying most of its visual spark as well as its conceptual nerve. In the process, as we'll see, the superhero genre was revived, even reinvented. All this happened little by little.

The tentativeness of the process is often overlooked. Claims for Marvel's greatness, or Lee's, or Kirby's, are usually couched in terms of what Marvel achieved over the long haul as it consolidated the early Kirby/Lee and Ditko/Lee creations into a single working "universe," a mythos through which other artists and writers could romp and to which they could add their own notions, spin-offs, and revisions. That achievement took time. Again, to reread the formative Marvel Comics, circa 1961–63, is to see just how unsteady the beginnings of this universe were, and how raggedly and unselfconsciously it grew.

Lee, Kirby, and company were determined to make the most of a small, contractually cramped line of comics, and so they set about redirecting existing titles and pruning other titles to make way. There was no master plan in late 1961 when *Fantastic Four* was launched; the superhero books arrived bit by bit, and at the outset each character—Ant-Man, the Hulk, Thor, Iron Man, etc.—was in its own world, without either an overarching continuity or the self-conscious shaping presence of Lee's editorial persona (still inchoate in 1962). What's more, the early issues of the *FF* show much shifting about and uncertainty in tone and direction, and much unevenness of quality; the series does not arrive at its prototype identity for at least two years. During that period Marvel continued to publish quite a few non- superhero titles, including teen humor, romance, and westerns. In (cover date) January 1963, for example, Marvel published—besides *The Fantastic Four*, *The Incredible Hulk*, and the several "mystery" anthologies—*Gunsmoke Western*, *Kid Colt Outlaw*, *Two-Gun Kid*, *Love Romances*, *Millie the Model*, and *Linda Carter, Student Nurse*. There were still other Marvel titles besides these; Lee kept them rotating on a bimonthly basis.[3] What Lee and Kirby started in late 1961, then, was the germ of something that took time to grow. As Jordan Raphael and Tom Spurgeon note, the "birth" of Marvel did not come as one signal event, but rather through the "lively but considered transformation of an existing comic-book line" (88). That transformation forced other kinds of comic books out.

Part of this process involved the hijacking or redirection of the mystery/monster books, which converted to superheroics fairly quickly starting in 1962, after *Fantastic Four*'s launch. This transition testifies to a growing confidence as well as the constraints under which Kirby and Lee, et al. were working. Between August and October 1962, *Amazing Fantasy* (formerly *Amazing Adult Fantasy*), *Journey into Mystery*, *Tales to Astonish*, and *Strange Tales* all turned toward the costumed hero (*Tales of Suspense* followed in March 1963). By late 1963 the anthologies were dominated by costumes. By late 1964 all the other features had disappeared. Interestingly, Marvel's superhero comics during this period remained close to the monster comics in style and tone; the debt was obvious. Villains and storylines blatantly echoed Kirby's many monster and alien-invader tales. Early episodes of *The Fantastic Four*, *The Incredible Hulk*, "Ant-Man and the Wasp," and "Thor" featured monstrous villains who echoed the earlier monsters in appearance and/or name: Kurrgo, Mongu, and the Creature from Kosmos; giant monsters summoned by the Moleman, the Miracle Man, and the Sub-Mariner; alien invaders like the Skrulls, the Toad Men, and the Stone Men from Saturn; and so on (regarding such, *Fantastic Four* #2 contains a droll bit of self-mockery: Mr. Fantastic scares off the invading Skrulls by tricking them into believing that the creatures in a Marvel monster comic are real!). More importantly, the superhero strips shared the monster comics' penchant for the chunky and grotesque, and conjured the same drive-in movie atmosphere of general dread. In short, the early Marvel superhero stories were a hybrid of heroics, drive-in sci-fi, and fantastic horror. Only gradually did they shed their early formulaic roots and begin to build a universe.

So, that universe did not suddenly appear *ex nihilo* in 1961. The company's vaunted "crossovers," in which characters appear in each other's magazines and thus strengthen the illusion of a consistent world, did not begin until Kirby & Lee's *Fantastic Four* #12 (a Hulk crossover) and Ditko & Lee's *Amazing Spider-Man* #1 (a Fantastic Four crossover), both cover-dated March 1963.[4] *Amazing Spider-Man*, continuing Spider-Man's adventures from *Amazing Fantasy* #15 (Aug. 1962), was the first Marvel title to be launched with the larger continuity in mind: during *Amazing*'s first two years Spider-Man would cross over with the FF, the Human Torch alone, the Hulk, and, in 1964, the newly launched Daredevil (and from then on an early Spider-Man crossover was *de rigueur* for most new Marvel heroes). The Hulk, whose own title, drawn first by Kirby and then by Ditko, was cancelled after just six issues in March 1963, would be the first of the Marvel characters to wander from book to book, appearing in *FF* #12 (the same month his own book was scrapped), then in the first three issues of a new supergroup title, the Kirby-drawn *Avengers* (Sept. 1963–Jan. 1964), and later still in *Amazing Spider-Man* #14 (July 1964).

By late 1963, Lee, Kirby, and company knew they had a comet by the tail. The early continuity of *The Avengers* exemplifies Marvel's new approach to exploiting crossovers: *Avengers* #1 brings together a handful of preexisting heroes, Thor, Iron Man, Ant-Man, and his sidekick the Wasp, to capture the Hulk, who abruptly joins the newly constituted team, then quits just as abruptly with #2. The third issue pits the enraged Hulk against the team, now joined by the equally wrathful Sub-Mariner (the revived Golden Age antihero, by then recast as an antagonist for the Fantastic Four). The Fantastic Four and Spider-Man make cameos in these early issues of *The Avengers*, leading up to #4's revival of Simon & Kirby's Golden Age hit, Captain America, revealed to have been frozen in suspended animation for the better part of two decades. Captain America eventually becomes the leader of the Avengers, recruiting in #16 (May 1965) a new lineup that includes several reformed villains previously introduced in the *X-Men* and "Iron Man" (*Tales of Suspense*) series. Kirby himself disappeared after #9, then returned, briefly, as layout artist of #14–16, long enough to usher in #16's new lineup (under artist Dick Ayers).

In short, by 1964 Marvel continuity had tightened enough to encourage frequent crossovers and to sustain entire series spun off from other titles, such as *The Avengers*. One of the first moves toward consolidating the Marvel Universe came with such a spin-off: a Kirby-launched solo series (1962–1965) for the Fantastic Four's Human Torch in the *Strange Tales* anthology, joined in later issues by his teammate the Thing. Such series by their nature encouraged crossovers. In 1964 the crossovers began coming fast and furious: *Fantastic Four* #25–26 (April–May) featured a Hulk/Avengers clash—actually the first cliffhanger in the FF's history—and #28 (July) a set-to with the X-Men. Spider-Man tangled with the Hulk, Daredevil, and (repeatedly) the Human Torch. By year's end the revived Captain America, again drawn by Kirby, spun off from *The Avengers* and grabbed a solo spot in *Tales of Suspense*, where he shared billing with Iron Man. By the end of 1964 the Marvel formula was in place, and the crossovers were constant: in *Fantastic Four* #31 (Oct. 1964), the Avengers make a cameo notable for its matter-of-factness (they argue with the FF over who will subdue the Mole Man); then, in *X-Men* #9 (Jan. 1965), the Avengers are full-blown guest stars. At the same time *The Avengers* series crossed over with Spider-Man (Dec. 1964) and took on a pair of Fantastic Four villains, the Mole Man (again) and the Red Ghost (Jan. 1965). Traffic in the Marvel Universe was getting hectic. Finally, the oversized *Fantastic Four Annual* #3 (late 1965) comes as something of a climax to this trend: as two members of the team, Reed (Mr. Fantastic) and Susan (Invisible Girl), wed, their ceremony is crashed by just about every hero and major villain thus far introduced in Marvel Comics, turning the nuptials into an all-star donnybrook and cross-promotional extravaganza. It's a very crowded comic book.

## KIRBY'S LEAP

Throughout this formative period (1961 to early 1966) Marvel's core artists, its workhorses and pillars of style, were Kirby and Ditko. The latter handled *Amazing Spider-Man* and, from 1963, the hallucinatory "Dr. Strange" series in *Strange Tales*, Dr. Strange being a spell-chanting super-mystic who defended Earth from magical and otherworldly menaces. Dr. Strange and Spider-Man, both imbued with Ditko's moody evocativeness, would become his signature Marvel characters, so that, despite the diversity of his Marvel work, Ditko is now mostly linked with these two properties. The eerie urgency of his art contrasted well with the brawling dynamism of Kirby, adding a different kind of emotional depth to the Marvel Universe.

It was the more prolific Kirby, though, who launched most of the other superhero series: *Fantastic Four*, "Ant-Man" (in *Tales to Astonish*), *The Incredible Hulk*, "Thor" (in *Journey into Mystery*), and the solo "Human Torch" (*Strange Tales*) in 1961–62; *Avengers* in 1963; *X-Men* and the "Captain America" revival (in *Tales of Suspense*) in 1964. In addition, Kirby designed the initial version of the character "Iron Man" in *Tales of Suspense* (dated March 1963, drawn by artist Don Heck) and was soon pressed into penciling three more Iron Man stories. He also contributed design and perhaps plot points to the first issue of *Daredevil* (April 1964, drawn by Bill Everett). What's more, he penciled the attention-getting covers for *Amazing Fantasy* #15 (Spider-Man's debut) and *Amazing Spider-Man* #1. At the same time, Kirby continued working in other genres, helming the revived western series *Rawhide Kid* (from 1960); contributing to another western, *Two-Gun Kid* (from 1961); launching *Sgt. Fury and His Howling Commandos* (1963), a WWII comic that became part of the Marvel Universe; and doing scattered stories for other comics, including further anthology stories. He also provided pencils for many covers. Eventually he presided over the transformation of Sgt. Fury into the James Bond-style super-spy, "Nick Fury, Agent of SHIELD" (in *Strange Tales*, 1965), a character that would be closely tied to the Marvel superheroes. Clearly, Kirby was the artistic dynamo of the Marvel line, designing most of the new heroes and co-creating, in *The Fantastic Four*, one of the two main engines from which Marvel's sixties continuity would spring (*Amazing Spider-Man* being the other).

Marvel's growth remained uneven, however, and what Kirby did from month to month varied. Other artists quickly succeeded Kirby on some of the above series: for example, Joe Sinnott briefly followed Kirby on the "Thor" feature in *Journey into Mystery*. Also, some of the early series would prove short-lived, such as *The Incredible Hulk* or the "Ant-Man" (later Giant Man) series in *Tales to Astonish*. Nonetheless, Kirby's energetic pencils kept Marvel in motion. His storytelling and character designs were hallmarks of the company circa 1961–1964, and, by 1965, he was providing layouts, at Lee's behest, to help break in other artists on such books as *Avengers* and *X-Men* (an extension of his earlier role as contributor to the early "Iron Man" and *Daredevil*). His fingerprints, in short, were all over the Marvel line. Despite the reliable presence of artists such as Sinnott and Heck, despite continuing work from veterans such as Bill Everett and Wallace Wood, despite the growing stable of Marvel freelancers at mid-decade and the crucial return to Marvel of artist John Romita in late 1965 (Romita had not worked for Marvel since 1957), the company's style was built squarely on Kirby, and the characters he helped create typically suffered as soon as he stepped away. For example, there was a notable falling-off in dynamism and visual imagination when Kirby departed "Thor," *Avengers*, and *X-Men*. Other artists were urged to follow Kirby's lead, but initial results were tepid. For instance, Sinnott's breakdowns and figure work lacked Kirby's solidity, narrative drive, and brisk action (note that Sinnott would end up becoming *Fantastic Four*'s definitive inker, indeed one of Kirby's best, by the late mid-sixties). The unappreciated Heck was a lukewarm superhero artist at best; he would have been more at home in down-to-earth, realistic genres (Heck too would sometimes serve Kirby as inker). Eventually Kirby was deployed by Lee not only as a guiding example but also, for a time, as the layout artist whose breakdowns other pencilers were directed to complete: in this way, others were set up to follow Kirby on *Avengers*, *X-Men*, "Captain America," and *Daredevil*. In essence, Kirby's storytelling skill was used to undergird the drawing of others.

In providing breakdowns Kirby performed much of the work of narrative drawing for other artists: establishing page design, composition, the staging of action, and narrative flow. He also supplied plot notes, penciled directly onto the margins of the art boards. (Though reproductions of Kirby's pencils are common, copies of his rough layouts with notes are rare; telling examples can be found in *The Jack Kirby Collector* issues 48 and 50. Gartland's "Failure," Part Six, discusses the layout process and gives examples of its results.) The various "finishers"—pencilers and inkers—supplied the final rendering, including, probably, anatomical precision, nuances of expression, dramatic lighting, and the enticements of technique. Kirby supplied the narrative architecture. He worked incredibly hard during this period, laying out stories in *Daredevil*, *Strange Tales*, *Tales of Suspense*, and *Tales to Astonish* while simultaneously taking *The Fantastic Four* and *Thor* to new heights. Simply put, he was Marvel's power plant.

Veteran Gil Kane (who by 1967 was freelancing steadily for Marvel) was one of many artists Lee urged to follow Kirby's lead, even though he already had drawn more than two decades' worth of comic book art in his own right. Years later he recalled Kirby's central and overwhelming role: "Jack's point of view and philosophy of drawing became the governing philosophy of the entire [Marvel] publishing company and, beyond the publishing company, of the entire field." Marvel, he noted, managed "to take Jack and use him as a primer. They would get artists, regardless of whether they had done romance or anything else and they taught them the ABCs, which amounted to learning Jack Kirby. [. . .] Jack was like the Holy Scripture and they simply had to follow him without deviation. That's what was told to me, that's what I had to do." This, Kane realized, was how Marvel "taught everyone to reconcile all these opposing attitudes to one single master point of view ("Peer Pressure" 109). The "Marvel" point of view, then, was the Kirby point of view—he was Marvel's blueprint. His relationship with the company animated it and kept it going.

That relationship was at its peak circa 1966-67. Creatively, Kirby erupted: even before his layout duties eased off in late 1966, the power of his artwork took a hurtling, headlong leap forward, its degree of detail and nuance once more living up to the strength of his underlying layouts and rivaling the intensity of his best pre-Marvel cartooning. It was as if his art was galvanized by the sheer pressure. His design sense frothed over; his costumes, gadgets, and characters hit a new level of baroque lavishness. At the same time, he began to treat the superhero as a vehicle for high fantasy and science fiction. Mythopoesis—uninhibited world-building—was the order of the day. Kirby chased ideas and visions superhero comics had never before had the nerve to approach.

In short, Kirby outreached his prior work both visually and conceptually. His work on *Fantastic Four, Thor,* and *Tales of Suspense* (later *Captain America*) ripened and overgrew all previous limits. This period crystallized his style, establishing the definitive and oft-imitated late Kirby: the visual template from which so much subsequent superhero work has derived and which, indeed, Marvel embraced as something like the ultimate style during the latter sixties. From late 1965 to late 1967, Kirby was in peak form in terms of both visual splendor and narrative inventiveness.[5] The fruits of this period made Kirby into the "Kirby" best known to present-day comic book fans and the default stylist for superhero epic.

The year 1968 saw Marvel's sudden expansion (a lure for buyers, perhaps?) and subsequent sale to Perfect Film. Kirby's relationship with Marvel soured. His relationship with Lee was already strained by the creative gap between them and his growing resentment of Lee's editorial control (see Fischer, "Unmasking"; Gartland, "Failure," Part Four). In 1969 came a downturn in the whole comic book market. Marvel turned increasingly to the consolidation of the gains made in mid-decade, and its output became more self-involved and derivative—the bloom was off. But what had happened before then had been a little revolution, not only changing visual storytelling in comic books but also, as I'll discuss in our next chapter, enabling much that has happened narratively in superhero comics since, pushing back the genre's thematic horizons so that the grand ambitions of late-sixties Marvel (and Kirby's subsequent Fourth World) are now common.

Consider such Marvel and DC comic book titles of the last thirty years as *Secret Wars, Infinity War* and *Infinity Crusade, Cosmic Odyssey, Age of Apocalypse, Crisis on Infinite Earths,* or *Final Crisis.* Everything is cosmic now. So much of what has happened to superheroes in the direct market era, for good or ill, involves raveling out the implications of Kirby's mature style, his go-for-broke sense of epic, his apocalyptic imagination. This is what Marvel accomplished, and could not have accomplished without Kirby. This is why Kirby's estrangement from the myth of the Marvel Bullpen, a myth he helped to create, came so bitterly, inevitably coloring his remaining years in comics and prompting a still-unresolved struggle over his creative legacy.

3

# HOW KIRBY CHANGED THE SUPERHERO

Heroes and villains
Just see what you've done
— BRIAN WILSON & VAN DYKE PARKS

Thus far I've tried to untangle Kirby's relationship with Marvel, the publisher with which he is most closely linked. Much of the lore and conversation of American comic book fans has to do with that relationship, because the Marvel of the 1960s was pivotal to comic book history and Kirby was pivotal to Marvel. By now it is obvious that Marvel did something important to comic books, particularly to superheroes—and the previous chapter uncovered the gradual process of *how* Marvel did it, making the case that Kirby was Marvel's essential co-author. But, content-wise, what exactly is it that Kirby brought to Marvel, and thus to the superhero genre?

This question invites a flurry of others, some about genre, some about Kirby. What was the superhero genre like prior to the Marvel sixties, and how has it developed since? How did Marvel become pivotal to the genre, opening new possibilities and straining to new limits? Regarding Kirby, how did his contributions to Marvel draw from his own talents and sensibility, and how did his subsequent work unearth that sensibility, teasing out elements or qualities first glimpsed at Marvel? How did that later work go on to influence the superhero genre? Finally—and here is a question for the remainder of this book—how did these changes in the superhero in turn spur Kirby's further artistic growth, and thus set the terms of his subsequent recognition as cartoonist and author?

To tackle these questions, I propose first to step back and reconsider the superhero genre as such, with and without Kirby. This may seem like a detour from our main interest; admittedly, it takes us far from Kirby's narrative art. Yet it's a step we must take, because, I will argue, Kirby reshaped the entire genre. This he did in pursuit of a kind of *graphic mythopoesis*, essentially an impromptu world-making that granted him a new sense of license, or new set of affordances, for his graphic imagination. To understand the impact of this, some consideration of the genre's history and status is in order.

First, the blindingly obvious: superheroes are still regarded by many as the core of American comic books. The best-known examples of the genre, the familiar Batman, Spider-Man, Superman, or X-Men, epitomize what fans know as mainstream comics, a designation that in itself shows just how much influence the genre has exerted. I'd argue that "mainstream" is a misnomer, given the degree of specialization now required to navigate the world of superhero comics; nonetheless, the clichés of the genre are very widely recognized, easily turned to parody, and ever ready for scrambling and revision on page and screen. The rise of corporate entities like Marvel Studios and DC Entertainment has cemented the general sense that comic books act primarily as superhero mills for other media (movies, videogames, etc.). Appreciation of the larger history of comic books, of which superheroes are but a fraction, lags behind knowledge of the key superhero brands.

The genre, I submit, is neither as sorely limited as its severest detractors insist nor as malleable and promise-crammed as its apologists believe. Superheroes can do much, but I don't share the faith, most fervently expressed by comics writer Kurt Busiek in *Astro City*, that the genre's possibilities are "endless," that its symbols and metaphors are limitlessly adaptable, and that, in a nutshell, it can accommodate almost any kind of story (8). Rather, I think the genre, though rich and plastic, is thematically pretty tightly bound. The precincts of the superhero are definitely circumscribed. That said, much of the freedom Busiek finds in the genre stems from the expansive and transforming contribution of Kirby.

Essential to the genre from the get-go, and still important now, are fundamental contradictions that are played out in ritualistic fashion, so that social and psychological conflicts are continually rehearsed and renegotiated. I take my cue here from John Cawelti's notion that formula stories simultaneously excite and quell our anxieties, inciting uncertainty and intense feeling even as they offer reassurance via redundance and familiarity (15–16). *Tension* is the keyword: not only formal but also ideological. This may be why superheroes, as Richard Reynolds observes, can support various contradictory readings (83). Conflicting codes and desires are part of the genre's basic makeup. Of course this quality is not unique to superheroes; other genres such as the romance novel, detective story, or western also act out basic animating tensions. That is why they are so volatile.

For example, Jayne Ann Krentz has argued that romance fiction makes the central male character, typically a super-masculine alpha male, both hero and villain, for, whatever the other plot elements in a romance, the central man is the "real problem" the heroine must solve. Fundamentally, the heroine must place herself at risk with him, so he becomes the source of both anxious excitement and, ultimately, tenderness and reassurance ("Trying to Tame the Romance" 108–09). This suggests the romance genre embodies a tension between the desire for intimacy and the fear of vulnerability that goes with it. Romance novels constantly reimagine and play out this most basic contradiction, this tremulous and fascinating balance (hence the polarities, the charged ideological positions, that have developed in the criticism of the genre).

Just so, the irresolution of certain conflicts animates the superhero. The most obvious of these are, first, the contradiction between an agonistic individualism, often violently expressed (*power*), and an altruism that turns violence to prosocial, regenerative ends (*responsibility*); and, second, the contradiction between the spirit of antinomianism embodied by the figure of the vigilante (*justice*) and the spirit of obedience under law (another kind of *justice*). To these two may be added a third, less often acknowledged if no less fraught: a contradiction between self-effacement (Clark Kent) and flamboyance (Superman), the latter leading easily to the queering of this mostly male-addressed genre and often tipping over into a knowing, nudging campiness. After all, superhero stories typically rehearse masculinity via the extremes of deficiency—geekiness—and excess—a hyperbolic, almost self-parodying machismo.

Superheroes, in sum, are a strange genre, though arguably no stranger than other genres based on the continual rehearsal and readjustment of social and cultural contradictions. Historically, the genre has comprised (of course I'm speaking in terms of dominances, not absolutes) starkly gendered adventure tales replaying the conflicts between aggression and altruism, vengefulness and law, and psyche and society, typically through the lens of individual agon: internal struggle, self-conflict, duality. Sometimes the tone is boisterous, even humorous (the rowdy insouciance of the original Superman), sometimes borderline tragic, but the fundamental tensions remain. There is more to the genre than this, however, and that something "more," which is a matter of extended range, of expanded scope and possibilities, has a lot to do with Kirby.

In any case, the genre poses a problem for comics studies, one that the present study will, I have to admit, do nothing to fix. The ascendancy of the superhero in comics fandom has tended to cloud the historiography of comic books and give a distorted and impoverished impression of the medium's development. In spite of the vital work going on in other areas, the superhero marks an event horizon from which comics and comics studies cannot quite escape. The genre's preeminence in the comics culture creates a problem inasmuch as it distracts from and fogs over other aspects of the medium; fixation on superheroes makes it harder for the general reader to see comic books for what they have been, historically, and what they can be. In sum, the superhero's influence on the prevailing view of comics has been disproportionate and mystifying. There are historical reasons for this, of course; the genre's outsized influence testifies to its impact during three formative periods in the history of the comic book.

The first of these periods was the dawn of the so-called Golden Age in the late 1930s, that is, the period of rapid growth shortly after the very birth of the comic book industry. During this period, as we've seen, Kirby made key contributions in terms of genre, characters, page design, and narrative technique. The Golden Age (a problematic term, but common currency) is typically dated from the advent of superheroes in 1938 with Jerry Siegel and Joe Shuster's series *Superman*, the *locus classicus* of superheroes, and, depending on your sources and your loyalties, either ended with the end of WWII in the mid-forties, after which superheroes sorely declined, or continued into the early fifties with the happy mushrooming of non-superhero genres—by which time the comic book had become a staple if controversial element in American youth culture. Secondly, superheroes reemerged during a so-called Silver Age of partial revival after the near-collapse of the industry in the mid-fifties, a revival keyed to the superhero genre and most often dated to 1956, though most vital and energetic from about 1960 to 1968. Of course Kirby made essential contributions during this period as well: the subject of our previous chapter, indeed the starting point for this whole study. The Silver Age is impossible to imagine without Kirby and without Marvel. Third came a period of redirection in the wake of the sixties counterculture and underground comix, most obvious after the heyday of the undergrounds (circa 1968 to 1973). This third period was distinguished by two trends: one, the influx of devoted superhero fans into professional comic book production; and, two, the entrenchment of comic book specialty retailing, that is, the comic book store or so-called direct market, with its focus on active superhero collectors (regarding which, see Hatfield, *Alternative Comics* 20–29). Since the rise of the direct market, which both rescued and, if you will, typecast the comic book, superheroes have come to represent, for many fans and detractors alike, the core of the comic book as a medium.

Indeed superheroes are often presumed to be the signal contribution of American comic books to popular culture worldwide. But this viewpoint hides as much as it reveals: privileging the superhero this way, as the quintessence of comic books, hides the genre's dormancy from the late forties to the late fifties. Bear in mind that, sales-wise, the comic book medium peaked in the early fifties when superheroes were scant (regarding which, see Gabilliet,

Ch. 4). So the superhero has not always been the life force of comic books, let alone comics. The genre's seeming preeminence owes something to revisionism on the part of fan historians, who until recently have been largely responsible for writing the history of the comic book and who have uncritically taken the superhero as the core and basic measure of the medium. Fandom has been reluctant to place the genre, and its fluctuating popularity, in a larger historical context. Again, this has something to do with Kirby and with Marvel, whose joint achievement was to reestablish the superhero as the life raft if not very *raison d'être* of commercial comic books.

## WHAT SUPERHEROES HAD BEEN

Admittedly, over the past forty-plus years the fortunes of the superhero truly have dominated comic books, a dominance only reinforced in the public mind by the recent flood of blockbuster superhero films (the box-office power of which has re-intensified the traditional Marvel and DC rivalry). There is no disputing the superhero's current importance for a certain vision of comics. Today the genre enjoys a notoriety that recalls the Golden Age, when superheroes, then often called simply "costumed" heroes, energized the nascent comic book industry, even jolted it to life. Superman was the catalyst: as has often been recounted, the kernel of the genre arrived in 1938 with Siegel and Shuster's original "Superman" strip, launched in the monthly *Action Comics* published by DC. Siegel and Shuster's landmark series fused the graphic energy of newspaper comic strips, the vigilante ethos of dime novel and pulp adventure heroes, and the pop futurism/utopianism of early pulp science fiction. Superman trumpeted a new formula: the disguised, thus socially mobile, hero with near-godlike abilities. This formula centered on both "powers" and costume.

If the superhero's powers conferred an almost divine status, ratifying his vigilante activities in the name of a greater good, the costume became the superhero's instantly recognizable trademark, branding each character and conflating in one ripe, vivid image the genre's many appeals: graphic, commercial, moralistic, and wish-fulfilling. Most often the costumes were form-fitting, evoking circus strong men and early twentieth-century physical culture. Yet, as Michael Chabon has pointed out, they typically had nothing to do with realistic depictions of any kind of clothing. Seldom did a superhero's costume look like cloth draped on a body; instead it was purely a graphic device, a "notional" or "illusionary" convention that most often served to depict, through a haze of color, "the naked human form, unfettered, perfect, and free." Far from concealing identity (the prosaic explanation), the costume served to make manifest the hero's identity and origin, "function[ing] as a kind of magic screen onto which the repressed narrative [might] be projected" ("Secret Skin" 20–21). At the same time, the costume perhaps carried a whiff of subversion or welcome disorder, a reminder of the "violation of cultural categories" and "intoxicating reversal" of social hierarchies that Terry Castle finds in the practice of masquerade. Castle notes provocatively that masquerade serves both psychological and social functions: while denying "unitary notions of the self" and embodying the experience (and pleasures) of "double-ness," it also provides a temporary release from and stylized commentary upon social convention. The relationship between costume and wearer, she suggests, is inherently ironic (*Masquerade and Civilization* 4–6). Indeed the superhero's disguise, mask and/or costume, enabled its wearer to invert his usual identity. The heroes thus achieved an ironic class mobility à la so many versions of Robin Hood, a quality shared by pre-comic book predecessors such as the Baroness Orczy's Scarlet Pimpernel (1903) and Johnston McCulley's Zorro (1919). They also achieved an equally ironic reaffirmation of beleaguered masculinity. Here masculinity was made triumphant, queerly enough, through flamboyance: the adoption of colorful, circus-like attire. Critics have inevitably remarked the homoerotism or gender ambiguity implicit in this trope; the notion of a closeted superbeing, forced to hide his uniqueness for society's sake, would seem to beg for such readings (examples are rife: see the readings of Batman in Medhurst and in Brooker, Chapter 2, or Catherine Williamson's reading of *The Mark of Zorro*).

The prevalence of mythological and folkloric motifs—the orphaned or homeless hero, the mask, and attributes associated with animals such as bats, birds, and spiders—testifies to the mythic or archetypal underpinnings of the superhero. In fact archetypal interpretation à la Jung and Campbell has become one of the most common strategies for drawing critical attention to (and attempting to confer some borrowed dignity on) the genre. Yet the peculiarities of the formula, as codified by Superman and his many imitators, reflect conflicts specific to early twentieth-century America, whose popular depictions of heroism transplanted the vigilante ethos of the frontier into densely populated, socially volatile urban settings (see Coogan 2003; Coogan 2006, Chapter 6). The city was almost always the hero's HQ: as Scott Bukatman has pointed out, superheroes served, still often serve, as "vehicles of urban representation," super-mobile navigators of the impacted spaces of utopian modernity (and the dark dystopian underworlds of same); they "exist to inhabit the city, to patrol, map, dissect, and traverse it," to render it legible (222). Again, the formula is specifically *modern*. So, while much criticism has focused on the putatively timeless, archetypal aspects of the superhero, just as much attention ought to be given to the genre's historical and distinctly American character. Not universal archetype, in the sense of Campbell's heroic monomyth, but culturally specific *formula* may be the more helpful guidepost here (regarding which, I again refer readers to Cawelti).

*Superman* demonstrates the formula and its evolution. Stenciled from the science-fiction premise of Philip Wylie's pseudo-Nietschzean pulp novel *Gladiator* (1930) but jettisoning its pessimistic viewpoint in favor of an almost childlike embrace of New Deal liberalism, the original Superman became a radical "champion of the oppressed," actively seeking social as well as criminal justice through his vigilante exploits. The character was explicitly utopian, and his first few adventures were tinged with progressive politics, proletarian sympathies (see Worcester 30–31; De Haven 70–73), and a staunchly anti-war, even isolationist spirit. Soon, though, various factors—including licensing opportunities, the conscious gearing of story content toward young children, and the increasingly anxious nationalism of the pre-war period—undermined the populist and radical leanings of the character, redefining the superhero as simply a jingoistic national symbol. This was to be his most familiar guise. Campy reinterpretations of superheroes (notably the popular *Batman* television series of 1966–68) tend to riff on this unquestioning law-and-order patriotism, in spite of the antinomian spirit of the earliest stories.

Superheroes in the forties, such as Superman, Captain Marvel, and (obviously) S&K's Captain America, were linked to the war effort and served as effective instruments of wartime propaganda, targeted particularly at children and servicemen. Scholar Chris Murray has labeled such entertainments "popaganda," and the label fits. Timely's heroes were especially tied to the war effort, and their stories were nakedly jingoistic. Their nemeses were grossly stereotypic, indeed inhuman, Germans and Japanese, typically rendered as monstrous grotesques or knowing, gleeful sadists: outright voluptuaries of pain. The very shamelessness and perversity of such comics was part of their energy and appeal. They were brutal, and encouraged in comics a pervasive violence that outlasted the superhero and came to disturb many parents, teachers, and social guardians in the postwar period.

S&K created popaganda during this period—*Captain America Comics*, *The Boy Commandos*, and so on—and their eager, brawling style epitomized what WWII-era comics were all about. However, they turned away from superheroes after the war, as did most everyone else in the business. Seemingly dependent on the war, costumed heroes fell sharply in popularity in the latter forties, displaced by a variety of other genres. Whereas costumes had dominated comic books during the war years—from about 1940, prior to U.S. engagement, to roughly 1944—their popularity wilted after the mid-decade, as culture in the United States shifted from wartime jingo about the common defense to anxieties about domestic tranquility, for example, the reintegration of veterans, the restructuring of the economy, and the widespread perception of violence and unease among youth (regarding the latter, see Gilbert). At this same time, of course, the Cold War conjured a new—or newly menacing—and more diffuse enemy, an enemy at once international and potentially domestic. Wartime fears of subversion did not end, but simply spread—looming, hazy, and ever-present, like a cultural smog. Comic books dealt with these fears implicitly, and, at times, explicitly (as argued by Savage, particularly of the Korean War period).

From circa 1947 to 1954 the key genres were westerns, romance (thanks to S&K), *Archie*-style "teen" humor, and, to a lesser though important extent, crime and horror comics—and the best-selling genre of all, the funny animal and children's humor titles epitomized by the mega-selling *Walt Disney's Comics & Stories*. As Gabilliet points out in *Of Comics and Men*, comic book publishers sought to diversify their audiences to include more adolescents, older girls, and adults, while holding on to and expanding the very large audience of preadolescent children that, often with parental sanction, already supported funny animal comics (29–37 passim). This was the comic book industry's absolute commercial peak. Superheroes were thin on the ground, and dying. Of the prominent costumed heroes of the forties, only DC's Superman, Batman, and Wonder Woman survived uninterrupted throughout the fifties and beyond, while other prominent lines of superheroes, from such publishers as Timely, Fawcett, and Quality, fizzled. Attempts at reviving the genre were short-lived and marginal. So the fortunes of the comic book were not tied solely to the fortunes of the superhero.

Superheroes would slowly reappear, in sanitized form, after 1956, now even more strictly defined as purveyors of pietistic morality and obedience under law. Their antinomian qualities were denied by the strictures of the industry's self-policing Comics Code, adopted in 1954, which effectively forbade not only political critique and violent vigilantism but also anti-institutional satire more generally (as is recounted in Nyberg's *Seal of Approval*, the best history of the Code). The genre's unsteady balance between vigilantism and law, between violence and civility, tipped markedly toward the law-abiding and conventional: the superhero as model citizen. This all-pervasive civic moralism, shorn of the most extreme violence of the WWII-era superheroes, was epitomized by DC's upstanding, unquestioning, and brightly optimistic superheroes, as rendered by such clean and elegant, if sometimes aseptic, visual stylists as Carmine Infantino (*The Flash*), Gil Kane (*Green Lantern*), and Curt Swan (*Superman*). By 1960 the new, state-of-the-art superheroes were DC's crisp, well-favored suburbanites: utopian science heroes for the Space Age (regarding the graphic qualities of which, see Schumer). These were, however, soon to be rendered obsolete.

## THE MARVEL SUPERHERO

Launched in 1961–62, Marvel's superhero line broke with the DC formula, complicating and to a degree undercutting the unfaltering moral clarity of the new heroes by offering a tense, ironic, and, over time, increasingly specialized, hermetic, and self-reflexive treatment of the genre. Marvel's characterization stood out: under Stan Lee, the byword became "superheroes with super problems" (Lee recognized the formula for what it was and ran with it), while, thanks to Kirby's vital artistic input, the protagonists became increasingly monstrous, pitiable, and alienated, their superpowers often implicitly linked to the Cold War through such tropes as genetic mutation, accidental exposure to radioactivity, and the Space Race. Crystallized by Lee in concert with Kirby and Steve Ditko, both of whom had a yen for the grotesque, the Marvel ethos demanded heroes whose superpowers were counterbalanced by deformities, disabilities, or social stigmas. For instance, the antiheroic Spider-Man was often persecuted as a criminal menace, and the bestial Hulk hunted as a monster. Daredevil, a dashing, acrobatic hero, in some ways an anachronism, was made distinctive by a handicap: though empowered by a radioactive accident, he was also blinded. Iron Man, initially designed by Kirby though drawn by Don Heck, depended on his metal armor to keep his wounded heart beating. The characters' internal self-conflicts—mirroring the genre's own contradictions—were intensified to match. DC's heroes didn't have it so hard.

Something of Marvel's formulaic monster comics, circa 1959–62, resonated in their new superheroes. A venerable theme in science fiction and horror is the questioning of the very boundaries of the human, and indeed one of Kirby and Lee's freshest moves, in the context of superheroes, was to test that boundary, turning subhuman monsters into heroes, a move anticipated by few characters during the genre's 1940s heyday. (Points of comparison might be Bill Everett's antiheroic Sub-Mariner or Jerry Siegel's Robotman, both hybrid, half-human figures, or, on a more obvious visual level, Mort Leav and Harry Stein's swamp monster, the Heap. Of these, only Robotman was purely a hero.) Kirby and Lee went further with the tragic antihero than the genre had before, introducing the Fantastic Four's Thing, alias Ben Grimm, and his more savage counterpart the Hulk, alias Bruce Banner, just six months apart. These were creature-heroes, spiking the genre's potential for antisocial aggression and violence. Both were pitiable fall guys whose power—basically, mind-boggling strength—came at the cost of monstrosity, social ostracism, and alienation.

The debt to that urtext of science fiction, *Frankenstein*, was obvious. Both the Thing and the Hulk were self-contradictory, embodying the concept of the *fusion figure* set forth in Noël Carroll's theory of horror: a composite figure that "unites attributes held to be categorically distinct and/or at odds in the cultural scheme of things in *unambiguously* one, spatio-temporally discrete entity" (*Philosophy of Horror* 43, original emphasis). Each is, like Stevenson's Jekyll and Hyde, two-men-as-one. Each performs what Carroll calls categorical transgression, that is, the flouting or jamming of categorical distinctions: hero/horror, human/inhuman, man/monster. (As the cover to *The Incredible Hulk* #1 puts it, "Is he man or monster or . . . is he both?") The Thing looked like an animate lump of clay, or, later, a patchwork of terra-cotta shards, but at least he retained his voice and personality when transitioning between human and monstrous form. The Hulk was a green (originally gray) giant whose personality radically changed when he transitioned: a true Jekyll/Hyde figure, though closer in appearance to popular film versions of Frankenstein's monster. The scenes of each character transforming from human to monster, or vice versa, were among the most dramatic in the comics, often accomplished through panel triptychs (a recurrent device of Kirby's, as we saw back in fig. 5). Later Kirby characters, such as Orion and Etrigan the Demon, would likewise be monstrous composites.

At the outset, both the Thing and the Hulk were horrific characters. The Thing, however, was softened right away with a touch of ironic humor: "I live in a world too small for me! [. . .] Why must they build doorways so *narrow?*" (*FF* #1, pages 3–4). As Carroll observes, horror is closely aligned to humor based on incongruity ("Horror and Humor" 154–56). Over the years, the Hulk too has sometimes been a funny character, given the mismatch between his monstrous strength and his frequent childishness. This ironic dance between horror and humor derived partly from the comics' visual/verbal sparring.

More obvious, though, was the characters' status as angry and dangerous malcontents. For example, the possibility that the Thing's anger might turn him against his teammates was often reused as a plot tease. Related plot mechanisms were the guilt that the Fantastic Four's leader, Reed, felt for "causing" Ben's condition and, on the other hand, the possibility that Ben might be forever cured, that is, made "a man" again (a boon for him and Reed, a letdown for readers, surely). All three ideas come together as early as *Fantastic Four's* second issue. Within a few issues, of course, the Thing eases off: his surliness is tempered by a sense of humor, the repartee between him and the other team members (particularly the Human Torch) becomes a reliable engine of comic relief, and, with issues 8 and 9, his friend and love interest Alicia (a blind sculptress, no less) helps to bring out his winning qualities. So, within a year of the series' launch, his tragic qualities are sidelined—and yet never forgotten, as Ben's alienation and angst were inevitably revived and stoked in future stories.

The Hulk, on the other hand, was usually an outright pariah, a rootless, aimless, uncontrollable monster. *The Incredible Hulk* (1962–63) and its follow-up series in *Tales to Astonish* (from 1964 on) was an attenuated riff on the Jekyll/Hyde formula: a divided creature whose human side, Banner, struggled for ascendancy, but whose Hulkish self, bestial and brash, inevitably took control. The character's dialogue was famously inconsistent, a glitch rationalized by saying that Banner's mind was "clouded," or receding into the Hulk persona. Beyond the Hulk's childish insistence that he was "strongest" and that no one could "beat" him, Stan Lee didn't have a secure hold on the character. At times the Hulk spoke like an arrogant supervillain (*Get out of my way, insect!*), at times like a Ben Grimm-esque tough guy (*Nuts! I don't want any part of this crummy world!*), and at times like a small and confused kid, one who referred to himself in the third person as if dissociated (*Nobody tricks Hulk!*). Inevitably, though, the Hulk became a hero, pitted against villains either hyper-cerebral, such as the Gargoyle, the Leader, and the Stranger, or monstrously Hulk-like, such as the Abomination, and often having to come to the rescue of Banner's love interest, Betty Ross, in a drawn-out "Beauty and the Beast" formula (indeed the story in *Incredible Hulk* #5 is titled just that). Hulk was frequently forced to do the bidding of villains, like a draft animal or mindless slave; in a sense, the whole series was about powerlessness, though the Hulk's continual boasting belied that theme.

Of the two monster-heroes, the Thing was the more humanly varied and multifaceted. He was a Golem of sorts, thus visually interesting, but also a chip off the Kirby block, part braggart, part white knight, a mixture of East Side roughness, buffoonish humor, corny sentiment, and reluctant heroism. Many readers have seen Kirby himself in the character. In any case, the Thing was a masterstroke, a fusion figure uniting the living (human) and unliving (rock), man and Golem, hero and horror. He paved the way for further superhero grotesques: the X-Men's Beast, for instance, or the varied cast of the Inhumans, some of whom (Medusa, Gorgon) first appeared as enemies of the Fantastic Four.

Made familiar by repetition, Marvel's grotesque, freakish heroes ultimately lacked that fearsomeness Carroll argues is essential to horror—but they successfully reclaimed and juiced up the superhero genre by supplying an edgy,

urban ethos at odds with the neat, suburban sensibilities of DC. They brought
to the fore, once again, the genre's potential for untrammeled (or barely tram-
meled) aggression. Until then, DC's shiny, ever-optimistic lineup had unquestionably led the superhero revival post 1956 (later dubbed the Silver Age). DC,
spurred by editor and sometime science fiction fan and literary agent Julius
Schwartz, had taken steps toward redefining the genre by recasting established
1940s heroes such as the Flash and Green Lantern in an updated, sleekly modern science-fiction milieu. These SF- and Cold War-oriented revivals dovetailed smartly with a new nationalistic emphasis on science and science educa-
tion in the post-Sputnik era (and comic books, of course, happily participated
in the then-worship of astronauts as culture heroes).

Moreover, editor Schwartz, who, like Siegel and Shuster, had participated
in the earliest science-fiction fandom—he had co-edited the seminal fanzine
*Time Traveller* [*sic*]—fostered comic book and superhero fandom by printing names and addresses of fan correspondents within his titles, a move that
encouraged the rise of fan communities and amateur publishing (Schwartz
105–06). His colleague Mort Weisinger, another early SF fan and sometime SF
pulp editor—in fact Schwartz's collaborator both on *Time Traveller* and in the
first SF literary agency—did the same in the Superman titles, which he edited
(De Haven 117, 136–37). Superhero comics, in other words, followed the example of SF fandom. In this way the superhero genre had a salutary, though
of course also blinkering, influence on the rise of comic book fandom as an
organized, self-aware subculture. Here is where the previously neglected geek
culture of comic book fans came into its own and began, gradually, to influence the production of the comics directly. Over time, this newly ascendant
fandom was charmed by Marvel's outcast heroes, who ditched DC's paternal-
istic, wholly incorporated worldview in favor of a scruffier look and attitude
that was equal parts anguished Romanticism and hipster street cred. Marvel,
in short, empathized with the freaks.

If Marvel was a space of resistance, then its graphics were the way in. In
contrast to DC's coolly modernist streamlining, the Marvel style was vigorous,
even brutal, and arose from a process in which speed-drawing and narrative
improvising were indistinguishable. Marvel favored energy over smoothness.
In contrast to the scripter-dominated DC, Marvel's production method (as
seen in our previous chapter) favored the bold, energetic, narratively *generative*
artwork of Kirby and Ditko. The Marvel method, as noted, placed a greater
storytelling burden on narrative drawing than on wordsmithing. Plots were
built mainly through cartooning, not text. Ditko brought a weird moodi-
ness and psychological urgency to the genre, while Kirby brought an increasingly grand, even Olympian quality, leading to stories of cosmic scope and

pretension—though leavened by a streak of humor, by Lee's self-mocking editorial persona, and by a soap opera-like emphasis on the domestic travails of the protagonists.

Kirby in particular was on a tear. Lee scurried alongside. Tension between word and image, and among generic elements, was felt at every level. Irony erupted everywhere. For example, the Fantastic Four battled world-threatening menaces from other dimensions, lost kingdoms, and far-flung planets, even as their members, most notably the Thing, were routinely stricken by failed or uncertain relationships, self-hatred and self-doubt, and other everyday problems. A long-running subplot had Susan (the Invisible Girl) wavering romantically between Reed (Mr. Fantastic) and the group's enemy, the Sub-Mariner. If graphic fantasy was *The Fantastic Four*'s foundation, tragicomedy was the reigning mood—that, and paranoia. In hindsight, the Marvel characters' origins, invoking radioactivity and scientific accidents, reveal a fearful or at least cautionary view of emerging technologies, a view often confirmed in stories of high-tech menace on a global scale: a pop paranoia that resonated perfectly with the jittery mood of the era's sci-fi and monster movies. The stakes rose ever higher, in keeping with the Cold War and its barely acknowledged technological terrors. Marvel had the edge.

The result, after mid-decade, was a never-ending series of near-apocalyptic situations, later to be revisited endlessly by faithful fans and writers: a background against which the personal lives of the heroes, far from fading into insignificance, ironically came to assume the utmost importance. Here, gradually and with much hedging and uncertainty, the superhero genre began to transform. Earlier conventions, including the disguise or secret identity and the hero's ritualistic self-denial, became less important and in some cases were dropped, though the strong sense of irony embodied by the secret identity trope remained (in some cases stronger than ever, as in Ditko's Spider-Man). Protecting secret identities mattered less than exploration, expanding casts, group dynamics, and causal chains that remained open at episode's end. Endless battle, without the comforting, ritual closures of earlier superhero adventures, was Marvel's métier, encouraging the development of an overarching fictive history shared among Marvel's many superhero comics. This so-called intertextual "continuity" became a golden idol to fans, indeed, Marvel's strongest commercial asset and the putative source of its unique style. Rival DC would eventually adopt the principle as well. In-depth knowledge of continuity became a shibboleth of fandom.

Suffice to say that Marvel accomplished a lot during this germinal period. Understanding of this accomplishment, though, is often clouded by two misapprehensions:

**1. That Marvel made superhero comics "realistic."** As noted in Chapter 1, fans have invoked the idea of a growing realism to explain each new innovation in the genre. Realism, though, is a relative term; any standard of realism in superhero comics must be defined relative to the genre's history, its seminal productions, and its key contributors. Granted, Marvel played its part in bringing a new degree of illustrative realism to superheroes, partly by apprenticing already-accomplished illustrators like John Romita and John Buscema (both probably more technically facile than Kirby) to the Kirby style and partly by making room, eventually, for a new generation of stylists for whom photorealism and commercial design were privileged points of reference, beginning in the late sixties with, as noted, Neal Adams (whose brief run on *X-Men* in 1969 represented a new take on characters Kirby designed, and is considered seminal). What's more, story-wise Marvel allowed for a greater degree of emotional complexity in its characterizations, greater, that is, than had previously prevailed in superhero comics. This quality bears out the lasting influence of romance comics (of which both Kirby and Lee had done quite a few). Yet what energized the Marvel comics of the sixties, what accounts for their heated tone, is a clash of sensibilities, a volatile intermixture of image and text that consistently pitches toward melodrama and overstatement. Yes, Marvel's aching, emotionally fraught characterization brought a greater degree of psychological realism to the superhero, if only because Marvel admitted a wider range of emotions than, say, the staid, constricted superhero books of DC; realism, however, was not, and arguably still isn't, a goal in itself.

Tom Crippen makes the interesting observation, apropos of more recent superhero comics, that the appeal of "superhero realism" lies in the perceived difference between the grand, fantastical qualities of the heroes and the quality of realism itself. The "gap" between them, Crippen observes, the way the two "bump" up against one another, yields "a kind of humor [. . .] produced by seeing different realms of thought fail to align" (134). If the genre's grounding in fantasy is, as Crippen says, what "gives the realism its kick," then that "kick" cannot help but partake of irony. Certainly neither of Marvel's great founding artists, Kirby or Ditko, aspired to realism; both practiced narrative drawing at its most telling, emotionally fraught, and graphically expressive. Their work was brusque and strange. The vaunted "realism" of Marvel—which is the quality most often highlighted in discussions of Lee's scripting, in contrast to that of other comic books of the era—served to recover an adolescent and young adult audience for superhero comics, inoculating the genre with a dose of topicality and pathetic irony. This approach was comparatively realistic, but only for the sake of anchoring the elements of the bizarre, otherworldly, gargantuan, and operatic that played just as big a part in the Marvel aesthetic.

Rather than realism, the operative principles of vintage Marvel were *irony* and *graphic energy.*

**2. That Marvel was created with continuity in mind, and the Marvel Universe grew out of a careful publishing program brainstormed by Stan Lee.** As established in Chapter 2, there was no settled plan at Marvel in late 1961 when *Fantastic Four* made its debut. In fact Marvel's tight fictive continuity developed *ex post facto.* The company's superheroes arrived gradually, tentatively, and, until the arrival of *Amazing Spider-Man* in early 1963, without a sense of an overall world. Note that Marvel did not grant a new solo title to a character previously introduced in another superhero title until *The Silver Surfer* (1968–70), spun off from *Fantastic Four.* Note too that it took quite some time for solo characters to gain multiple series: aside from the Human Torch/Thing feature in *Strange Tales,* the first Marvel character to star in two different titles at once was the non-superhero Nick Fury, star of both the WWII-era *Sgt. Fury and His Howling Commandos* (1963–74, then reprints to 1981) and "Nick Fury, Agent of S.H.I.E.L.D.," the Bond-inspired spy series in *Strange Tales* (1965–68) that spun off into its own short-lived book in 1968 (both incarnations of Fury were launched by Kirby and Lee). Marvel did not make a practice of publishing multiple interlocking titles starring the same character until *Peter Parker, the Spectacular Spider-Man* appeared in 1976 to complement the long-running *Amazing Spider-Man.* (The character's third monthly would follow in 1985, and of course a plethora of *X-Men* spin-offs came in the early mid-eighties and after.) As argued in the previous chapter, the Marvel Universe is a piecemeal work accrued over decades; indeed its fiction of continuity came about as much through retrospective efforts like *The Official Handbook of the Marvel Universe* (1983, revised and reissued multiple times since) as through the original comics of the sixties era. Marvel continuity, then, is the co-achievement of Marvel and its fans: witness the continuity-reinforcing efforts of such fanzine writers, later comics professionals, as Peter Sanderson and Mark Gruenwald. The former, Sanderson, became Marvel's archivist; the latter, Gruenwald (1953–1996), co-published and co-edited the continuity-oriented fanzine *Omniverse: The Journal of Fictional Reality,* which, in token of its scholarly dedication, bore footnotes (see Gruenwald). He then went on to mastermind Marvel's *Official Handbook* and, later, to serve Marvel as an executive editor and continuity maven.[1] Such fans-turned-pro had as much to do with solidifying Marvel's continuity as had any of its contributors in the sixties. In essence, the Marvel Universe as it is now known was the result of incorporating fan fiction into the company's official lore.

Clearly, the development of ever-stronger continuity in superhero comics dovetailed with the increasing influx of fans into professional positions within the comic book industry. This trend began prior to Kirby's departure from Marvel in 1970 (most famously, fan Roy Thomas was hired at Marvel in 1965), and then accelerated in the early to mid-seventies, urged on by the increasing cohesiveness of fandom and, over time, the development of the direct market. That market, consisting of hobby shops that specialized in the collection and trading of comics, nurtured a subculture that encouraged the free intermingling of fans and professionals. It also provided a life raft for the superhero. Though partly "underground" in origin, testifying to the liberating effects of underground comix, the market was especially beholden to superhero fandom (again, see Hatfield, *Alternative*); in the late seventies, it was increasingly colonized by new, up-and-coming publishers of pulp adventure fare, including superheroes, sword-and-sorcery fantasy, and space opera, all redolent of the frontier romance and belonging to the metagenre of the vigilante hero. By 1980 the market was by and unquestionably *for* superhero fans. Marvel and DC, by then wholly dependent on superheroes, co-opted the direct market with ingenious and aggressive marketing and a growing number of exclusive (that is, direct-only) publications. By 1982 Marvel depended on the direct market for as much as half its sales (Gabilliet 87; Rogers 66). Both Marvel and DC, the only two mainstream comic book publishers to resist the overall plunge in sales during the seventies, understood that the direct market represented the future of the industry. Traditional newsstand sales accounted for an increasingly small percentage of Marvel and DC's revenues (on this crucial transition, see Rogers 56–57, 64–67; Parsons 68, 76–77; Gabilliet 71–74, 138–45).

In the early to mid-eighties, under these conditions, Marvel's best-selling *X-Men* and its spin-offs were the direct market's dominant comic-book franchise, distilling and extending the company's soap opera approach to superheroics. Populated by outcast "mutants," whose sense of persecution at once traded on adolescent fears and inspired moral fables about prejudice and xenophobia, the *X-Men* franchise sought to trump the Marvel comics of the sixties in terms of both pomp and sentimentality. Its emphasis on the heroism of the persecuted and misunderstood (perfect for a marginalized subculture!) also questioned, to a degree subverted, the genre's once-absolute insistence on the need to contain the superhero and, as Reynolds has pointed out, preserve the social status quo (77). More and more, the Marvel heroes rearranged and redefined their world; more and more, Marvel continuity diverged from (while still attempting to comment on) current events in *our* world. All the while, fan patronage proved to be the medium's lifeline and the professionalization of fans resulted in more complicated, continuity-driven comics. No one working at Marvel circa 1961–62 would have predicted this.

The changes wrought by Marvel and its fandom would have ideological as well as commercial consequences. These came to a head in the 1980s when the recognition that superheroes might transform their worlds, combined with the relative freedom offered by the direct market (freedom from the restraints of the Comics Code if nothing else), led to the publication of darker, morally ambiguous, at times subversive stories, culminating in a so-called revisionist or adult trend within the genre. This late-eighties trend popularized not only increasing violence but also archly self-conscious examinations of the genre and its implications, for example, the role of superheroes in a fractured, disunited society and the problems posed by vigilantism. Such revisionary works sought, through either speculative realism or satiric excess, to question rather than simply reinscribe the genre's basic assumptions. This trend, though more strongly linked to rival publisher DC (*The Dark Knight Returns*, *Watchmen*), drew inspiration from Marvel's large-scale treatment of the genre, in particular from Marvel's twinned impulses toward tighter intertextual continuity and more obvious topical relevance. Spurred by the Marvels of the sixties and seventies, the direct market superheroes of the eighties and nineties followed both of those impulses, on the one hand questioning the repressive yet reassuring moralism upon which the Comics Code insisted, and, on the other, moving toward ever more cosmic crossovers and "event" series—vast, intricately knotted, and apocalyptic. The latter represent a sort of metastasis of the continuity principle. The influence of Marvel, more particularly of Kirby's penchant for grand-scale world-building and world-threatening, fairly saturates the American comic books of the past thirty years.

## THE MARVEL MYTHOS

It has often been said, though not so often convincingly, that superheroes constitute "a modern mythology," and that the Marvel Universe in particular called forth or made more obvious this mythic quality. Such arguments are inexact. If Marvel constitutes a *mythos*, then it is one that does not carry all the meanings that attach, or once attached, to the word: it does not consist of traditional stories built around putatively historical events; it does not constitute, at least not in any sacred or authoritative way, a body of widely shared beliefs about the world; it does not bear the cosmogony or eschatology of a people (though it has its own privileged stories of genesis and Armageddon, making and unmaking). In short, the Marvel mythos does not seem to perform much of the cultural work performed, or once performed, by the traditional mythoi so often invoked for the sake of the comparison. Notwithstanding Richard Reynolds' useful *Super Heroes: A Modern Mythology* (1992) and other, lesser books, no thorough study has yet been done to substantiate the notion of superhero comics as a mythology, at least in terms other than metaphorical (for a critique of Reynolds on this point, see Nevins).

Yet, if the comparison is too often loosely made, Marvel did draw inspiration from mythology, particularly Kirby's appetite for mythic tales, a hankering seen even very early in his work (in such features as 1940's embryonic "Mercury"). From such tales Kirby inherited a sense of scope, a habit of representing moral and philosophical conflicts by using godlike and symbolically counterpoised characters, and a penchant for creating families of such characters that both reinforce and yet also blur the differences between "good" and "evil." Explicit borrowings from ancient myth, including internecine feuds and symbolically opposed figures, structured Kirby's *Thor* and "Tales of Asgard," in which Kirby tended to design characters by the handful rather than singly (ditto for his later Fourth World and *Eternals*). These myth-making gestures weren't just tokens of archaism; they were very much at home in Cold War America, testimony to the beliefs and fears of the time. Implicitly, Kirby's personal mythologies testify to and make sense within the Cold War's totalizing ideological conflict. This is why Marvel's vintage superhero comics have a time capsule-like quality. They also attain, not least because of Kirby's graphic mythopoesis, some of the timeless, deeply resonant qualities of mythology and legend.

Under Kirby, Marvel's approach to superheroes became more complex, less settled, and, if I may hazard the word, pantheonic. By this I mean that, over time, Marvel's heroes and villains came to counterbalance each other, in a sort of rough-hewn grand design defined by symbolic symmetry. All of them, heroes and villains, belonged to a great, sprawling, superhuman family whose interweaving, often violent relationships were tangled and confusing, but also compelling. Good and evil forces were paired in a Manichean struggle in which the victory of the good, though expected and hoped for at the end of each tale, turned out to be temporary, provisory, and fragile. Conflict reigned. The heroes' omnipotence was not guaranteed (though the coddling moralism of the Comics Code did ensure that heroes almost always won the battle if not the war).

To some extent this pattern of unceasing conflict had always been the case for superheroes; Superman's career, after all, was famously described as a "never-ending battle." But the Marvel characters were not blessed with that forgetfulness which, in earlier superhero comics, almost always ushered the antagonists back, in ritualistic fashion, to an atemporal stasis, or what Neil Gaiman has called a "state of grace," between episodes, so that the beginning of each new story could be a fresh starting point (see "Change or Die!" with Gaiman et al., 195–196). Instead, the Marvel characters remembered—and so did their readers.

Gaiman's concept of the "state of grace" echoes Umberto Eco's famed analysis of narrative time in his essay "The Myth of Superman" ("Il mito di Superman e la dissoluzione del tempo," 1962, rev. and trans. 1972), which was one of the earliest and is still one of the smartest academic analyses of superhero comics (and of "time" in popular series fiction more generally). Eco, writing in the early sixties prior to Marvel's big changes, argues that Superman comics, indeed superhero comics on the whole, embody a "paradoxical" approach to narrative temporality, so as to reconcile the demands of the mythic—that is, the archetypal, the "emblematic," the fixed and predictable functions of the superhero—with the different demands of the popular romance, that is, the novel. Per Eco, the novel depends on the invocation (yet also violation) of the everyday and "typical," and thrives on unpredictability, "the ingenious invention of unexpected events," and, above all, the possibility of development (148–49). The demands of novelistic development call for the hero to *accomplish* something, that is, "to ma[k]e a gesture which is inscribed in his past and which weighs on his future." Such accomplishments, such meaningful happenings, constitute, Eco says, "a step toward death"—for to act is to "consume" oneself, to use up or foreclose some of one's future possibilities and to add to the archive of events that will shape (and hem in) one's future actions (150). To act is to surrender to time's passage. Superman comics therefore depend on a temporal paradox, not because the "time" depicted within a given story is odd (though time travel stories were common in Superman comics then) but because the inferred time "which ties one episode to another" is canceled or ignored or continually rewound to a notional status quo, denying change (153). In short, Superman comics—and by extension all superhero comic series of that era, according to Eco—neglected time between episodes, or treated it only very selectively. They followed a logic of repetition rather than development: what Eco calls an *iterative* structure, in which "each event takes up again from a sort of virtual beginning, ignoring where the preceding event left off" (157).

This had already begun to change before Marvel, Tom De Haven argues, in the Weisinger-edited Superman titles circa 1958 and after. During that era, Superman developed a supporting cast of other survivors from his native planet of Krypton, his alien status was increasingly stressed, and the stories tilted hard in the direction of science fiction, focusing on Kryptonian lore.

Weisinger, De Haven notes, "devised a preposterous yet consistent series history and culture," so that, gradually, "the permanent cast members were endowed with charged and significant memories" (115). Indeed memories and revisitations of Krypton proved a reliable story engine for years. Superman and his story-world were thus greatly enriched: "In depicting, for the first time, Superman *as* an alien, *as* an immigrant, *as* a survivor, and in presenting these attributes as consequential and defining, the comic books [. . .] developed a coherence and an inviting, elevated *meaningfulness* [. . .]" (117). This, De Haven notes, presaged the developed of tighter continuity at Marvel, and had the unintended consequence of hooking a new, more dedicated kind of reader (137).

By this light, Eco's analysis of Superman had already become outdated by 1962. Yet Eco does note that Superman stories take place in an "oneiric climate" that selectively admits time and enables a kind of ritualistic return to and elaboration of the character's origins and history (153–54). His analysis acknowledges the embroidering of the Superman universe under Weisinger, including Weisinger's frequent recourse to "imaginary" (what-if) stories and "untold" or retold tales (154–55). What does *not* happen in these comics, Eco argues, is anything that would draw Superman into developments likely to dictate his future actions. Yes, the Weisinger-era Superman had backstory, that is, a history, but not one that necessarily imposed on each successive installment. Despite the many recurrent motifs and the burgeoning cast of characters in Superman comics during this period, almost every tale was self-contained. New readers could jump on with any issue. Between-issue temporality was still vague or deniable.

In contrast, Marvel became addicted, soap opera-like, to continuing storylines and unresolved problems. Marvel's heroes and villains had baggage. They shared memories and carted them around, seldom forgetting. As Kirby, Lee, and company chased the notion of continuity, those memories often (though not always consistently) impinged on present struggles. For example, the Fantastic Four were haunted by villains-at-large such as the Sub-Mariner and the Frightful Four, whose escapes left the team with troubling loose ends between issues. References to preceding issues became common. Even as inter-title continuity became Marvel's main selling tool, individual titles such as *Fantastic Four* and *Amazing Spider-Man* began to experiment with cliffhanger stories of two or more issues each. By late 1964, *Amazing* was a nonstop soap opera, and the same was true of the *FF* by mid-1965. If these serials lacked the cohesiveness of the ideal novel, if over the long term they were still indefinitely repeating *series* rather than whole stories published by part, still they boasted, individually and collectively, an additive and even genealogical quality that turned them into an unending "saga." A saga, as Eco has said elsewhere, entails the passage of time; it is able to let characters grow, change, and perhaps even die; it is prone to a treelike branching into various narrative lines. Admittedly, an open-ended, commercial saga is still, as Eco observes, essentially "a series in disguise," repeating, albeit in a pseudo-historical framework, the same old story, the same ideas; there is a contradiction between the saga's effort toward novelistic development and the series' effort to avoid consumption, so as to maintain the infinite exploitability of the characters (*Limits* 87). Yet a saga at least allows the potential to develop an immense, ongoing fictive network, what scholars Pat Harrigan and Noah Wardrip-Fruin have called a *vast narrative* (2–3). Marvel, building on hints in Superman and other comics, activated the idea of vast narrative for comics.

Again, bear in mind that this vast narrative—the Marvel Universe—started tentatively, and only later was consolidated and elaborated on by diverse hands. It represents a case of multiple authorship on a massive scale, carried out over the decades following Marvel's first success. However—and this is key for our present interest—some of the elements that made this mass effort possible were present early on in Kirby's work. Indeed they arose from his drawing board. For example, one of the keystones of the Marvel saga was (and is) *family resemblance*: the fact that heroes and villains often come from common roots and boast similar or complementary powers. Kirby introduced this idea to Marvel, specifically the topos of symbolic pairings or matches between hero and villain. This fretful dualism spoke to the cultural moment: to the Cold War, to its global diffusion of conflict, its comprehensiveness, and its insistence on ideological opposition and mirroring (clash of civilizations, ahem!). What this meant, practically, is that good villains never stayed dead and never stayed away for long. They became regular supporting characters.

Superheroes had always required super-antagonists, of course. From the forties on, many heroes had faced recurrent signature villains who seemed, always, to escape captivity and renew the old feuds. Batman's rogues' gallery is probably the best-known example (Joker, Penguin, et al.). But at Marvel the villains often evaded capture and simply withdrew at the end of an episode, leaving plot points dangling. Earlier superhero comics, by contrast, typically jailed or even killed off the villains at story's end, only to bring them back later. For instance, the Brain Wave is one of the signature villains for the Justice Society of America (the team featured in DC's *All Star Comics* between 1941 and 1951), yet he faced the JSA only four times during the Golden Age, each time ending in "death" or capture. Super-villains who appeared much more frequently, so frequently as to become part of a hero's supporting cast, were unusual: the best example would be Captain Marvel's archenemy Dr. Sivana, who appeared continually in Fawcett Comics' various Captain Marvel series (1940–1953) and who often evaded capture. Sivana's absurdly comic presence became a staple ingredient of Captain Marvel's world (this Captain Marvel, note, was no relation to Marvel Comics the publisher). More typical were villains who recurred often but whose presence was not considered essential to a series' premise: Batman's Joker, Superman's Lex Luthor, Captain America's Red Skull.

By contrast, Marvel in the sixties not only let the villains get away but also made the unresolved threats they posed a continual and defining aspect of the heroes' world. By the mid-sixties Marvel had developed powerful pairings of hero and villain whose continual conflicts could sustain stories indefinitely: the Fantastic Four and Dr. Doom, Thor and Loki, Spider-Man and Dr. Octopus, Spider-Man and the Green Goblin, the X-Men and Magneto. What's more, Marvel's villains were often tied to the heroes by shared origins—connected symbiotically, almost like family. There were few precedents for this in earlier superhero comics. One example could be Black Adam, a villain introduced in Fawcett's *Marvel Family* series in 1945 who shared the same magic origins and basic costume design as the heroes (again, this *Marvel Family* was unrelated to Marvel Comics). Black Adam, however, was originally a one-shot character, and would not be reused for some thirty-two years. Marvel took this idea of the villain as hero's counterpart and, over the years, ran with it: for example, the Fantastic Four's resident scientist, Mr. Fantastic, nearly met his match in Dr. Doom, a mad genius whom he had met and tried to befriend years before when both were in college. Doom often seemed to be motivated as much by fraternal rivalry with Mr. Fantastic as by innate evil; a popular villain, he became a near-constant presence in the lives of the Fantastic Four and a pillar of the Marvel Universe (he has starred in several series of his own). In the *X-Men* series, the hate-filled Magneto fulfilled a similar but even more central role, growing in stature so much that, long after Kirby's tenure, the character would hover uncertainly between villain and misguided antihero.

Nemeses were everything. Numerous Marvel comics in Kirby's wake pursued the idea of the villain as inverted hero, as rival and opposite. The Hulk clashed with other radiation-induced monstrosities, the Abomination and the Leader; Iron Man battled a rival armored character, the Titanium Man; and Dr. Strange faced off against rival sorcerer Baron Mordo, who shared his origins. Meanwhile, Ditko's Spider-Man faced foes such as Dr. Octopus and the Sandman, who, like Spider-Man, gained their powers through nuclear accidents and who, equally like Spider-Man, were freakish in power and appearance (indulging Ditko's penchant for elastic, ever-morphing body types and curving, serpentine shapes). Much, much later, well past Ditko, Spider-Man would face evil doppelgangers whose looks were closely patterned after his own costume (Venom, Carnage). The villains often seemed to be distorted shadows of the heroes.

Surely Kirby cannot be credited or blamed for most of this? Of course not. These trends did not pop out suddenly in 1961–62, but over time as the Marvel Universe grew, fitfully, erratically, at first more the result of cross-promotional improvising than some considered, long-range plan. Many creators beyond Kirby and Lee were involved in its growth. It was under Kirby, though, that Marvel decisively latched onto the idea of unresolved, never-ending conflict between superpowered opposites, and, revealingly, Kirby's subsequent work often explores this kind of dualistic premise in distilled or exaggerated form. This sort of mirroring obviously appealed to him, as both a storyteller and a designer of characters.

The *X-Men* series, launched in 1963, is the keystone example. It introduced the germ of an idea that was to emerge full-blown in many of Kirby's later creations: that of superhuman heroes and villains springing from a common origin, vying with each other like rival gods in some epically dysfunctional family. Humankind, of course, was caught in the middle. *X-Men* approached this concept through the then-novel idea of mutants, that is, superbeings who were simply born that way. *X-Men* #1 (Sept. 1963) establishes the blueprint straight off: a perpetual conflict between "evil" mutants, represented by Magneto, and "good" (that is, pro-human) mutants, represented by Professor Charles Xavier and his young students, the titular X-Men. Linked by a common name and nature (*mutant*), yet starkly divided by philosophies and means, Xavier and Magneto define opposite poles in a struggle that was to become a foundational element in the Marvel Universe: Magneto seeks to rule over humankind as "homo superior," while Professor X seeks peaceful coexistence with humans and strives to defend the world from Magneto's ambitions. This fundamental conflict is at work even in the first story.

Originally, neither Magneto's specific origin nor Xavier's was important. Their common mutanthood was a given. What mattered was the struggle between X-Men and evil mutants to define the relationship between mutantkind and humankind. In this struggle, humanity became the fulcrum and victim, just as, so often in ancient mythology and epic, humans are proxies in or victims of conflicts among gods and goddesses. In the *X-Men*'s premise, then, there was a promise, a seed, of mythological scope. There had never quite been anything like this in comic books before: never had super-villains played such a fundamental role in a series, and never had comic books focused on a "race" of superbeings simply born with their unique powers. The X-Men needed no magic words, no mystic thunderbolts, no cosmic rays or attacks by radioactive bugs to explain their abilities. Neither did their most potent and enduring antagonist, Magneto. From this simple idea came, gradually and without fanfare, a new approach to the superhero.

Granted, Kirby and Lee did not fully exploit this potential in the early X-Men. The Lee & Kirby X-Men of 1963–66 was an underachieving series that, after a promising launch, came to seem cramped and uninventive alongside Kirby's best work. Kirby departed the series on the cusp of 1966 to focus on other work; by then he had fully penciled X-Men issues 1–11 and provided layouts for other artists, mainly Werner Roth, in issues 12–17 (dated July 1965 to Feb. 1966). He would provide covers or cover layouts for most issues through late 1966. But this was not his sharpest work; frankly, X-Men was a second-stringer. Lee handed over the scripting to protégé Roy Thomas as of #20, and what followed was largely undistinguished until the arrival of artist Neal Adams in 1969. Shortly after the fondly remembered Adams/Thomas run, the series died, only to be revived as a reprint book, in which status it continued quietly for almost five years before its widely touted revival in 1975, years after Lee and Kirby. Even the earliest issues of X-Men, those penciled fully by Kirby, had been comparatively weak: the only essential villains introduced in the early run were Magneto and the robotic Sentinels, and, as had The Fantastic Four before it, the series cast about uncertainly for subplots, hooks, and distinctive characterizations. Kirby and Lee returned to Magneto monotonously throughout their two-plus years on the title, without deepening the conflict among mutants or expanding the scope of the action in such a way as to capitalize on the series' premise. Though said premise held extraordinary promise, when handled in an ordinary way it confined and hobbled the series, making it dully repetitive. Truthfully, the X-Men languished in the shadow of the Fantastic Four; the series demanded a bigger treatment than it got. The early issues remained trapped in month-to-month superheroics, often against colorless villains, the only novelty coming from Professor X as teacher and the hovering presence of Magneto as antagonist. Years would go by before other creators (Chris Claremont et al.) would begin to extrapolate from the original and exploit the series' potential.

Though X-Men had the glimmer of an idea, it was Kirby's peak period on Marvel's Thor that most successfully explored a pantheonic approach to superheroes. The mythological Thor had held a special fascination for Kirby for decades: witness "Villain from Valhalla," a 1942 Sandman story by Simon & Kirby, or "The Magic Hammer," another Thor-related story for DC's Tales of the Unexpected in 1957. However, the early Thor stories in Marvel's Journey into Mystery failed to capitalize on the character's mythic origins. Like many of the early-sixties Marvel series, Thor began with one foot in the Kirby/Lee monster comics; then, after Kirby's brief initial run, it had little to offer besides standard crime-fighting stories in mythological drag. However, once Kirby returned to the series and hit his stride—especially in 1966 and after—his *Thor* became a launch pad for epics of unprecedented scope and mythic resonance. Building on, though also offhandedly distorting, the patterns laid out in Norse myth, Kirby and Lee made Thor's unpredictable half-brother Loki into a pure villain and central figure, while also spotlighting other mythic characters, both heroic (e.g., Sif, Balder, Heimdall) and villainous (e.g., Hela, goddess of death; various giants and trolls). Thor's pitiable human alter-ego, the lame but well-intentioned doctor Don Blake—in superhero parlance, his *civilian identity*—disappeared for issues at a time, as Kirby's interest in conventional superheroics waned and he instead explored the possibilities of a godly pantheon.

Prior to this, *Thor* had been dominated by romance-styled plotting about Thor/Don Blake's stymied relationship with love interest Jane Foster, his nurse. This was *Superman* with a vengeance: Blake, kindly, lame, and a bit dull if not outright "mild-mannered," desired Jane, but his true self, Thor, could not cleave to her because his godly father, Odin, forbade him to love a "mortal." Jane was often in need of being rescued; Thor/Blake was torn by his divided nature. In essence, Don Blake was a mashup of Clark Kent and the then-popular Dr. Kildare. In the *Thor* of the mid- to late-sixties, though, things were cosmic: often, nothing less than the end of everything was at stake. Jane Foster was eventually shunted to the side and the series went Blake-less for long periods. Plots occasionally wobbled back to earthbound crime-fighting and soap opera, but most often slipped the traces, giving free rein to Kirby's off-the-cuff mythopoeic barnstorming. Kirby's design and drawing went wild (as I'll discuss in our next chapter), the elastic plots giving affordance to spectacular graphic invention.

Equally grand in scope from the mid-sixties onward was Kirby's *Fantastic Four*, which used the team's science-fiction roots to explore a range of hidden worlds, alternate realities, inhuman species, and space-spanning superbeings. In fact it was the *FF* that first and most clearly heralded Kirby's new, outsized approach to the superhero genre. The much-praised "Galactus trilogy" in *FF* #48–50 (March–May 1966), which first introduced the seminal characters Galactus and the Silver Surfer, is similar in outline to many of the conflicts acted out in the peak-period *Thor*: the Godlike Galactus, not so much a villain as an amoral, impersonal force, struggles with his once-servant, the Silver Surfer, to decide the fate of the world. Again, humanity is the fulcrum: the Silver Surfer's sympathetic regard for humans resembles Thor's own, and, eventually, the Surfer would be cast as an almost Christlike sufferer for humanity's sins (a symbolic burden most weightily depicted in the Stan Lee-scripted, post-Kirby *Silver Surfer* series of 1968–1970). In the Galactus trilogy, even the most powerful of humans, the Fantastic Four, are forced into the role of bystanders—until the intervention of another Godlike extraterrestrial, the Watcher, helps humanity save itself. Humankind thus tips the scales, though in an almost childlike, unknowing way, in a mythic struggle to decide its own destiny.

The "Galactus trilogy"—which, as our next chapter will show, is a prime example of Kirby's technological sublime—was to prove supremely influential, indeed epochal, for Marvel and its fans. Tellingly, it isn't so much a cohesive trilogy as three months' worth of issues placed within a larger continuity. *Fantastic Four* #48 actually begins with the resolution of the Inhumans storyline launched several issues earlier, while #50, though titled "The Startling Saga of the Silver Surfer," resolves the threat of Galactus halfway through, quickly ushers off the Surfer, and then concentrates on domestic happenings in the lives of the FF: tension between newlyweds Reed and Sue, the tortured wanderings of Ben, who is convinced that his girlfriend Alicia has rejected him for the Surfer, and—this was evidently a selling point—Johnny's first day at "Metro College," where he meets new supporting character Wyatt Wingfoot. The "trilogy," then, has none of the formal separateness or claims to historic importance that we might expect in the marketing of "event" series in today's comic books. Rather, the operative mode is that of a soap opera. Yet what these three issues are remembered for is their unprecedented scale: Galactus intends to devour the earth's energy not because he is malicious or evil (the usual super-villain stuff) but because he is a force "above good and evil," to whom the Earth's inhabitants are simply beneath notice. The story's resolution hinges on forcing Galactus, through the Silver Surfer, to *take* notice. The central character, as it turns out, is the one who mediates between the human and the godlike, the Surfer, who unpredictably blossoms from a mere functionary of the plot—a cold, unemotional harbinger of doom—into an articulate and tormented hero.

Much of the story's drama stems from the Surfer, as he transitions from plot device (his arrival heralds the coming of Galactus) to character. Introducing the Surfer, as eccentric a gimmick as any Kirby had come up with, was an ingenious narrative stroke, brought to the boards by Kirby without Lee's input in order to foreshadow the threat of Galactus on a more human scale. The device of the Surfer allows us to approach Galactus obliquely, to imagine what kind of being would need a "herald" this imposing to prepare the way for his arrival. The first chapter's climactic splash, a full-page panel dominated by the big "reveal" of Galactus, derives its power from the way it fulfills the suspense generated by the dozen or so pages preceding it. The chapter's title,

"The Coming of Galactus," anticipates its end, for which we are prepared in two ways: first, by seeing the Surfer's progress through space, toward Earth; second, through apocalyptic signs—a sky filled with flames, then with floating rocks or "debris"—that strike terror into the people of New York City. These unexplained phenomena inspire panic in the streets, provoking confrontations between Johnny and Ben and a fearful crowd. (Ben knocks out one man with a tap of his finger, a bit of comic drollery that offsets the story's lowering sense of threat.) Afterwards, the omniscient Watcher, a frequent supporting character in *Fantastic Four*, appears at the group's headquarters and reveals that the "fire-shield" and orbiting debris were his own unsuccessful attempts to hide the Earth from the Surfer, Galactus's "advance scout" (oddly enough, the orbiting debris does nothing to dim the light of the sun!). Even as the Watcher speaks, the Surfer slips through the barrier of debris and lands—as luck or narrative economy would have it—right on the roof of the FF's headquarters. Ben dispatches the Surfer with one punch, but to no avail: the signal having been given, Galactus arrives suddenly, announced by a full-page photomontage splash that shows the opening of his spherical starship. Galactus disembarks, in a costume of baroque complexity festooned, funnily enough, with a "G" on the chest (like Superman's "S" chevron or the FF's own "4" logo). Arm outstretched, dwarfing even the giant Watcher, Galactus makes a singular impression: "My journey is *ended*! This planet shall *sustain* me until it has been drained of all elemental life! *So speaks Galactus!*" (20). Part of what makes this work so well, in spite of its unselfconscious absurdity, is the cumulative effect of the narrative teasing that leads up to this moment. This cliffhanger must have been quite a stunner to Marvel readers in 1966.

The Silver Surfer, a clear example of the kind of improvisation that characterizes mid-sixties Marvel, is the device that makes this first chapter tick. He is introduced as a cosmic traveler "zooming along the starways like a living comet—with the freedom and wild abandon of the wind itself," but also as an object of terror for the villainous Skrulls "of the Andromeda Galaxy," past enemies of the Fantastic Four, whose fearful determination to hide their entire solar system already tells us something about the scope of the threat the Surfer represents (7–8). The Surfer is later shown surfing the cosmic explosion of a "super-nova" and then detecting our own solar system, all the while shooting through Kirby's overstuffed, decorative idea of outer space, which is alive with closely packed stars, planets, and fizzing energy (apparently it didn't occur to Kirby that space is mostly emptiness, or dark matter). When the Surfer arrives, he is a portent, a promise, of impending apocalypse. What's interesting about the construction of this drawn-out narrative tease is that it apparently came from Kirby alone.

Plate 1. Panoramic violence: an example of Jack Kirby at his peak. Jack Kirby, with Mike Royer (inks and lettering), "Unleash the One Who Waits." *The Demon* #1 (Aug.–Sept. 1972), pages 2–3. © DC Comics.

Plate 2. Cap's origin, retold. Jack Kirby and Stan Lee, with Syd Shores (inks) and Artie Simek (lettering), "The Hero That Was." *Captain America* #109 (Jan. 1969), page 15. © Marvel. Original art reproduced courtesy of Marc Kardell.

Plate 3. Photo-collage as sublime vista. Jack Kirby and Stan Lee, with Joe Sinnott (inks) and Artie Simek (lettering), "This Man . . . This Monster!" *The Fantastic Four* #51 (June 1966), page 14. © Marvel.

Plate 4. The Promethean Galaxy: beyond lies the greatest of mysteries. Jack Kirby, with Mike Royer (inks and lettering), "Spawn." *The New Gods* #5 (Oct.–Nov. 1971), pages 2–3.

CONTINUED AFTER NEXT PAGE

Plate 5. Over the dimensional barrier. "This Man . . . This Monster!," page 13.

Plate 6. Norton faces "the change": a kind of self-annihilation. Jack Kirby, with Mike Royer (inks and lettering) and George Roussos (colors), "Inter-Galactica." *2001: A Space Odyssey* #6 (May 1977), page 16. © Marvel, "based on material © 1968 by Metro-Goldwyn-Mayer, Inc."

Plate 7. Izaya reaches the turning point. Jack Kirby, with Mike Royer (inks and lettering), "The Pact." *The New Gods* #7 (Feb.–Mar. 1972), page 18. © DC Comics.

Plate 8. Himon speaks of the Source: *It lives! It burns!* Jack Kirby, with Mike Royer (inks and lettering), "Himon." *Mister Miracle* #9 (July–Aug. 1972), page 21. © DC Comics.

Stan Lee, in his book *Son of Origins of Marvel Comics* (1975), credits Kirby with creating the Surfer. According to Lee, Kirby penciled the first chapter of the story after an informal conference with Lee, in which the two agreed on the broad concept of a huge, godlike being "who could destroy entire planets at will" (205)—a pretty generic idea, it must be admitted, and of course Lee's account is so short on specifics as to be unconfirmable. What is most specific about Lee's account is that, when Kirby eventually delivered the pages for the trilogy's first installment, Lee was, he said, startled to see an unfamiliar figure on a flying surfboard, upon which Kirby explained that a being as powerful as Galactus ought to have a herald, "an advance guard" to come before him and pave the way—a good call, but, one is tempted to say, a storyteller's call, not one justified by any logic other than that of the narrative. Lee recalls being intrigued by, even "wild" about, the Surfer, whom Kirby had created on his own, out of whole cloth (206). What this tells us is not only that Lee did not have a hand in the initial design of the character, but also that he was not in control of the pacing of the narrative, since the Surfer is critical to the dramatic structure of the story's first chapter. He is the story's pacemaker. Lee's account thus inadvertently reveals much about the nature of the Kirby/Lee collaboration at this stage and about the central role Kirby played as a conceptualist and storyteller. By inventing/inserting the Surfer, Kirby in effect plotted the story. He paced the telling. He even provided the character that, in the end, would steal the show, in "The Startling Saga of the Silver Surfer."

In other words, the Silver Surfer is a character that grew out of Kirby's process of narrative drawing rather than a prior intention or any literary considerations. As established in our previous chapter, the bulk of the "writing" (in the sense of story-plotting and storytelling) was in the art. Character design and movement, facial expressions, the composition of panels, the leap from panel to panel, the gridding of the page: all of these crucial cartooning/storytelling elements were the province of Kirby, the artist. Regarding this particular story, Mike Gartland unpacks the process of its creation in *The Jack Kirby Collector* issues 22 and 23, which provide facsimiles of penciled pages from *Fantastic Four* #49 that include Kirby's original plot notes. Gartland concludes: "Despite whatever input Stan might or might not've had at the conceptual phase, these margin notes show the action and dramatic impact of this pivotal episode [. . .] begin with Kirby" ("Failure," Part Two 38). In his role as dialoguer, Lee responded to what Kirby gave, at times seriously, at times playfully, always adding a new layer to the total work. In the case of the Surfer, a character for whom Lee has great affection and over whom he reportedly tried to exert a proprietary claim for a while (McLaughlin 98), the meeting between Kirby's pencils and Lee's script resulted in a new layer of characterization. As the story builds (#49–50), the treatment of the Surfer deepens, infusing Kirby's initially cold, enigmatic conception—a being of energy, wholly alien and unfeeling—with a "nobility" and an awaking "conscience" that will shape the story's outcome and in fact provide the crucial stalling action: the Surfer will turn on his master, Galactus, and battle him, buying time for Johnny Storm to fetch the cosmic super-weapon with which Galactus can be overcome. In short, the Surfer, at first improvised by Kirby simply for the sake of storytelling, ended up becoming the story's thematic linchpin and thereby a major Marvel character.

It would seem that, during the production of *FF* #48, both Kirby and Lee saw something they wanted to use in the Surfer, and so Kirby elaborated. As Lee recounts in *Son of Origins*: "Later, as I started to write the dialogue for the strip, I realized that The Surfer had the potential to be far more than just a high-flying, colorful supporting character. Studying the illustrations, seeing the way Jack had drawn him, I found a certain nobility in his demeanor, an almost spiritual quality in his aspect and his bearing. [. . .] I was tempted to imbue him with a spirit of almost religious purity" (206). Accordingly, issues 49 and 50, as they emerged from Kirby's drawing board, pushed the Silver Surfer to the fore. Out of Kirby's improvisation, then, came a signature character, one in which both Kirby and Lee developed a keen interest. They would return to the character repeatedly, first in *Fantastic Four* #55, then in the epic *FF* #57–61 and subsequent issues, often casting the Surfer as a victim and emphasizing his innocence and suffering, qualities that Lee, finally, underscored in the *Silver Surfer* series of 1968, with its pathetic, blatantly Christlike hero. By the late sixties Lee had been so charmed by the character that he came to regard it as specially his, and, insisting on an anguished, Romantic and sacrificial treatment of the character, took it far from what had emerged on Kirby's drawing board (McLaughlin 97; Raphael and Spurgeon 123). Ironically, Kirby's impromptu narrative problem-solving resulted in one of Lee's most self-consciously ambitious literary efforts—a testimony to the odd results often achieved through the Marvel method.

The Silver Surfer, then, is Kirby's fingerprint on the Galactus trilogy. Most relevant to my interest, though, is the way the character's expanded role affected the shape of the story. The Surfer's rebellion against Galactus constitutes a key example of Marvel's signature dualism: master versus herald, with humanity in the middle. *The Fantastic Four* thus experimented with the same sort of conflict hinted at in the early issues of the *X-Men*. It also opened the door to the grand-scale, cosmic adventures that would appear in *Thor*. Other ideas introduced in the *FF* likewise recalled the *X-Men*'s premise: most notably, that of the Inhumans, a race of beings superhuman by nature yet forced to live in a Hidden Land, shielded from human eyes. In the first Inhumans story, immediately prior to the Galactus trilogy (Nov. 1965–Jan. 1966), Kirby and Lee again discarded the conventions of accidental origins and secret identities in favor of a more mythic approach, creating a pantheon of good and evil characters (the Inhumans' royal family) with a shared origin and destiny. One senses Kirby—the evidence shows that it *was* mainly Kirby plotting the series at this point—straining at the limits of formula here, cramming whole series' worth of concepts into *The Fantastic Four*. The existence of other worlds or dimensions allowed for similar explorations; new settings, such as the Negative Zone and Wakanda, became breeding grounds for new characters and ideas. In Kirby's run on *The Fantastic Four*, then, and especially between late 1965 and late 1967, the Marvel Universe began to sprout.

This sudden afflatus may in part have been due to Martin Goodman's plans to expand the Marvel line: biographer Ronin Ro claims that Kirby had been apprised of such plans and even promised a share of the profits from expanded merchandising, and thus was incentivized. By Ro's account, Kirby, when he realized that Goodman in fact could not expand the line so quickly, ended up grafting his new ideas onto *The Fantastic Four* (98–99). In any case, as the Marvel Universe went through this growth spurt it began to diverge drastically from the ordinary life-world of its readers, blooming into a strange world all its own. The month-to-month *Fantastic Four* serial—the cornerstone of Marvel—gestured toward a saga, a vast, rambling narrative. To the low-fantastic appeal of the costumed urban hero was added an emphasis on invented landscape and infinite powers akin to high fantasy. The frontier ethos of the vigilante hero—and the questions of justice, vengeance, and law that go with it—were sidelined in favor of pure, marvelous invention.

## THE EPIC APPROACH, AND ITS CONSEQUENCES

Kirby's transformation of the superhero dates back to the basic, then-unfulfilled premise of *The X-Men*. Through the ongoing conflict between good and evil mutants, Kirby felt his way tentatively toward what would become, for him, an irresistible new idea. Instead of defending the status quo, that is, the everyday life-world assumed by their readers, the X-Men redefined the world by their very presence. Instead of defending against random "crime," the X-Men battled other mutants, for humanity's sake. Unlike the superhero comics that came before it, then, *The X-Men* started from a premise that was not conservative but potentially transformative. Harking back to the genre's science fiction roots (recall Wylie's *Gladiator*, for example), it had the potential to make the whole world look different. This possibility would be more fully exploited as Marvel's continuity developed into an ever-tighter generative (and restrictive) mechanism. *X-Men*, in short, opened the door to a speculative approach to superheroes, an approach much influenced by Kirby's reading of SF. Kirby then gladly walked through that door in *Fantastic Four* and *Thor*, taking those series to new heights.

In sum, Marvel under Kirby introduced an epic approach to the superhero genre that was "mythic" both in its scale and in its pantheonic complications. At Marvel, heroes and villains shared common origins and each side was defined by its constant struggle against the other. This idea has had a great impact on the structure and iconography of the genre in the years since. By establishing pantheons of rival superbeings, Kirby infused a once tapped-out genre with the potential for more complex character relationships, sustained and meaningful conflict, and spectacular narrative drawing. Drawing of course was at the heart of it all: Kirby the designer was questing for new things to do. But the narrative consequences were far-reaching. Kirby's outsized take on the genre at last gave superheroes threats worthy of them, villains and dangers that could fill the historical gap left by the defeat of "the Axis" at the end of WWII, the genre's first boom period. Thus superhero comics could implicitly rehearse the ideological struggles of the Cold War without sinking to naked jingoism (though early on there was plenty of that too), and could speak to the era's looming sense of apocalypse. This mythic approach of Kirby's paved the way for series in which heroes not only saved the world but redefined it. It also gave the contemporary superhero a reason for being. With *X-Men* and *Thor*, Kirby began to weave into comics the kind of complex narrative designs found in classical myth or the Old Norse Eddas, while yet upholding a stark, sharply drawn, Code-sanctioned moral dualism, a Manichean tug-of-war between Good and Evil.

Admittedly, said dualism fails to capture, in fact refuses, the frequent moral ambiguity of so many myths and Eddas, with their capricious, often self-serving, sometimes self-destructive gods and heroes. For the most part, the Marvel Comics of the sixties skirt tragedy and uphold a staunchly prescriptive morality. As Code-approved superhero comics of their era, they remain locked into a pinched, earnestly moralistic idea of children's fiction; as partial heirs to the bathos of muted, post-Code romance comics, they work on emotional registers that call to mind formula adolescent fiction. These are stories conceived with young readers—or, rather, a frankly conservative, moralizing approach to young readers—in mind. Their explorations are often blunted by that assumption. And yet Marvel's fallible heroes, the moments of genuine pathos scattered through their stories, and the expanded story-world in which they adventured, all these took the superhero comic book in vital new directions. Monster-heroes like the Thing and the Hulk, as well as misfits like Spider-Man, sharpened the superhero's internal agon, his driving self-conflict, resetting the genre's basic tensions. At the same time, Marvel's super-groups—its families of heroes and villains—introduced complex interpersonal dynamics, far from either solo hero tales or the blandly collegial, clubhouse-like atmosphere of DC's then-Justice League (which gave no hint of personality conflicts, nor indeed of distinct personalities, among its members). The ever-expanding storyscape around them, meanwhile, was stuffed with things to respond to, recurrent menaces to fight, dreamlike locales to visit, and the possibility of relationships to rekindle.

In sum, Marvel made formula superhero comics both more welcoming of emotional complexity and much wider in scope. In the latter quality, their epic scope, Kirby's handprint shows through especially clearly; Marvel's new sense of scale afforded him a grand canvas. It liberated him. As a result, the Marvel of the sixties boasted some of the most inventive graphic design and cracklingly vital narrative drawing ever seen in comic books. But this accomplishment did not end in the sixties, for Kirby would go on, after his classic period at Marvel, to explore still more shaded and conflicted characters and more expansive worlds.

If, fortified by Kirby, Marvel rebuilt and revitalized the superhero, then this success prodded Kirby further, stoking his ambition. He began to see that he could treat superheroes as vehicles for personal expression and for the conflict of ideas, at a time when ideas seemed to animate conflict on a global scale. As the rhetoric of the Cold War pitted rival ideologies against each other in a bid for world dominance, so Kirby worked out the conflict of ideas with a rugged graphic immediacy. More and more, he assayed themes that haunted and provoked him. More and more, he made abstract concepts leap off the page, personified. In his hands, some of the genre's axial conflicts—between justice and authority, for example—became less important, while others—such as the superhero's status as both insider and outsider—were boldly redefined. A peculiar *otherness* crept into his superheroes: they became gods, and pulled humans into the orbit of their conflicts. They worked the cosmos, not just the city, but brought the cosmos *to* the city too, imbuing the city with layers and mysteries. Asgard and New York, Supertown and Metropolis—Kirby made the mundane settings of the earthbound hero and the grand settings of mythology part of one vast narrative design. He was perhaps less interested in the kinds of conflictedness that first gave life to the superhero—masculine self-doubt, urban paranoia, the allure and wickedness of crime—but very interested in doing new things with what was there, the established and understood language of the genre. He turned this language toward mythic fantasy. His best work gave ideas an embodied urgency and an archetypal obviousness, but at the same time a quirky and surprising visual richness.

Kirby's work, in short, pursued the possibility of superheroics as allegory, a possibility he broached at Marvel, then went on to plumb in his visionary and bizarrely eccentric Fourth World for DC. Through the Fourth World—which I'll begin dealing with in depth in Chapter 5—he introduced multiple innovations that have influenced superhero comics ever since. One such innovation, the idea of simultaneously launching several new series within a single larger storyline, has since become common industry practice. Other innovative features of the Fourth World were its deliberate symbolic parallelism; its ideological subtext, if indeed we may call it *sub*text (it's pretty obvious); and the way it used an overarching conflict and shared cast to revive and exploit various subgenres. Like *The X-Men*—and indeed it underscores in hindsight Kirby's distinct contribution to *The X-Men*—the Fourth World establishes a conflict among demigods, of which humans become the focal point and deciding the fate of humanity the main objective. The saga's titanic villain, Darkseid, attacks Earth in the hopes of plucking a fateful secret from human minds, while Darkseid's opposites, the gods and heroes of "New Genesis," spring to humanity's defense. This is where *The New Gods* begins: with human life, ever the disputed stake in Kirby's epics. Here Kirby's mythic approach to the genre emerges in its pure form; here archetypal figures are locked in world-defining struggle. Having established this struggle, Kirby developed, as we'll see, symbolically fraught characters and cast them in variations of traditional comics genres.

It may be that, in 1971, all this was too much for the comic book's tottering newsstand market to handle. After all, the original incarnation of the Fourth World proved short-lived. However, the concept has been revived repeatedly, insistently, over the decades since, usually in diminished or more readily containable form. Even though the series posed trouble for the putative continuity of the DC Universe, subsequent writers have found its concepts irresistible and sought to reintroduce them, or versions of them, into the company's expansive menu of characters. In fact Kirby's pantheonic treatment of superheroes, of which the Fourth World is the very distillation, has since transformed the narrative strategies of the whole superhero genre. As Chapter 5 will show, the superhero "universes" introduced into the market over the last twenty-five or so years (including variations on the Marvel and DC universes as well as startup universes published by other companies) demonstrate the lasting appeal of Kirby's innovations to comics creators. Four decades after the Fourth World began, creators intuitively recognize that superheroes demand not only worthy antagonists but also coherent worlds and shared origins. So this is how Kirby reshaped the superhero genre: the notion of "continuity" prevalent in superhero comics today rests not only on the phenomenal success of the Marvel Universe that Kirby did so much to create, but specifically on the mythic approach to the genre that emerged, tentatively, in *The X-Men* and then blossomed into the Fourth World. More than any other creator, Kirby opened up this rich and habitable space.

I make this claim not to exult in an easy triumph, nor to make a case for Kirby as the only important contributor to Marvel. We've already affirmed that Kirby was not the sole architect of Marvel; the company's achievement was collective and contingent on a set of circumstances impossible to be repeated, including the facts of Kirby's availability and financial desperation. Moreover, despite his contributions to the Marvel aesthetic, thus to superhero comics in general, Kirby did not vault directly from Marvel to due recognition, compensation, or a genuine sense of ownership—editorial, financial, or professional—over his own work. Though gush about Kirby as "King" was common enough, his co-authorship of Marvel remained veiled behind company rhetoric. He had to wait until retirement for a measure of vindication, critical reappraisal, and partisan fan support. Finally, as I aim to show in the coming chapters, Kirby was not interested in the workmanlike upkeep of continuity, nor did he have much share, in later years, in the Marvel continuity he had helped to create. Rather, he was interested in high concepts and the overflowing of ideas, designs, and visions. By the mid-seventies, continuity was his nemesis. He professed disinterest in subsequent revisions of his characters by other creators, did not return to old series with the intention of recreating the terms of their earlier success, and was sometimes held to task for either wrenching old properties in new directions or failing to notice that new directions had already come. That Marvel continuity post-1970 fostered a sense of comparative realism only proved to be a thorn in Kirby's side, and, in later years, the freewheeling, childlike qualities of many of his comics frankly alienated many of the very fans that had lapped up his work (under Lee's imprimatur) back in the sixties. The Marvel Universe, more generally the settled and hyper-rationalized version of the Marvel aesthetic that overtook the comic book field, turned out to be inhospitable to Kirby's talents.

Kirby's position vis-à-vis the superhero genre is therefore a curious one. In Marvel he co-created a vast narrative that, on the one hand, fired his ambitions and pushed him further along artistically, and yet, on the other, bred a fan culture whose expectations for consistency and systemization would only have straitjacketed him, had he been able to meet them at all. If it is possible for one person to be both a father figure and an outcast, Kirby has been both of those. While the repertory of contemporary superhero comics, specifically the vast narratives of Marvel and DC, is based largely on his work, today's comics are so thoroughly enmeshed in the custodial upkeep of continuity that the actual history and rude specificity of Kirby have been effaced, and the daffier, more outré elements of his comics have been kept at arm's length. Perhaps this is why writer Chris Roberson has referred to Mark Gruenwald, only half-jokingly, as the real "father of modern superhero comics": "The current state of superhero comics, with its obsessive attention to continuity and rationalization, line-wide crossovers, multiple realities, and increasing divergence from the real world, resembles nothing so much as a Mark Gruenwald comic writ large" ("Mark Gruenwald" n. pag.).

This "current state" is as much the achievement of fandom as of publishers. It is designed for sharing. We know, after all, that genres are not simply formulas or lists of conventions or clichés, but social compacts, ways of acting and relating in the world. We know that the superhero genre isn't simply a textual but also a social network, that knowledge of continuity grants cultural capital within said network, that continuity generates both fan fiction and professional comics, and that by now the difference between the two is practically no difference at all. The superhero genre and its collective, its fandom, are now online, "cross-platform," and invested in the shared-universe model; the genre has become a big playground. Why not?

Recent genre theory has reminded us that a genre's social purposes are at least as, if not more important than, its formal and aesthetic components; indeed, Amy Devitt has shown that genres are defined "less by their formal conventions than by their purposes, participants, and subjects . . ." (698). The "purposes" of fandom include participation—on a social level as close by as one's local comic book shop—in the vast narratives of superhero comics, and fans have collectively embroidered on those narratives in ways quite alien to the original comics of Jack Kirby. Indeed, vast narratives may function best for fans when their points of historical origin are elided, when launch points are multiple and slightly blurry, and when there is no single, unquestionable, canonical source text to follow (or when claims to canonicity are bracketed off). In any case, Kirby provided the raw material for shared universes that have gone on and will continue to go on without him.

Here's the rub: in the mid-seventies, Kirby himself posed a glitch in Marvel's vast narrative. This ironic turn of events will be explored in our final chapter, a study of his late and in a sense anticlimactic Marvel series *The Eternals* (1976–78). That chapter will address the ways in which Kirby found himself crowded out of the very world he had helped create.

But now, to explain more fully how Kirby's style and sensibility transformed the superhero, hence the comic book, I propose to examine the tendency in his late work toward the technological sublime. That tendency emerges clearly in *The Fantastic Four* and *Thor*, then suffuses his subsequent comics (*The Eternals* being a grand example). After that, we'll proceed to Kirby's most personal exploration of the sublime, what he reportedly considered his magnum opus: the Fourth World, the climax of his career in superheroes.

## 4

# KIRBY'S TECHNOLOGICAL SUBLIME

For the effect of genius is not to persuade the audience but rather to
transport them out of themselves.
— LONGINUS, *On the Sublime*, Fyfe translation

He didn't seem so concerned with the wiring of plausibility
but more with the nuts and bolts of what makes us tick.
— DEAN HASPIEL, "Jack Kirby Makes Me Stupid"

Kirby and Lee's *The Fantastic Four*, on which they worked in tandem from
1961 to 1970, was Marvel's flagship and, along with Ditko and Lee's *The Amazing Spider-Man*, one of the signature superhero comics of its era. It led the
sudden surge in creativity which, as we've seen, overtook and transformed
Marvel between 1961 and about 1963 and that laid the foundation for the
since much-elaborated Marvel Universe. Understandably, a great deal has
been written about *The Fantastic Four*, mostly in the fan press, and many
comic book creators have weighed in on its significance and on what it is
like to take up the reins of the franchise (see for example DeFalco et al.). As
the prototypical superhero "team" book of the sixties, it has been variously
reimagined, dismantled, alluded to, and parodied in numerous other comics,
from market-minded relaunches of the sort typified by the *Ultimate Fantastic
Four* series (2004–2009); through the auteurist one-off, *Unstable Molecules*
(2003), by James Sturm and Guy Davis, et al., which casts the team in a domestic tragedy—a critique of 1950s middle-class conformism and sexism—in
a naturalistic style that evokes alternative comics; to Warren Ellis and John
Cassaday, et al.'s *Planetary* (published not by Marvel but by DC/WildStorm,
1999–2009), an allusive metastory about pulp culture archetypes in which the
villains, known simply as "the Four," represent a nightmarish spin on the Fantastic Four, essentially a dystopian shadow of Kirby and Lee's heroes.

All such retakes of the FF have two things in common. First, they exploit, sometimes spectacularly, the idea of scientific and technological development, often going so far as to treat the advancement of science (in keeping with the Cold War vibe of the original) as a race or bid for power. Second, they testify to the FF's reputation as not only superheroes but also explorers and futurists—in current Marvel parlance, "imaginauts"—in an endlessly unfolding cosmos, a reputation that, implicitly, acknowledges *The Fantastic Four*'s importance as Marvel's earliest generator of new characters, settings, and concepts, in effect the cornerstone of its Universe. (Even the ironic *Unstable Molecules* ends with a paean to escape, exploration, and "real knowledge.") *The Fantastic Four* is known for inventing, then consolidating, key elements of Marvel's vast narrative—the results of what I've called Kirby's graphic mythopoesis—and its mid-sixties peak is celebrated as a crazily fertile period of "research and development," a spike in creativity coexistent with and undeterred by the cosseting constraints of the Comics Code. Within the straitened, post-Code world of comic books, *The Fantastic Four* was a salutary kick in the pants.

The truth about Kirby and Lee's *Fantastic Four* is that it was neither consistent nor consistently excellent. Its high points, though, are very high. The series is beloved among fans for its bounding excess, graphic dynamism, eye-popping designs, archetypal characters (a common claim is that its four heroes represent earth, water, fire, and air respectively) and, above all, sheer imaginative fecundity. In fact, inconsistency or patchiness would seem to be one of its strengths, for *The Fantastic Four* "works" by "not" working, by embodying, as argued in the previous chapter, an unresolved clash of sensibilities. This clash is not simply that between the contrasting outlooks of Kirby and Lee, as has often been argued (see, for example, Wells), nor even the prevailing irony that, as we've seen, marks Marvel comics. Rather, it is the clashing of narrative strategies drawn from different genres. *The Fantastic Four* was a stew in which soap opera elements informed by Kirby's and Lee's respective work in romance comics (I thank fellow scholar Craig Fischer for insight into this) mix with Kirby's interest in science fiction, in particular his growing fascination with the technological sublime.

I derive the term *technological sublime* from many sources, notably Leo Marx's book *The Machine in the Garden* (1964) and a web of related work by other scholars, notably Perry Miller, John Kasson, and David Nye (Miller appears to have coined the term, informing Marx). Each has written about the history of cultural attitudes toward technology, more particularly America's worship of science, technology, and industry. The phrase *technological sublime* indeed suggests an attitude of worshipful awe. It seems to me, however, that Kirby's work reveals a less celebratory, more ambivalent sense of the technological sublime, something more in keeping with how I read Burke's definition of the Sublime as put forth in his seminal *Philosophical Enquiry* (1757). That definition is fearful—or, rather, *fear-based*. The technological Sublime in this Burkean sense is a favored mode of Kirby's: the use of high-tech motifs to represent vast forces that not only are ineffable and awful (in the original sense of the word) but also may result in shock, estrangement, or madness. This "awful" sense of the Sublime is increasingly evident in Kirby's work as the sixties progress. In tune with his ever more mythic take on the superhero, Kirby pushed his drawing to extremes, indulging an ecstatic, newly heightened graphomania and shooting for grand, cyclopean images. This was his way of not only, so to speak, pumping up the volume of comic books but also opening them to disorienting new vistas, from which everyday human perspectives might be reframed and questioned. Creations such as Galactus and the Silver Surfer were means to this end.

With its vaulting sense of crisis, *The Fantastic Four* of the mid-sixties obeys a logic of escalation that bears witness to its Cold War roots, as the series typically involves threats to the entire world. Exploration of the technological sublime, as both delight and terror, marks the book's peak period: witness its utopian technological settings, such as that of the Black Panther's make-believe African kingdom, Wakanda (*FF* #52–53), which, as Adilifu Nama argues, represents a provocatively "Afrofuturistic" fusion of super-science and progressive anti-colonialism, a "hi-tech African Shangri-La nation-state" (137–39); or its super-scientist characters, notably Mr. Fantastic (Reed Richards) and his counterpart, the villainous Dr. Doom, who is both "scientist" and "sorcerer"; or the mingling of ancient mysteries and high-tech science fiction, as in, for example, the adventure with Prester John, the Wanderer (*FF* #54). This last point in particular, the blending of the archaic-occult and futuristic-technological, is a notable Kirby fixation (about which, more below).

Witness too a preoccupation with the question of what defines humanness vis-à-vis the superhuman, as in the tales with the Silver Surfer, the Inhumans, or "Him," the so-called creature in the Beehive. These various examples, and many others, betray a fascination with the magical potential of technology, echoing Clarke's law: that *any sufficiently advanced technology is indistinguishable from magic*, as we observed of our *Demon* example back in Chapter 1. If, as Reynolds points out, superhero comics indiscriminately blend science and magic to foster a sense of wonder (16), then Kirby is one of the main perpetrators of this confusion, because he so often strains toward the cosmically wondrous. Above all, he is fascinated by the human experience of the Sublime, in the Burkean sense: the awe-inspiring, the unassimilable, and the existentially dizzying or terrifying. *The Fantastic Four* and much of his later work gesture toward this Sublime via his awestruck blurring of magic and technology.

As handed down from philosophical aesthetics and critical theory—I hope readers will forgive a brief excursus—the concept of the sublime typically describes the human experience of vastness, grandeur, irresistible power, ineffability, or existential threat. A privileged term in the aesthetics of Romanticism, the sublime ambiguously evokes both the loss and the exaltation of the self in the face of greater things. Romantics took the natural sublime as impetus and backdrop for their stress on heroic isolation, self-scrutiny, and the transporting extremes of poetic subjectivity—in Wordsworth's formula, the overflow of powerful feelings. As such, the sublime has played a critical role in framing and aestheticizing individual experience (regarding which, see Ferguson). At the heart of the concept, I note, is a quivering uncertainty.

A core text in this connection is Kant's *Critique of the Power of Judgment* [*Kritik der Urteilskraft*] (1790). Kant posits the sublime as an aesthetic experience wherein beauty arises from, as Wendy Steiner aptly puts it, "a confrontation with the unknowable" and "the superhuman" (Steiner 5). In Kant's view, we experience the sublime when we face something in nature that represents "limitlessness" or exceeds human limits (Kant 128; *gesammelte Schriften*, vol. 5, 244; all references are to the Cambridge edition of 2000). Whereas beauty, Kant says, implies a "purposiveness," as if the beautiful object were meant to present itself for our delectation, sublimity appears "unsuitable" for aesthetic judgment and, as Kant has it, "do[es] violence to our imagination," giving us a "negative pleasure" that essentially derives from pain though it is nonetheless sublime *and* pleasurable. We are at once attracted and "reciprocally repelled" (129). For Kant, then, the experience of the sublime is a provocation, something that, as Mary McCloskey so well puts it, "affronts and outrages the imagination" (McCloskey 97). Those words, *affront* and *outrage*, well describe Kirby's appeal.

Despite his emphasis on repulsion, Kant's idea of the sublime is—this is important—ultimately affirmative. From his perspective, the experience of the sublime entails a recovery of Reason in the face of something initially overpowering. To experience a thing as sublime, Kant argues, "we must see ourselves as safe" from its immediate threat, and must be aware of our independence from said thing and of our own capacity to think about it:

[T]hunder clouds towering up into the heavens, bringing with them flashes of lightning and crashes of thunder, volcanoes with their all-destroying violence, [. . .] the boundless ocean set into a rage, [. . .] etc., make our capacity to resist into an insignificant trifle in comparison with their power. But the sight of them only becomes all the more attractive the more fearful it is, as long as we find ourselves in safety, and we gladly call these objects sublime because they elevate the strength of our soul above its usual level, and allow us to discover within ourselves a capacity for resistance of quite another kind, which gives us the courage to measure ourselves against the apparent all-powerfulness of nature. (Kant 144–45; *gesammelte Schriften*, vol. 5, 261)

In other words, for Kant the sublime puts us in a paradoxical position, at once aware of our seeming powerlessness before the object and yet reminded of our own independence from it and thus our "superiority over nature" (145). The Kantian sublime, in short, is about finding something fearful "yet not be[ing] afraid of it" (McCloskey 100). For Kant, experiencing the sublime means having an aesthetic encounter—a distanced, contemplative, and therefore finally safe and unthreatening encounter—with the chaotic, the wild, and the infinite. That encounter, he insists, ultimately exalts rather than diminishes us. In fact the important thing about the sublime, from Kant's point of view, is not something present in external objects but something called forth from within us, affirming our intellectual and spiritual elevation.

Kant's sense of the sublime, then, entails the triumph of intellect over nature. Scott Bukatman explains it well: if the sublime "initiates a crisis" within us by threatening our habitual ways of thinking and our presumed mastery, still its total effect is positive because "it is almost immediately accompanied by a process of appropriation of, and identification with, the infinite powers on display," a process whereby that which "cannot be contained" is, in fact, contained (92). By this argument, the sublime admits anxiety but finally rewards us with a sense of "cognitive mastery" (Bukatman 82). As Bukatman argues—ingeniously applying the Kantian model to the ravishing effects sequences in science fiction films—the encounter with the sublime, though initially overwhelming, even stunning, may become for us a means of scopic mastery and even "cognitive play" (110). If at first the sublime threatens us with loss of control and helplessness, eventually it flatters us and shores up our self-estimation, our vaunting sense of importance.

This is not quite what I get from Kirby. Certainly it is a more flattering perspective than what I take from Kant's most important predecessor on the issue, Burke, whose *Philosophical Enquiry* had sought to codify ideas of the sublime and the beautiful. Burke describes the feeling of the sublime as arising from sheer terror: in the words of David Nye, "an ecstasy of terror that fill[s] the mind completely" (Nye 6). Whereas the beautiful, according to Burke, arouses delight and tenderness, the feeling of the sublime instead stirs up fear. Kant too speaks of fear, but for him the experience of the sublime represents the intellect's victory over what is frightening: the reassurance of the mind confronted by vast forces. For Burke, by contrast, the experience is neither wholly rational nor graspable by the intellect. The *Enquiry*, as William F. Byrne has remarked, privileges the *immediacy* of aesthetic experience, and in fact seeks to free the aesthetic from its dependence on reason (19–20). This emphasis is subtly but crucially different from Kant's. Burke's Sublime belongs to, but fails to tame, things that are both "great" and "terrible": qualities such as vastness, infinity, obscurity, darkness, impenetrability, and irresistible power. A feeling of "delightful horror," he says, is the "truest test of the sublime." Hence his importance to the Gothic and to the whole aesthetics of terror that sprang from Gothicism (compare in this light H. P. Lovecraft's seminal essay on "Supernatural Horror in Literature," with its emphasis on fear of the unknown). Despite Burke's reputation as a conservative political and moral theorist, one whose views were grounded in respect for tradition, mistrust of passion, and distaste for political spectacle, his aesthetic theory, as Byrne argues, appears radically Romantic.[1]

Admittedly Burke, like Kant after him, acknowledges that "distance" is needed to make the terrible "delightful"; otherwise, the terrible is simply terrible (Burke 40). In a sense, both men speak of vicarious experience, defused of immediate danger. But with Burke there is a telltale difference in stress. Unlike Kant, he does not see the aesthetic experience of the Sublime as entirely canceling our initial fear and astonishment. On some level, Burke argues, the Sublime renders the reasoning mind helpless, and some residue of this helplessness remains even in our pleasure.

This Burkean sublime—what up to now I've denoted as the capital-S Sublime—is one in which delight and terror mingle. It fairly describes Kirby's work at its most intense and hallucinatory. Despite his tough-kid pragmatism, I'd say Kirby was a Romantic at heart, stretching toward the Absolute; in his peculiar way, he sought to invest comics, particularly superhero comics, with feelings of grandeur, sublimity, and cosmic awe, while yet still cartooning in a rowdy, childlike fashion. His enthusiasm for science fiction, which was so much a part of *The Fantastic Four*, had less to do with wonkish technological extrapolation and more with a spiritual question: How do we respond when facing the limits of what is humanly comprehensible? Life, Kirby said, was "a series of very interesting questions, and very poor answers" ("Kirby Speaks!" 6). He believed that part of his job as storyteller was to evoke the questions, in heightened, dramatic form.

We know Kirby was an avid reader and viewer of science fiction from an early age: early for him, and early for science fiction as a market genre. He created a lot of SF, though this aspect of his work is under-studied alongside his costumed heroes. *The Fantastic Four*, at its best, is a science fiction comic. This is not to say that Kirby had a disciplined scientific mind; frankly, the evidence doesn't lead me to believe that he did. But science fiction need not depend solely on discipline or verisimilitude, and, what's more, it can and often does address spiritual questions through technological metaphor. For all its ties to legitimate science—and this is a vital point argued by Adam Roberts in *The History of Science Fiction* (2005)—science fiction need not subscribe to the positivist ideal of a "scientific method" strictly governed by logic, falsifiability, and uniformity of method (6–8). That is, the science in SF need not be disciplined; it can be "soft" as well as "hard." Science fiction, after all, includes the fantastic, the dreamlike, the surreal and the allegorical. It is an aftereffect of Romanticism. Roberts makes the intriguing twofold argument that science fiction, one, constitutes "a mode of doing science," and yet, two, embraces a view of science that is anarchic, along the lines of that advocated by Paul Feyerabend in *Against Method* (1975). Feyerabend, rejecting scientific orthodoxy, argues that insisting on uniform methodology, and on firmly dividing legitimate science from pseudoscience, has the potential to suffocate inquiry (Roberts 7). "The only principle that does not inhibit progress is: *anything goes*" (Feyerabend 14). I admit I'm not persuaded by this argument with respect to real-world science, but its advantages for fiction are obvious, and Kirby's scientific imagination was certainly anarchic in this sense. As Roberts points out, such a freewheeling view of science makes room for the exploration of phenomena typically consigned to the fringe of pseudoscience or quackery, for instance, the kinds of pseudoscientific phenomena eagerly explored on cable television, or, in Kirby's day, in paperbacks and tabloids. These phenomena—ESP, psychokinesis, UFOs, "gods from outer space," et cetera—fascinated Kirby, as did any science so far in advance of the familiar that it served to confirm Clarke's law (again, that, to the unfamiliar, advanced science is magic). Kirby was a tabloid futurist and unabashed fabulist, not above liberally borrowing from Erich von Däniken's *Chariots of the Gods?* to set up the fictional world of *The Eternals* (to which we'll return later).

Grabbing hold of such pseudoscientific notions, Kirby's unruly imagination outraced the conservatism of scientific method. At its mid-sixties peak *The Fantastic Four* practiced pseudoscience as poetry, both visual and verbal. At the same time, it tilted toward the Sublime: a potential implicit in the series from the start but more fully realized after 1965. In brief, *The Fantastic Four* was about Kirby doing superheroes as science fantasy. After all, the team's origins were pseudoscientific (involving a rocket ride and an inadvertent bath in "cosmic rays"), its villains were usually technologically oriented and/or extraterrestrial, and its problem-solving tactics often involved pseudoscientific gadgets. World-building, gadgetry, the posthuman, and the inhuman: these were all parts of the *FF* from the get-go, but they fairly boiled over between

1965 and 1967. No surprise, this, for Kirby was working flat out during this period and (despite Lee's grip on the tether) following his whims, and he was a science fiction fan who had grown up with the genre.

Consider that the first so-called SF pulp, Hugo Gernsback's seminal *Amazing Stories*, launched when Kirby was eight years old (1926). In later years Kirby vividly recalled the life-changing impact of an issue of Gernsback's *Wonder Stories* (possibly *Science Wonder Stories* or *Science Wonder Quarterly*: the magazine had several incarnations) that he fished out of a gutter circa age twelve (Theakston, *Treasury, Vol. 1*, n. pag.). Biographers report that Kirby read SF hungrily, and his memories of and affection for pulp-era SF remained strong; he is said to have collected quite a bit in the genre over the years. In essence, he was a child of SF's formative era, as indeed superhero comics from Siegel and Shuster onward were offspring of an emergent SF fandom. Evidence of this influence is everywhere in Kirby's comics, which often operate in a breathlessly prophetic mode that testifies to the formative power both of SF magazines—*Amazing, Wonder Stories, Astounding*, and their kin—and also of a more general pop futurism, the sort promoted by putatively nonfiction magazines like *Popular Science* and *Popular Mechanics*. In fact pulp SF grew out of such popular nonfiction (for instance, Gernsback's science journal *Modern Electrics* [1908], later *Science and Invention*, was the direct precursor to *Amazing*). Kirby probably read a lot of both. Futurism, after all, was a way out and a way up from the crushing facts of his origins on the Lower East Side. When given free rein, then, his comics often migrated toward the scientific romance. Simply put, Kirby had a hunger for the future. If science fiction is, as has often been claimed, a "literature of ideas," he was interested in ideas early on, for both their revolutionary potential and the escapist excitement they offered. The arrival of the Space Age, as a technological and socio-political reality, must have seemed to him a blossoming of ideas into fact. As the Space Race loomed in reality, Kirby's scientific imagination revved up to match and indeed overtake the facts. At Marvel his ideas got even wilder.

In short, Kirby, though his imaginings often carried the whiff of something touchingly Old World, *Mitteleuropean*, and folkloric, was an avid forecaster of the future (just one of many contradictions in his character). In the late fifties, not long before *The Fantastic Four*, he had had ample opportunity to indulge this tendency, producing work in a Space Age science fiction vein: from DC's *Challengers of the Unknown* (1957–59) through Harvey's *Race for the Moon* (1958) to the syndicated *Sky Masters* (1958–61). This was the peak of Kirby's "hard" science fiction, running apace with Sputnik and the Mercury program. Around the same time, Kirby's brief run on DC's "Green Arrow" (1958–59) sought to infuse that character, essentially a pale knockoff of

Batman, with outlandish SF elements. Perhaps this direction was encouraged by DC's welcoming of SF under Julius Schwartz, signaled in such titles as *Strange Adventures* (from 1950) or *Mystery in Space* (from 1951). As noted in Chapter 3, Schwartz steered DC's revival of superheroes in futuristic, SF-oriented, Cold War-inspired mode: "John Jones, Manhunter from Mars" (1955), The Flash (1956), Green Lantern (1959), and The Atom and Hawkman (both 1961). A kind of revamping was at work. If, as Roberts argues, the superhero genre is informed by SF's "longstanding mediation of the dialectic between 'material' (scientific) and 'spiritual' (religious)" worldviews (225), then the late-fifties period saw a notable shift toward the modern, scientific superhero in preference to the magical or spiritual. It was DC under Schwartz—enabled by scriptwriters such as John Broome and Gardner Fox—that pioneered this change, cannily exploiting the nation's then-fevered emphasis on scientific advancement. In concert with artists such as Carmine Infantino and Gil Kane, Schwartz and company pioneered a visually cool, suburbanized re-creation of the superhero genre. Concepts like "Adam Strange" (from 1958) and the "Guardians of the Universe" (in *Green Lantern*, from 1960) were essentially science fiction in superhero dress (as had been the less-celebrated "Captain Comet," in *Strange Adventures*, 1951–54). DC also ran other SF strips parallel to its superhero revival; for example, after 1959 *Strange Adventures* featured "The Atomic Knights," "Star Hawkins," and "Space Museum." This was the first notable flowering of SF in American comic books since the early fifties—a propitious moment, one would think, for Kirby.

Yet DC was not to be the place where Kirby could indulge his manic futurism. DC's workplace culture, dominated by scriptwriters and editors (for example Schwartz and Mort Weisinger) and constricted by a stodgy editorial ethos, proved inhospitable to Kirby, whose outré, high-energy work ran counter to the house aesthetic and often repelled DC staff. Though SF strips like *Sky Masters* and "The Three Rocketeers" (*Race for the Moon*) would have been at home in the DC stable—and *Challengers* was indeed a hit for the company—DC's general preference for sleek, streamlined, suburban-moderne aesthetics clashed with Kirby's violent approach, which in some ways remained beholden to the seminal Gernsback-era pulps. Kirby's yen for the gigantic, probably influenced by the towering inventions of pioneering magazine illustrator Frank R. Paul (Gernsback's foremost artist), linked him to the SF of the formative pulp period. The sheer violence of Kirby's style also harked back to the pulps, and the momentum of narrative drawing drove him to extremes. Though DC's comics were loopy enough, the company shunned this sort of graphic brazenness, preferring temperance and smoothness. Some editors at the company were known to dislike the comparative crudeness of

Kirby's cartooning and the convulsive, herky-jerky outrageousness of his plotting. Reportedly, he was criticized for not following DC's "style" (Evanier, *King* 101). In any case, the souring of Kirby's business with DC's Jack Schiff (as previously noted) forced Kirby to fall back on the former Atlas, which later, transformed into Marvel, became the home for his rather different SF concepts, chief among them *The Fantastic Four*.

The science fiction on offer in *Fantastic Four*, indeed in comic books generally, was in a sense retrograde, a throwback to the gosh-wow effusiveness and social naïveté of the seminal SF pulps. Marvel in particular partook of a childlike sense of wonder: the young reader's sense of being overawed by a huge, looming world. Mainstream SF comics of the mid-sixties skirted, or just didn't know anything about, the contemporaneous trend in literary SF toward the so-called New Wave, with its experimentalism, radical dystopian satire, and existential dread: that phase of taboo-flouting avant-gardism which Damien Broderick has aptly characterized as a disruptive "reaction against genre exhaustion" ("New Wave and backwash" 49). Kirby may not have known then about SF's New Wave, and in any case it is doubtful he would have shared its ideological precepts and penchant for narrative fracturing, willed confusion, and entropic hopelessness. The question is moot, since superhero comics under the Code were aimed at children, rather a certain ideological description of children, and so would not have allowed such aesthetic and political radicalism. What possibilities were there, then, under the narrowness of the market and Code, for experimentation? What outlet for the visionary?

The most visionary and invigorating element of Marvel was Kirby's graphic mythopoesis, that is, his talent for ideation and world-building *through drawing*. The worlds he made were not merely notional but visual, fundamentally the results of an improvisatory graphism: the propulsiveness of the sketch. He drew worlds into being. As Harry Morgan has pointed out, the drawings in comics have an "autopoetic" quality; they generate worlds ("Graphic Shorthand" 30). Kirby's ideas didn't arrive as ideas only, but as drawings. Donald Phelps's observation that drawing is not merely "the inscription of imagination" but "imagination's vehicle" (38) is splendidly borne out by Kirby's work at Marvel, for, whatever else his Marvel comics are "about," they are surely about delirious graphiation. Not only the obvious action sequences but also the settings, the character designs, the crazy gadgetry—everything—is charged with the energy of speed-drawing and reflects the spontaneous outpouring of an essentially *graphic* imagination. Granted, everything was entrained to the rhythms of an unfolding story, everything subserved the narrative; that narrative, though, did not arrive in the abstract. It came to life on the page, conducted by Kirby's drawing. Kirby's graphic performance imbued the ideas with a visionary quality and sold every concept, no matter how barmy—the Silver Surfer, the Cosmic Cube, Lockjaw the teleporting dog—or how alien. This is what infused the retrograde science fiction of Marvel comics with a newness befitting its era, and this is why the Marvel of the sixties appeals strongly to fans of so-called psychedelic art and design. Kirby inadvertently provided a graphic accompaniment to the psychic unstitching, the mind-bending excess, of that era. *Drawing* was key. After 1965, the technological sublime would give Kirby license to draw new and grander things.

When given free rein, Kirby's science fiction was high fantastical. Despite his flirtations with hard SF, he was drawn to wildly speculative visions that were, in essence, magical. His imagination was rooted in folklore and mythology, and his scientific thinking loose (even as a kid I recognized scientific gaffes in his comics). What attracted Kirby was the chance to depict the godlike, the superlative, and the cyclopean: in a word, the sublime. He was fascinated by the question of how encountering the Absolute, in the sense of the infinite or cosmic unknowable—what he sometimes called the ultimate knowledge—might shake the human mind to its foundations. At times he associated the quest for knowledge with terrible danger: witness for example the Fantastic Four's ventures into that fearsome and scarcely logical otherworld called the Negative Zone (see plate 3), a reliable story-generator for Kirby and Stan Lee. At times he associated scientific questing with alienation or cruel punishment. For example, in *The New Gods*, flagship of the Fourth World project, he created a place called the Promethean Galaxy (*New Gods* #5, Oct. 1971), which is a region of space filled with the gigantic, frozen, yet still-living figures of beings who sought to penetrate the "final barrier" and achieve the "maximum state," that is, to plumb the mystery of the Source: the very originary principle of the universe (see plate 4).

What these eternally tormented figures did, essentially, is seek to understand the Absolute, or God, through scientific means. This Promethean vision holds special fascination for *The New Gods'* Metron, the "knowledge-seeker" and supreme technician, who rides the spaceways in his so-called Mobius [*sic*] Chair, a gimmick that at once points to infinity (as in a Möbius strip) and yet ironically underscores Metron's sedentary and passive nature (he's usually depicted sitting). Metron too would like to probe the enigma of the Source—the wellspring of existence—but he has no spiritual connection to it. Rather, he seeks to apprehend it intellectually, to, as his very name suggests, *measure* it. Kirby once referred to the character—in an interview for a college student paper no less—as an "academic god" (Interview with Lane and Wisenbaker 19–20). Basically, Metron is an amoral mechanist whose desire for the ultimate knowledge prompts him to sell his technology to the highest bidder, as indeed he does to the villainous Darkseid (as I'll discuss in Chapter 6). His hubristic hunger for knowledge will be the very thing that compromises him morally. Implicitly, Metron is like the shattered, frozen giants of the Promethean Galaxy, in that he too would dare challenge the Source in order to satisfy his curiosity. Obviously, Kirby saw terrible risks in trying to answer life's "very interesting questions."[2]

Notions like the Negative Zone and the Promethean Galaxy provided a visual playground and a challenge to Kirby, prompting him to try new ways of representing the sublime. His photo-collages, for example, strain against the limitations of the coarse, four-color comics printing of their day and seem designed to suggest, rather than *draw* in a literal sense, the otherworldly and ineffable (see Bryant, "Cut & Paste"). According to Kirby biographer Mark Evanier, the Negative Zone was created specifically to give license to Kirby's collages and was meant originally to be rendered entirely in collage form (*King* 171). In any case, Kirby's use of photos to evoke something dreamlike is consistent with the Surrealist impulse to suggest dreamwork or the unconscious through détournement and collage. The character of Metron, noticeably, is also associated with photo-collage: Kirby's first-ever presentation drawing of the character, circa 1969, was a vaguely scientific-looking collage, while the Promethean Galaxy sequence in *New Gods* #5 begins with a splash that poses a drawing of the character against a collage background. When Kirby actually gets down to depicting "the place of the giants," however, he delivers a gigantic drawn image of torment that intensifies his habitual use of exaggerated foreshortening, with the looming central figure splayed out in a distorted, almost anamorphic "X" signifying, somehow, both grandeur and abjection. As ever, the point is made visually—and Metron and his words are dwarfed by contrast.

Though Metron is Kirby's clearest embodiment of the hazards of scientific exploration, the idea of trying to plumb the infinite appears often in his earlier work too, most clearly in *The Fantastic Four*. Indeed Reed Richards, "Mr. Fantastic," could be an antetype of Metron: the explorer and inventor par excellence. Yet, where Metron sees in the cosmos only a spur to his intellect, the Fantastic Four are often humblingly aware of their comparative smallness and fragility. In *The Fantastic Four*'s aforementioned Galactus trilogy, Johnny, that is, the Human Torch, aided by the superhuman Watcher, undertakes a journey across the universe in order to retrieve a super-weapon from a vast space station. Said station is in fact the home of the Earth-threatening Galactus (fig. 8). This part of the plot is practically necessary, a *deus ex machina* solution to the unsolvable problem Kirby and Lee have set up in the story: how to stop the unstoppable Galactus, godlike eater of worlds. Yet this cosmic

Fig. 8. Across the cosmos to Galactus's home. Jack Kirby and Stan Lee, with Joe Sinnott (inks) and Sam Rosen (lettering), "If This Be Doomsday." *The Fantastic Four* #49 (Apr. 1966), page 16, panel 3. © Marvel.

journey also allows for some interesting reflection: when Johnny returns from his extraordinary voyage, he is stunned by the experience, to the point that he is rendered helpless, almost babbling:

> I travelled [*sic*] through worlds . . . so big . . so *big* . . . there . . there aren't *words* . . !
> We're like ants . . just *ants* . . *ants!!* (*Fantastic Four* #50, page 7)

Clearly Johnny has experienced something we could call sublime. This scene, indeed the whole story, focuses on contrasts of scale and perception, specifically the contrast between humanity's antlike smallness and Galactus's power "beyond the limits of [. . .] comprehension." Humans are likened repeatedly to insects alongside Galactus's outsized majesty.

Ultimately, of course, the tale yields to a human perspective, taking a sentimental tone and sidelining the awesome threat of Galactus in favor of the heroes' human ordinariness. An ardent optimism and softening taste for soap opera, traits often imputed to Lee, work to bring the story back to human scale, leavening its strange, alienating qualities. In addition, grace notes of human comedy are scattered throughout (these are attributable as much to Kirby as Lee; note how the Thing's bumptious physical comedy serves to rev up the action and offset the story's seriousness). Yet, despite all this, Johnny's staggered reaction to his journey strikes the story's dominant note: even though by issue's end he has gone to college and resumed pining for his girl, he continues to be bemused by his, as Lee has it, "glimpse of the wonders of the unknown *cosmos*" (19). Though the series formula of *The Fantastic Four* does require a retreat from cosmic pomp back to the human scale, it turns out that completely ignoring what has happened is impossible. Ditto for superhero fans, among whom the Galactus trilogy came to be seen as a turning point—after which the parameters of the genre were irreversibly changed.

Coming on the heels of the trilogy, *Fantastic Four* #51 (June 1966) goes it one better, pitting the sublime against the domestic in a volatile single-issue story that epitomizes Marvel's new take on the genre. This story, a sententious fable about heroism and self-sacrifice titled "This Man . . . This Monster!", includes equal measures of moralizing, melodrama, and delirious visual-verbal poetry. In this, the first "Negative Zone" story, Lee's dialogue struggles to make sense out of Kirby's wild graphic flights, which represent the next step after Johnny's cosmic trip in #49–50. At the same time, the tale reverts to the familiar theme of Ben Grimm's bitterness and alienation from the group (a plot hook used as recently as #41–43). The now-married Reed and Sue, the former in scientific explorer mode as he seeks to crack the barrier to "subspace," the latter tugging at him anxiously in what had already become a plot convention, serve as foils to Ben's self-pity, which is goaded on by his fear that he has lost his girlfriend. His loneliness comes to life via a rain-drenched opening that slathers on the pathetic fallacy with haunting power: standing in the middle of a raging downpour—a haze of vertical strokes, courtesy of Kirby and ace inker Joe Sinnott—he is lost and alone. The plot, building outward from this evocative splash, has two engines. One is that Ben's misery makes him vulnerable to the story's nameless science-villain, himself a social outcast, whose envy and ambition spur him to steal Ben's identity so that he can "destroy" the Fantastic Four and thus prove he is Reed's "mental superior." To gain fame and power and silence all doubters, this mad scientist drugs the Thing and then *becomes* him, causing the genuine article to revert to his human, non-Thing self.

The other plot engine is Reed's determination to master "the *space-time* principle," that is, to learn how to travel "faster than light, to any part of the universe!" (8). In order to defend the Earth against extraterrestrial threats "such as Galactus"—Lee's script contrasts the selflessness of his aims with the villain's selfish vanity—Reed insists on entering the transdimensional realm of sub-space, which would later be rechristened the Negative Zone. To this end, Reed has invented a towering machine he calls a "radical cube" (it isn't really cube-shaped) that can create a dimensional portal. In a move typical of *The Fantastic Four*, Reed has done this almost entirely on his own: work "crews" have helped with the building but no one else has been privy to, much less partner in, Reed's planning. In the clench, of course, he turns to The Thing for help. "For the good of mankind," Reed walks into the radical cube, tethered to this world by a lifeline held in The Thing's—actually, the false Thing's— hands, and takes the plunge into sub-space.

There Kirby's graphic inventiveness runs riot, and Lee's verbiage tries to keep up. The resultant visual-verbal tension lunges toward the ineffable and gloriously nonsensical:

> I've shredded the very fabric of *infinity*—where all *positive* matter is transposed into *negative* form! [. . .]
>
> It's almost more than human eyes can *bear!* I'm actually witnessing a *four-dimensional universe*—but the effect of seeing it with *three-dimensional vision* is indescribable! (13)
>
> I've *done* it!! I'm drifting into a world of limitless dimensions!! It's the *crossroads of infinity*—the junction to *everywhere!* (14, see plate 3)

These attempts at visual-verbal repartee engender a bemusing sense of paradox that is offset and enlivened by the sheer dynamism of Kirby's narrative drawing. Here we are definitely in the territory of the sublime. In a single page of four even panels (see plate 5) Reed, first, strides through a corridor of Kirby-tech; second, plunges through a dimensional "void," that is, nearly dissolves in a cloud of crackling dots (much like our Captain America example in plate 2); third, marvels at the almost abstract "four-dimensional" geometry of this new world, against which backdrop he is antlike in his smallness; and, fourth, finally approaches the verge of sub-space, where he slips through wavy bands of energy and color: abstract cosmic doodles, again recalling the graphic obstacles and portals seen in Johnny's earlier space trip. Radiating lines of force are just about omnipresent. Color is near-abstract, used to fill out and delineate shapes but unconnected to discernable mimetic goals. The results of the visual-verbal interplay are oxymoronic and almost incoherent; clearly, Kirby and Lee are trying to take us somewhere *else*.

The two plotlines intersect because the man anchoring Reed to "our" world, that is, the false Thing, becomes the one who must save Reed's life. When Reed's lifeline fails and he plummets into a vortex that promises certain death, the false Ben, shamed by Reed's selflessness, chooses to follow the real Ben's heroic example: he dives into sub-space, uses his great strength to hurl Reed to safety, and sacrifices himself in the process. In other words, Reed's heroism converts the villain, who repents his pettiness and plays the hero himself. He seeks to live up to the image of the one whose identity he has stolen. To bring off this reversal, the plot is patently rigged: Reed and Sue accept the false Ben rather too easily, disbelieving and rejecting the true Ben when he returns to the team's headquarters in human guise (both Bens freely go in and out of the headquarters without raising security concerns); what's more, the final realization that the false Ben was false, the true one true, raises no further questions from anyone. Sue's role is perfunctory and, as was often the case in the series, hemmed in by sexist clichés. The telescoping of the plot into the comic's twenty pages takes it toll on credibility, and the tale rings to an abrupt close, slamming shut with a bit of preemptory moralizing typical of Marvel: "[h]e paid the *full price*—and, he paid it—like a *man!*" (20).

If, plot-wise, some jury-rigging is present, still the story works. It works like a fable, its compression enabling the stark moral contrast hinted at by the title. That phrase—this man, this monster—with its nifty, typically Lee-like parallelism, takes on several potential meanings at once. Outwardly, Ben Grimm is a Golem, a "monster"; inwardly, he is a man and a hero, an exemplary figure who, though he falters momentarily, sheds his self-pity and returns to the FF's headquarters to warn Reed and Sue. Alternately, Ben's doppelganger, an exaggeration of the original's alienation and self-pity, is the monster, though more so when he looks like a man. He becomes a true "man" only when he takes a monster's guise. By the story's logic, Reed is the truest man, a paradigm of selfless courage; his envious counterpart, by contrast, must cast off selfishness in order to become that kind of man and thus cinch the story's resolution.

The plot twists a classic Kirbyism, the spectacular contrast between brain and brawn. Reed's would-be rival, another "brain," comes disguised as "brawn," and then the motives of the two brains are contrasted. One is humble and self-sacrificing—even Reed's reclusiveness and secrecy are portrayed as heroic—while the other is overweening, jealous, and tragically flawed, though capable, in the last analysis, of using brawn to save his rival and thereby redeem himself. One has made an incredible scientific leap in order to guarantee, in good Cold War fashion, Earth's security against sudden attack. The other has also made an incredible scientific leap (he has stolen someone's very identity), but for the wrong reasons. Reed challenges the cosmic unknown, we note, not for glory, nor even to advance scientific knowledge for its own sake, but to protect and serve. In sum, "This Man . . . This Monster!" invokes Kirby's sublime so that it can serve as backdrop for a moralistic and ideological contrast as clear as it is fraught.

Of course another contrast is at work in the comic as well, that between Kirby's extravagance and Lee's: the sheer improvisatory momentum of narrative drawing versus the anchoring exertions of the script. Lee has the last word insofar as his moralistic verbal signposting does the work of (in Roland Barthes's sense) anchoring the images, that is, telling us what to think about them and underscoring the ideological perspective on which the story's title insists. But the tension between visual and verbal brings the story to life. In my view, the main source of interest in this morality play is the way its pages open out to make room for sublime spectacle, and, conversely, the way that the spectacle sharpens and clarifies the morality.

It's worth noting that this story, though tightly wound, contains, besides its rain-soaked opening splash, two other full-page panels, one revealing the "radical cube" and the other comprised of the photo-collage depicting Reed's plunge into sub-space. Such a use of two full-page panels in mid-story was unprecedented in *The Fantastic Four* (the closest equivalents being the full-page chapter headers in #7, from October 1962, and a scene-setting two-page spread at the start of *Fantastic Four Annual* #1, from 1963). In the year preceding #51, including issues 39 to 50 plus the "wedding" story appearing in *Annual* #3, the series had used full-page panels other than opening splashes and pinup pages just five times. It's worth noting that among these were three photo-collages, one depicting gadgetry in Reed's laboratory (#39), one evoking travel through "the fourth dimension" (*Annual* #3), and one, of course, depicting Galactus's ship descending to Earth (#48). Kirby had already used photo-collage panels in the *FF*—to be precise, in eight different stories starting with #24, plus on the cover of #33—typically for the sake of showing either strange, otherworldly vistas such as outer space and undersea realms, or high-tech machinery. More often than not these were full-page images. Yet "This Man . . . This Monster!" leapfrogs his previous efforts, combining a full-page collage depicting otherworldliness with a full-page drawing depicting a mind-bending, "radical" piece of high-tech. The plot is squeezed into the constraints imposed by these grandstanding images and by its requisite twenty-page length. The resultant hastiness and compression, and, more generally, the comic's visual/verbal repartee, impart a dynamism and tension that simultaneously propel the story and arrest the eye. Everything is governed by the tremulous, dynamic (il)logic of paradox, of oxymoron. Partly because of the frayed circuit between Kirby and Lee—a problem posed by the very Marvel method—and partly due to a new ambitiousness, this story is a collision of multiple elements: visual splendor and high-flown text; proto-psychedelic fantasy and soap opera domesticity and pathos; superheroes, romance, and science fiction. Kirby's and Lee's backgrounds in multiple genres are evident: consider the romance comic tropes that contrast with and complicate the heroic action, a switch from the simple boyish adventure of early costume comics (though the tale's treatment of gender roles remains far from progressive). Equally clear are the opportunism and sheer adaptability of the superhero genre, its nature as a mega-genre capable of absorbing disparate elements from other genres, modes, and styles. If we are looking for a single-issue quintessence of Kirby and Lee's Marvel manner, "This Man . . . This Monster!" will do.

Similar collisions mark the *Thor* series circa 1965–66. Appearing in *Journey into Mystery* from issue 83 to 125 (mid-1962 to early 1966), "Thor" had been launched by Kirby and consistently spotlighted in covers penciled by him, yet early on most of the stories had been handed off to other artists, notably Joe Sinnott and Don Heck. Likewise, scripting up to issue 96 had been handled not by Lee but by Larry Lieber or "R. Berns" (Robert Bernstein), though Lee is assumed to have had plotting input. The series was at first a second-stringer, and clearly shows it, a textbook example of how the Marvel heroes found their footing—and outgrew their host anthologies—only after periods of vague, stumbling hesitancy. Although Odin, Loki, and other gods had been introduced as early as the series' third issue (*Journey* #85), "Thor" had remained, as noted, devoted to standard superhero tales with a mythological gloss, enlivened perhaps by Loki's hovering presence but generally spare, self-contained, and formulaic. Other villains—Mr. Hyde, the Tomorrow Man, Carbon-Copy Man, and so on—had nothing to do with the hero's mythological roots. Stories were short, typically thirteen pages in length. In fact, *Journey into Mystery* continued to run unrelated short short stories in Marvel's "mystery" vein, drawn by Ditko, Lieber, and others. Kirby's artistic interest, despite his long-standing love of mythology, was minimal. However, *Journey* #97 (Oct. 1963) signaled a change: it introduced the spin-off series "Tales of Asgard," a myth-oriented five-page backup drawn by Kirby and scripted by Lee that continued monthly for the next four years. "Tales of Asgard" greatly expanded the scope of Marvel's "Thor" mythos; as Mark Alexander has pointed out, the series galvanized both Kirby and Lee, giving artistic free rein to the former and eliciting a mock-Shakespearean eloquence from the latter ("Quest" 52–54). The graphic freedom it provided was crucial: it was to be the seedbed of much of Kirby's later work, including the Fourth World. Moreover, *Journey* #97 installed Lee as regular scripter of the "Thor" series, and, soon after, Kirby rejoined "Thor" as lead artist (#101). Within a few months (as of #105) all other backup comics except "Asgard" dropped out so that the lead "Thor" story could become longer (at first eighteen, later sixteen pages). In short, everything about *Journey into Mystery* became Asgardian.

The conversion became complete as of #126 (March 1966), when, at last, *Journey* stopped being *Journey* and was retitled simply *Thor*—another pivot point, and an overdue acknowledgment of how important the series had become for Kirby and for Marvel.[3] This occurred at exactly the same time as the Galactus trilogy in *The Fantastic Four*. Kirby had hit a new high. In this brief, intense period, he abruptly expanded the Marvel Universe as if for the sake of future exploitation—recall that by 1966 Marvel's Martin Goodman may have been planning to expand the line—in the process introducing a bevy of new characters and concepts that would later be developed into new series. At just the moment when Kirby was upping the stakes in *Fantastic Four*, *Thor* too came into its own. With Lee's editorial tether looser than ever, and Kirby's imagination running free, the books went wild. Kirby's narrative drawing clearly determined the plots. The issues of *Journey* and *Thor* before and after the transition at #126, say up to a year before and a year after, show Kirby falling headlong for the technological sublime—the results a crazy, whirling blend of myth and science fiction.

The nominal first issue of *Thor*, #126, finds the Greek demigod Hercules (first injected into the series the previous year, in *Journey into Mystery Annual* #1) locked in a godlike brawl with Thor. This is the opening move in a multipart story that involves Pluto and Zeus—true to form, this promiscuous blending of mythologies does not bother Kirby at all—and ends with Thor fighting to save Hercules from Pluto's realm, "the Netherworld." Even as this story peaks, in issues 129–130, a new plotline is introduced via Jane Foster's new roommate, a mysterious woman called Tana Nile, who turns out (in #131) to be a "Colonizer" from the constellation Rigel, a revelation that leads to an outer space epic spanning several issues. Suddenly Kirby tacks hard in the direction of science fiction: the Rigel story not only introduces the Rigelians but takes Thor to the Black Galaxy to encounter Ego, the Living Planet. Accompanying Thor on this cosmic quest is another new character, the robotic cosmic historian known as the Recorder: an expository mechanism rather like the Watcher or Silver Surfer before him. Even Galactus makes an appearance. On the heels of this spacey adventure comes the earthbound but still science-fictional tale of the kingdom of Wundagore and its master the High Evolutionary, a costumed, Dr. Moreau-like experimenter who has bred "new-men," that is, beast-men created through genetic engineering (#134–135). Wundagore is a dazzlingly abstract, high-tech fortress patrolled by "knights" who crisscross the skies on "atomic steeds," that is, flying machines (fig. 9). Somehow *Thor* has become a science fiction series.

Fig. 9. Mythic SF: Thor encounters the futuristic-archaic. Jack Kirby and Stan Lee, with Vince Colletta (inks) and Sam Rosen (lettering). "The People-Breeders!" *Thor* #134 (Nov. 1966), page 9, panel 3. © Marvel.

At the same time, "Tales of Asgard" develops an overarching continuity via a quest plot with apocalyptic leanings. Said plot (launched in #117, June 1965) makes the series, doled out in five-page episodes, essentially a breathless string of sudden, slam-bang cliffhangers with plenty of license for unleashed narrative invention and epic-scale drawing. The hook goes like this: dispatched by Odin, Thor and his fellow "argonauts" sail through the cosmos in a godly vessel searching for clues to the threat of Ragnarok, the apocalypse of Norse myth.[4] This expedition involves all manner of mythic spectacle and happy design challenges for Kirby. It also allows for the fleshing-out and/or introduction of several Asgardian supporting characters who join Thor's crew, including the Warriors Three: Hogun, Fandrall, and the stout Falstaffian humbug Volstagg, a splendid comic rascal. This mission ends rather abruptly, however, with the crew summoned back to Asgard to witness the unfolding of a dire prophecy: "The Meaning of Ragnarok" (#127) and "Aftermath" (#128), two chapters that, with their eschatological sense of an ending and new beginning, supply the conceptual kernel of what would eventually become, for rival company DC, Kirby's Fourth World. Indeed these episodes could be tacked onto DC's *New Gods* (which we'll study in our next chapter) with few changes. Suffice to say that during this period "Tales of Asgard" became very important to Kirby. What he was able to do in that series, and in its sister, *Thor*, would stay with him and haunt him from then on.

*Thor* and "Asgard" recast mythology as science fiction. Their modus operandi is like that of Roger Zelazny's SF of the period, notably *Lord of Light* (1967) and *Creatures of Light and Darkness* (1969), with their futuristic pastiches of Hindu and Egyptian mythology respectively. These novels, reconciling New Wave experimentalism with mythopoeic splendor, made ancient mythoi over in contemporary dress, rife with anachronistic nods to the modern (interestingly, Kirby contributed development art to a never-realized *Lord of Light* movie adaptation). While *Thor* does not have Zelazny's ironic knowingness, it is ambiguous in a related way: a pageant of elaborate costuming, scenery, and devices midway between mythic archaism and sleek futurism; a farrago of ancient legend and modern space opera, at once resistant and totally beholden to the look of modernism. This approach liberated Kirby not only story-wise (Rigelians? Living planets? Why not?) but also graphically. It gave new affordances not only to his careening plots but also to his design sense. This can be seen before the *Journey/Thor* transition in, for example, the advent of the Destroyer, an implacable, robotic character that is essentially a weapon, a living machine built by Odin as a doomsday device (#118–119). That Odin should build a life form encased in a metallic body, replete with a visored helmet for a face, and that Odin should see a need for a doomsday device at all, may seem odd. But such elements are intuitively right in Kirby's graphic world, where, after all, the gods use television-like monitor screens ("universal mirror," "cosmic crystal," etc.), chemical weapons, suspended animation, "attractor beams," and other technological gimmicks whenever the plot, or Kirby's ecstatic drawing, demands.

If *The Fantastic Four*, with its familial sparring, warm characterization, and Space Age balderdash, supplied the blueprint for most of the Marvel team books to follow, *Thor* created an alloy of science fiction and mythic fantasy that proved equally important to the company's, and indeed the superhero genre's, design sense and graphic vocabulary. *Thor* posits a premodern world of myth and legend in which, curiously, costuming, armor, armament, and settings tend to be streamlined and eminently modern, a method seen in everything from Thor's outfit (a far cry from the "Thor" in Simon & Kirby's 1942 *Sandman* story) and Odin's imperial pageantry to the argonauts' cosmic ship and the design of other godly characters like Hela (from #102 onward) and the Enchanters (#143–145). Though the settings are mythic, the design sense bespeaks a sort of make-believe modernism, sans any recognition of industrialization and its travails. Again, magic and technology are clasped together, drawing out both the mythical and the science-fictional roots of the genre in a sustained improvisation whose underlying logic is Kirby's graphic sense—and whose motive force is Kirby's obsessive striving for the sublime.

## THE MAXIMUM STATE

All mutuality is blocked or denied in the sublime as the puny self shivers
in the presence of the unknowable immensity of the Other.
— WENDY STEINER, *Venus in Exile* (5)

These mid-sixties comics, in their treatment of the technological sublime, point forward not only to later *Fantastic Four* and *Thor* comics, post-Kirby, but also other, less celebrated examples of Kirby's own work. Consider for instance Kirby's adaptation (for Marvel, 1976–77) of Stanley Kubrick and Arthur C. Clarke's *2001: A Space Odyssey* (1968), a project that fairly invited him to riff on the sublime. Though Kirby lacks Kubrick's sophisticated coolness, likewise Clarke's scientific authority, his *2001* represents a personal take on the film's spiritual themes. It was an odd project, extending from a faithful one-shot adaptation of the movie itself to an ongoing monthly consisting of original stories patterned on the movie's basic plot, albeit with new characters and settings. Lacking an ongoing continuity, the monthly offered, in stuttering iterations, a series of riffs on the film's premises, invoking both the prehistoric primitive and the Space Age high-tech. In the series' most interesting episode (#5–6), Harvey Norton, a superhero fan from a dystopian future version of New York, undergoes the consciousness-raising *2001* experience, but only after coming to the rescue of an extraterrestrial whom he dubs the "princess" (this character resembles *Thor*'s Tana Nile). To save the princess, who is mute and basically unknowable, from her anonymous pursuers, Norton runs a mind-blowing race through the cosmos, replete with Kirby's trademark fizzing detail. The chase leaves him shattered, thus to be transformed by the appearance of the Monolith, that silent visitor which, in film and comic alike, seems to trigger "evolutionary" leaps. (*2001* gets plenty of mileage out of a popular misconception: that evolution is something that can happen to individuals, as opposed to species.)

The cosmic trip here, echoing the sublime "astral gate" sequence of Kubrick's *2001*, also calls to mind Johnny's trip in *Fantastic Four* #49–50, which preceded Kubrick by about two years. The "shattering" of Norton similarly suggests that making the "leap" is a transformative if not ego-destroying process. First Norton, we're told, is "almost unhinged by the trauma of abject disorientation" (page 14); later, he is reduced to a "battered shell" and must "endure the *change!*" (26–27). Ironically, Norton lives out his last minutes fantasizing about being a superhero—a cheeky tribute by Kirby to his fans, I'd say—only to wither away and be replaced by the so-called new seed or Star Child, whom Kirby describes as humankind's means of "admission to a *wider* universe" (31). On the one hand, the vision of Norton as superhero reinforces his egotistical romantic fantasies; on the other, this interlude sets the stage for Norton's ultimate leap to something post-ego, and posthuman.

This story, indeed the whole *2001* series, shows that late-period Kirby was increasingly preoccupied with, as Christopher Brayshaw says, "how to represent events and psychological states that have no prior equivalents in human experience" (58). Norton reaches something like the "maximum state," and it is self-annihilating: facing the Absolute means hazarding one's very identity. The point is made visually by a climactic splash panel (see plate 6) in which Norton, splayed out in an improbably large cruciform shape—like the Promethean giant in *The New Gods*—lies at the foot of the Monolith, the blue-black surface of which, seen dead on, becomes, or hides, rather, the panel's implicit vanishing point. Norton is at once magnified and reduced by this awful image. Like Johnny's journey in the Galactus trilogy, Norton's trip is about profound disorientation and a challenge to his human sense of scale and importance. Once again Kirby leans hard on the technological sublime.

Both the Galactus trilogy and the peak period of *Thor* anticipate Kirby's mid-seventies series *The Eternals* (subject of our Chapter 7), in which the "gods" that created our species are figured as inscrutable giants from outer space who have come to pass judgment on our world, perhaps to destroy it (there's another echo here of Clarke, specifically of *Childhood's End*). Chief among these so-called Celestials is Arishem, the Judge, on whose thumb is inscribed the formula for destruction (fig. 10). Arishem and all its fellow Celestials are faceless unknowns, and do not speak directly to any of the characters in the series, at least not in any way that we readers are privy to. Instead they communicate by proxy, or simply go about their business silently, methodically. There's something dispiriting about going from Galactus to these less approachable figures: at least Galactus has a face and speaks in a human idiom (an absurdity, granted); at least Galactus can express emotions. By contrast, the Celestials have no personalities, only ominous titles (though, tellingly, Kirby cannot bring himself to give up anthropomorphism). While they represent the zenith of Kirby's obsession with godlike figures, the Celestials are ciphers, sublime precisely because they are distant and impenetrable. Conceptually,

Fig. 10. Arishem, planet-killer: the next step after Galactus. Jack Kirby, with Mike Royer (inks and lettering) and Glynis Wein (colors), "The Fourth Host." *The Eternals* #7 (Jan. 1977), page 17. © Marvel.

they are the next step after Galactus, but they are even more limited in their emotional appeal and dramatic use.

One cannot help but think of Kirby's "Interpretations of God," a series of drawings made for his private pleasure circa 1970 though later made available as a limited-edition portfolio (Dark Horse, 1996). For a time these drawings hung on the walls of the Kirby home. One of them shows the gigantic figure of God, a naked patriarchal figure—rather like William Blake's Urizen—with streaming hair and beard, his back to a suppliant humanity and his face turned away, distant, unanswering, unknowable (for reproductions of the series, see for example *Jack Kirby Collector* issues 26 and 46). This figure, Promethean yet conventionally anthropomorphic in guise, resembles a riff on Kirby's Odin or Highfather characters. Notably, it gives no comfort. Arishem is another take on that sort of Old Testament God, but refigured as a machine-like functionary, inorganic, almost robotic: the destruction principle couched in anthropocentric form, yet imbued with no character per se. The emphasis here on humanoid shape and godlike gigantism is almost absurdly conventional—a distillation, perhaps, of the child reader's sense of being outmatched, dwarfed, by the scale of the adult world—but the sense of utter coldness and aloofness remains severely potent. What Absolute lies behind Arishem's grille-like mask?

Kirby's cartoon Sublime, once one looks past the touching preposterousness of the ideas, offers a mingled pleasure and terror, or pleasure *in* terror. His repeated replaying of the confrontation between human smallness and superhuman gigantism suggests a protracted struggle with life's "interesting" questions. Whatever spiritual or religious understandings gave Kirby meaning and reassurance in his own life—a question we will revisit in Chapter 6—his work reveals a fascination with the limits of human understanding and with the minuteness of humanity in the face of cosmic things. He strove to take the cartoon idiom of the superhero in that direction, that is, toward the Sublime, in the process creating a grandiloquent brand of science fiction that addressed themes of spirituality, ultimate knowledge, and measureless power—*extremes*, as Kirby once said, "extreme situations, extreme relationships" (Wyman, "Conversations" 11). *The Fantastic Four* rendered these extremes accessible via roughhousing playfulness and frank sentimentality. In a sense, it wrestled the Sublime to the ground, domesticating it with soap opera subplots and a zingy sense of irony. However, once Kirby was untethered from Stan Lee and cast as an author in his own right, he could drift, and sometimes did, away from the sentimental grounding of the *FF* into stories of provoking strangeness, even chilly inhumanity. The teetering balance struck in stories like "This Man . . . This Monster!" sometimes tipped in the direction of the distantly cosmic, as Kirby's preoccupation with the technological sublime became even more extreme.

Because of this late-period tendency, some have surmised that Lee alone gave Marvel its air of emotional warmth and fervent optimism, and that Kirby's outlook was either (depending on one's loyalties) more pessimistic or less facile, or perhaps not as humanly engaged. Indeed, Earl Wells argues that the tonal differences between Kirby's work with Lee and his later solo work prove "once and for all" that Lee was the essential authorial voice at Marvel: the company's ideological guiding star, the one that believed in and sold the Marvel ethic of nobility, self-sacrifice, and moral certainty (82–85). Lee elevated the human. His scripting recuperated and reaffirmed our importance (rather like Kant's view of the sublime). By contrast, Wells argues, Kirby's view is frightfully ambivalent and offers no easy assurances about the nobility and efficacy of heroic sacrifice. Instead he undercuts glib heroism, questions our capacity for self-destruction, and views the drama of human survival and evolution on a much grander, albeit more remote and less simplemindedly optimistic, scale (86–87). This is an intriguing and sensitive argument inasmuch as Wells recognizes Kirby's love affair with fear and dismay: the sublime and terrible. Wells, though, underplays the fact that the comical and sentimental elements in Marvel had to be generated as much by Kirby as by Lee, bearing in mind that narrative drawing, just as much as scripting, is responsible for Marvel's tone. Also, Wells overstates the case for Kirby's later work as a sharp "about-face" from, rather than outgrowth and response to, Marvel. I argue that there remains a through-line connecting Marvel and Kirby's later comics, and that Kirby did not simply careen in a different direction because Lee was no longer at the wheel. He grew. He sought to fulfill the potential of Marvel, to exercise the capacity for sublime invention that working for Marvel had opened up in him.

Admittedly, this did produce tonal changes in his work. Other tonal shifts are evident as well: disappointment if not bitterness shadows much of his late period, and, as we'll see, there is a great welling darkness behind some of his solo comics. There are memories of war—more genuine and troubling than anything he channeled at Marvel—and nightmarish projections of dystopian futures. As Wells says, late Kirby often seems ironic and "doom-haunted" (87). Yet humor and tenderness and even schmaltz remain parts of Kirby's post-sixties repertoire, tugging at his sleeve as it were. Paeans to youth and ardent hopes for the future are constant; optimism coexists with bad dreams and trembling hearts. A splendid example can be found in his last Marvel period (1976–78) in a time-traveling tale scripted by Kirby himself, the awkwardly titled *Captain America's Bicentennial Battles* (1976)—a frantic, often dark whirlwind tour of American history that somehow ends on a warmly optimistic note. In this tale, Cap becomes unstuck in time and experiences various eras, confrontations, and traumas, from meetings with Ben Franklin,

Geronimo, and John Brown through the first atomic bomb test to the Great Chicago Fire; essentially, he finds himself on a quest to see "America and the truth at the heart of it!" (72). The comic ends with a one-two punch, first satirizing phony Hollywood exploitations of patriotism via a star-spangled Busby Berkeley-style musical number, then easing off into a quiet sequence that celebrates dreams of peace and opportunity via homespun examples of ordinary people. Finally, it resolves into a two-page spread that depicts Cap sitting among children—boys and girls of several ethnicities—who share his dream that "we can be *anything* we want to!" Even as the final caption invokes "a threatening tomorrow," even as Cap talks of "disappointment, despair and the crunch of events," he and the children bespeak Kirby's "stubborn *confidence*" that we all "can become like *super-heroes*"—that "we can become strong and *smart* enough" to beat our problems. What's more, Cap says, America offers us *the chance of making life meaningful!!* (78). Here, among the kids, Cap is an almost grandfatherly presence (Kirby would have been about fifty-nine at the time). This heartfelt, and, if you like, corny, resolution gives us a rare double-page image by Kirby that does not evoke either spectacular violence or sublime vistas. Despite the text's warning that keeping peace is impossible, that life is struggle, *Bicentennial Battles* ends with real hopefulness—and in a noticeable retreat from the cosmic Sublime.

This example is unusual, granted, not only because *Battles* was a one-shot timed to cash in on America's bicentennial fervor but also because Kirby's comics of the period did tend to stress threatening tomorrows over optimism and peace. *Battles* includes a sequence envisioning futuristic warfare on the moon, and throughout the comic cyclopean images evoke a feeling of helplessness in the face of overwhelming powers. Even this "birthday" celebration of America depicts a hero carried along unwillingly by events—and moments of dizzying sublimity. By 1976 Kirby had clearly become uninterested in simple heroic affirmations and overtaken by a sense of vast and ineffable forces. What changed for Kirby after the mid-sixties, as I hope to show over the next several chapters, was his desire to wrench superhero comics in the direction of allegory and so raise the philosophical stakes of the genre. It was the Marvel of the sixties, more particularly *The Fantastic Four* and *Thor*, that provided the fuel for this vaunting, quixotic effort: a bolder, more extravagant indulgence of the cartoon Sublime. And Kirby indulged mightily in the years following.

It seems clear that Kirby was interested not so much in the details of real-world scientific development as in what science fiction makes available narratively: the encounter with the Sublime, with awe-inspiring, fearful visions that push the reader toward the limits of what is comprehensible. That he strove to depict these visions in a graphic idiom that was boisterous, exaggerated, and caricatural—in a word, cartoonish—is one of the lingering and delightful ironies of his career. What happened to Kirby after Marvel—creative delirium, then cruel disappointment, and, over the long haul, enduring influence—would serve to rewrite the rules of comic books yet again.

5

# THE GREAT BUST-OUT: KIRBY'S FOURTH WORLD

There came a time when the old gods died! The brave died with the cunning! The noble perished, locked in battle with unleashed evil! It was the last day for them! An ancient era was passing in fiery holocaust!

The final moment came with the fatal release of indescribable power—which tore the home of the old gods asunder—split it in great halves—and filled the universe with the blinding death-flash of its destruction!

In the end there were two giant molten bodies, spinning slow and barren—clean of all that had gone before—adrift in the fading sounds of cosmic thunder . . .

Silence closed upon what had happened—a long, deep silence—wrapped in massive darkness . . . It was this way for an age . . .

THEN—THERE WAS NEW LIGHT!

— JACK KIRBY, *The New Gods* #1 (February 1971)

Two worlds: the one green and flourishing, overlaid with forests and clean waters, a free-breathing, fertile world orbited by a floating city crystalline in its beauty, where the inhabitants rejoice in an unending dream of peace; the other a metallic husk, its surface scabbed by hideous machines and cratered by huge, seething fire pits that choke the very life's-breath of the place, its atmosphere smoke-clotted and its inhabitants shadowed always by misery and fear. These are, respectively, New Genesis and Apokolips, sister worlds. The first is governed by Highfather, the unquestioned yet benevolent elder whose "wonder-staff" enables him to commune with the divine Source, the wellspring of all things. The second is ruled, with crushing absolutism, by Darkseid, despotic and cunning, his gray face nearly a graven mask, his person like a block of stone. Each ruler leads a great and varied cast of gods and creatures, and each clearly embodies a certain principle. Highfather honors freedom and creativity; for him, choice is life (even the divine guidance of the Source is but counsel, not command). Above all, Highfather celebrates youth, its freedoms and its potential, its continual promise to recreate the world afresh. Darkseid, on the other hand, personifies the desire for absolute power; he honors only Darkseid. Had he his way, every atom of life in the universe would be but a function of his will. In sum, Darkseid is about control: *Anti-Life*. He believes himself to be the force "at the core of all things," and he intends to bend all things toward him.

Between these two diametric forces, New Genesis and Apokolips, is a third place, fragile and promise-crammed: our Earth. Darkseid is searching on Earth, among humans, for the secret of the Anti-Life Equation, a secret that would enable him to control all life in the universe with but a single word or thought. To shake this secret loose from humankind, Darkseid will sow chaos and fear, holocaust and death, over the Earth, dispatching multiple underlings and working on multiple fronts. Conversely, the gods of New Genesis will come to Earth's defense. Chief among these is the fierce and enigmatic warrior, Orion, whose brutal nature belies his commitment to the cause of New Genesis. Orion will walk among humans in order to challenge Darkseid directly. Others, including the Forever People, that is, a team of young gods from New Genesis, and Scott Free, an escapee from a so-called orphanage (in fact a prison and indoctrination center) on Apokolips, will fight battles of their own against an array of Darkseid's functionaries. This is a "Super War," and the stakes—well, the stakes are everything.

Such is the premise of the comic-book saga Jack Kirby originally pitched to DC Comics as *The New Gods* but that finally came to be published as four different periodicals: first, a surprising stint on the preexisting series *Superman's Pal, Jimmy Olsen* (Kirby did fifteen issues in 1970–71), where, in a reckless gust of improvisation, Kirby's grand scheme was obliquely introduced; then three new titles in which his ideas were more fully realized, *The Forever People* (1971–72), *The New Gods* (1971–72), and *Mister Miracle* (1971–74). Together, these comics, sometimes referred to as a trilogy, sometimes a tetralogy, came to be called Kirby's Fourth World, a title whose meaning has never quite been clear (the term caught on among fans before becoming canonical at DC). Unprecedented in scope among superhero comics, the Fourth World was regarded by many fans, and apparently the artist himself, as Kirby's most personal work.

Regrettably, the Fourth World was canceled after just over a year and a half (although *Mister Miracle*, cut loose from the larger saga, shambled on for roughly another sixteen months). Over time, however, the Fourth World's characters and concepts would prove remarkably durable, eventually becoming linchpins in the putative continuity of the DC Universe. Variously revived between the late mid-seventies and the early 2000s, the Fourth World would be absorbed fully into continuity in the eighties; reprinted in part (*New Gods*) in 1984; capped with *The Hunger Dogs*, a widely regretted new "ending" by Kirby, in 1985 (see Morrow, "Production"); and reprinted in full via a series of trade paperbacks between 1998 and 2004. Meanwhile, the Fourth World would be colonized by others besides Kirby (for an overview, see Toole). As early as 1976, writer/editor Paul Levitz (formerly of the fanzine *The Comic Reader*, later President and Publisher of DC) wrote an article for DC's in-house "fanzine," *The Amazing World of DC Comics*, in which he posited that Darkseid's search for the Anti-Life Equation might become the pivot point of DC's future continuity, that is, a way of reconciling DC's various SF comics with futuristic or post-apocalyptic settings, among them Kirby's *Kamandi* ("Earth After Disaster!"). Sometime later, in *The Legion of Super-Heroes*, Levitz collaborated with artist Keith Giffen to produce a multipart story titled *The Great Darkness Saga* (1982, compiled in 1989) that served to popularize Darkseid as a major villain for the DC Universe as a whole—a role he would continue to play in various company-wide "event" series, from *Legends* (1986–87) to *Final Crisis* (2008–09). No longer confined to the Fourth World, Darkseid became DC's greatest cosmic schemer, a patient, cunning manipulator of continuity, and in this role he paved the way for reintroducing other Fourth World characters in different contexts. Since then, Superman comics have occasionally spotlighted Fourth World concepts (often drawing on Kirby's *Jimmy Olsen*), while various short-lived series have starred the characters Scott Free and Orion, Walter Simonson's series *Orion* (2000–2002) being the most fully informed by Kirby's ideas.

In fact the Fourth World has become a crux of DC continuity. Certain event series, such as *Cosmic Odyssey* (1988–89) and *Genesis* (1997), have focused on Kirby's characters, while others, such as *Crisis on Infinite Earths* (1985–86) or *Kingdom Come* (1996), have not failed to invoke the New Gods at least briefly, at critical moments. Most recently, writer Grant Morrison has spearheaded efforts to revamp the New Gods, first via *Seven Soldiers* (2005–06) and then via *Final Crisis*, billed as the climax of DC's long series of apocalyptic "crises." These are not so much stories as baroque intertextual networks. In *Final Crisis*, which opens with the murder of Orion and centers on the machinations of Darkseid, Kirby's Fourth World is superseded by a so-called Fifth World and many Kirby characters are redesigned if not reborn. Oddly, this "final" crisis was directly preceded by another last outing for Kirby's characters, *The Death of the New Gods* (2007–08), a self-cancelling exercise in housecleaning described by author Jim Starlin as a "mercy killing" (Ekstrom n. pag.). Outside of comics, meanwhile, toy lines (most famously Kenner) and animated television series produced between the eighties and early 2000s (*The Super Powers Team: Galactic Guardians, Justice League Unlimited*, and others) adapted some Fourth World characters, especially Darkseid and his minions. *Superman: The Animated Series* (1996–2000) cast Darkseid as a major villain, recalling Superman's interactions with the New Gods way back in Kirby's *Jimmy Olsen* and *The Forever People* (and featuring plot elements and even specific images lifted from the Kirby originals). Most recently Darkseid has appeared in video games, a direct-to-video animated film, and the live-action *Smallville* TV series. In short, the Fourth World properties have received a lot of play since their original "cancellation." If not as generative as, say, *The Fantastic Four*, whose publication has continued uninterrupted since 1961 and which has spawned countless spin-offs and branching narratives, the Fourth World has nonetheless been a perennial.

In fact, among fans the Fourth World is regarded as one of DC's prestige properties. Besides providing fodder for future projects and merchandising, revivals of the series served to renegotiate and redefine the company's relationship with Kirby as creator and brand, so that DC could play a role in the growing auteurist appreciation of Kirby among serious readers. Inviting Kirby to redesign Fourth World characters for toy and TV tie-ins in the early eighties, DC arranged to pay Kirby and his family royalties for these properties, giving him an incentive to return to them late in his career (Evanier, *King* 199–200). What's more, DC made sure that the tagline "The New Gods created by Jack Kirby" (or something similar) would appear on most future appearances of the characters. Revivals and reprintings after 1997 would usually feature Kirby's name above the title (*Jack Kirby's New Gods*, and so on). When the controversy over Kirby's struggle with Marvel erupted in 1985, DC was able to contrast its own policies toward Kirby with Marvel's very unpopular position (see Dean, "Kirby and Goliath" 92). In other words, the company took a stand for Kirby that mitigated its reputation for treating him poorly years before. Crucial to this change was DC's continuing revival and promotion of the Fourth World as a singular work of Kirby's genius. Ironically, having canceled the Fourth World abruptly in 1972, DC now hypes the saga as one of the jewels in its crown. This process began in the mid-eighties and was completed in 2007–08 with the republication of the saga in a four-volume hardcover set, *Jack Kirby's Fourth World Omnibus* (ironically, at the same time as *The Death of the New Gods*). By way of this handsome repackaging, the Fourth World has become a major site of negotiation between DC's carefully burnished image as a publisher and the artist-myth of "Jack Kirby." The idea of the saga as Kirby's masterwork has definitely taken hold.

So, *is* the Fourth World Jack Kirby's masterpiece?

Sure, in several senses. I consider it the pivotal work of Kirby's career. But the notion of the "masterpiece" implies a degree of completeness, self-containment, and formal *apartness* that a mainstream comic book series, in Kirby's day, could not expect to achieve. Practically speaking, the Fourth World was a grouping, or better an interlocking, of periodical (in most cases roughly bimonthly) comic books, each with its own logo, cast of characters, continuing storyline, and, most importantly, tone. Each book, in short, had its own identity. Yet each also displayed a deadline-driven changeableness, a capacity for sputtering, unevenness, and misdirection. Together and separately, these several series, in the manner of most comic books, were spotty, erratic, and immediately responsive to their times. By contrast, a masterwork tends to possess, or so we assume, a certain inviolate separateness: not only a deliberateness and consistency of craftsmanship but also a discrete, sharply delimited character. A masterwork is *by itself*, distinct from its surroundings. Such a view does not accommodate the fitful highs and lows, the continual ups and downs, of a deadline-hounded periodic series in a popular format. The idea of the masterwork implies a degree of artistic autonomy seldom available to mainstream comics, and hardly available at all until more recently, for mainstream comics have always been, at bottom, beholden to the heteronomous principles of the marketplace. Part of the spectacle and inescapable irony of the Fourth World lies in Kirby's attempt to negotiate a sphere of relative autonomy within the strictures of an inhospitable market, and in DC's concomitant attempt to foster and exploit an auteurist appreciation of Kirby—even though they originally enforced on him a stringent, close-fisted contract typical of anonymous work-for-hire.

The Fourth World does represent something "apart," in that Kirby saved up the idea behind the saga for some time, approaching it with uncharacteristic deliberation and a growing ambition. Yet, when he actually got around to doing it, he ended up relying as much as ever on sudden improvisation. This is why the Fourth World at once reflects Kirby's conscious shaping—there's a basic symmetry, a symbolic neatness, about the whole saga—and at the same time keeps branching off suddenly into seeming tangents and what would turn out to be unexplored dead ends. Bear in mind that during this period Kirby was contractually bound to produce at least fifteen pages of comics a week, and in fact produced on average more than three full comic books' worth of material each month. He was working not only on the Fourth World but also on various other concepts. In short, he was, as usual, insanely busy.

Part of that busyness was about trying to redefine the very nature of his profession. For example, Kirby spent time in 1971 working on what he had hoped would be a line of slick, full-color magazines for DC. In the end, these were downgraded to cheap black-and-white magazines comparable to the output of Warren Publishing (*Famous Monsters of Filmland*, *Creepy*, and such). Kirby had at first pitched these magazines to DC as a way of working toward a more "adult" audience, sidestepping Comics Code restrictions, and more effectively competing on newsstands; biographer Mark Evanier reports that Kirby suggested a slew of themes for such magazines, from which DC picked only a few ("The Unknown Kirby" 7). These magazines were to feature a substantial amount of comics, along with other graphics and sensational, tabloid-style text features. DC did eventually publish two such magazines, the crime-themed *In the Days of the Mob* and the horror-themed *Spirit World*, both in the fall of 1971 (coyly marketed, not under the DC logo, but under the imprint "Hampshire Distribution Ltd."). Both, however, were scotched after just a single issue. A third title, *True Divorce Cases*, was axed before publication, but only after Kirby had produced an issue's worth of material (a spin-off of sorts, the Black-themed *Soul Love* or *Soul Romance*, was also developed but discarded). So, at the same time that Kirby was creating the Fourth World, he was also producing magazines that he hoped would bid for adult readers outside superhero fandom. These were saddled with, arguably, retrograde content (note the reversion to genres typical of fifties comics: crime, horror, and romance), but it was hoped that they would make a splash with their slick production values, an idea that, in the end, DC did not go for. The Fourth World, which Kirby apparently envisioned as not only a series of comic books but also, in the long term, a collected work—what today we would call a graphic novel—should be seen as part of this larger effort to find alternatives to the then-foundering comic book format (Evanier, Afterword, *Omnibus* I, 389).

Simply put, Kirby imagined taking comic books into more upscale and durable forms, so as to reach a more adult (and more dedicated) audience. However, in almost every instance Kirby's initial vision, something larger and more attention-getting than the standard comic book, something that would involve other proven talents besides himself, ended up being reduced to another comic book assignment for Kirby alone, heaped onto his already-crowded schedule. Admittedly, solo Kirby is probably more interesting than the kind of collaborative work he had originally envisioned—but the hoped-for coherence of the Fourth World no doubt suffered due to his grinding schedule.

The premise of the Fourth World came to Kirby in fits and starts, beginning in the late sixties as a notional follow-up to Marvel's *Thor*, which, as we know, Kirby had been plotting and penciling for some time. *The New Gods* could have been a direct sequel to *Thor*, taking place after the fall of the Asgardian "old gods" as prophesied in "Tales of Asgard." Indeed, as noted in our previous chapter, the "Asgard" episodes in *Thor* #127–28 (April–May 1966) precisely anticipate the opening pages of *New Gods* #1:

> [. . .] *Asgard* itself is finally torn asunder by a monumental explosion, which shakes the very foundations of *infinity* itself!!
>
> Finally, nothing remains . . . but *silence!!* Silence . . . and grim, utter, endless desolation . . . the awesome remnants of an age, a glory, that is forever gone. . !
>
> [. . .] Until, at last, naught remains of Asgard but a charred, smoking mass . . . a celestial cinder which shall smolder and glow while the long years pass . . .
>
> Lo, the centuries turn to ages, and the ages to eons [. . .]

In time, we are told, new life flourishes on the once-dead world, life "shared by [a] young, new race of gods" that springs up, "takes dominion" over the land, and "spawns a new civilization . . . a new golden age . . . a new *rebirth* [. . .]" (*Thor* #128, "Aftermath!", pages 2–4). Clearly we are just steps away from *The New Gods*. However, any immediate plans Kirby may have had for this "new race of gods" fell prey to his growing disenchantment with, in fact outright anger at, Marvel, with the result that he uncharacteristically withheld the idea, along with a handful of concept drawings he had commissioned fellow Marvel artists Don Heck and Frank Giacoia to ink circa 1968. At this time, according to Evanier, the basic premise of what would become the Fourth World had not been elaborated much beyond the idea of a cosmic war against Darkseid (Afterword, *Omnibus* I, 390). Whatever Kirby had in his head, it was inchoate, undisclosed for the most part, and changeable. On paper, what he had was a set of handsome drawings, only some of which would actually inspire characters used in the Fourth World. Since Kirby was not in a position to develop the premise further while at Marvel, he let whatever he had in mind remain in his head until he made the transition to DC in 1970.

At that time, Evanier suggests, Kirby envisioned taking superhero comic books in the direction of epic fantasy, so as to expand their horizons and appeal to an audience that already collected comic books with near-religious fervor (Afterword, *Omnibus* I, 389–90). This is just what comic book publishers are doing today, of course; Kirby was ahead of the curve. Apparently he pitched such ideas during his negotiations with DC, when the exact form of his epic-in-the-making had not yet been decided. DC instead requested three bimonthly comic book series in the traditional format. Kirby, determined as ever to make the most of what he was offered, agreed, opting to channel his epic, now tentatively known as *The New Gods*, into three interlocking series, to be titled *The Forever People*, *Orion*, and *Mister Miracle*. It appears (again, Evanier is our best source) that Kirby saw these three as assignments that, once established, he could pass on to other artists and writers. He foresaw working with established artists such as John Romita, Don Heck, Steve Ditko, and Wallace Wood, all of whom worked or had worked for Marvel. He also thought he would break in new writing talent to help him steer the books (Afterword 389–90). In short, Kirby imagined taking a supervisory role not unlike Stan Lee's editorship at Marvel—with the crucial difference that Kirby would be serving as conceptual artist and plotter.

Instead, DC asked Kirby to commit to writing and drawing the new books himself for an indefinite period. These three, *The Forever People*, *The New Gods* (retitled from *Orion*), and *Mister Miracle*, would be the backbone of Kirby's contract. However, the contract, which was demanding, called for still more work—or placed him in the position of needing more work to support his family—and so Kirby was required to take on an existing DC title. This he did by radically revamping the existing Superman spin-off, *Superman's Pal, Jimmy Olsen* (lifespan: 1954–74), under the editorship of Murray Boltinoff. In fact *Jimmy Olsen* #133 became the first-published of Kirby's new books for DC (cover-dated October 1970, though actually released in August, it competed against Kirby's final jobs at Marvel). Perversely, *Jimmy Olsen* also became the inroad for the Fourth World: the three issues of Kirby's *Olsen* that came out before the other Fourth World titles appeared laid seeds for what was to come. In particular, *Olsen* introduces Darkseid, who is glimpsed in #134–35 as a vague figure on a video screen (thumbnail-sized at first). Darkseid's human underlings, Inter-Gang, figure in the *Olsen* stories from the start, and two characters from Apokolips, the geneticists Simyan and Mokkari, are featured villains starting in #136. Yet Kirby played his cards close to his chest, revealing little. Only later, with the first issues of *The Forever People* and *The New Gods* (both dated Feb. 1971), did the natures and origins of the warring gods become known.

So even Kirby's masterwork came in the side door, unexpectedly. Everything about his run on *Jimmy Olsen* bespeaks a frantic spirit of improvisation. From within a series assignment that he undertook only reluctantly, and after he had conceived "The New Gods" as a trilogy, Kirby did something startling: he instantly changed the tone of the preexisting series and used it to lay the groundwork for the three new books, in effect sneaking up to the larger cosmic stakes of what would become the Fourth World. His *Olsen* was in fact a peculiar mashup of elements: something old, that is, the Newsboy Legion and the Guardian, Simon & Kirby characters of the forties, now revived; something new, meaning not only Inter-Gang and Darkseid, but in fact a raft of new things; and, of course, something borrowed: Superman and his pal, Jimmy Olsen, now drafted into Kirby's realm. Whether or not he had meant for Superman to be part of the Fourth World from the start, Kirby gave the Man of Steel a central role, casting him as a reluctant, sometimes disapproving, protector and father figure to Jimmy and the Newsboys. The boys, for their part, became explorers of a wondrous if murkily defined realm: that of the Wild Area, the Zoomway, and the Project, a veritable feast of ideas, all of them introduced in Kirby's first three issues of *Olsen* in a mad, spilling rush, what Grant Morrison has aptly called a "breathless conceptual overflow" (Introduction, *Omnibus* I, page 7).

Here the grand and puzzling nature of the Fourth World is introduced straightaway: one part considered planning, two parts reckless ad-libbing. Even the title "Fourth World" seems to have developed by accident. As Evanier has said, for Kirby "everything was in a state of flux until he actually put it down on paper," and, once he had, the results were perhaps as surprising to Kirby as they were to his readers ("Unknown" 5). If the Fourth World premise had been gestating for years, and gave Kirby's new work a certain grandeur and solidity, the project's actual launch, via *Olsen*, was antically inspired, marking Kirby's most hectic period of idea-spewing since his full-to-bursting mid-sixties run on *The Fantastic Four*. Evanier reminds us that Kirby's "schedule was such that there wasn't time to pause, reflect, and plan" (Afterword, *Omnibus* I, 395). This astonishing surge of creative energy represents, for some, a flailing exhibitionism sadly distant from Kirby's more carefully edited work at Marvel, as if he was determined at any cost to prove himself an idea man apart from Stan Lee. For others, including this writer, the Fourth World represents Kirby's professional zenith. Apart from its other virtues, the saga treats us to, in Morrison's words, "the spectacular harvest of a mind at play" (8).

Calling the Fourth World a singular masterpiece would downplay the elements of improvisation and, frankly, inconsistency that give the work its wild, drum-hearted, insistent strangeness. It's tough to separate what works in the Fourth World from what doesn't: the lunges that don't pay off, the occasional flatfooted or dated story elements, as in *Olsen*'s calamitous drop-off starting with issue #139 (starring the likeness of comedian Don Rickles!) or, for those readers put off by idea of the Black Racer, the sudden inclusion of that bizarre character in *New Gods* #3. In this sense, the Fourth World is a mixed bag. But the bravura, hell-for-leather quality of the several series—taken as a month-by-month, peaks-and-valleys joyride—more than compensates for the moments Kirby seems to lose his grip. In other words, you can read the Fourth World two ways: as an overall epic (in which only certain chapters shine), and as a project whose life was in the doing. If we cannot also enjoy the Fourth World in this second way, in its manic changeability and inconsistency, then few periodical comics preceding the graphic novel era will likely charm us.

These two ways of reading are pitted against each other in the four-volume *Jack Kirby's Fourth World Omnibus*, which attempts, at last, to present the Fourth World stories to a larger audience and in the order of their original publication.[1] Rereading the stories in this format is at once gratifying and frustrating. It's gratifying because retracing the saga's publication history gives one a renewed appreciation for the sheer prolificacy and energy of Kirby at his peak and gives new insights into his working method. It helps to see, for instance, how, after an initial, explosive period of spitting out ideas and characters, Kirby begins to consolidate and clarify his world: in *Jimmy Olsen* #136 (dated March 1971), and immediately following in *Forever People* #2 and *New Gods* #2 (both April–May 1971), Kirby draws together the various threads of his saga. Seeing this in the Omnibus format underscores Kirby's continual tug-of-war between careful premeditation and sudden inspiration; the Omnibus, then, serves as a time capsule of his month-to-month working process. But it's also frustrating, because the several series comprising the Fourth World had separate storylines, which are continually interrupted in the Omnibus format. For instance, the cliffhanger between *Olsen* #136 and #137 remains hanging for some seventy pages (an interval that includes the first issues of the other three titles).

The lack of a precise fit, continuity-wise, between the titles can also be confusing. For example, Superman and Jimmy Olsen appear simultaneously in two disparate stories: in the *Olsen* run, of course, but also in *Forever People* #1, where the treatment of the Man of Steel is tonally quite different. Neither story refers to the other. (Production code numbers suggest that, though the *Olsen* storyline was published first, *Forever People* #1 was actually produced first, in fact was the first full story Kirby completed for DC [Cooke 48–49].) The very monumentality of the Omnibus edition tends to hide or confuse such issues, whereas, by contrast, the act of putting down one slender comic book and picking up another (each one a discrete object) helps to rationalize if not overcome the otherwise-glaring discontinuities. In its effects, then, the Omnibus edition cuts in two directions: on the one hand, its monumentality gives it a time-capsule quality or historical value that is most welcome; on the other, the gathering of the Fourth World titles into one package, one binding, and one determined sequence tends to throw the discontinuity between the titles into unwelcome relief. In a sense, the Omnibus works against its (presumably) intended aim of underscoring the Fourth World's putative unity and wholeness.

Thus, the Fourth World, as a whole, does not quite coalesce. It lacks the consistency to which today's graphic novels aspire, or even that of Kirby and Lee's *Fantastic Four* at its peak. Though the Fourth World presaged the graphic novel ideal, it was not created under a production model that could have given it coherence. What it does possess, in retrospect, is sheer, mad energy: a deluge of ideas and a mind-rattling intensity of execution. It also boasts remarkable graphic power: in monstrous beauty, if not consistency of finish, the drawing in the Fourth World marks a leap for Kirby as an artist, perhaps partly because his increased editorial control allowed him to chase after ever more bizarre and pregnant imagery. In other words, his narrative drawing hurtled forward because the narrative and graphic dimensions stimulated each other. From this reader's point of view, a change in inkers also proved salutary: starting with *New Gods* #5 (Oct. 1971), the inconsistent, at times slapdash, Vince Colletta was replaced, on all the titles except *Jimmy Olsen*, by a younger, lesser-known inker and letterer, Mike Royer, who brought a bolder, more fluid brush line in contrast to Colletta's fussy pen technique.

This change was more than merely cosmetic—or perhaps we should say, rather, that in comics there is nothing "mere" about cosmetics. Colletta, known in the fifties as a romance artist, began inking Kirby at Stan Lee's behest at Marvel in the early sixties, and typically softened Kirby's brusque drawings, bringing a feathered edge to Kirby's slashing lines and chunky, geometric forms. Often he would break Kirby's heavy lines, jagged squiggles, or rugged blacks—places where Kirby bore down hard on the pencil's edge—with fine pen-line hatching. While Lee liked and sought after this tempering effect, particularly on *Thor* (Colletta's longest gig as a Kirby inker), Colletta's delicate pen was at odds with the increasingly massive, geometric, and abstract aspects of Kirby's drawing over the course of the sixties and after. From the late sixties onward, and certainly at DC starting with the Fourth World, one sees Kirby, more and more, going after a total effect that is at once hallucinatory, wildly energetic, often frightening, and, not coincidentally, more starkly graphic. Colletta's inking, however, impeded this tendency. In addition, Colletta's work was uneven on its own terms, owing, presumably, to deadline pressures (Colletta had a reputation as a go-to inker for rush jobs). Study of his inks vis-à-vis surviving photocopies of Kirby's pencils reveals that Colletta sometimes erased or blacked out telling graphic details or even major compositional elements in Kirby's drawings, simplifying and diluting Kirby's designs. At their worst, Colletta's finishes decidedly diminish the end result.[2]

These niceties of production method have major consequences for comic art. Royer, who unlike Colletta was hired and supervised directly by Kirby, took a loyalist's approach, striving to uphold, through a lively brush line, the rawness and dynamism of Kirby's pencils. *New Gods* #5 marks an immediate and, to readers at that time, probably shocking change in rendering, with a more voluptuous line, deeper blacks, and more severe yet also more vibrant display lettering, now fully integrated into the drawings. Royer was slicker than Colletta. He began his career assisting cartoonist Russ Manning (whose style was handsomer than Kirby's), and later worked as a character artist and product designer for Disney. His own drawing is typically smoother, less ragged, and more rounded than Kirby's. Nonetheless Royer was determined to preserve, as indeed he was hired to preserve, the quirkily rugged look of Kirby's pencils (Royer, "Fastest Inker" 25; "Brush" Part 1, 72–74). He found a way to translate the roughness of said pencils into a distinctive shorthand. Kirby came to prefer this approach, which characterized all of his later work, even that finished by others besides Royer (though never again would Kirby be so well matched with a new inker).

Kirby's work with Royer, like his work with everyone else, was not consistent, nor did it improve past 1973. However, Royer was crucial because he helped Kirby toward an aesthetic that can be seen threatening to emerge in his late-sixties Marvel work but that fully arrives in the Fourth World. This aesthetic, the late Kirby style, jells in the company of two inkers, the first being Joe Sinnott on *Fantastic Four*, whose original brief, like Colletta's, was to soften, shape, and discipline Kirby's drawing. He did, with an elegant, liquid line, though over time he began to allow more of Kirby's unvarnished qualities show through (Sinnott, "Ordinary" 9, 19; Interview with Morrow, 27). The second was Royer, under whom Kirby's trademark tics of style, already apparent in comics like *Fantastic Four* and *Thor*, hardened into an eccentric graphic language, imitable, close to self-parody (as is any sufficiently intense form of artistic expression), and indeed constantly parodied in comics even now. This is of more than cosmetic interest because these inkers, the best of Kirby's late career, responded to Kirby's strivings and to the changes in his style, and Kirby in turn seems to have come closer to finding what he wanted when working with these two, Royer in particular. The Fourth World, which even under Colletta boasts some of the most electrifying pages in Kirby's career, blossomed under Royer into a work of violent and outrageous beauty, taking Kirby to another level. In fact the Kirby/Royer period from roughly mid-1971 (Royer's arrival) to early 1973 stands as a high-water mark for Kirby's art. The present-day appreciation of Kirby as an outsider artist, or primitivist, testifies to the importance of this period.

If the Fourth World is not a neatly finished masterwork, it was still a watershed for Kirby and for comics. The wonder of it is that, despite its influence, it retains its eccentricity, its irreducible individuality. Simply put, it is as personal a project as Kirby was ever able to pursue in his long career. Besides sheer vigor and splendid graphic execution, the saga exhibits three other qualities that set it apart from its forebears in superhero comics: one, the originality and later influence of its overall premise; two, the originality of its numerous secondary inventions, many of which are not simply gimmicks but potent metaphors; and three, of course, its fervent presentation of Kirby's values, courtesy of an obvious ideological subtext (if indeed *sub*text is the right word) and a hopeful if sometimes clumsy treatment of youth and youth culture.

## PREMISE

Admittedly, I've always been a bigger fan of contemporary comics than I am of these "classics." But more than once while reading the Fourth World comics, I was shocked and amazed at how much Jack Kirby's work has inspired the comics I read and enjoy today.
— Student Vaheh Hartoonian's response to reading Kirby in a seminar on superheroes

The Fourth World's premise—essentially, a superhero epic comprised of, as observed in Chapter 3, a pantheon of related characters and a symbolic dualism—is important not only for its own sake but also for its cascading influence. Structurally, Kirby's saga was something new for comic books, in that it introduced, *at the same time*, multiple series centered on a single fictive world. To say that this proved influential would be an understatement; this approach has since been imitated *ad infinitum* in mainstream comics, from the DC and Marvel universes to various other (mostly short-lived) superhero startups under other imprints. Consider for example Marvel's "New Universe" (1986–89), a separate world later absorbed into Marvel continuity whose heroes mostly derived their powers from a cosmic "White Event"; Marvel/Epic's Shadowline saga, consisting of three interlocking titles about the superhuman Shadow Dwellers (1988–90); the Valiant/Acclaim universe (1992–2000), which retrofitted a new continuity onto vintage characters from Dell and Gold Key comics while also launching new characters; the Ultraverse, a writer-centered line (several writers were gathered in "seminars" to plan it) launched at Malibu Comics but later purchased and gutted by Marvel (1993–96); Dark Horse Comics' superhero line, called Comics' Greatest World or Dark Horse Heroes, based around four fictional cities (1993–96); the Milestone universe, published by Milestone Media in partnership with DC and centered on the fictional city of Dakota, most of whose superhumans traced their origins to a single catastrophe called the Big Bang (1993–97); and the WildStorm universe (*WildC.A.T.s, Stormwatch/ The Authority, Gen[13]*, etc.), first launched at

Image Comics, later an imprint of DC and tied to DC Universe continuity (1992–2010).

Historically, most of these examples were launched during and contributed to a brief flush of confidence that accompanied the mushrooming of the comic book collector's market in the early nineties, at around the time of the much-hyped startup of Image Comics (1992). Most did not survive the bursting of that bubble, post-1993. All of them, whether consisting entirely of new properties or created by combining and revamping existing properties, were based on a "shared universe" model, featured common settings, characters, devices, and originary events. This model was conducive to the marketing of crossovers. Such projects, whether outlined by a single creator (such as Shadowline's Archie Goodwin) or by a team of creators (as with the Ultraverse), required the concerted efforts of large groups of editors and creators in order to get to market, in contrast to Kirby's barnstorming solo flight.

Obviously, the historical line that leads from the Fourth World to these various other comics began at Marvel in the sixties, when, under Stan Lee's supervision, the continuity principle was ascendant. The Fourth World, however, went Marvel one better in terms of preplanning, offering several variations on the same theme simultaneously. By contrast, Marvel's continuity (as established in Chapters 2 and 3) developed gradually, with 1963–65 being critical years of focus and consolidation. What Kirby did, with *Jimmy Olsen*, *The Forever People*, *The New Gods*, and *Mister Miracle*, was build continuity among a cluster of titles before they were published. He posited a conflict and a set of devices to be shared among all four series. The same approach characterizes the New Universe, Shadowline, the Ultraverse, Dakota, et cetera. The difference, of course, is that what Kirby originally envisioned but did not get (the opportunity to work with and guide other creators) is what later became standard.

Admittedly, few of the above-named superhero lines are of anything but historical interest. Most lasted only briefly, falling prey to summary cancellation, slow death by declining sales, changes in ownership, and/or absorption into larger, more famous brands (Marvel, DC). They were specific to the superhero-dominated direct market and sprouted during a precise window (the early nineties) due to economic inducements peculiar to said market. They rode a speculation boom; honestly, they were signs of decadence. What is worth noting is that, at that time of inflated expectations and frank opportunism, the market turned reflexively to the very sort of coordinated, inter-title continuity that Kirby had pioneered twenty years prior.

Naturally Kirby is no more to be held responsible for these comics than, say, Akira Kurosawa is for *A Fistful of Dollars*, but his influence was felt. His sense of scope, and something of his hyberbolic style to match, became part of the DNA of new superhero launches. As if in testimony, Topps Comics assembled a shared universe project titled the "Secret City Saga" out of castoff materials from Kirby's trove of unpublished ideas and drawings (1993), even as the artists of Image Comics invoked Kirby as a forebear in *Phantom Force* (also 1993), again working over unfinished Kirby concepts. The results, though mere footnotes from an artistic point of view, are revealing. The resurgence of interest in the then-retired Kirby at just that moment—during the high season, post-Image, of investment and speculation in newly made comic book series—underscores what a handy blueprint Kirby provided. What had crystallized in the Fourth World was the pantheonic, shared-universe approach to the creation of superhero worlds, an approach easily dulled by repetition but readily exploitable in the fevered climate of early-nineties comic book marketing.

The Fourth World, in other words, suggested a way of focusing and intensifying the effects of continuity as pioneered at Marvel by Lee and Kirby. As Chapter 3 argues, the conflict at the root of the Fourth World exaggerates the dualism already inherent in Kirby and Lee's *X-Men*, whose dialectical, good mutant/bad mutant premise would generate decades' worth of story material from 1963 onward. Kirby, intuiting that such conflicts were too big and too promising to be limited to a single traditional comic book, dreamed of something grander. Out of a compromise between his dreams and the practical constraints of his DC contract came a logical next step, dividing a sprawling epic into several new comic books that premiered simultaneously. In this sense, the Fourth World was a sequel to Marvel and its model of continuity. Even as the Marvel Universe, post-Kirby, deepened, so as to generate popular crossovers such as "The Kree-Skrull War" (*The Avengers* #93–97, 1971–72), Kirby demonstrated the possibility of building several new ongoing titles out of a single multifaceted premise. In essence, he tried to trump Marvel.

Though many fans saw the Fourth World as shockingly different from Marvel comics, the project represented an amplification of Marvel's continuity principle. The consequences of this move are still being played out today in ways Kirby could not have foreseen: in an ever-tighter emphasis on all-encompassing, company-wide continuity policed by staff editors (which arguably would have been anathema to Kirby) and in elaborately rigged event series that often retrofit Kirby creations so as to redefine preexisting universes. The Fourth World's byzantine multi-title continuity, in short, has been both gift and curse to subsequent superhero comics.

Besides what it did to superheroes in the long run, the Fourth World's premise was also a summation of Kirby's career to that point. In some ways it was achingly traditional. Though its premise promised a grand coherence, its division into bimonthly comic book series allowed for variety in character, theme, and tone, as well as, frankly, the rehashing of traditional genre elements. Innovative in scope, the project nonetheless enabled Kirby to revisit familiar neighborhoods. For instance, the adventures of Jimmy Olsen and the new Newsboy Legion, and for that matter of the Forever People, recall the S&K kid gang formula of the forties and early fifties, while Mister Miracle recreates the acrobatic hero type familiar from such S&K properties as Captain America, the Sandman, Manhunter, and Stuntman. The Fourth World dusts off these old formulas, with new twists.

*The Forever People*, for example, while recalling the original, youthful *X-Men*, departs from the kid gang premise by dispensing with the usual adult chaperone (for example, the Guardian in "The Newsboy Legion," Rip Carter in *Boy Commandos*, or even Superman in Kirby's *Jimmy Olsen*) and replacing him with the Infinity Man, a super-being who appears whenever the Forever People join together around their "Mother Box" and utter the keyword "Taaru!" Infinity Man functions somewhat as the Guardian does in the Newsboy Legion's adventures, but is no fatherly protector. Rather, he is a composite of or stand-in for the Forever People themselves, a mysterious figure summing up the power and possibilities of the whole group (and underscoring the series' emphasis on concepts of freedom and growth). Mark Moonrider, one of the Forever People, refers to the group as "the door for [Infinity Man] to enter" (#1, page 18). The character, whose invocation by "magic word" calls to mind Fawcett's *Captain Marvel* of the forties and fifties, admittedly lacks personality, but, as a counterweight to the lively teens of the title, is an ingenious stroke. Mister Miracle, meanwhile, takes S&K's acrobatic hero and gives him a new gimmick, one suited to Kirby's flare for balletic action: he is an escape artist. Scott Free's struggle to break free from his past—the great bust-out, as Kirby put it—is symbolically reenacted each issue by his daring escapes and stunts. Seldom has a superhero's ability or gimmick seemed so psychologically apt (a symbolism seized upon by Chabon in *The Amazing Adventures of Kavalier & Clay*, with its Kirbyesque character the Escapist).

It was the Fourth World's flagship title, *New Gods*, which represented something new. While its original working title and ostensible protagonist was *Orion*, and its mainspring was the conflict—the father-son conflict, as it turned out—between Orion and Darkseid, the series' wide-open title allowed Kirby to focus occasionally on other characters: the "Bug" Forager, for example, in a two-parter about the invasion of Earth by a "Bug" horde (#9–10), or Highfather and Darkseid himself in the saga's most-praised chapter, "The Pact" (#7). But even here there are hoary elements, particularly the echoes of crime comics in several chapters. There's something touching about Kirby's insistence on populating the series with so many gangsters and cops and fedoras (even Orion sports one!). Early chapters attempt to make the cosmic scope of the series more approachable and to move Orion around comfortably among humans—never an easy fit—so the crime comic elements represent a kind of self-reflexive fallback for Kirby. As a series, then, *New Gods* is all over the place: perhaps because Orion is such a difficult leading man, his book proves the most shiftable of the Fourth World titles, plastic enough to give rein to Kirby's constant improvising. Its combination of clichés and genuinely new ideas is startling.

## INVENTIONS

If the Fourth World's premise provided a new blueprint for superhero comics, Kirby's originality was just as evident in the series' arsenal of secondary inventions, its odd, often symbolically fraught characters, settings, devices, and contraptions. In fact the greater pleasure is in the details, rather than the schematic whole. Secondary characters are colorful and often frightful, especially Darkseid's legions: take for example the sadistic aesthete Desaad (the homophonic pun on or misspelling of *De Sade* is a typical Kirbyism), who delights in sucking fear from his victims; the bestial warrior Kalibak, Darkseid's son; the glib "revelationist" Glorious Godfrey, an evangelist for Anti-Life; the harridan Granny Goodness, a grotesque caricature of motherhood; the discarnate energy being Doctor Bedlam, whose lifeforce inhabits successive "animates" or living mannequins; the Female Furies, fighting women of Apokolips, each with her own power or shtick; and hordes of "Justifiers," flying "para-demon" sentries, "dog cavalry," and so on. The cast as a whole is an outlandish bunch, boasting shamelessly freakish character designs: Big Barda, fiercest female warrior of Apokolips; Sunny Sumo, wrestler; The Black Racer, airborne harbinger of death. Settings are equally weird and evocative. Consider Armagetto, the Apokolips ghetto that houses the "lowlies," the most abject of Darkseid's subjects; the Orphanage, Granny's house of horrors, where the young of Apokolips are broken to her will and to that of Darkseid; the Colony, home of Forager and the other Bugs of New Genesis; the aforementioned Promethean Galaxy, "place of the giants"; Happyland, a nightmarish amusement park-cum-death camp designed by Desaad (*Forever People* #4–6); or the Wild Area, land of *Jimmy Olsen*'s counter-cultural "dropout society," with its great treehouse city, Habitat, and the adjoining Zoomway, a "dragstrip" mined with obstacles that outlaw bikers risk death to ride. The gizmos too are legion. Among the obvious recurrent examples are the Boom Tube, the Whiz Wagon, the Super-Cycle, the Mountain of Judgment (a giant vehicle), Metron's space-traveling Mobius Chair, Orion's "power rods" (or Astro-Harness, or Astro-Glider), and Mister Miracle's "aero-discs" and other life-saving gimmicks. Even devices of only momentary importance are intriguing: meta-rod, dragon-tank, (Desaad's) Psycho-Fuge and Fear Siphon, or the murderous thinking machine, (Granny's) Overlord. Pouring out gadgets and gimmicks in a nonstop flood, Kirby runs wild, indulging to the fullest his yen for the technological sublime and in particular a favored trope, the confusion of organism and machine.

Overlord serves as an especially ripe example of Kirby's weirdly evocative, at times ironic, use of this trope. Introduced in "X-Pit" (*Mister Miracle #2*, May–June 1971), Overlord is both gizmo and character, and both more and less than he/it seems. First seen in a full-page splash (fig. 11), Overlord appears a looming figure of metal, a Kirbyesque blend of gigantism and techno-abstraction topped, unsurprisingly, with an outsized head—a symbol, as so often with Kirby, of intellectual or psychokinetic power, though in this instance also, oddly, of babyishness. Barely recognizable as humanoid, Overlord consists of a bigheaded hodgepodge of tubing, plating, and diagrammatic patterning: nested shapes compulsively layered, a Kirby trademark. Godlike, Overlord boasts, *I—AM—OVERLORD* [. . .] *I—CREATE—I DESTROY* (page 1). Yet Granny Goodness, who issues commands to Overlord from a remote terminal, describes it as "too *precious* to be *exposed* to the world"; her cringing minions refer to Overlord as Granny's "pet" (8). Granny orders the machine, first, to assassinate Scott Free (Mister Miracle) from a distance. Then, when that fails, she orders it to fashion a trap for Scott: a torture chamber known as the X-Pit, "every atom" of which, we are told, is "linked to Overlord *himself*." (21).

When Mister Miracle escapes the pit and kills Overlord, essentially by overloading its circuits with power, Granny mourns him: "Oh—my *heart* [. . .] Granny is *hurt!* Granny is *ruined!*" (A travesty of parenthood, Granny often speaks of herself in the third person, like a parent condescending to a child.) As it turns out, the reason Overlord is built with a baby's proportions is because it is a small, shoebox-sized figure, essentially a fragile, toylike gift from Darkseid—as Scott says, "a fraud." Basically, it is Granny's baby. Overlord's presence in the story serves to characterize Granny (here making her first appearance) as a monstrous parody of motherhood, perversely alternating between sentimental cream-puffery (*My soldier boys never fail their granny! My soldier boys are the best!*) and despotic "discipline." By killing Overlord, Scott—himself an escapee from Granny's "orphanage"—mocks Granny's maternal rhetoric and exposes

Fig. 11. Overlord, a living machine. Jack Kirby, with Vince Colletta (inks) and John Costanza (lettering), "X-Pit." *Mister Miracle* #2 (May–June 1971), page 4. © DC Comics.

the basis of her authority as illusory. The wrap-up of the story hints richly at an old, tense, unresolved relationship between Scott and Granny: he the rebellious son, she the sadistic "mother."

Another intriguing, perhaps disturbing, note is struck by this particular example, a subtlety that says a lot about the Fourth World. Scott kills Overlord using a device of his own, his Mother Box: again a symbol of motherhood. This is the same device Scott uses to comfort the dying Thaddeus Brown (the original Mister Miracle, from whom Scott inherits the mantle) in the previous issue (#1) and which saved Scott's life from Overlord's first attack. In fact, the Mother Box is an omnipresent idea in the Fourth World, a device that guides, reassures, and protects Kirby's heroes. The Forever People have one; Orion has one; Scott Free has one. A Mother Box has great and unspecified powers: the Forever People's Mother Box charts their course and enables them to summon the Infinity Man; Orion's hides the ugliness of his true face; Mister Miracle's helps him escape from trap after trap. Pioneered by Himon, a visionary scientist and revolutionary who haunts Apokolips, forever slipping just out of Darkseid's grasp, the Mother Box proves equally elusive. Though a machine, a Mother Box is sentient. Though powered by the Source and thus "linked to the *infinite*" (Darkseid's words), a Mother Box can be injured. It (she?) can also be healed, or revived, by an outpouring of "love" and "belief" (as in "The X-Pit"). Desaad, Darkseid's cruel lieutenant, attempts to murder one, only to have it disappear or disintegrate (*Forever People* #4).

Disturbingly, Orion does murder, or believes he murders, a Mother Box. In "Spawn" (*New Gods* #5, Oct.–Nov. 1971), Orion crushes the Mother Box belonging to the villain Slig, then gleefully, cruelly, cackles, "She *loved* you, Slig!!!" Here, in one of Kirby's darker moments, Orion is momentarily outed as a brutish killer. Reverting to his true face, Orion admits that, but for his own Mother Box, he would be, as Slig says, "a mad, tormented animal." Mother Box, Orion reflects, "*calms* and *restructures* and keeps me *part* of New Genesis!!*" (20). Then he kills Slig, remorselessly. A similar ambiguity slips into the climax of "The X-Pit," as Scott "jam[s] Mother Box into [Overlord's] torment-circuits" and her power "race[s] with vengeance" toward their source: "Somewhere, I could hear his *silent* scream—somewhere, I felt him—*die!*" (21). A Mother Box, then, though typically a warm and protective presence, can also strike out savagely, vengefully. What comes out of all this is a strange intermingling of organic and artificial life and a sense of interdependence between person and machine.

This figures most provocatively in "The Glory Boat" (*New Gods* #6, Dec. 1971–Jan. 1972), in which Orion's companion Lightray turns a battered wooden boat into the incubator for a gleaming, "techno-active" organism (fig. 12):

Fig. 12. The techno-active organism as weapon. Jack Kirby, with Mike Royer (inks and lettering), "The Glory Boat." *The New Gods* #6 (Dec. 1971–Jan. 1972), page 25. © DC Comics.

a machine that, once activated, grows of its own inward impulse into a sleek silvery missile, which Lightray then uses to destroy their enemies, the Deep Six. This techno-active process is a pure expression of Kirby's technological sublime, at once redemptive and destructive, healing and cataclysmic. It recreates the boat as a cosmic weapon while also causing the transformation and apotheosis of a human bystander in the gods' war, a murdered young man. This man's face has literally been wiped away—rendered blank, featureless—by the Deep Six, but is restored as the climax nears, moments before the missile explodes in an eye-boggling blaze of Kirby-dots. This rhapsodic episode suggests a glorying in, but also a fearful ambivalence about, the blurring of the living and the technological. Kirby's inventions throughout the Fourth World are fraught with such peculiar, multivalent symbolism.

## VALUES AND POLITICS

It's fair to say that, despite his crushing work schedule and the usual fitfulness of his thinking, Kirby was wholly engaged by the Fourth World. These comics were *about* something; they represented his boldest bid to turn the superhero genre into a vehicle for ideas. Their dualistic premise allowed him to use his heroes allegorically, to personify ideas that mattered deeply to him. Animating the saga is a not-so-subtle subtext: that the essence of human life is choice, and that Anti-Life represents the negation of choice, that is, absolute domination. As Serifan puts it in *Forever People* #5, "If someone possesses *absolute* control over you—you're not really alive!" Darkseid, in his quest to wield Anti-Life, is the ultimate totalitarian, a tyrant determined to bend all to his will. In contrast, the gods of New Genesis serve as champions of freedom. This conflict between control and freedom gives the Fourth World books their vaulting, headstrong, earnest quality. Kirby clearly believed in this struggle, for no matter how outlandish the concepts, or humorous or satirical some of the episodes, these comics are dead serious. If often preposterous, they are also free of condescension. They speak to Kirby's fears. Cartoonist and Kirby devotee Walter Simonson has observed that the Anti-Life Equation is Kirby's "comic book reification of fascism," and fascism's spread certainly impacted Kirby's life and his understanding of what it was to fight for freedom (Introduction, *Omnibus* II, page 8). Indeed fascism seems to have inspired in Kirby both fascination and horror.

Subsequent revisions of Kirby have reinterpreted the basic conflict in the Fourth World along different lines. For instance, Jim Starlin and Mike Mignola's *Cosmic Odyssey* miniseries (1988–89) interpreted Anti-Life as a malevolent, sentient being. Starlin's later *Death of the New Gods* went further, positing that the Source and Anti-Life are but facets of the same divided entity (a duality already suggested in Gerry Conway's *New Gods* revival of the late seventies). This downsizing, so to speak, drastically shifts the ideological axis of Kirby's story. Starlin's Source/Anti-Life duality suggests a theory of the unity of opposites, a Pop take on Taoism or perhaps another riff on the Freudian Eros/Thanatos binary that preoccupies Starlin's work from the seventies onward. *Death of the New Gods* ends with the fusing of New Genesis and Apokolips—a reversal of the image of the planets dividing in *New Gods* #1—so that they form one rather *Taijitu*-like (yin-yang) world. The result would seem to be an enactment of the predictable idea that good and evil, life and death, are necessarily intertwined, an idea already dramatized by Kirby on a personal level within the figure of Orion. J. M. DeMatteis's attempted *Forever People* revival (1988) diverges openly from Kirby's premise, making Kirby's heroes champions of "order" over "chaos," a common notion perhaps influenced by Michael Moorcock, in whose fantasy fiction the "balance" between Law and Chaos figures largely (a concept familiar to most *Dungeons & Dragons* players). This revamping too is unconvincing; in fact DeMatteis gets it exactly wrong, in that Kirby's Darkseid represents not chaos but order, a suffocating order robbing its subjects of choice and therefore life. Granted, Kirby's Darkseid conjures chaos in his assaults on Earth, but only with the ultimate aim of ferreting out the secret of Anti-Life and thus enslaving all beings. Darkseid, in short, is the State at its most monolithic and tyrannous. In sharp contrast, Kirby's treatment of characters such as the Forever People and Mister Miracle represents the possibility of radical freedom.

*Freedom* is a word easily abused, of course. Requiring superhuman champions to protect human "freedom" flirts with fascism itself, and, arguably, is inescapably ironic. Superhero detractors tend to find the genre more fascistic than freeing,[3] and, in any case, Kirby's premise contradicts itself, calling for violent heroes to, as it were, make the universe safe for democracy (in Cold War fashion). Underlying this is a belief that violence is inevitable and freedom must be bought with martial force—the Fourth World is, after all, a superhero tale. It is also a war story, the work of a man for whom WWII was the defining episode of his adult life and the Cold War the lingering aftermath. Characters such as Orion and the Infinity Man embody the culture and ideology of Cold War America, specifically the idea of righteous force in the cause of liberty. Orion, we note, is a monster, and Infinity Man a blank. There is also the question of whether Kirby's ordinary human characters live up to his notion of freedom: distressingly, many of the bystanders in the saga turn out to be just that—bystanders, ciphers to this great account. This deemphasizing of the human and the everyday (some readers sorely miss Stan Lee's lightly ironic, deflating touch here) seems to contradict the saga's very emphasis on human liberty. Kirby, working within the superhero genre and ratcheting up its violence to godlike scale, doesn't seem to recognize this problem as such; in essence, the Fourth World is about a war of powers. On the surface, it doesn't seem to have occurred to Kirby that the warrior gods of New Genesis, with their powers and their determination to intercede in human affairs, might be more like than unlike their counterparts from Apokolips. Or did it?

That the Fourth World is in dead earnest repels some readers. The tone of the saga, sincere and unpatronizing as it is, might be taken as high-flown, stuffy, or even tyrannizing. But that's not quite right. For one thing, the humor denied Orion keeps popping up in other parts of the tetralogy, not only in the absurd effervescence of much of Kirby's *Jimmy Olsen*, but also in, for instance, *Mister Miracle*'s supporting cast or the Forever People's run-ins with bemused bystanders. The byplay between gods and humans is at times poignant, as in the brilliantly drawn scene on playwright Eve Donner's penthouse terrace in which her curiosity and proffered tenderness are rebuffed by Orion's destructive rage (*New Gods* #9). And if the humans in the cast, such as Donner, are mostly walk-ons, they show up often enough: lovers on a rooftop, a neighbor in an elevator, people on the street.

Some stand out clearly, most notably police sergeant Daniel Turpin, titular hero of "The Death Wish of Terrible Turpin" (*New Gods* #8). Turpin, a thickset, cigar-chomping cop of the old school—one of several such characters identified by fans with Kirby himself—is a blunt, plainspoken, middle-aged hero whose philosophy is simply "to *give* as good as you *get!!*" (8). Granted, a narrating caption refers to Turpin as merely as supporting player to the story's "*principal* cast" (Orion and Lightray), for he is a man, "and men are no more than *pawns* in the larger game" (6). This dismissive remark, though, is surely ironic, for, despite the story's spectacular battle between Orion and Kalibak, Turpin dominates the tale, determined as he is to "haul in" the "super-weirdos" laying waste to his city. Even when battered, crushed, almost killed, he still attempts to place the gods "under arrest" (a moment of deadpan comedy). For Turpin, the city belongs to "us," not to the warring gods (22). If the overall story suggests that Turpin may be mistaken, he still has our sympathy. He even succeeds in stunning Kalibak, leaving a flummoxed Lightray to ponder the earthman's resourcefulness. At moments like these, the human characters, though absurdly overmatched by the gods, register dramatically. Turpin may be out-powered, but his self-determination in the face of near-certain death, his ability to "choose the fire and fury to become *more* than what [he is]," throws the gods' struggle into new perspective.

It is Kirby's "gods," though, who are most compellingly characterized, indeed most humanized. The saga turns out to be not so simple, for Kirby—and this is revealing—blurs the seeming idealized perfection of New Genesis, adding complexity to his gods. If the Fourth World entails a clear-cut conflict between good (freedom) and evil (totalitarianism), Kirby's characters don't have it so easy, or so simply. His champions are outsiders even among the gods. The Forever People are too restless, Scott Free too earthbound, and Orion too warlike to enjoy the peace of New Genesis. The very premise of the series demands these heroes come to Earth, but there is more to it than that. Orion, though raised on New Genesis, in reality is of Apokolips; he is torn and tormented. His true face is hidden from everyone, his full history hidden even from himself. Mister Miracle, Orion's flipside, though born of New Genesis, is a fugitive from Apokolips, a runaway from Granny's Orphanage, and Earth is his refuge. The Forever People, though less obviously conflicted, are still outcasts: they preach a message of truth, love, and friendship, but are ostracized as "hippies" and "savages." They are forced to set up base in a tumble-down tenement, with only an invalid boy and his (initially fearful) guardian for neighbors. Of all these characters, Orion is especially complex, for he is the son of Darkseid, struggling against his own fierce nature and destiny, yet also the saga's essential hero. Orion's character, in its savagery, hints at an ambivalence or despair on Kirby's part: a sense that freedom and peace may require a ferocious defense. Orion is, at heart, a killer. This entangles considerably the saga's Manichean, good-versus-evil premise.

Despite all this, the Fourth World is an optimistic work. Characteristically, the heroes of New Genesis are mostly youths, representing hope, energy, and enthusiasm. Kirby's identification with young people is obvious throughout, most notably in *Forever People* and *Jimmy Olsen*. These books broke new ground for mainstream comics by making heroes of hippies, such as the Forever People themselves or the super-scientific Hairies in *Olsen*, who "live in harmony with whatever and whoever [*sic*] they contact" (a utopian vision of the scientific pastoral not unlike the depiction of the Black Panther's Wakanda in *The Fantastic Four*). The *Forever People* in particular, with their Super-Cycle (a kind of high-tech buggy) and their outlandish, individualistic clothing, distill popular images of hippydom but in a wholly positive light. Reading their adventures now, in hindsight, is like diving into a utopian vision of "the sixties," cartoonishly distorted just as the sixties are cartooned in the American imaginary. "They belong to sunrise," as issue #1 proclaims (recalling, perhaps, "Let the Sun Shine In," from 1967's *Hair*); they are "new to this age."

In *Forever People* #2, the young "gods" are called hippies by anxious bystanders yet don't seem to know the term. Their knowledge of human lingo seems bookish and out of date. One man mocks them (*All ya gotta do is show him a bathtub—an' if he runs—he's a hippie!*), only to be knocked out flat by an uncomprehending Big Bear, largest of the group, who mistakes the man's sarcasm for brotherly good humor and crushes him in a bear hug. The scripting is inconsistent: on the one hand, the young gods casually use slang like "turn on" and "dig," but, on the other, Big Bear misuses phrases like "out of sight" and "groovy" as if unaware of their rightful contexts (in general, the gods seem puzzled and fascinated by earthly custom). Later, when the young gods seek to establish headquarters in a nearly abandoned tenement "wait[ing] for the coming of urban renewal," the boy Donnie takes to them right away, but Uncle Willie, "the security guard," draws a gun on them, calling them savages. The scene climaxes on an ironic note: Beautiful Dreamer, who has telepathic powers, probes Willie's mind for more comforting images and so is able to transform the group, in Willie's eyes, into something "familiar," that is, idealized, nostalgic images of youth, the kind "Willie *knows* and *likes*." Beautiful Dreamer suddenly wears a modest, square-neck dress (as opposed to her usual revealing minidress), Serifan an all-American baseball cap and letterman sweater (as opposed to his usual cosmic-cowboy look). "You used to know *lots* of kids like us! *Remember?*" Willie's fear is easily quelled by this illusionary change; he decides that the newcomers look "nice enough" after all, and offers to help them (8). How easily his prejudices are tapped.

Kirby relishes these ironic encounters between young people—open, new, challenging by their very appearance—and their elders—closed, hardened, fearful. Irony aside, the Fourth World idealizes youth as a means of salvation, a regenerative force whenever "man's civilization faces destruction" (*Forever People* #1). *New Gods* #1 makes the point clearly: Highfather, the gentle patriarch, is first seen listening to a children's choir, for, "as ever, he can be found where the voices of the *young* are raised in chorus!" Having summoned Orion to his presence, Highfather instructs him, "First we *bow* to the young—they are the carriers of *life!*" (7). The beauty of their song, he says, must not be allowed to fade. Even Orion, fiercest of warriors, swears himself to this cause. Though brief, this moment is a critical early signal of what the saga will be all about. (Indeed, *Forever People* #7 even shows Highfather answering a petition from "the Council of the Young.")

Oddly, Kirby reserves his most nightmarish stuff for his youngest heroes. His horror of and fascination with totalitarianism is most evident in *Forever People* #3–6, an extended story that depicts the preacher Glorious Godfrey and his "Justifiers," anonymous, masked soldiers only too willing to sacrifice themselves for Darkseid. To wear the mask, says Godfrey, is to be faceless and therefore "unified! Glorified! Justified!" (#3, page 4). In Godfrey's rhetoric, values are inverted: life is a threat, and Anti-Life, "the *positive* belief," is a gift: the gift of superiority, of license, "the *right* to point the *finger* or the *gun!*" Issue 3 begins with a chilling splash panel showing a throng of people with blank, dead eyes, rigid and expressionless in their conformity: "It's the *others*, Godfrey! Those who *don't* think right! / This is *our* world! *Our* world! They have *no* right to *meddle* with it!" (1). In the caption box at the top of the page, Kirby, tipping his hand, has placed the following epigraph:

"That is the great thing about our movement—that these members are uniform not only in ideas, but, even, the facial expression is almost the same!"
— ADOLF HITLER

The following two-page spread, depicting Godfrey in the pulpit, so to speak, presents a flurry of doublespeak: *Life has pitfalls! Anti-Life is protection* (on a heart-shaped sign); *Life will make you doubt! Anti-Life will make you RIGHT!* (a banner); *You can justify anything with Anti-Life!* (another sign). The ensuing plot is frightful: surviving an attack by a Justifier (a suicide bomber!), the Forever People seek out Godfrey, tracing him to an old-fashioned revivalist's tent like a circus big top. There Godfrey, abetted by a booming pipe organ (shades of Eisenstein's *Alexander Nevsky*), shares his "revelations." The Forever People summon Infinity Man, but he is banished by Darkseid. Then the young gods are knocked out and carted by Justifiers to "the camp of the damned," that is, Happyland, Desaad's horrific amusement park: Disneyland as death camp. Much of #4 is devoted to the tortures, both physical and psychological, gleefully meted out by Desaad, whose "Scrambler" manipulates images and thus conceals the terrors of the camp under the guise of theme-park entertainments. Beautiful Dreamer, for example, is immobilized and placed within a kind of Sleeping Beauty display; she appears to onlookers as "the Sleeping Robot Princess" who can be awakened only by the proper "magic word." From the customers' point of view, she is an attraction, while, from her point of view, the customers (all trying to get close to her and speak the word, of course) appear as monstrous grotesques. Evil is performed in plain sight, and terror is indistinguishable from banal enjoyments.

The suffering of Kirby's teens underscores the nature of Darkseid's evil. The Forever People are mis-recognized and victimized by crowds representing a vacuous conformism. In one extraordinary scene in #4, Darkseid strides out among the customers of Happyland, where he is mistaken for a performer (fig. 13). An overeager parent, getting into the spirit of things, tells his child that Darkseid is "a real, live spaceman"; on the other hand, an older man reassures his frightened granddaughter that Darkseid is only an actor. Darkseid

Fig. 13. Darkseid in Happyland. Jack Kirby, with Vince Colletta (inks) and John Costanza (lettering). "The Kingdom of the Damned." *The Forever People* #4 (Aug.–Sept. 1971), pages 13–14 (selected panels). © DC Comics.

corrects him, calling himself "the *real* thing" (13). Angered, the man leaves with the child, as Darkseid, his granite face working up to a smile, crows mirthfully:

> All young humans *recognize* the real thing when they see it! Young humans see me—even in *"Happyland!"* But you elders hide me with *"cock and bull"* stories to keep the premises smelling *sweet!* (26)

Darkseid erupts with laughter, drowned out by the anodyne music of Happyland. In effect, this scene undercuts sentimental conceptions of childhood innocence and gullibility, arguing that children, whatever their elders want to think, have a keen awareness of evil.

Though the young are the center of the Fourth World, an ambivalence about youthful rebellion still survives in the books, most obviously in *Jimmy Olsen*. Kirby's *Olsen* features several covers stressing generational conflict between Jimmy and Superman, two drawn by Kirby and others by Neal Adams (DC's go-to artist for covers at the time). These covers to some degree reflect conflicts within the stories inside, since Jimmy and the Newsboys often resent Superman's cloying, protective presence. But the covers exaggerate the conflict, presumably as a sales tease. The cover to #133, Kirby's first, depicts Jimmy and some Outsiders (bikers) running Superman down. That of #134 shows the Outsiders bearing away Superman's supine body. The following cover, #135, is downright misleading, showing Superman overwhelmed by tiny clones of himself unleashed by a gloating Jimmy (nothing like this occurs in the comic). Next, #136 shows a giant green Jimmy bashing Superman (more accurate, this).

Now, lures of this sort were nothing new for *Olsen*: plenty of covers before Kirby's run, whatever the contents of the comics inside, showed Jimmy asserting his independence, blowing off or getting the upper hand over Superman. For example, #109 (March 1968, about two and a half years before Kirby) featured "Luthor's Pal, Jimmy Olsen," with a cover depicting Jimmy torturing (!) Superman to make him reveal his secret identity. Issue 118 featured "Hippie Olsen's Hate-In," with a cover depicting a bearded Jimmy and a "hippie gang" picketing the Man of Steel (a far cry from Kirby's treatment of the hippy type). Issue 120 features "Jimmy Olsen's Super-Punch," with a cover showing Superman felled, in fact killed, by one punch from a puzzled Jimmy. This theme of role reversal, the powerful Superman placed at the mercy of young Jimmy, seems to have been *de rigueur*, an obligatory motif that simply came along with the *Olsen* assignment. Though Jimmy was Superman's "pal"—a tag evoking friendliness, boyish camaraderie, and dependence—the series often sought to startle readers with images of Jimmy's agency and Superman's physical abjection. Messages were mixed: at times the covers show a defiant Jimmy (Jimmy the villain, Jimmy the "hippie"), at others a contrite and confused Jimmy ("Can you ever forgive me?").

Related to this was the shtick of transforming Jimmy into *something else*, gigantic or super-powerful or just plain weird: a "giant turtle man," a human porcupine, even his own superheroic alter ego, Elastic Lad (indeed, DC published the nostalgia-themed collection *The Amazing Transformations of Jimmy Olsen* in 2007). Kirby worked this angle as well, pitting Jimmy, Superman, and company against a giant green "clone" of Jimmy (#135–36) and turning Jimmy into a ferocious "caveman" (#146). All this was in keeping with past practice. A bigger problem for Kirby was finding space for Jimmy in the midst of complicated stories stuffed with supporting characters, outré concepts, and, of course, outriders from the Fourth World.

Kirby's treatment of adolescence in *Olsen* seems to have been a tardy response to images of youthful rebellion already bubbling up in the popular culture by the sixties' end. Such responses were common then; interestingly, though, Kirby's treatment of youth is more affirmative than cautionary, and his responses less disapproving than those of his predecessors on the series. Though from the start he pushes the trope of generational conflict, he doesn't choose sides in an easy, automatic way. Kirby's Jimmy is ambitious, eager to make his mark as a reporter, and impatient with Superman's protective hovering; he sees the Man of Steel as a wet blanket. Superman knows better, for he understands that Jimmy is over his head. However, the youth-dominated Wild Area into which Jimmy and the Newboys so recklessly travel turns out to have many facets, both dystopian and utopian.

When Superman first enters the area (#133), he encounters a hippy sitting lotus-style on an elevated platform, a mix of Lewis Carroll's mushroom-topping Caterpillar and a pillar-saint. "Welcome to the *Wild Area*, brother!" says the hippy. "You are now *free* to do your *own* thing!" (14). Achingly dated dialogue ensues, as the pillar-hermit rebuffs Superman for interrupting his "meditation" and tells him to "split." Superman then comes across a self-appointed border patrol that tries to shoot him down: "We dig only our *own* vigilante group! So—it's like you're *doomed!*" The Man of Steel himself then adopts hippyspeak: crushing one of his assailant's guns, he says that his costume is "for *real*, brother! Only it stands for *peace*—something you should dig—but *fast!*" (25). The arrival of the Outsiders and Jimmy, bikers all, breaks up the scene.

Our initial impression of the Wild Area is none too positive, and Superman thinks the very thing one might expect adults of the era to say about youth culture: "There are no *rules* here! This is a place of complete *anarchy!*" (16).

There is more than a hint here of late-sixties biker movies such as *The Wild Angels* (1966), *Hell's Angels on Wheels* and *The Born Losers* (both 1967), and, of course, *Easy Rider* (1969), but in fanciful, high-tech dressing. (This issue hit the newsstands about nine months after the Altamont Speedway Free Festival, or concert, in California, in which members of the Hell's Angels played such an infamous role.) Jimmy is now the head of the Outsiders, having bested their former leader in combat. Incredibly, the bikers possess a weapon powered by kryptonite (Superman's weakness) and so, on Jimmy's command, are able to knock Superman out and take him captive.

Superman wakes, to his amazement, in the fabulous treehouse city of Habitat: a striking example of Kirby's technological sublime in blended rustic-futuristic mode (fig. 14). This storybook environment—one big clubhouse—makes imaginary concessions to functionality and has its own make-believe ergonomics (including, oddly enough, wooden ramps that accommodate motorcycles). It's a lovely, loopy vision of a "green" city, where living is a fantastic fusion of *civitas* and wildness: a Romantic vision that epitomizes Kirby's melding of nature and high-tech and anticipates current visions of the ideal eco-city. It is also a perfect setting for *Olsen's* eager and utopian, if inconsistent, treatment of the counterculture. The series' ideological uncertainty, its simultaneous caricature and fond embrace of youth culture, are reflected in the spatial and thematic incongruities on this page: the lack of a clear vanishing point, the seeming clash of perspectives, the way Habitat seems to jut this way and that, and the juxtaposing of high-speed, high-tech elements with humbler, domestic elements such as couples walking. The fanciful concessions to practicality, the way the odd railing, streetlamp, or ladder tries to appeal to our sense of everyday function, belie the inspired craziness of the vision and the ideological tensions beneath.

Superman is impressed to see that the dropouts of the Wild Area can be so "industrious" (20). Jimmy, however, informs him that the Outsiders simply inherited, or "took over," Habitat from its builders (perhaps they really are too wild to build such things for themselves?). Nonetheless the Outsiders have a society and a code of behavior, one that has put Jimmy in charge. Here again we see Kirby trying to, as the saying goes, surf the zeitgeist: his entire depiction of a youthful "dropout society" brings to mind such pop landmarks as the 1968 film *Wild in the Streets*, with its over-the-top vision of a hedonistic, youth-controlled America—a dream of social collapse though also crazy, utopian possibility.

To make things still blurrier, Jimmy's explorations of the Wild Area lead to the discovery of another hippy-inspired group, the Hairies. Their home, a gigantic armored "missile carrier" known as the Mountain of Judgment,

Fig. 14. Habitat, a high-tech hippy utopia. Jack Kirby, with Vince Colletta (inks) and John Costanza (lettering), "The Newsboy Legion." *Superman's Pal, Jimmy Olsen* #133 (Oct. 1970), page 20. © DC Comics.

constitutes in itself a democratic, high-tech utopia: more of Kirby's breathless futurism. A benevolent commune of (as it turns out) genetically engineered super-hippies, the Hairies have formed "a new, mobile, scientific society" (#134, page 22). They seek only "to be left alone" to develop their talents to the full. Superman embraces the Hairies' society unreservedly, and in fact already knows something about them. Here Kirby is guilty of an inconsistency: when Superman first meets the Hairies, he acts surprised, but subsequent issues suggest that he is their old friend and indeed has participated in the very "project" that birthed them. If the Outsiders are dropouts from mainstream society, the Hairies are their counterparts, beneficent dropouts from what Kirby calls simply the Project, or, sometimes, "the D.N.A. Project" (DC would later re-christen it Project Cadmus, as if in tribute to "The Cadmus Seed," a Kirby story about cloning for Harvey's *Alarming Tales* [1957]).

Surprisingly, the Hairies become the entryway for an extended, multi-issue arc about the risks and possibilities of genetic engineering, all set within the Project's militaristic and, frankly, unnerving setting. Muddying his utopian-hippy themes, Kirby likens the Project to the Manhattan Project, for it turns out that the government is behind it all! The tone of this story is hard to place: on the one hand, Kirby presents the possibilities of genetic tampering with a gosh-wow air of excitement, but, on the other, he has two geneticists from Apokolips hijack the same technology, as if to sound a cautionary note (they are the ones responsible for Jimmy's transformations). In any event, Kirby populates this byzantine science fantasy with images of free-spirited youth: surrogate Jimmys, miniature Newsboys, and, repeatedly, the Hairies, with whom Jimmy, the Newsboys, and Superman ultimately commune in a musical trance, their minds tuned to a Hairy invention that "gathers in the *radio-signals* from the stars" and arranges them into "patterns of *harmony*" (#137). Jimmy presides over, or conducts, this transporting ritual, an occasion for two cosmic splashes in Kirby's signature photo-collage style. As one of the Hairies says, "We *hear* as one! We *see* as one! We *soar* as one!" Jimmy puts it more succinctly: "*Groovy!* This is a real gas!" (5–6). The vibe is unmistakably psychedelic and utopian.

In sum, despite *Olsen's* uncertain milking of generational conflict, Kirby's envisioning of the Hairies, the Forever People, and other young characters suggests a sympathetic and, for a person of his generation in that era, surprisingly optimistic outlook on youth culture. With its bald, often clumsy hippy dialogue but idealized young characters, the Fourth World is clearly the work of a middle-aged man earnestly trying to keep pace with and understand the youth of the time. Not for nothing did Kirby devote sporadic backup stories to "Young Scott Free" and the "Young Gods of Supertown": his young characters embody the idea of freedom that underlies the saga, and in them we see his wistful identification with the trials and potential of youth.

In fact the Fourth World is a story about children: not only the obvious examples, i.e., the Forever People and the boisterous kids of *Jimmy Olsen*, but also those grown children of Apokolips and New Genesis, Orion and Scott Free, protagonists of *The New Gods* and *Mister Miracle* respectively. Their childhoods were determined by the war of worlds. The two central stories in the Fourth World are concerned with the causes and consequences of an exchange that brought Apokolips's son to New Genesis and, vice versa, New Genesis's to Apokolips. These twinned stories testify both to Kirby's hatred of totalitarianism and to his ambivalence about the necessity of war, shaped by his implicit unease regarding the then still-raging American war in Vietnam. These tales are told in "The Pact" and its companion piece, "Himon," which focus on, respectively, a father and son. Because these twin stories come closest to bringing unity and focus to Kirby's jigsaw masterpiece, I offer close readings of them in the next chapter.

Like much of Kirby's work, the Fourth World suggests a fiercely active mind—untutored but intellectually engaged, even supercharged—always searching for ways to personify grand ideas. This synthetic mythos represents his boldest attempt to give life to abstractions, to turn a battle of concepts into rip-roaring adventure. It was a project in which, inevitably, the grand ideas spiraled beyond even Kirby's original aims, so that the premises, so clear at first, became humanly messy and unpredictable. Kirby was engaged heart and soul in this effort, the most complex creative undertaking of his career. One can hardly blame his fans for saying, as they often do, that it's a shame he did not get the opportunity to see this dream through to a proper end while still at the height of his powers. (The ill-regarded *Hunger Dogs* sought to ring the curtain down, but by then Kirby was in decline.) That said, it is difficult to imagine how the saga could have ended in such a way as to do justice to its sprawling, inexhaustible, endlessly explorable worlds. How could Kirby have satisfactorily brought the Fourth World to an end? It was too rich, too exploitable. As Doug Harvey observes, its fragmentary, incomplete, yet end-lessly suggestive nature is the essence of its power; its "every character, event, and detail is saturated with potential meaning," and the sheer proliferation of its ideas suggests an infinitely receding horizon (18–19). Little wonder that, decades after the fact, the Fourth World has become the reactor core of the DC Comics universe. The ideas—the ideological focus—that first got under Kirby's skin and goaded him to do the work have, of course, been jettisoned along the way. His work, happily, survives.

## 6

# KIRBY AT APOGEE

Both "The Pact" (*New Gods* #7, Feb.–Mar. 1972) and its counterpart "Hi-mon" (*Mister Miracle* #9, July–Aug. 1972) are flashbacks, detours from the forward-thrusting narrative of the Fourth World. Kirby described them as "supplement[s]" and begged his readers' indulgence. In fact, these stories are the core of the Fourth World, and among the most deeply personal comics Kirby ever made. As such they demand a closer look.

### "THE PACT"

"The Pact" is a war story, full stop. It is a Vietnam-era myth-fiction about the moral ambiguity and terrifying costs of war. The tale deals with the way war distorts the warrior and the fact that warring to defend something can lead to the betrayal of the very thing defended. As backstory, it tells us how things came to be, but it also fulfills *The New Gods'* very premise of warring powers. After all, *New Gods* follows (as the Source Wall counsels in issue #1) this simple outline: *Orion to Apokolips—then to Earth—then to war.* The series is about a second war of worlds. But "The Pact" tells us about the first. Above all, it is the tale of Izaya (Highfather) and how he came to be the foster father to Darkseid's child Orion. The child, hostage to the war, becomes the very means of establishing a fragile cease-fire: a treaty. On the shattering of that treaty, the Fourth World saga rests.

A creation myth of sorts, "The Pact" reverts to the high-scriptural tone of *New Gods* #1, starting with the ritual phrase "In the beginning" and even invoking, Genesis-like, the idea of form rising out of chaos. Though it will turn out to be a story of war—the Great Clash, as Kirby calls it—"The Pact" is more concerned with the personal than the panoramic. It begins on New Genesis, with an idyllic splash page of Izaya the Inheritor and his wife, Avia, happily resting in Edenic comfort (fig. 15). Back to back they sit in the grass,

# IN THE BEGINNING —

THE *NEW GODS* WERE FORMLESS IN IMAGE AND AIMLESS IN DEED!!! ON *EACH* OF THEIR *TWO* NEW WORLDS, THEIR RACES HAD SPRUNG FROM A *SURVIVOR* OF THE OLD!! THE LIVING ATOMS OF *BALDUUR* GAVE NOBILITY AND STRENGTH TO ONE!! — AND THE SHADOW PLANET WAS SATURAT- ED WITH THE CUNNING AND EVIL WHICH WAS ONCE A *SORCERESS*!! FOR AN AGE THESE NEW GODS PURSUED THEIR OWN DESTI- NIES — UNTIL THE TIME OF THE *GREAT CLASH*!!! IT WOULD START ON *NEW GENESIS*—WITH THESE TWO—*IZAYA THE INHERITOR* AND HIS WIFE *AVIA*—AND HAPPINESS— THE *FIRST* SIGN OF COMING TRAGEDY—IN AN *IMPERFECT* STATE!!!

IN MOMENTS LIKE THESE, WIFE, THE WARRIOR *SOFTENS*—AND SEES THE LAND IS *NOT* A MERE LOGISTICS-MAP!!

ARE WE *MADE* FOR WAR, IZAYA? YOU KNOW—I'VE *NEVER* HEARD YOU SING!!

FROM TIME TO TIME—THIS KIND OF SEGMENT WILL SUPPLEMENT THE LARGER TAPESTRY OF THE NEW GODS. THANK YOU—*JACK KIRBY*

Fig. 15. Edenic splendor, but in "an imperfect state." Jack Kirby, with Mike Royer (inks and lettering), "The Pact." *The New Gods* #7 (Feb.–Mar. 1972), page 1. © DC Comics.

two lovers idling, in dress and demeanor like figures out of myth. Kirby's opening caption, though, warns of "coming tragedy" and establishes that this is no Eden but rather "an *imperfect* state." Izaya, maned with leonine hair like a robust young version of an Old Testament patriarch, calls himself a warrior;

in reply, Avia asks, "Are we *made* for war, Izaya?" Wistfully, she urges him to raise his voice in song rather than in battle. Already one gets a sense that Izaya is war-weary, though why is not clear. The second page follows this thread, with Izaya telling Avia he cannot sing as yet, but that she "*feeds* [his] aching spirits." At this point the lovers' idyll is abruptly shattered as Izaya and Avia are beset by Steppenwolf of Apokolips and a band of his "demon raiders," out for brutal sport. Over the ensuing four pages, "tragedy" comes and the foundations for the Fourth World are laid.

Even as the raiders attack, a small, half-glimpsed figure warns "Uncle" Steppenwolf to take care. Avia flees off-panel, and Steppenwolf, ever the proud hunter, grapples with Izaya hand-to-hand. The subordinate raiders, urged by the unseen nephew, interfere in the combat, to Steppenwolf's displeasure. Izaya smashes through them with his staff, then rounds on Steppenwolf, threatening him with death. But Avia suddenly reappears and shouts to Izaya to stay his hand. Startled, Steppenwolf whirls and kills her with a fatal bolt of power. As the still-unglimpsed nephew chastises his uncle for his rashness, Izaya's features tighten in fury. Before he can get revenge, however, Izaya is shocked into seeming death by a metallic glove that delivers a jolt of energy to his head. The "killing-glove," as we see at the end of the sequence (page 5), belongs to the nephew: Darkseid.

Darkseid urges uncle Steppenwolf to leave the scene quickly. Steppenwolf, though distrustful of his scheming nephew, takes for granted that Izaya is dead. Their dialogue reveals that Darkseid's mother (Steppenwolf's sister) now rules Apokolips, for at this early point in the saga Darkseid has yet to seize power. Steppenwolf knows his nephew to be ambitious, "clever and cunning—and a *plotter!!*" (5). Indeed: as they depart in a flying machine (each page taking us further away from the opening's sense of ancientness and toward the props of high-tech combat), we learn that it was Darkseid who suggested this "foray" on New Genesis, and that, contrary to what Darkseid has said and Steppenwolf believes, Izaya remains alive. One senses that everyone is playing roles that Darkseid has scripted, for a final caption tells us that "as he has engineered the *incident*—Darkseid has *begun* the *war!!*" Turning the page, we run headlong into the story's title, in a frenzied, archetypically Kirbyesque double-page spread that fulfills the story's logic of escalation, depicting what Kirby calls "techno-cosmic" warfare. Izaya, vowing vengeance, now wages war on Apokolips, and we are bombarded with smoke, fire, splintering metal, and high-tech weaponry.

Thus, in a handful of pages—less than a score of images—"The Pact" establishes its milieu and symbolic conflicts: New Genesis versus Apokolips, war versus the desire for peace, cunning versus valor, vengefulness versus mercy and forbearance, and Edenic nature versus hellish technology. The themes are appropriately biblical, the scope epic. In succeeding pages, Kirby, although concerned more with the emotional and spiritual consequences of the war than with spectacle, will serve up striking images of impersonal mass violence, grand but punctuated by grim close-ups of the dead to remind us of the personal costs. The story presents a panoply of killing machines, rendered with Kirby's flair for mythic futurism: Izaya's flying "monitors" drop "de-energizing bombs" that violently disperse the power sources of Apokolips, leaving behind massive craters; Apokolips replies by sending fire-belching dragon-tanks across the "matter threshold" (a kind of transporter) to grind across the fields of New Genesis. Here Kirby's technological sublime is in full sway. Metron, supreme scientist and technologist of the Fourth World, is outed as a willing pawn in this war, for it is he who, in return for access to Darkseid's mysterious "X-element," invents the matter threshold for Apokolips. As the battles get closer and more personal, Kirby's antic inventiveness froths over: "destructi-poles," dog cavalry, "electro-axe," blast-shooting glove—a veritable torrent of notions, all affordances and prods for his graphic imagination. Steppenwolf himself, on dog-back, presses the attack on New Genesis; he breaks through enemy ranks to face the masked "leader" who, it turns out, is Izaya, "the risen dead." Izaya slays him with his war-staff. In the cold silence that follows, Metron appears, and a curious exchange ensues between Izaya and the scientist:

> IZAYA: I could *sense* a silent witness to this fight! Have you come to *survey* your handiwork?
> METRON: This war is *your* doing, Izaya!! Can I help it if *both* sides seek to use me!?
> IZAYA: And when it *serves* your purpose, you *cooperate!!*—And warriors *die* because of it!! (16)

This exchange, a debate over the ethics of using technology to wage war, is surely a post-WWII, post-atomic bomb moment, with Metron standing in for the bombmakers and rocket-scientists of Kirby's own lifetime. Undermining Kirby's spewing delight in high-tech invention, and our own delight in his inventiveness, is a grim recognition of war's technological horrors and of the fact that scientific progress is often underwritten or prodded by military R&D (for both the matter threshold and Metron's traveling Mobius Chair, the consummate explorer's craft, are built with X-element technology). Metron and Izaya alike recognize that it is "obscure and humble" Darkseid who is the master manipulator behind the war, for in fact Darkseid, as Metron reveals, knew all along that Steppenwolf would face Izaya and be killed. "By intrigue, he got *war!* By war, he got *power*!! By power, he got *Steppenwolf*!!" The scene ends with the realization of another mind-boggling, almost farcical idea: Darkseid is literally raining down planetoids on the surface of New Genesis, using "Metron's methods" to hurtle space debris at his enemy.

At this point the story reaches a nightmarish absurdity, with a disjointed series of panels sketching out the ever-accelerating escalation of techno-cosmic war: monstrous, laboratory-bred mutations (a kind of biological warfare); seismic weaponry; massive solar lasers; and, the crowning, almost incomprehensible touch, a panel (see plate 7) depicting a planet-sized "impacter" sent hurtling into "an enemy-captured sun!!!" *Huh?* The desired effect seems to be a kind of ineffability, an overspill of the technological sublime, as the gods' warfare lurches toward the inexplicably grand and cataclysmic. It's both ridiculous and awe-inspiring: beyond human ken. (The sound effect accompanying this image is distinctly unhelpful: *VRAWWWW!!* What does that signify?) The caption here is even ambiguous regarding which "enemy" has captured the sun and whose impacter is crashing into it, though the preceding sequence would suggest that the sun-capturing enemy is Apokolips. The vaulting ridiculousness of the panel makes a point: the escalation of the "god-machines" has become a meaningless, leapfrogging absurdity.

Yet what really matters about this panel is that it ushers in a page that suddenly, drastically, wrenches gears, drawing us back to the personal dimension on which, Kirby has already told us, the story must focus. The remaining four panels on this page are devoted to Izaya, the Inheritor.

As our eyes move downward, from the impacter to the second panel, we see something rather different from the impersonal images of carnage on the preceding page. Now we see Izaya as if from a low angle, looking up. His face is graven, his mouth downturned, severe, his eyes literally empty. He appears spiritually evacuated. But for his mane of hair he looks more like Darkseid than like himself, though his features also bear a touch of sorrow. Inside of Izaya, the caption tells us, something dies with each new ratcheting-up of the war. "*Where* will this *end?*" the narration asks. How can Izaya presume to "save" New Genesis while destroying so much? This cosmic arms race is killing what's inside him. In the next panel, Izaya's face is unseen, buried in his hands. A pivotal moment. "This is *Darkseid's* way," he says. "I am *infected* by Darkseid!!" Izaya realizes he must find himself: not the warrior, but, as he states in the following panel, "the *true* servant of those he leads!!" (a line that reveals much about both Kirby's conception of leadership and Highfather's role in the saga). At the bottom of the page, Izaya heads out, alone and quiet, into the ruined and blasted landscape that was New Genesis.

The following two pages represent one of the most unusual "origins" in comics and one of the strangest and finest scenes in Kirby's career. Izaya wanders over the scarred and ravaged land, littered with the remains of war machines and infested with bacterial agents. It's a wasteland, he realizes bitterly, but seeing this devastation only solidifies his resolve: he will, he must, change his ways. Like Steppenwolf, he realizes, "I've allowed myself to *follow* the mad dreams of Darkseid!!—From which *no one* can survive!!!" And so Izaya doffs his armor, discards his war-staff, and declares, even as the elements begin to fizz and crackle around him, that he has renounced "the way of war." This is not something easily done; it is a desperate, angry renunciation. Shouting into the mounting wind, Izaya proclaims himself free of Darkseid's way. And yet he does not know what he is looking for or where his authentic self resides: "*Where is Izaya!!!??* WHERE IS IZAYA!!!??" The excess of punctuation matches the sudden, eruptive intensity of the images: Kirby begins to slash the page with lines of hurricane force, laying on the pathetic fallacy with a vengeance. As "violent electrical flashes twist and *stab* across the *darkened* land," Izaya is reduced/freed/exalted to the point of simply screaming his own name into the wind. In intense, borderless close-up, almost nothing remains to define his face except so many violent ink-strokes (Mike Royer's masterful rendering of Kirby's no-doubt frenetic pencils—*go see it for yourself!*). Form is defined by movement: a true Kirbyism. One can almost imagine Kirby's pencil point strafing the page.

As we turn the page (fig. 16) the echo of Izaya's scream becomes a roar, then the tattoo of a "thousand drums beating," urging Izaya's "questing spirit" onwards, onwards, through Kirby and Royer's slashing wind-strokes, toward—well, toward God. Such a reading is irresistibly tempting. But there is no anthropomorphic God here, no outsized echo of humankind like Galactus, but rather an "ageless, inscrutable" presence, waiting not to make itself known, but "for Izaya to communicate!" (20). It is simply a wall, a bare wall of rugged whitish stone standing in the middle of nowhere (one is reminded of the Monolith in Kubrick's *2001*, which Kirby would adapt into comics form a few years later). Suddenly things are calm. Here Izaya is no longer seen in close-up, indeed he is hardly seen at all. We see him from behind as he approaches the wall. His ragged arms and his staff do the work of foreground framing, directing our attention to the wall and defining the imagined distance between it and Izaya. If we think a still, small voice should follow Kirby's crackling atmospherics, we are mistaken, as Izaya's voice in bold, bold lettering bellows: "IF I AM IZAYA THE INHERITOR—WHAT IS MY INHERITANCE!?" This is the moment of Izaya's spiritual crisis and exaltation, and, for Kirby, such moments are usually wrestling-with-an-angel moments, violently rendered (for violence *is* Kirby's coinage) and fully in tune with human suffering, dismay, and anger. If the wall represents God, Kirby's hero comes before him with a booming question, almost a demand. After a momentary calm,

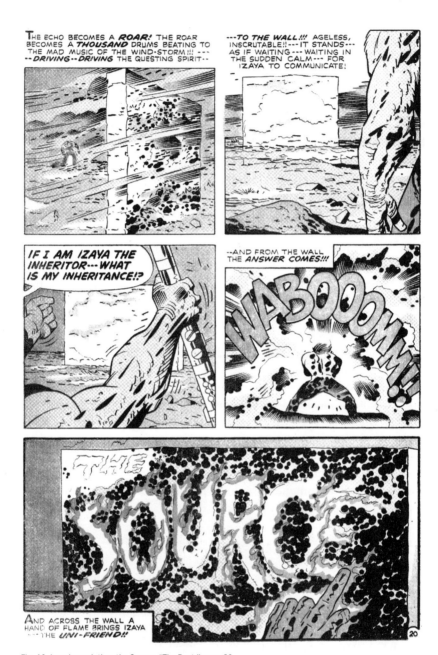

Fig. 16. Izaya's revelation: the Source. "The Pact," page 20.

then, comes a burning-bush moment, for the wall answers with an explosion (WABOOOOMM!!) and then, unexpectedly, gives a sign of comfort etched in fire, for "across the wall a hand of flame brings Izaya" the Source, which, the caption tells us, is "the Uni-Friend." Said caption, though, belies the fierceness of the images. We are on the horns of paradox: the wall, aloof and inscrutable, has answered first in an explosion (like God's rejoinder to Job, it's no comfort) but then also, curiously, in the written, the graphical, words of a "friend." A friend to all.

Such a highpoint in Kirby's narrative drawing: the crux of the Fourth World, delivered with vehemence and poignancy that seem to bring the artist's whole worldview to light. Notably, it's a religious scene, and "The Pact" is a religious story.

My point is not that the story is theologically rigorous, nor that it may be explained away as a precise allegory; that kind of programmed approach was, I believe, alien to Kirby, and in any case I am not suggesting a univocal religious interpretation. There have been such readings of Kirby comics (in fanzines, for example, when the subject of his "gods" comes up), and to my thinking they are unconvincing to the extent that they are decisive and closed. Like most mainstream comic books, Kirby's can have little to do with religion as conventionally depicted—religion in its institutional guises—but on occasion they point toward a kind of inward spiritual grappling. "The Pact" is one such occasion, probably the starkest in Kirby's published work. My sense is that "The Pact" tries to locate the crucial difference between Highfather and Darkseid, between New Genesis and Apokolips, and that that difference entails, finally, Izaya's (and Kirby's) questing and questioning relationship to a higher power, alternately an inscrutable presence and a sustaining "friend." That relationship crystallizes in one inevitably graphic confrontation, a moment of self-reflexivity that refigures God as the divine graphiator: a hand of fire, messaging, inscribing.

Kirby's paradoxical sense of the divine has everything to do with the vital tensions animating this tale. "The Pact" is not Pollyannaish in its morality; in fact, the gods of both Apokolips and New Genesis are capable of cruel warfare, indiscriminate destruction, and murder. Kirby's gods are human in their refusal to fit entirely into bipolar, good/evil categories. If the larger premise of the Fourth World seems to insist on such a Manichean schema, the best stories in it slip from the schema and into vivid, conflicted life. "The Pact" is one such story, rife with moral ambiguities, some of which Kirby may have even let slip through his fingers unawares. Izaya kills and, then, through struggle, anger, and confusion, renounces killing. If the Fourth World is about a super-war, "The Pact" says no to war. The effect is confusing, but this is what makes the story irreducible—and great.

It is also what makes the story responsive to its time. Created on the cusp of 1972 in the Nixonian Vietnam era, indeed during the so-called Vietnamization of that proxy war, "The Pact" enacts a deep ambivalence about the moral and psychic costs of war to a beleaguered United States. Reportedly, Kirby opposed Nixon and developed deep misgivings about the war in Vietnam (Evanier, *King* 177 and Afterword, *Omnibus* I, 395), though he never expressed such views openly in his work. Around this time he purportedly promised a strip about Vietnam to *The Someday Funnies* (Michel Choquette's unrealized countercultural comics anthology, an idea born at *Rolling Stone* magazine), but then abandoned the idea because he found the subject "overwhelmingly sad" (Levin 56).

In any case, *The New Gods* had already implicitly addressed the war in "The Glory Boat" (#6), which is animated by a conflict between two humans, one a hawk, one a dove: on the one hand the Nixon-esque industrialist and militarist Farley Sheridan, a hectoring WWII veteran who remembers "the beach at Normandy" (a scene whose aftermath Kirby himself, as a GI, waded through); on the other, his son Richard, a conscientious objector who ironically turns out to be the more heroic when facing death, sacrificing himself to save his father (a twist on the father/son duality embodied by Darkseid and Orion). "The Glory Boat" leaves Farley to live out his dearly bought life in regret and wonder, as Kirby asks, "*What* is *man* in the last analysis—his *philosophy*—or *himself!?*" (26). This bedrock ambiguity calls into question both Farley's hawkish posturing—he caves in when confronted by the terrors of Apokolips—and Richard's nobly presented pacifism, for he fights back when his family is threatened. Richard's rejection of violence is likened to that of New Genesis (says Lightray, "I know of a place where *everybody's* like that!!"), but New Genesis itself is shown to be morally shaded by the realities of war, since both Orion and Lightray must kill. "The Pact" runs further with this same ambivalence, and is one of the rare moments in Kirby's oeuvre when he explicitly questions the code of violence that underlies his heroic tales. When Kirby was working full-tilt on the Fourth World, he seems to have been alive to the contradictions both in the world and in his work.

Further moral ambiguity—a constitutive ambiguity, without which the Fourth World makes no sense—rears up in the final four pages of "The Pact," which recount how a ceasefire between New Genesis and Apokolips is brokered via a strange "secret" bargain. This "pact," involving an exchange of heirs, will buy the peace. Darkseid consents, not because he wants peace but because he wants time, time to plot. So he arranges to send his son, raised in exile without knowing his father, to New Genesis; in return, Izaya's child is to be brought to Apokolips. The two children will be exchanged across the matter threshold. This pact, tardily revealed here, well into the saga (issue #7, remember), is the underlying secret of the Fourth World.

As Granny Goodness delivers Izaya's son, a mere baby, Darkseid's words hint at both Old Testament sacrifice (Abraham and Isaac?) and a Blakean contrariety: "Izaya's *whelp*, eh? This will *hurt* him!! He's surrendered his prize lamb——for a *tiger!!*" Even as he consigns the New Genesis child to Granny's "orphanage," Darkseid anticipates the boy's eventual escape from that cruel place. That escape, he prophesies, will constitute a breaking of the pact, which is exactly what he wants. With gleeful irony, therefore, Granny christens the boy "Scott Free" (no other name is given, nor any information about his mother or his birth). Then Darkseid's own fierce son, somewhat older, and long since wrested from his equally fierce mother, Tigra, is forced into the matter threshold and dispatched to New Genesis. Raging, mistrustful, vicious, and uncomprehending, the boy finds himself in a strange place, where sits a white-haired "elder" at a table, head bowed to the tabletop in grief, hands clutching a staff. Drawing a dagger, the boy prepares to attack (fig. 17):

> I was told I'd find my *father* here!! If *you're* my father, *speak!!*
>   You *won't* speak to me! You'll *never* speak to me! *You hate me!!* HATE ME!!

Furious, he swings the knife, but the elder speaks, his words halting the dagger in mid-plunge: "'Hate' is *no* longer a word in this place!! *Put down that weapon!!*——son——!" The elder, Izaya, stands. His lionlike mane of hair has gone white. He holds, not an elaborate war-staff as earlier, but a simple Mosaic shepherd's crook. When the boy asks Izaya if he is his father, the elder replies simply, "Only if *you* wish me to be! I am *Highfather!!*" Stretching out his hand, Izaya proffers friendship to the boy, saying that they "have *need* of each other." The boy, Orion, hesitates, but Izaya urges, "The hand, or the *weapon*, Orion!! I, *too*, had to make that choice!!" Orion drops the dagger. Though he does not clasp Highfather's hand, he follows him, declaring his trust "for now." *Thus*, Kirby tells us, *it began*.

As origin stories go, "The Pact" turns out to be an ironic one, muddying the Fourth World's putative moral certainty. The tale shows us not only how war devastated and degraded New Genesis, but also how Scott Free's sufferings were ordained to end that war, thus to purchase the planet's rebirth. Without the pact, New Genesis cannot be restored to its paradisiacal state. In

Fig. 17. Orion meets Izaya, now Highfather. "The Pact," page 24.

other words, the rebirth of that Edenic world hinges on the "orphaning" and effective sacrifice of young Scott Free on the nightmare world of Apokolips. The ethics of this tradeoff are never openly discussed by Kirby, but, tellingly, when Orion first meets Highfather the old man is bent over with grief, and indeed Highfather admits that he has "need" of Orion. This seems to speak to emotional loss as well as strategic necessity. Clearly Highfather has given up something (someone) dear to him.

If Scott Free's suffering is the price of peace, then, conversely, Orion's up-bringing on New Genesis is a way of assimilating and retraining the warlike. Izaya teaches Orion the value of a hand extended in friendship, even though Orion retains something of his ferocity and capacity for violence: an inheri-tance that forms the nucleus of his internal agon, his animating self-conflict. Ironically, Orion's stature as the champion of New Genesis will depend upon this conflictedness and anger, in essence on his origin as Apokolips's exiled son. That inner conflict, we are to understand, gives Orion his edge, and will be essential to defeating his father. By the same token, defeating Darkseid be-comes the goal that channels if not tames Orion's helpless fury. As Highfather tells Superman in *Jimmy Olsen* #147 (March 1972), "There was a *fierce* young one [. . .] But we found a *need* for him here!! And it *helped* him mightily!!" (23). It is symbolically crucial that Orion, the exile of Apokolips, is brought up by Highfather and so given the family he never had, whereas Scott, the exile of New Genesis, is deprived of family and consigned to an orphanage. If both Orion the Hunter and Mister Miracle are shaped by nature and by nurture (or in Scott's case lack of nurture), Kirby implies that the development of both will be critical to stopping Darkseid, and that New Genesis, ultimately, will get the better end of the pact.

Curiously, Orion, who is older than Scott Free at the time of the pact, will turn out to be the one more profoundly influenced by his surroundings. He will take up the cause of his adoptive world, while, in contrast, Scott, who is depicted as a baby at the time of the exchange and thus presumably will un-derstand his origins and himself even less, will resist the values of his adoptive world. Scott will remain a hero in spite of the brutalizing treatment meted out to him on Apokolips, an argument, perhaps, for his innate goodness. One might be tempted to say that, in Kirby's view, nature will out, but this does not seem to be case with Orion, whose connection to New Genesis changes him profoundly (though without soothing his inner turmoil). As it turns out, it is not simply and automatically the case for Scott either, for he too needs a patriarchal mentor to guide him, a teacher who, from within the nightmare world of Apokolips, prompts, challenges, and inspires Scott to seek escape. That figure is Himon.

## "HIMON"

The story "Himon" is companion to "The Pact," though published about six months later (*Mister Miracle* #9). The crowning chapter in the *Bildungsroman* of Scott Free, "Himon" serves as the prequel to Scott's various adventures as Mister Miracle, super escape artist. It delivers on hints and promises dropped in prior issues (#5–7) in a series of short backup stories titled "Young Scott Free" that depict key moments from Scott's adolescence in Granny Goodness's horrific "orphanage." Capitalizing on all that came before, "Himon" shows just what sets Scott on the path to freedom and how he escapes from Apokolips (and thus inadvertently fulfills Darkseid's larger plan).

Himon—master of disguise, escape artist par excellence, and above all the "master of theories"—is Kirby's embodiment of imagination.[1] A protean genius, Himon has a disconcerting tendency to "phase" in and out of anyplace, anytime; he can go and escape from anywhere. He has the power to shake off bodies like dry husks, thus to sidestep death again and again. Though Kirby offers a prosaic explanation for Himon's impossible escapes—that he can create convincing replicas or stand-ins for his body by scientific means, echoing Nick Fury's "Life Model Decoys" at Marvel—more than anything Himon is a metaphor. Every literal-minded explanation of his powers falls short. Himon is imagination personified: the inspiration for designers, craftsmen, dancers, artists. His visionary energy threatens Darkseid's suffocating, totalitarian world order.

On Apokolips free exercise of the imagination carries terrible risks. Himon's students often die for dreaming. When young Scott Free witnesses dreamers tortured and destroyed, he cracks, and finally fully commits to freeing himself from Apokolips. For Scott, Himon becomes no longer merely a source of furtive escapism but a genuine means of escape. The story of "Himon," then, is about the horrors that break Scott's conformism and harden his resolve for imaginative freedom—as the cover of the issue says, to bust out.

The tale is unpleasant, yet exhilarating. Its setting is the nightmare of Apokolips, and its pervasive violence is cold, appalling. Apokolips, though dulled by decades of reuse, remains one of Kirby's most frightening ideas: a blotted, smoking, industrialized hell that makes mythology out of the author's formative experiences, fusing Lower East Side squalor with visions of a thumping, jackbooted, Nazi-like technocracy. "Himon" depicts this worldscape without much grandeur but with an astringent, unsentimental, brutal clarity. Few dark places in Kirby's oeuvre can match it (the City of Toads, perhaps, from *Eternals* #8–10, or the chilly dystopia of *OMAC* #1). In keeping with this setting, the tale metes out torment and death—a sudden surplus of outrageous violence—with a steely matter-of-factness.

This story underscores Kirby's larger ambitions for the Fourth World, insofar as it assumes a knowing audience that is following *Mister Miracle* and *New Gods* at the same time (and indeed a note on page 1 links it with "The Pact"). The tale foreshadows how Scott's escape from Apokolips will factor into, if not spark, a new war; darkly prophetic dialogue between Himon and Metron hints that Scott's moment of decision may be a turning point in the whole saga. These hints reveal just how much narrative and thematic material Kirby had in his head at the time, and how meaningful the larger tapestry of the Fourth World had become for him. This was a decisive moment in Kirby's career. For one whose work had most often been driven by the tyranny of deadlines and whose degree of engagement (not his work ethic, which was tireless, but his artistic interest) would often vary even within a single month, Kirby was unusually focused and committed, again fully alive to the nature of his work, during this period. His engagement was at its fiercest, and his maintenance of continuity, so often a trouble spot for him, most deliberate.

The scripting in "Himon" boasts, for Kirby, unusual compression and elegance. The cadences of his script are relentless, incantatory, and hypnotic. More importantly, the frantic prose is tuned to the tale's overriding themes. Consider for example the opening description of Greyborders as the "raw and dirty edge" of Apokolips from which Darkseid siphons his power (1). This caption gives crucial insight: that the taproots of power are often found among the powerless. The key here is the concept of belief, invoked by the next page's reference to "endless gods" (2). The line may be puzzling at first, but when Kirby suggests that the so-called lowlies of Armagetto *believe* in Darkseid, that they "glory" in his service, and that Darkseid will allow them to worship only him, then the idea of Kirby's gods takes on new relevance: here Darkseid is indeed godlike. The central problem in "Himon" is that most of the lowlies do believe in Darkseid, so much so that they fear and hate the very figure who might be the agent of their liberation, Himon. Kirby's lowlies, though downtrodden and wretched, are not idealized sufferers waiting for the possibility of freedom, but instead cringing devotees of Darkseid's order. Behind this is a bleak and pitiless understanding of totalitarianism: its logic, its strategies, its stunting effects. The lowlies have been raised with a slave mentality, so that they cling to their role as "nothings," mere objects or functionaries in Darkseid's repressive regime (as Himon remarks, page 7). They have swallowed the oppressors' cant: what is done to the lowlies is justified in terms of being done *for* them, on their behalf. And what threatens Darkseid's reign is construed as "infection" (3). Willik the "protector," a soldier for Darkseid, claims to defend the lowlies' "pride and spirit" even as he orders the immolation (by flamethrower) of an entire crowd of them, one of the more shockingly offhand moments of violence in all Kirby's work. Willik's aim is to drive Himon from

Fig. 18. Himon's hand reaches out, beckoning. Jack Kirby, with Mike Royer (inks and lettering), "Himon." *Mister Miracle* #9 (July–Aug. 1972), page 5, panel 2. © DC Comics.

hiding. Bleakest of all is Himon's tacit acceptance, or, if not acceptance, then simple businesslike acknowledgment, of this terrible price: the murders are taken as a given, and Himon, as ever, moves on. The story registers the shocks of war with alarming bluntness.

For the reader, Himon is a hand before he is a face (fig. 18). As Willik incinerates the crowd, Himon stands amidst the flames of sacrifice, a silhouette in quick pen-strokes à la Kirby's Human Torch, and what emerges from that fire is a hand: a clenched fist, goading Willik toward confrontation (5). The hand beckons toward the fire—*Step in, Willik!*—but Himon then vanishes. Turning the page, we find ourselves in a new scene, and Himon's hand now reaches out from a blank and shimmering wall toward "Young Scott Free," beckoning his aid. If Willik was lured into the flames, Scott too is invited to reach out. One is forcibly reminded of the hand of flame, writing its divine words on the Source Wall. Himon is like that hand.

Scott does extend Himon a helping hand, pulling him free of the wall. This is ironic, for in truth it is Himon who is extending *his* hand to liberate Scott. Even as Scott pulls him free, Himon provokes him with mocking epithets, pointing out the slave mentality within him: "You're a *nothing!* You're an *object!* Your body is a *weapon!*——And your mind is its *trigger!*" His words underscore the story's axial conflict: that of the hive mentality, with its notions of status and hierarchy, versus the power of the freed imagination. Though Scott proudly identifies himself as "an aerotrooper of Darkseid's *own* elite," Himon gives the unflinching gloss: that Scott is in essence a function of Darkseid's will, and a killer. Only when he confronts Scott face to face do we see Himon's face full-on for the first time (page 7, panel 3). The moment is shocking because it makes obvious, retroactively, how Himon's identity has thus far been hidden from view. At last we see him, just as band of his "misfits" does, and this matters.

Himon's gang of young misfits is an odd bunch: Kreetin, Bravo, Zep, Weldun, and the mute artist Auralie. Together they comprise yet another Kirby-klatch of representative types, recalling the X-Men or the Forever People (even down to an inwardly and outwardly "beautiful" dreamer, in this case Auralie). These particular youths, though, are different, for they are mostly frustrated and incomplete. Scott, a prideful young stormtrooper (a "skinhead," as Himon calls him), is embarrassed to be among them, the so-called dregs of Apokolips society, but at the same time he is drawn to what Himon has to offer. He admits that what Himon has shown him "works" (8). When Scott likens himself to Kreetin, who, he says, "despises [Himon] as much as *I* do," the comparison is revealing, for though Kreetin has constructed a Mother Box, he lacks the animating spirit to activate it. Kreetin's problem is that he thinks mechanistically: he sees the Mother Box as a mere bundle of "gadgets." In short, he is myopic, unimaginative. When an angry mob comes for Himon, Kreetin's Mother Box does not allow him to "phase out" and get away, but Himon barters himself to ensure Kreetin's escape (12). Running from the scene, Kreetin encounters Metron, who, getting to the heart of the character, observes that Kreetin's sense of self-preservation has saved his skin but cost him a Mother Box (13–14). Kreetin does not know how to value what he has lost. For him, imagination is "worth mere dust" and Himon's cryptic words are "garbage." This is why Kreetin doesn't "work," as Himon observes: his crude idea of survival forecloses his imagination, his spirit. The slave mentality bends him to the ground (note how he grovels before Metron: page 13). Even the vicious Willik understands that Kreetin has technical skill but no "mystic fire" (17).

That Kreetin should run into Metron, the super-scientist, makes sense, for Metron too is a technician rather than a visionary. Though elsewhere Kirby likens Metron to Prometheus in his ambition, his "boldness and hunger" (*New Gods* #5), "Himon" reveals him to be a mechanist who translates Himon's inspired theorizing into hard, usable fact. Himon, likewise a scientific genius, is a technician too, but not only a technician. The crucial relationship between the two is divulged in a pregnant and disconcerting scene set "on a gutted slag heap near Armagetto" (fig. 19), where, we are told, the mind of the visionary must be "eternally *grounded*" (16). This intriguing paradox—the visionary rooted to the slag heap—scarcely has time to register before Kirby reveals that Himon, "master of theories," is also the one whose ideas "*fostered*

Fig. 19. Himon, master of theories, clasps hands with Metron, master of elements. "Himon," page 16.

Darkseid's power." Tellingly, Himon admits this even as he clasps hands with Metron, who has been a figure of compromise and cunning ever since *New Gods* #1 (as we know from "The Pact," Metron has supplied both sides of the god-war with technologies of mass destruction). That handclasp is electric: again the hand of Himon reaches forward, bathed in glowing energy, communicating ideas and power to someone else, in this case Metron, master of the physical elements.

Because he has abetted Darkseid's evil, Himon declares that he must be on hand "at its end." A kind of penance is at work. The allegory could be read this way: imagination can be harnessed in all sorts of ways, even for the sake of oppression, yet, if not stamped out, it will ultimately subvert the oppressor's cause. Like Metron, then, Himon is a shadowed character, connected by chains of complicity and consequence to the larger god-war. This is why he grows in complexity with repeated readings. Again Kirby implicates good in evil, compromising the Fourth World's starkly drawn Manichean clash of values so as to become more challenging and provocative. Most provoking is the thought that Darkseid, as prophesied in "The Pact," *wants* Scott to escape, or to die in the attempt, thus to sunder the Pact with New Genesis, precipitate war, and propel Darkseid's larger plan of conquest. Metron's goal, it seems, is to make sure that Scott does not die in the attempt, but aside from this he remains enigmatic: one never knows quite what Metron is up to. These larger-than-life characters seem to be watching to see how Scott will react, which is, again, disconcerting. One is reminded of the way the "sons of God" and Satan enter into the Book of Job, the latter with God's permission. Why? Similarly, why is Metron able to maneuver freely on Apokolips? Why does Darkseid appear at story's end, yet let Scott go?

What prompts Scott's ultimate escape is the death of the dreamer, Auralie, at the hands of Willik, who in turn is executed by Himon. This final movement starts with the death of another: ironically, Kreetin, the self-preservationist, who is bluntly dispatched by Willik with a single blow. In another offhandedly cruel moment, the corpse of Kreetin is hung alongside the other misfits, all dead, their bodies limp as empty sacks (18). The offhand manner of Kreetin's death is a surprise, given Kirby's yen for drawn-out, nimbly choreographed violence. By contrast, Kreetin dies by summary execution: once again, death comes matter-of-factly, without Kirby's usual frenetic buzz and without platitudes. Worse by far is the fate meted to Auralie, the dreamer among Himon's misfits, who "creates *beauty*" even in the nightmarish climate of Granny's orphanage. Gazing into a glassy cube, she can make dancing visions appear (9). Thus "poor, brave Auralie" (as Himon calls her) strives to protect and give outward form to her own "inner beauty." Caught by Barda and her female warriors, Auralie is shielded so that her "crime" will go un-discovered, for both Scott and Barda, despite identifying themselves by rank and function like good soldiers, realize that Auralie's uniqueness is important. Barda covers for her (a promising chink in Barda's armor of toughness), and Scott, even as he first encounters Barda, invokes Auralie to explain his own desire to explore further, to seek "*other* roads [and] *other* tricks" (11). Auralie's slender fragility stands for an idea of gentleness; her silent conjuring of danc-ing images represents a vision of art in contrast to Kirby's own hectic and vio-lence-filled world. She becomes the story's key, the character whose sacrifice at last compels Scott to escape. The torture she suffers at Willik's hands—a pair of immobilizing "shock boots" to end all dancing—is symbolically apt and horrific, though, thankfully, more implied than shown (19).

If this scene of implicit torture feels very dark, the sequence that follows is literally so. Its ensuing emotional climax, however, beautifully recalls the turning point of "The Pact." Himon assassinates Willik; immediately after, he speaks to Scott and Barda in a sequence clotted with shadows (page 21, see plate 8). Here Kirby's words and drawings collaborate beautifully, force-fully linking Himon's visionary imagination to the generative power of the Source. Himon explains to Scott that it is the Source that powers his Mother Box, and Scott realizes that this same power makes Darkseid afraid: "Then Darkseid fears us all! He fears what he can't control!" Inky shadows dominate until we see Scott, full-on, his face at once troubled and hopeful (panel 5). Again the close-up, long withheld, comes as a culminating, affirming shock. On this same page, Himon's own face is again shaded, and, in panel 2, almost graven in its mysteriousness and intensity: an up-angle view of his face, with eyes pupil-less and blank, recalls the very moment in "The Pact" when Izaya rejects the way of war. The blank whites of the eyes suggest both emptiness and inspiration; as in "The Pact," the image occurs as Kirby's thoughts turn toward the Source. Though Himon's execution of Willik has cast harsh shad-ows over him, he acknowledges that the Source is the root of his power, and, as he speaks of it, he seems inspirited, invigorated, and deeply alive: "I *dream!* I *roam* the universe!!" As in Izaya's confrontation with the Source Wall, so here there is a sense of awe and connection, enlivening if not entirely comforting. The scripting waxes eloquent as Himon describes the nature of the Source: "It *lives!* It *burns!* When we reach out and touch it——the core of us is *magnified!*"

This too is one of the most heavily fraught pages in the Fourth World, and one of Kirby's most moving scenes. The narrative drawing here, a tense play of shadows, reaches beyond "Himon" to the greater saga and shows Kirby at his most shrewd and focused. The synergy of art and text is taut, and the emotional payoff tremendous, especially for those who have followed the trials of "Young Scott Free" from the outset. The ironic juxtaposition of (graphic) darkness and (thematic and textual) insight lends the scene an animating tension. Royer's inking is faithful to the dark tonal quality of Kirby's under-drawing (as confirmed in *The Jack Kirby Quarterly* #11, which reprints copies of Kirby's pencils for this page), boosting the heft and eloquence of the scene.

After this understated climax, the resolution of "Himon" is lurching, un-even: the requisite breathless action, disguising the fact that the most impor-tant stuff has already happened. The last five pages careen through an abrupt transition and into a headlong chase toward, finally, Scott's longed-for escape. Yet this last sequence is formally intriguing as well. If, as he bolts for freedom, Scott often runs directly "toward" us readers, at other times, especially in the final two pages, he runs "away" from us into the distance. This visual logic is forecast by the comic book's cover, on which Scott hurtles toward us but at the same time seems to be yanking "back" the gate or barrier that confines him, turning his body, graphically, into a tense, exploding "X" of motion: his body is leaping for us but his arms are wrenching backwards. The cover is one of Kirby's strongest and most relevant of the period, in that it underscores the point that Scott's headlong flight is checked or frustrated by obstacles he must tear apart by violence. The tense shot/reverse-shot exchanges during the escape sequence follow this same logic: mostly they show Scott affronting the picture plane, that is, the plane of the page, moving alternately toward and away from the reader. Kirby understood intuitively that the picture plane is a site of confrontation between text and reader: panel bordering works not only as a means of organizing the page and parsing the action, but also as a dynamic constraint, a barrier toward which and away from which the action moves, often threatening in an illusory way to burst "through." A tremendous amount of graphic conflict—crackling, energizing conflict—goes on at the picture plane, drawing both artist and reader into the action. This is to say that Kirby knows that we readers are there, and organizes the action into a series of feints toward or away from us.

Affronting the page, as if to tear through it, is a large part of what makes certain Kirby stories work ("The Glory Boat" being another outstanding ex-ample). Yet here, intriguingly, Scott's final escape occurs inward, so to speak, away from the reader, away from Darkseid and Himon for that matter, into a Boom Tube (fig. 20). This moment of escape comes just after Scott's climactic cry—*LET ME BE SCOTT FREE—AND FIND MYSELF!*—and is the only mute panel in the story. Scott's shout is in response to both Darkseid and Himon, and for this he faces us, resolute, angry perhaps, craving liberty and self-understanding. Himon, instead of bidding Scott remain with him, urges him on to liberty, and so Scott sets out on an echo of his father Izaya's same

Fig. 20. Scott's escape. "Himon," page 26, panels 1–4.

quest in "The Pact," that is, to find himself ("Where is Izaya!!!??"). Having at last spoken up for himself, Scott turns from us and leaps into the distance, sans text, to freedom. Retreating from the space of violence (the picture plane), he throws himself after receding possibility (the Boom Tube). The moment recalls Orion's crossing of the matter threshold at the end of "The Pact," and leaves us with a similar open-endedness (Scott's journey will take him to Earth, where *Mister Miracle* #1 finds, or found, him).

"Himon" is bound to strike, indeed has struck, some fans as an autobiographical cryptogram. The tale, after all, meshes with our understanding of Kirby's public career and private circumstances, including his experience of war, his professional frustrations, and perhaps his faith. Reading Kirby's stories, particularly later stories, through an autobiographical lens is common. But what matters most is that "Himon" deals with the liberating power of the imagination not in some hollowly sentimental way, sans complexity and friction, nor in some narrow, obscurely personal way, but in a grandly complex, at times unsettling, and always dramatic fashion.

"The Pact" and "Himon," conceptually paired, are among the several chapters that urge fans to call the Fourth World, yes, Kirby's masterpiece. In "The Pact," Kirby's misgivings about war—war being one of his constant subjects—blossom into a pained and eloquent parable that assays spiritual and religious themes with, for him, unusual directness and clarity, but also a haunting ambiguity. Implicitly, the story testifies to the mood of a culture mired in endless and incomprehensible war, the aggrieved, self-accusing, spiritually unmoored America recognizable in so many artifacts of the Vietnam War period. "The Pact" bears out Kirby's reported opposition to that war. In "Himon," meanwhile, Kirby's noted fascination with the promise of youth, implicit in *Jimmy Olsen* and *The Forever People*, collides head-on with his understanding of totalitarianism. Scott Free is like a member of the *Hitler-Jugend* in need of deprogramming, and Himon, the agent of his liberation, is nothing less than the walking principle of imagination unfettered. For all the story's violence and darkness, it is about waking up and busting out.

Together these two stories show Kirby the narrative artist at his zenith. They represent a period of explosive growth and sheer runaway enthusiasm, coupled with searching, motivated content. They are examples of that which, from the outside, seems so unlikely and yet has occurred again and again in mainstream comics: a bid for artistic autonomy and personal expression within the very idiom of a heteronomous, mass-produced art. Kirby never got quite what he wanted, but in these comics he did, for a moment, break free.

## 7

# "UNEXPECTED CONSTANTS"

## Kirby's *Eternals* versus the Marvel Universe

Consider the following comments culled from the letter column of Marvel's *Black Panther* during Jack Kirby's 1977–78 tenure on that series:

> [Don] McGregor's storylines were as complex as the real world, and his characters were genuine human beings. After [McGregor's] "The Panther's Rage" and "The Panther vs. the Klan," there is only one word to describe [Kirby's first issue]: obscene.

> . . . The Panther as originally depicted in the *Avengers* was deeply concerned with the position of blacks in America, and again [McGregor's] storyline . . . developed this original background in an adult fashion. Please, please don't abandon this real world to go careening throughout the universe. (#3, May 1977)

> I was unhappy to see Kirby take over the series, because he approaches comics with a different type of fantasy. His version of T'Challa [the Black Panther] detracts from the character as [previously] developed . . . I'm in the strange position of liking Kirby's work very much, but detesting what he has done to a character I had really come to like. (#4, July 1977)

> I'm not sure which technique you used while operating on him—psychosurgery, electroshock therapy, lobotomy, or thorazine treatments—but whatever it was, it wiped out the Panther's character completely. (#5, Sept. 1977)

. . . to have this realistic Panther exist at the same time as Kirby's fantasy Panther detracts from both characterizations. Would it be possible to draw some sort of distinction between the two . . . say, Kirby's T'Challa exists in the past, while the Panther currently appearing in *The Avengers* is the modern man? (#8, Mar. 1978)

. . . one of the disturbing qualities of Kirby's projects is that they seem too unrestrained, too outrageous, too "comic book-ish." I find myself cringing at bits of dialogue. (#6, Nov. 1977)

No offense, but a lot of the time your writing is childish. (#5)

These comments, and others like them, pepper the "Panther Postscripts" column throughout most of Kirby's run. They represent, if not a gathering consensus, then apparently a vocal plurality of fans.

Consider likewise the following commentary by letter-writer Larry Twiss during Kirby's 1976–77 run on *Captain America and the Falcon*: "When the King returns, he returns. All of the wonder and power of the old Marvel magic is with us once again. It's really like a step back to what everybody is always calling the good old days. But the good old days change to what-is-to-be the good old days of tomorrow, or today. And today, characterization plays such a big part. I miss it in Jack's current work, especially since we all have the subplot-filled days of Steve Englehart fresh in our minds" (#200, Aug. 1976). Twiss' comments appeared in *Captain America*'s "bicentennial" issue, the climax of Kirby's lengthy "Madbomb" story (issues 193–200). But such comments echoed throughout Kirby's run, occasioning a protracted debate in the series' letter column (whose title, "Let's Rap with Cap," nicely sums up the spirit of the era). Fan criticism ran from the mild or bemused, such as "The extreme changes in personality that occurred in the heroes when you took over were unsettling" (#206, Feb. 1977), to the downright vituperative: "I suppose it's fitting that the man who created Captain America be allowed to destroy him, but I can't let it go unnoticed . . . Does Jack know how to write in the real world?" (#206). In these columns there is the persistent, nagging sense that Kirby might be an anachronism, a concern encapsulated by a letter in #207 (Mar. 1977) that begins, "The problem, put simply, is that Jack Kirby is scripting 1963 comics." This same letter underlines a question asked by many fans, namely, why is Kirby regarded as "a law unto himself? Why ignore the last six years . . . ? Why sacrifice logic and realism in the name of action?" In fact, the letter columns of both *Black Panther* and *Captain America* were preoccupied during Kirby's tenure with questions of logic, consistency, and verisimilitude, questions tethered to assumptions about Marvel's efforts at social realism and, above all, its maintenance of continuity. Kirby's return to Marvel in the late mid-seventies, then, was no unalloyed triumph. Actually, it was disastrous.

Between Marvel's first gestures toward continuity in the early sixties and its fetishizing of continuity in the mid-seventies, Kirby had left, then come back again. In the interim at DC, he had enjoyed a brief period of limited editorial autonomy during which he had created the Fourth World, wreaking havoc with (though also laying a seedbed for) DC's as-yet inchoate continuity. His return to Marvel ostensibly came with a similar promise of freedom: Kirby would be editor of his own books, and get to tell his stories, his way. Although some Marvel fans had been repelled by his DC work, his return was keenly anticipated: Marvel's "Bullpen Bulletins" (i.e., hype pages) were speckled with teasers about his upcoming comics; also, in September 1975, just as his new Marvels were about to begin, the company's in-house fanzine *FOOM* ("Friends of Ol' Marvel") devoted an issue to Kirby's homecoming, proclaiming "Jack's Back!" and "The King is Here!" Expectations were high. Yet disappointment was unavoidable, for the Marvel to which Kirby returned in late 1975 was not the Marvel of the previous decade, the Marvel he had done so much to build. In a sense, it had become more chaotic, with a succession of editors-in-chief—heirs to Stan Lee—to mind the store. Paradoxically, however, it had also become more fanatical than ever about the idea of continuity. To Kirby that entangled continuity would prove more restrictive than generative.

In the Marvel of the mid-seventies, scripters, rather than pencilers, held the reins: an ironic reversal of the situation in the early to mid-sixties, when Lee, Kirby, and Steve Ditko had pioneered the "Marvel style" of production. These scripters, many having come out of organized comic book fandom, had colonized concepts birthed by Kirby in the previous decade, investing these concepts with their own meanings via long, elaborate story arcs: for example, Roy Thomas's Kree/Skrull War in *Avengers* (1971–72), or Steve Englehart's *Avengers/Defenders* war (1973). Characters originally designed by Kirby had become vehicles for cultural argument in terms more explicit than what Kirby was used to. As Bradford Wright observes, the comic books of the time participated in the general "culture of self-interrogation," opening "a window into the chaos" and social anomie of the period and admitting a "sense of disillusionment, resignation, and even nihilism"; they had begun to engage, as the mainstream never had before, in overt criticism of social norms and ideology, as well as in trippy philosophizing (155–156). For example, circa 1973–74 Englehart had posed issues of patriotism, duty, and political disaffection, post-Vietnam, in the typically super-patriotic *Captain America*, even attacking the

Watergate-ensnared Nixon in veiled form and having the hero abandon his star-spangled identity in favor of that of the Nomad, an estranged and rootless wanderer. Meanwhile Don McGregor's "Black Panther" run (in the ill-titled series *Jungle Action*) had spotlighted issues of race and racism blithely ignored by Kirby and Lee, the Panther's creators. The *X-Men*, fallow for years, had recently been revived (1975), and its scripter Chris Claremont would soon exploit its obvious potential as a means of criticizing prejudice and xenophobia, issues lightly hinted at by Kirby and Lee but brought to the fore by Thomas and then doubly underscored by Claremont. Even as these writers sought to bring real-world issues explicitly to the forefront of Marvel's stories, they also shepherded and extended the company's burgeoning continuity.

Marvel was now a scripter's world. Its inter-title continuity was rigorously defended by writers both fannish and professional. From its pell-mell origins, the days when Kirby had tossed out one absurd, glorious idea after another, Marvel continuity had stabilized—or, if not stabilized, then at least reached a point at which stability was taken as the necessary goal—under the scripters' touch. The once-radical high concepts of yesterday now served as pillars of a "Universe" that both inspired and hemmed in creativity in the present. Continuity, along with editorial mass, pressured production, and writer-editors (as opposed to cartoonists) were the era's stars. Until the imposition of a tighter editorial regime near the end of the seventies, these writer-editors developed personal fiefdoms and basked in the relative freedom afforded by Stan Lee's retirement from the editor-in-chief's position. At the same time, they reveled in the sprawling complexity of Marvel's vast narrative, its Universe.

Lee had hardly been forgotten, however. In his role as publisher, he continued to be Marvel's paterfamilias, its grand old man and revered public spokesman. Indeed, Lee's influence, in the corporate mythology of Marvel and in the self-imaging of its star writers, had never been greater. Lee's star was ascendant, despite his virtual retirement from comic-book making years before; the lessons he had taught were all-pervasive. But at the same time newer, younger writers—such as McGregor, or Steve Gerber—dared to do work that, though hedged by the conventions of the superhero, was unusually personal, even bizarre and quixotic. The Marvel "revolution" of the sixties had certainly done its work, for projects of a decidedly subversive cast, adolescent in spirit and imbued with a countercultural sensibility, were sneaking in to what had been mainly a medium for young children, that is, the Comics Code-era comic book. Lee had been the guide and model for the new writers, and, having progressed from editor-in-chief to publisher to corporate icon, had his name added to every masthead (*Stan Lee Presents . . .*). He had drawn in a flock of writers determined to work in his name, but also determined to do their own thing. Again, many came up out of the fan subculture.

At this point wordage was dominant: under Thomas and subsequent editors, verbiage had crowded and cropped the visual. Scriptwriters, at least as much as artists, defined the new Marvel, and, in the new fan-oriented environment, a succession of young editors-in-chief sought to give shape to what was, in truth, a rather anarchic enterprise. The new editors were determined to conserve and extend what "Stan and Jack" had started, but in the offices there was also a sense of freedom and, frankly, disorganization. Things had changed since 1968, the year of Marvel's sudden expansion and its sale to Perfect Film and Chemical, later Cadence Industries (the big change that had driven Kirby away in the first place). Things had certainly begun to crumble by 1972, when Martin Goodman retired and Lee succeeded him as publisher, appointing his protégé Roy Thomas as the new editor-in-chief. Despite his nominal publishership, Lee had quickly grown tired of, and stepped back from, the day-to-day business of running the company and, as his biographers have put it, had instead "channeled his boundless energy into a vocation that suited him equally well, if not better—publicity" (Raphael and Spurgeon 157). In short, Lee had lost touch with editorial. Meanwhile, the editor-in-chief's job had become a revolving door: Thomas had had several successors in short order. By mid-decade the "freedom" of the Marvel office went hand in hand with disorder and declining sales (in fact, true of comic books generally).

Marvel seemed rudderless in the mid-seventies. To fill the vacuum created by Lee's withdrawal, Cadence hired Al Landau and then James Galton to serve as Marvel's president and assume command of practical business dealings (McLaughlin 162–63). Lee told an interviewer for *FOOM* in early 1977: "I, as publisher, should be responsible for the business end [. . .]. But I don't function that way. I work with Jim Galton, who's president of the company, and is involved in management—in contracts, licensing, circulation, financing, and all that sort of thing. I limit myself just to the creative aspects" (McLaughlin 64). But in fact Lee had little to do with the creative aspects; his role was far different from what it had been in the sixties, and those who worked under him during this period remember him as "hands-off" (Raphael and Spurgeon 151–52). In any case, Marvel's editorial shambles continued until 1978, when former fan and *wunderkind* comics writer Jim Shooter would take to the editor-in-chief position and, controversially, impose tighter order over both production and continuity.[1]

Even before Shooter, though, in the aimlessness of the mid-decade, Marvel's writer-editors cared about continuity. They liked extending and complicating it; they liked moving through it, as fish move through water, pushing and being pushed by it. Even when Marvel was an anarchic mess, the company and its freelancers depended on inter-title continuity for their very identity. Despite how social and ideological change crept in, affecting everything from

*Captain America* to *Doctor Strange* to *The Defenders*, continuity informed, spurred, disciplined, and constrained both writing and art to an ever-greater degree. Marvel and its fandom blurred together.

Some writers produced spirited work under these constraints, and it is no exaggeration to say they loved the depth and complexity of the Marvel Universe. Moreover, Marvel's iconic characters could weather, and exploit, social and ideological change. But Kirby was something else again. Brashly imaginative and congenitally restless, he had never had a taste for the yeoman-like upkeep of continuity, and his new creations at Marvel fit poorly into the cosmology he had midwifed years before. The one that caused the most trouble, the most innovative and ambitious of his new Marvel books, was *The Eternals* (1976–78), an outburst of graphic mythopoesis that offered to rewrite the very history of the world. Like the Fourth World before it, which hijacked aspects of DC's Superman mythos for Kirby's purposes, *The Eternals* threatened to make a wreck of corporate continuity—and suffered for it.

What *The Eternals* had going for it was a terrific concept, perfect for indulging Kirby's preoccupation with the technological sublime. It was a comic book Apocalypse, in the sense of both revelation and End Times narrative. It boldly riffed on Clarke's Law: again, the maxim that technology, sufficiently advanced, seems like magic. Kirby, like Clarke, took this insight as far as it would go, reimagining God as a host of technologically advanced extraterrestrials.

Updating the premise of an old Simon & Kirby five-pager, "The Great Stone Face" (*Black Cat Mystic* #59, Sept. 1957), folding in ideas from Clarke's *Childhood's End* (1953), and cashing in on the then-popularity of Swiss author Erich von Däniken's cryptoarchaeological humbug *Chariots of the Gods?* (*Erinnerungen an die Zukunft*, 1968, U.S. ed. 1970), *The Eternals* not only posits a potential Armageddon—a last Judgment—but also reworks the past in one fell swoop. Humanity, we are told, has never been alone on this world; we are but one of three related hominid species created by the godlike Celestials. Beneath the sea lie the Deviants, genetically unstable upstarts driven into hiding by the Celestials as payment for their world-conquering hubris, while above the clouds, and hiding among us, are the graceful, immortal beings known as the Eternals, friends and protectors of humanity. Though Kirby's earlier working title, *The Return of the Gods*, was nixed in favor of *The Eternals* (perhaps due to editorial caution?), the series' premise in fact unites all three species in their hour of judgment, going *The New Gods* one better in apocalyptic urgency.

Like much of Kirby's work, *The Eternals* was baldly opportunistic, exploiting and extending a popular fad. In this case, the fad was the seventies' mania for pseudoscientific speculation about humanity's origins, specifically the "gods from outer space" thesis of von Däniken's *Chariots* and related books: science fiction dressed up as real-world archaeology. Von Däniken's popular idea, whose evidentiary basis seems to have been in inverse relation to its entertainment value, was that humankind had been visited, millennia ago, by highly advanced extraterrestrials whose likenesses and activities were set down in human artifact and legend as those of the gods. These "space gods" played crucial roles in fostering the development of human civilization. Though von Däniken's thesis makes a hash of archaeology and logic, at its heart is a kernel of brilliance: the merging of "unsolved mysteries" of the past with the then-popular fascination with UFOs and alien visitation. What force could have enabled humankind to construct the pyramids? The stone heads of Easter Island? The lines on Peru's Nazca plain? Gods from outer space, according to von Däniken, and for a brief time the idea gave off plenty of heat. Of course, von Däniken had not invented the idea *ex nihilo*, but he popularized it skillfully, in effect creating a cottage industry of pseudo-archaeological "nonfiction" and establishing in popular culture what is often called the "ancient astronauts" or "paleocontact" thesis. Kirby glommed on to this thesis—yet another example of scientific speculation, in the anarchic, Feyerabendian sense—and ran with it. The premise obviously echoes Clarke: high technology misremembered as heavenly magic.

If the idea of visitors from space offers a slate on which we can inscribe our various popular obsessions (as, for example, *The X-Files* combined "alien abduction" with conspiracy theory and anti-government paranoia), then von Däniken ingeniously used this *tabula* to revive and lend new urgency to the mystery of humanity's origins. This blend proved popular enough to spawn many sequels and imitations, in print and on film. So popular was *Chariots* that by 1974, less than two years prior to *Eternals*, the book had gone through at least thirty-three U.S. printings, reportedly topping four million copies (Story's *The Space-Gods Revealed*, published in 1976, claims 34 million for total worldwide sales of von Däniken's books, which then numbered at least five in English). Another index of its popularity would be the rash of polemical, debunking books from both scientists and religious figures that appeared in the seventies (of which Story is a key example), testifying to anxiety about von Däniken's influence (see Kelly). That influence peaked late in the decade, for, though von Däniken cranked out other, similar books of cryptoarchaeology after *Chariots*, his stardom proved brief. By decade's end his fame had contracted as rapidly as it had grown, finally shrinking to cultishness. However short-lived his stardom, though, von Däniken's influence spread well beyond the printed page, diffusing into popular culture. For example, *Chariots'* German-made film adaptation (dir. Harald Reinl, 1970), improbably nominated for an Academy Award for Documentary Feature, had a long shelf life, running on American television in redubbed and adapted form under the title *In Search of Ancient Astronauts* (5 Jan. 1973), then exhibiting in theaters under the title *Chariots of the Gods* (1974), where, per the Internet Movie Database, it earned a reported 25 million dollars (see also Story, *Space-Gods* 1–3).

Its box-office success helped kick open the floodgates to a series of theatrically distributed pseudo-documentaries in the decade following, as well as speculative television programs such as *In Search of* (1976–1982). Kirby had a yen for this kind of pseudoscientific fantasizing, or, as he called it, "flapology"; indeed, critic Tom Spurgeon has rightly described *The Eternals* as "a bombastic run of episodes from *In Search Of*. . ." ("*The Eternals* #4," n. pag.). Lest any doubt lingers about the series' debt to such stuff, a blurb on the cover of #2 makes that debt explicit: "More fantastic than *Chariots of the Gods!*" In fact the series is a time capsule of the era's pseudoscientific obsessions.

Kirby was timely in his choice of subjects, but also highly idiosyncratic in his delivery. His own preoccupations are evident in *The Eternals'* drastic, world-encompassing, perhaps world-destroying premise. Humanity, we are told, is caught up in a struggle between two sister species: on the one hand, the deathless and reclusive Eternals, graced with powers such as telepathy and levitation; on the other, the miserable Deviants, cursed with an unstable genetic makeup that causes each new generation to breed new, unprecedented horrors. The Eternals, favoring peace and seclusion, interfere but rarely in human affairs, and only in the subtlest ways, while the Deviants, nursing bitter memories of a lost empire, scheme of conquest in their undersea hideaway, Lemuria, the last remnant of their erstwhile kingdom. The series begins with a cosmic event that brings both Eternals and Deviants out of hiding: the return of the gods (again, at one time a working title). These "gods" are the so-called Celestials: gigantic, faceless, unfathomable superbeings who first bred humans, Eternals, and Deviants by tampering with our common ancestor, "the dawn ape." The Celestials have returned to judge the success of their experiment. Specifically, the newly arrived Fourth Host—that is, fourth visitation—of the Celestials promises a final, irrevocable judgment, an apocalyptic reckoning that will come after fifty years of observation. Fifty years from *now*, Kirby tells us, the earth will pass muster, or die. Thus, in a few bold strokes, Kirby provides not only angels (Eternals), demons (Deviants), and gods—a richly populated cosmography—but also an eschatology: this is the way the world might end. Such a drastic pitch, summarily linking origins and endings, humans and gods, had no precedent in mainstream comic books.

Admittedly, *The Eternals* bears obvious similarities to the Fourth World. Though it poses a different ideological problem—life under judgment, not freedom versus totalitarianism—its title characters, The Eternals, frankly echo the demigods of New Genesis. They too are graceful and sublime (notwithstanding a capricious and quarrelsome few). In effect they are the superheroes of the series. In costuming and powers they recall *The New Gods* and *Forever People*. Their mountain-top retreat, Olympia, recalls Supertown, the flying city of New Genesis, while also echoing the earlier Attilan, hidden city of the Inhumans (from *The Fantastic Four*). The Eternal "Ikaris" (read *Icarus*), insofar as his likeness appears on every cover, anchors the series much as Orion anchors *New Gods*, though again Kirby draws on a larger repertory company. More engaging than Ikaris's stolid Nordic heroism—he lacks Orion's tragic dimensions, and, to be honest, isn't nearly as interesting—is the antic unpredictability of Sersi (*Circe*), a gorgeous, witchlike Eternal whose fey yet often childlike demeanor and ripe sensuality steal the show. Kirby also adds great Zuras (guess who), patriarch of the Eternals, resplendent in scarlet hair and beard, and Thena, daughter of Zuras, who provides a more stable though still-dynamic female counterpart to Sersi. Makarri, the lightning-fast runner, and Ajak, leader of the Celestials' "ground crew," complete the core group of Eternals, abetted by various supporting players over the series' run.

The series, though, isn't solely concerned with these characters, despite their status as humanity's defenders. Rather, *The Eternals* is about confronting a final challenge that subsumes Eternal, Deviant, and human alike. The fact that the book is named for the Eternals, rather than the gods, suggests an editorial feint to stem the radical implications of the series, or perhaps to blunt any comparisons to Kirby's other "Gods" series or charges of infringing on von Däniken's turf. Yet the earlier title *The Return of the Gods* (visible in Kirby's pencils for early issues) is more fitting, for the Eternals are not the series' only focus. What concerns Kirby is the wakeup call that the gods' return sends to all three species: will Earth be found wanting, and swept away like other Celestial experiments before it, or will it pass judgment and thus live to see the vaguely promised "day of Alpha"? Everything that happens in the series falls under the shadow of that judgment.

If the Eternals are dimmed by the fact that they too are subject to the gods' verdict, then the Deviants, likewise, are something less than Darkseid and company, the villains of the Fourth World. Darkseid has no peer in *The Eternals*. After all, he *is* a god: an immanent idea given eminent form. He represents a drive or hunger made flesh. By contrast, the Deviants in *The Eternals* are mere upstarts, flinging bombs at the gods but unable to get out of their shadow. Driven undersea millennia before by the harsh disciplining of the Celestials' Second Host, the Deviants burn with tragic memories as well as the curse of their volatile genetic inheritance. What they lack is grandeur.

Great Tode, tyrant of Lemuria, is a typical Kirby autocrat, cold and imperious, but also absurdly froglike in appearance (more Jabba the Hut than Darth Vader, one is tempted to say). Tode never stirs from his throne of privilege, on which he squats much like his namesake. More noble than Tode, though subject to his whim, is the series' chief villain, the Deviant warlord Kro. He begins as a mere functionary, and in truth is not very interestingly designed, but he soon shows a heroic if absurdly futile pride. "Yes, we lost," Kro rails in #2, and "we were *driven in shame* to the bowels of the earth!! *But we shall rise again!*" Granted, his character is inconsistent, for at times he is called upon to do things that ill become his dignity, such as playing the part of "the Devil" to excite humanity into rash action against the gods (the driving idea behind #3–5). Yet as the series progresses, Kro reveals surprising depth and develops into a fascinating character, capable of heroic gestures, even warmth. In #6 he consents to appear with Ikaris and company at an anthropology lecture at "City College," and in #8–10 he leads his erstwhile lover Thena (!) into Lemuria in an effort to win back her sympathy. As he boasts in #8, Kro is "noble, wise, and brave," capable of more than evil and low cunning. He is not a villain on par with Darkseid, but that is not what is called for here.

The humans in *The Eternals* unfortunately suffer a fate like that of most of the onlookers in *New Gods*: they are generally colorless, and often forced into mouthing an elevated expository prose that doesn't suit conversation. This handicap is obvious from the first issue, when bewhiskered archaeologist Daniel Damian and his daughter Margo are overwhelmed by the "cyclopean" (a word that reverberates through the series) setting of an ancient Incan ruin. They are guided by one "Ike Harris," a rugged young man in dark glasses who knows more than a mortal should. Ike soon reveals himself to be Ikaris, the Eternal, and so his mannered and stilted speech patterns begin to make sense; unfortunately Doctor Damian and Margo are saddled with high-flown language of their own (for example, in #3, "A-as an archaeologist, I-I'm *dumbfounded* at the sight of an ancient myth come *alive!*"). In the first few issues Kirby seldom, and never effectively, attempts to bring their dialogue down to earth.

This weakness betrays Kirby's vision, for what he is interested in here, clearly, is not sheer scope but rather the human predicament—human fears and aspirations—as enacted on a cosmic stage. Kirby is not indifferent to the humans in his story. Sadly, though, the wordcraft the premise demands most often eludes him. Issue 3, for instance, presents a human dilemma and thus an interesting crisis: when Doctor Damian elects to stay behind at the landing site of the Celestials, thus to live out the remainder of his days within an impenetrable "atom shield" erected by the gods, can young Margo afford to stay too? The decision is made for her by a chivalric—that is, chauvinistic—Ikaris, who scoops her up under his arm and carries her off, finally zapping her with an energy beam to quell her protests. (The scene echoes *Fantastic Four* #48, in which a distraught Johnny is dragged forcibly away from the Inhumans' city just as it is encased within a "dome" or force field.) The Damians' moment of parting has a certain resonance, but the doctor's dialogue, again, is stiff: "What I'm *trying* to say is that *you can't* sacrifice your youth for *my* dreams! [. . .] Good bye, Margo . . . be *happy*, child!" (7). In fairness, Kirby does not let it go at that, for Margo does suffer from the loss, and Ikaris knows it: "The loss of a father is a *great* price to pay for a full life—in time the gods will *exact* such payment from us *all*!!" In her grief, Margo begins to take on life and dimensionality. Kirby, however, does not sustain this, for throughout the run of the series she is consigned to the role of passive onlooker. Kirby does have fun, however, with another human character, City College professor Samuel Holden, who, unlike the bearded, safari-ready Doctor Damian, represents professional respectability at its deadly dullest—a respectability that Sersi, enamored of the professor, tweaks at every opportunity. For instance, when Holden's "discourse on anthropology" bores his guests right out of the room (#8), Sersi conjures a big band and invites him to dance. By #12 Holden is a bundle of nerves, "ready to pass out from the sheer *thrill* of it all," as Sersi quips. Faced with the unknown, the professor cries out in a fearful close-up, "Don't leave me, Sersi!!", a far cry from his stuffy, hobbling dialogue in #6. As Kirby knocks the stuffings out of Doctor Holden, he also burns some of the fat out of his scripting.

There are other engaging characters in the series, including the mischievous Sprite, youngest of the featured Eternals, a puckish squirt who likes to sow confusion and so ends up getting a spanking over Ikaris' bended knee. Sprite comes to the rescue in #13, "The Astronauts," by summoning the enigmatic "Forgotten One" to counteract a Deviant threat. The Forgotten One, an Eternal long banished from sight by Zuras for his insistence on meddling "in human affairs," represents (implicitly, was) all the great strong men of human history: Gilgamesh, Hercules, Samson. Dispatched by Sprite, he now redeems himself by stopping a foolhardy Deviant assault on the Celestials' orbiting mothership. Stories like these, dispensing with the usual star players, show Kirby's imagination at its most restless and protean. Clearly, Kirby was less concerned with stars, and more with the apocalyptic situation he had established.

So *The Return of the Gods* really would have been a better title. The Fourth Host of the Celestials, Kirby's voiceless, inscrutable giants, are, on the one hand, an extraordinary achievement: a grandiose concept that might be absurd, fatal, in less interesting hands, but that Kirby brings to life graphically. They are often majestically drawn. On the other hand, as I argued in Chapter 4, they remain chilly ciphers, notions rather than characters. Arishem, Jemiah, Eson, Tefral: these Celestials are god-engines with curiously Old Testament-sounding names, epitomizing Kirby's familiar tendency to promiscuously blend science and myth, body and machine, yet they lack personality. Typically for Kirby, these "gods" are massive humanoid forms encased in metal, possessing a grandeur at once elegant and ponderous. Here, for one of the last times, Kirby's trademark style—reconciling fluid, organic form with a huge, architectonic complexity—finds apt expression. The gods are living machines, their bodies organized masses of symbol and ornament, mysteriously hinting at function but really testifying to Kirby's love of swirling, technoglyphic detail. They well demonstrate Christopher Brayshaw's point that Kirby's drawing enacts a fierce dialectical tension between figuration and design and also between organic and monumental, inorganic forms (56–57).

Colossally inhuman, the Celestials are, in concept, sequels to Dr. Doom in his armor or Metron in his Mobius Chair: machines that live. Here as in *Thor*—and the design sense is very similar—Kirby's love of the technological crisscrosses his sense of the mythic and primal. Arishem, in particular, his thumb branded with the equation for doomsday, is an inspired vision, so much so that Kirby returns to him repeatedly, stressing the significance of his fifty-year vigil over the Earth. He resembles a larger version of the Destroyer, the robotic doomsday machine built by Odin in *Thor*. Towering over the gods' landing site, armored in red, face hidden behind a metallic grille, Arishem is a character only in the remotest, most inaccessible sense, lacking even the anthropocentric touches of a Galactus: "Inside the impregnable armor is a mind incomprehensible to man!" (#7). This technological God, sentinel of the Celestial host, distills the premise of *The Eternals* into one anthropomorphic symbol: the shadow of judgment, a titanic *memento mori* standing on a pylon. This is quintessentially, spine-shiveringly, Kirby. In fact Arishem's upraised hand replays the arrival of Galactus in *Fantastic Four* #48: huge, imperious, arm outstretched.

Throughout the series, the Celestials remain aloof, unknowable and immune to any physical assault, revisions of Galactus but without voice. Atomic bombs detonate in their hands, but they remain unmoved. Ballistic missiles targeted at them remain locked in their silos, unable to launch. Deviants and Eternals alike scheme for the gods' destruction, but their schemes prove pointless. Ikaris himself entertains fears of a "war" with the gods (#19), but we are never given any reason to believe such a war could be waged, let alone won. Issue 7's encounter between three gung-ho espionage agents and the gods of

Fig. 21. High technology as mythology. Jack Kirby, with John Verpoorten (inks), Gaspar Saladino (lettering), and Glynis Wein (colors), "The Day of the Gods." *The Eternals* #1 (July 1976), page 4. © Marvel.

the Fourth Host is such an uneven match as to be ridiculous: the men cannot begin to grasp the extent of the Celestials' power. Of all the characters in *The Eternals*, these "gods" most clearly represent a stretch for Kirby the artist—and yet, despite their humanoid forms and eye-entrancing designs, they are utterly immovable, enigmatic, and cold.

Cyclopean elements like these are the most persuasive elements in *The Eternals*. Frankly, the series deserves a larger format: more width, more height. Artistically, Kirby runs riot in the first several issues, yielding one spectacular splash after another. Issue 1 begins with monumental visions of "the legendary *Chamber of the Gods*": giant statues and carvings depict enormous helmeted figures in machines, their high-tech trappings rendered as ancient glyphs (fig. 21). "Outer space technology translated in terms of mythology," Doctor Damian enthuses. "Incredible!" Indeed. Kirby's high-tech style reigns supreme in these pages, but with a weathered, rough quality befitting stone. The doctor's remark in effect describes the reverse of the procedure Kirby follows throughout *The Eternals*, that is, mythology translated in terms of pseudoscience: the same reckless splicing of genres, of science and fantasy, seen in *Thor* and in the Fourth World (and, I can't resist pointing out, seen today in everything from *Stargate* to *Indiana Jones and the Kingdom of the Crystal Skull*). Graphically, the translation is a happy one, despite the inconsistency of the inking and production on the book, for Kirby's love of technological detail meshes well with the ancient cultures evoked in the settings. Issue 2 represents the series' visual apogee, boasting some five full-page splashes in addition to an extraordinary two-page spread of the Celestials' spacecraft. This in a seventeen-page story—such indulgence! And yet these huge images are not mere visual stunts, for each splash, ingeniously composed to guide the eye, is freighted with significance.

Regrettably, neither visuals nor storytelling in *The Eternals* is consistent in quality. Even the first few issues, though energetic and promise-packed, are marred by distracting and deflating inconsistencies. Once the book's whopping premise is established, Kirby strains to follow his first act with a brisk, fast moving tale about Kro fomenting panic in New York City, but the story's gimmick (Kro posing as the Devil) is inadequate to the sense of scale established in the first two issues. The carnage in #3–6 is relentless and sometimes impressive, as when armored Deviants drop from a flaming sky, but the skirmishes seem relatively minor, even diversionary, and the concept too prosaic after the cosmological revelations of #1–2. The art too is inconsistent: Kirby's sense of scale sometimes falters, and visual glitches knock some air out of his grand concept (a problem Evanier imputes to Kirby's worsening vision [*King* 187], though at its best the drawing is so staggering that this is hard to credit). Issue 4, the last inked by John Verpoorten, Marvel's then-production manager, is ragged: the finishing is unstable, varying from panel to panel, and the lettering, by two different hands, is glaringly inconsistent. (In the original comic books, inferior printing made for dark and clotted artwork throughout the series, in contrast to the cleaner production values of Kirby's then-recent work at DC.) There is a jaggedness about the work, in both the narrative drawing and the scripting, that bespeaks haste and editorial disarray.

If #3–6 lose the thread of Kirby's larger story, #7–10 recover it with gusto, and are the most interesting of the run. Issue 7, "The Fourth Host," which shows the impact of the Celestials on the human world, reasserts the scale, significance, and sheer chutzpah of Kirby's premise. The blend of story and art peaks in #8–10, a three-issue arc that adds weight and texture. Here the Deviants cease to be one-dimensional villains and take on a more tragic if not sympathetic shading, and we get to know the Deviants at home in Lemuria, their sunken kingdom. Lemuria has its share of horrors, yet the greatest are moral rather than physical. Most horrific is the spectacle of Deviant eugenics at work: the mutates [*sic*], monstrous yet pitiable offspring of the Deviants' unstable genetic code, are swept into the furnaces at "Purity Time," a cathartic cleansing ritual that rids Lemuria of anything *too* loathsome. When Thena asks Kro where the wretched creatures in the "Death Wagons" are being sent, he replies flatly: to the place "from which they will *never* return to haunt us." Pointing to a distant structure spewing flame and smoke, he says simply, "It is *there*, Thena." Here Kirby manages an understatement on par with the best of his writing in the Fourth World: a moment of quiet horror, deftly handled. (This scene compares well to the evocation of fascism in "Himon.")

Alternately, some mutates are consigned to the arena to amuse Tode and his family. Here only the ability to kill is valued; mercy and tenderness are worse than handicaps. Again Kirby aims high as a scripter, hammering the point home with an incantatory rhythm:

> In the City of the Toads, the price of life is *high!!*
> In the City of the Toads, the fight for life is a daily routine!
> In the City of the Toads, the mask of *cruelty* is more valued than the living *heart*!!
> *Woe* to him who lives in this city! For here, peace is a shadow—and *shame*, the daily bread. (2)

In counterpoint, Kirby's drawings enact the pointless violence of the arena with brutal force. "The City of Toads," in sum, is cruel and obscene, a culture founded on genetically inherited shame, but it is a believable setting, not a mere catalog of sideshow horrors. The Deviants' grudge against the gods, nursed for so many centuries, begins to make sense; at last the Deviants' bitterness begins to register. This story is the Deviants', and Kirby does his best to give it to us on their terms, even if that means upsetting the tidy dualism of his moral conflicts.

The series' most surprising moments of characterization come in these three issues, as Thena descends into Lemuria alongside Kro. That Thena and Kro should have been lovers in a bygone age is surprising in itself, but welcome, for both characters gain in stature and complexity from this twist. Kirby goes further, though, introducing in the arena the series' strangest pair: the scaly red giant Karkas, a reluctant fighter, noble in character but horrific in appearance; and a nameless character who becomes known simply as "The Reject," a savage killer, ignorant of all tender feelings and civilized nuances despite his very handsome and even human countenance. Other Deviants turn in horror from the Reject's beautiful features, while Thena mistakenly interprets them as a sign of "value." The story arc comes to a startling end when, in "Mother" (#10), Thena severs her connection with Kro and adopts Karkas and the Reject as her charges, even as an inquisitive Celestial, Eson, wreaks havoc on Lemuria. This expert balancing of small- and large-scale crises is aided by artwork that captures both intimate nuance and panoramic violence. Throughout this arc Kirby, ably inked by Mike Royer (on board since #5), brings Lemuria's underwater setting to vivid life. The art enjoys a consistency and beauty not seen since #1–2: the scenes of arena combat, undersea travel, and Purity Time are splendidly atmospheric, and the Deviants' futile struggle with Eson spectacular if ironic.

After this point, *The Eternals* declines, at first slowly, then in spectacular freefall. Issues 11–13 lack the tragic undercurrents of the Lemuria trilogy but are still tense and involving; after #13, however, the drop in quality is precipitous and depressing. Issues 14–16 involve Ikaris (now conventionally positioned as the series' superpowered star) in a misguided crossover with Marvel's Hulk, although in this case it is merely a mechanical replica of the Hulk, brought to temporary life by an overflow of the Eternals' energy. This parodic "Hulk" is exclusively Kirby's, a pseudo-Hulk as he puts it, who exists only to stir up trouble, not to knit *The Eternals* more securely into Marvel continuity. The story plays coyly with said continuity, but it seems clear that Kirby by this point was out of touch with, and reluctant or unable to conform to, the contours of the Marvel Universe. Granted, the conceit of an ersatz Hulk has satiric potential, and Kirby does get in some digs: one scene shows a crowd of onlookers, Marvel fans essentially, vainly hoping that other superheroes will join the fight against this "Hulk." But the story overall is pointless, the art wan and flavorless. Whether by editorial fiat, or by simple lack of enthusiasm, the expected splashes and spreads are mostly denied (a poorly composed one in #15 reveals Kirby's slackening interest).

The writing is on the wall: after #13, the series' spark gutters and fades, sputtering out over a few remaining months of contractual make-work. This comes as a dispiriting collapse after the bravura narrative drawing and conceptual reach of the early issues. In the last two issues (#18–19) the idea of the Celestials recurs, but on a scale much reduced; the shopworn plot is *Thor*-like, pitting Ikaris against his Loki-like cousin Druig. A serviceable annual from October 1977 (concurrent with the Hulk storyline) completes the run, capitalizing on Karkas and the Reject but again neglecting the Celestials and thus the book's basic premise.

This collapse is but part of the larger story of Kirby's bitter final tenure at Marvel, a period that, obviously, left neither Kirby nor Marvel nor the most vocal of Marvel's fans satisfied. Jonathan Lethem's essay "The Return of the King," a retrospective critique, condenses what was then the prevailing view in Marveldom: Kirby's second coming was "a clumsy misstep" (13), a paradoxical collision of "clunkily old-fashioned virtues" and "a baroque and nearly opaque futuristic sensibility" that deterred and alienated fans (5). During this tenure Kirby's brand-new creations, such as *The Eternals* and *Devil Dinosaur*, were criticized by fans (and reportedly by members of Marvel's editorial staff) for their outmodedness and labored scripting, while his revisitings of familiar Marvel properties, in particular *Captain America* and the *Black Panther*, both of which he had co-created, were very often pilloried for departing, without transition or explanation, from then-recent and putatively more sophisticated, at the least more self-consciously political, versions. Kirby's final period at Marvel, though busy enough and now regarded with some affection—most of his work from this period has since been reassessed, and some of its concepts revived and fine-tuned—was at the time considered a whopping failure. *The Eternals* was the one great, radical, mythopoeic premise to emerge from that period, but it was specially, cruelly hobbled by its (non-)relationship to the Marvel Universe.

In fact the Marvel Universe, more specifically the ideology of continuity that ascribed coherence to that universe, could not accommodate *The Eternals*. The series offered (to quote Simon & Kirby's "The Great Stone Face") "something so important that all the history books would have [had] to be rewritten." Its re-visioning of human history threw a wrench into Marvel continuity, already brim-full with gods, demigods, secret histories, and hermetic lore. This is why the question of whether to slot *The Eternals* into said continuity, and if so how, quickly spawned a debate within the very letter column of the book, a development that Kirby could hardly have foreseen and to which he could not adapt. In the "Eternal Utterings" column of issue 3 (Sept. 1976), fan and soon-to-be Marvel staffer Ralph Macchio uncorked the question with a letter at once eloquent and puzzling, addressed to "Jack" but in fact talking of Kirby in the third person (an inconsistency typical of the fan letter genre: after all, these things are addressed as much to editors and other readers as to any creative presence). While praising *Eternals* as "a new excursion into myth" and a "perfect vehicle for exploration" of the great existential issues, Macchio urges (not Kirby, presumably, but the editors) to "keep the world of the Eternals separate from the Marvel Universe, and let each evolve separately."

Macchio's reasoning is threefold: Kirby's cosmology threatens to "contradict already established laws of the Marvel Universe"; Kirby's answers to the big questions posit "unexpected constants" that will not allow other writers "sufficient latitude in storytelling"; and, conversely, the Marvel mythos will not allow Kirby to flex his imagination "to the fullest extent." In sum, the collision of Kirby's vision with Marvel's long-tended mythos will sacrifice both continuity and verisimilitude, two goals that, Macchio argues, "make Marvel Marvel." At the same time, avoiding such a smashup will liberate Kirby editorially. Thus, says Macchio, it is "imperative" to separate the two.

Back in 1976, as an eleven-year-old Kirby devotee with only patchy knowledge of Marvel continuity, I could hardly follow Macchio's reasoning, much less share his anxiety. Nor did I notice when, in the time between issues 3 and 7, Macchio (Marvel's "correspondent from Cresskill [NJ]," as he is called in #3) arrived at the company as a professional, where he has promoted Marvel continuity to this day. Back then I thought of letter columns as some far-away, exclusive province, populated by readers aloof to my interests, caught up in things I often didn't understand. But Macchio did help stir a revealing debate in the pages of *The Eternals*, and in hindsight, his argument was prescient. His letter recognizes, to a degree possible only to the most devoted fans of the period, the pressures of continuity (pressures even more evident today, in the wake of the so-called event publishing of the eighties onwards). Macchio was at the vanguard of fandom based on continuity; like his sometime collaborator Mark Gruenwald, Macchio represented the influx of *continuity fans* into the comic book's editorial sphere.

Arguably, Macchio was right: bracketing off *The Eternals* from the Marvel Universe would have served Kirby, and the series, better. In any case, he was not alone in his concerns. Indeed, the very same issue contains a letter from one Dennis Millard, who dubs *Eternals* a "new classic," yet hopes that "the Eternals stay in their own universe and away from the other Marvel heroes." While the unnamed letter column host doubts that "our newly-revealed race of Eternals will contradict any of the already established Marvel Universe"—a claim that had already been proved wrong by #3—he does invite other comments on the issue from "Marveldom Assembled." In fact many letters in subsequent issues continue to pick at this topic, building on and responding to Macchio's initial points. A letter in #4 raises the issue briefly, while in #5 two correspondents assume, and indeed hope, that *Eternals* will join Marvel continuity, the opposite of Macchio's view. One of these, though, Kurt Cruppenink, worries that Kirby's stories may not mesh with "the more realistic Marvel Universe" (there's that concern with realism again). In #7 the floodgates open, as Marveldom Assembled takes the editorial bait dangled in #3: seven letters weigh in on the continuity problem, three in favor of Macchio's suggestion that *Eternals* take place in a parallel "dimension" (this idea would provide an in-continuity rationalization for an out-of-continuity series), three against, and one undecided. The "debate" continued to rage for most of the series' remaining run.

Decades on, this controversy may seem like the proverbial tempest in a teapot, yet it reveals the importance of continuity to fandom's understanding of comics. In #7, Jana Hollingsworth effectively distills the pro-Macchio argument: "It would hurt both [continuities] if either Kirby had to curtail his mythologizing, or the rest of the Marvel Universe had to warp itself around Kirby's mythos." Curiously, the opposite camp, in favor of folding *Eternals* into the Marvel Universe, also grounds its arguments in the conservation of continuity: "alternate worlds," they say, are too messy and confusing. As Ryan Hollerback complains, this solution "smacks too much of what DC did to their characters," a reference to DC's proliferating "parallel" universes with their variant versions of the same superheroes. On either side, no-one seems to consider the possibility that *Eternals* might be simply *unrelated* to the Marvel cosmology, that is, a story in its own right that happens to be published by Marvel.

Paul Carlsen finally raises this possibility in #9, as he urges the editors "to keep the Eternals off in a world of their own—the real Earth, not another dimension." Other letters in #8–10 try to reconcile Kirby's world with Marvel's, though one reader demurs in #10 (too late). In #11, Scott [here misnamed *Sam*] Taylor expresses dismay that *Eternals*, "the best thing [Kirby's] ever done in comics," has apparently been jammed into Marvel's already overcrowded "mess." Mike W. Barr (another fan destined to turn pro) advises Marvel simply to let Kirby "have a totally free reign," with no thought to "inconsistencies" or "contradictions." Dennis Mallonee (another pro-to-be) sounds the clarion of consistency in #12, calling the inclusion of *Eternals* in Marvel continuity a "mistake." Other posts in #11–12 continue to fret over the issue, though by this time only the pro-Macchio position is voiced, the other viewpoint having been satisfied, presumably, by tentative nods to Marvel continuity in #6–7. The anonymous column host attempts to "officially" ring the debate to a close in #14, but the problem resurfaces in #16, and, inevitably, in #18, as baffled and disappointed readers at last weigh in on #14's "Hulk" crossover. At this point Kirby seizes the reins of the letter column, inviting mail directly to his post office box in California—implicitly, a sign of tension between the artist and Marvel's New York-based editorial establishment.

No matter: by then only one issue of the series remained.

In these letter columns, as in those of *Captain America* and *Black Panther*, we see a principle already enshrined in superhero fandom entering the editorial discourse of the comics themselves: clearly, continuity was becoming, or had become, the comic books' first, most important principle. This hothouse controversy over *The Eternals* was not a matter of grubbing for what Marvel fans affectionately call "no-prizes" (given for spotting continuity errors) nor simply of nitpicking editorial gaffes, but rather one of negotiating competing visions of a universe. The conflict was (is) invested with a sort of religiosity that, depending on your perspective, is either risible or fascinating. In the end, the anonymous editorial vision prevailed: *The Eternals* was deemed part of the Marvel Universe, whatever the contradictions. Perhaps Kirby wanted it this way; perhaps he did not understand just how snugly the straitjacket would fit. Perhaps the issue was so far from registering on him that he looked on the debate as a meaningless distraction. In any case, the loser in this instance was Kirby's vision of the series, his grandest after the Fourth World.

In hindsight, Marvel continuity increasingly exerts a distorting force on *The Eternals* as the series progresses. Issue 6 tosses off a gag about the Fantastic Four's Ben Grimm, though it is not clear from this gag whether, in the story's world, "Grimm" is to be regarded as a real person or a fictional character. What's more, #6–7 refer pointlessly to the espionage agency S.H.I.E.L.D., one of the linchpins of Marvel continuity, as three secret agents come face to face with Kirby's Celestials. Their identification as "Nick Fury's men" (Fury being the director of S.H.I.E.L.D. and a popular Marvel character) is gratuitous, and one is left to wonder whether Kirby came up with or simply acceded to the idea. More puzzling still, #14–16, as noted, sidestep the series' apocalyptic premise for the sake of an aimless, ambiguous concession that serves neither Kirby's creations nor the high-profile guest star (the pseudo-Hulk). This mistimed crossover waylays the larger storyline without satisfactorily answering the question of whether *Eternals* is "canonical" in the Marvel sense.

The Hulk episode, in essence, pushes the series' self-destruct button, trashing Kirby's own continuity in such a way as to confirm Marvel's intellectual ownership of *The Eternals* but not to make any sense. The story may be winking satirically at us, since the pseudo-Hulk is actually the creation of some college students, a conceit that, as noted, allows Kirby to blow a mild raspberry at fandom's fetishizing of continuity. (One is reminded of Kirby's *Kamandi* #29, in which a cult of apes worships Superman and preserves his costume but Superman himself does not appear.) But this interpretation does little to redeem an expendable and diversionary arc. By the end of *The Eternals*, a hollowing out has taken place comparable to the loss of depth evident in the last handful of *Mister Miracle*s, after DC had pulled the plug on the overarching Fourth World. The drop-off in energy and inspiration is similar, and equally disheartening. By series' end *The Eternals* has lost its grandeur and terror. Everything seems shrunken and ordinary.

Beyond the usual cursory explanations of Kirby's professional unhappiness at Marvel, it is hard to know exactly how this happened (and why so suddenly). We do not know exactly when or why Kirby decided, or shrugged his shoulders and agreed, to bridge the gap between his mythos and Marvel's, and on such vague terms. Nor do we know what sort of editorial negotiations or demands spurred him behind the scenes. Aside from the negative comments in the letter columns, what were Kirby's interactions, and how extensive, with his editors and readers? Did he merely accede to editorial pressure? Did he continue to nurse long-term ambitions for his series, or did he despair of it? Kirby fans have blamed editorial gerrymandering in the letter columns: staffers who conspired to fill Kirby's titles with a disproportionate load of fan criticism; editors or subeditors determined to rein in Kirby's expansive vision or pave over what they saw as potholes in Kirby's scripting. Whether anything like this happened remains a matter of dark, unspecified rumor. Evanier alludes to Marvel employees who resented Kirby's neglect of established continuity (see for instance *King* 185–87); Ronin Ro, sourcing Evanier, reports conflicts between Kirby and Marvel staff, a string of complaints from Kirby regarding unapproved changes to his published stories, and damaging, defamatory comments about Kirby made to fanzines by certain Marvel employees (186–88).

Blaming editorial interference for Kirby's loss of heart is tempting. Such interference—and it's a fact some did occur—compromised Kirby's nominally independent, California-based editorship of his own work. It violated the terms of his understanding with Marvel, at least as he understood them. Yet the mixed, often hostile reception of Kirby's mid-seventies work among both fans and professionals had as much to do with the centripetal force of continuity as it did with any shadowy, undocumented aspects of Marvel's workplace culture. One need not envision a conspiracy to understand why Kirby's free-wheeling talent ill-suited the Marvel of the mid-seventies. The conservation of continuity increasingly defined both fan taste and the editorial environments into which fandom served as an entryway, but Kirby was not a conservator. He was too restive and curious and impatient for that. The problem was, he had supplied so much raw material to Marvel in the sixties that he had virtually crowded himself out of his own neighborhood, leaving behind a flock of preservationists who, confronted by his return in the mid-decade, worried that his newest plans might call for nothing less than the wrecking ball. Kirby's neglect of inter-title continuity, his summary rewritings of history and cosmology, and his departures from Lee's familiar style made him anathema to a newly serious generation of fans weaned on Marvel's inbred universe and putative realism. He was the right artist at a spectacularly wrong time.

All this carries a whiff of irony, since Kirby had practically invented continuity by giving so much of his energy to Marvel, most obviously by way of his rambling, character-packed runs on *The Fantastic Four* and *Thor*. Moreover, his post-Marvel work on the Fourth World, with its interlocking modules, represented the next big elaboration of the continuity principle. So it seems odd that said principle should have boxed in and frustrated him so much. That it did is a measure of how much continuity had changed, since the late sixties, from a generative to a confining practice.

Since Kirby, *The Eternals* has been an on-again, off-again property, too promising to be let lie fallow but too troublesome to be incorporated fully into Marvel continuity on Kirby's original terms. The history of the property post-Kirby has been one of incremental revisionism, with, first, scattered guest shots and then a twelve-part series (1985) leading to the thorough absorption of Kirby's Celestials, Deviants, and Eternals into the Marvel Universe. Prerequisite to such absorption was a diminution in scope. Whereas Kirby had outlined a new creation myth for humanity, later writers demoted the Celestials to a mere influence on human development. Most of these later stories, even the aforesaid twelve-parter (scripted by Peter Gillis, then Walter Simonson), give the impression of someone batting cleanup, trying to make the most of a mess. A long Thomas-scripted run in *Thor* (now collected as *Thor: The Eternals Saga*) led to the Gruenwald and Macchio-scripted #300 (Oct. 1980), the effect of which was to downsize the Celestials and put the apocalyptic claims of Kirby's original to rest. Yet it was hardly a sturdy patch job; later efforts to redo *The Eternals* continued to be confused or half-hearted. The *Thor* run, in hindsight, is an earnest but numbing example of continuity-splicing, blunting Kirby's premise through relentless tinkering and rationalization. Such episodes are of only historical interest. The most commercially successful of the *Eternals* revampings has been that offered by best-selling fantasist Neil Gaiman and penciler John Romita, Jr., in a seven-part series in 2006–07 (collected in

2008), which in turned spawned a new ongoing series based on the Gaiman/ Romita template (2008). In Gaiman's scenario, the outlines of Kirby's premise are honored—Celestials, Eternals, Deviants—but the Eternals themselves have forgotten their nature and powers and become "human," their memories stolen from them. The anomie they suffer is like that of the many other bemused and passive protagonists in Gaiman's fiction (*American Gods, Anansi Boys,* etc.). Gaiman's taste for anticlimax seems to run counter to Kirby's instinct for the cataclysmic, but the resultant tension is at least interesting, investing Eternals and Deviants with heretofore unimagined dimensions and extrapolating from some of the strongest moments in Kirby's original. Like all of the latter-day *Eternals* projects, though, it dispenses with the fear of last Judgment.

The most peculiar revision of concepts from *The Eternals* can be found in Marvel's series of *Earth X* and spin-off titles from 1999 to 2003: a franchise based on designs by popular artist Alex Ross and set in a dystopian future that attempts to impose retroactively a single, overarching timeline on all of Marvel's history and characters. This series, comprised of *Earth X* (1999–2000), *Universe X* (2000–2001), and *Paradise X* (2002–03), practices continuity with a vengeance, and, far from trying to diminish the concept of the Celestials, makes them the centerpiece of the Marvel Universe: the Earth, we are told, is but an incubator for a Celestial seed. *Earth X* weaves together elements from numerous Marvel comics, many originally by Kirby, of which *The Eternals, Fantastic Four,* and *Machine Man* are only the most obvious. The huge cast, dominated by characters created or co-created by Kirby (the Inhumans, the Watcher, X-51, Captain America, and so on), becomes entangled in a byzantine plot in which the fate of the planet hinges on Galactus devouring the Celestial seed. This was to have been a possible future for the Marvel Universe, in response to DC's equally dark *Kingdom Come* (1996), but, I gather, has since been consigned to an "alternate Earth," that is, deemed uncanonical. Quintessentially post-Kirby, the *Earth X* series is vast in scope but neglectful of everything except superheroes (in this future, everyone has superpowers). It is swathed in an aura of religiosity and self-importance, and determinedly joyless and oppressive: a coming-together of vaulting, Kirbyesque scope and the publisher's latter-day pretensions to an airtight, hermetic continuity. Notwithstanding this experiment, Marvel has been unable to revive *The Eternals* with a stable, workable, in-continuity premise that cleaves to Kirby's template.

The promise and the failure of *The Eternals* prompt questions about the exact nature of the editorial interface between Kirby and Marvel in 1976–78. From its initial afflatus to its final, limping conclusion, *The Eternals* looks like the work of someone desperately in need of a trusted editor yet no longer able to commit himself to working under anyone else's editorial hand. Clearly *The Eternals* was yet another bid for artistic self-determination on Kirby's part; he could not have undertaken the project in a spirit of collaboration and compromise. Yet, despite his unwillingness to work with another writer or under another editor, his work was in fact still cramped by Marvel's editorial practice, its fan-based workplace culture, and its cultivation of "continuity" as the core principle of comic books. A fitful, often interesting, sometimes terrific series for its first year, *The Eternals* was compromised by bad choices evidently spurred both by editorial pressure and by Kirby's own unwillingness or inability to engage with Marvel continuity on a more substantive level. In *The Eternals*, as in his derided revamping of old favorites *Captain America* and *The Black Panther*, Kirby discovered that, as the old saw goes, you really can't go home again—even if you're the one that laid the foundations for the place.

Kirby's work from this period is now the object of nostalgic veneration. As of this writing, the bulk of his mid-seventies output at Marvel, including *Captain America*, *The Black Panther*, *The Eternals*, and even the oft-maligned *Devil Dinosaur*, is in print (or has just recently cycled out of print) in the form of paperback and/or deluxe hardback compilations aimed at fans. Much of Kirby's seventies work for DC is now in print as well, not only the Fourth World but also *The Demon*, *OMAC*, and *The Losers*, all in hardcover (two volumes reprinting *Kamandi's* early issues have lapsed from print, but an omnibus is pending). Images from Kirby's comics, early and late, are all over the Net, and wistful looks back at his mid-seventies work are common. At the same time, DC and Marvel have reintroduced ideas from these comics into present-day titles, everything from *Captain America* to *Final Crisis*, as part of the continual process of revising and revamping their highly specialized comics universes. Graphically most of the new comics have little in common with Kirby—stylewise, a surface realism and pseudo-cinematic, Photoshopped glamour are the state of the art—but the sheer throbbing excess of the comic book project appears still very much in thrall to Kirby's apocalyptic sense of scope and possibility. If fans are now mostly drawn to auteur-writers like Grant Morrison, Warren Ellis, and Mark Millar, and widescreen-style illustrators like Alex Ross and Bryan Hitch, the comic book and graphic novel culture still reveres Kirby in the abstract. Styles have changed, and Kirby's style is now something to be outgrown—or revisited once in a while, like childhood—and yet the comic book business continually returns to him as a fund of exploitable ideas. He is a totem. From a clamoring and critical adolescence to a beat-up, nostalgia-ridden adulthood, the core comic book audience has looked at Kirby as either embarrassingly or lovably old-fashioned, sometimes hemming a bit at his irrepressible childishness, sometimes longing affectionately to produce work as potent and unapologetic. For some, Kirby is not simply a beloved cartoonist but the patron saint of *comic book artists.*

It's hard to take perspective on such an artist, one to whom countless fans and comics professionals have paid homage and yet whose brash individuality has been so very often forgotten or misremembered or subdued to corporate origin stories. The publishing history of Kirby is very nearly the whole fascinating history of the comic book medium. Even if, as here, we confine our interest to the latter half of his career—even if we neglect decades of comics—Kirby's quixotic, meandering path, the half-effaced, smudged-out complications of his working life, and the sheer generous overflow of his contributions are enough to freeze you in your tracks. There is something irreducible about his story. Kirby's very influence makes the story urgent, yet hides or confuses the details: the way he worked, the setbacks he endured, the hopes he nurtured and had to leave unfulfilled.

The underlying problem for the critic has to do with, again, the need to locate Kirby's authorial voice, if not autonomy, in the face of a market and a genre justified mainly in heteronomous terms. Simply put, it is hard to find Kirby the Auteur amongst all the commercial imperatives, the "failed" projects, the unexpected hits, the feints and reversals, the very things that made his career arc in comics the looping, whirling, crazy dotted line that it was (and that have made this book, frankly, the methodological rover it is). Kirby was by no means a martyr, an unregarded, twilit figure or Romantic artist-hero indifferent to the market. He was a commercial comic book journeyman, by turns a shop man and a freelancer. He worked hard to make sales, and the stress of that work is written all over the hectic jumble that is his oeuvre. Yet it is my conviction that much of Kirby's work is personal and that it glows with a certain light.

Behind all the details and despite the rough edges, Kirby is there, a distinctive voice, an indelible cartoonist, and the quintessential insider-outsider artist: the comic book's myth-poet, eccentric godfather to an entire tradition. The great underlying point about him is the generative power of narrative drawing, the irresistible tug of graphiation as an improvised act of storytelling, an autopoiesis in which the story-world and its devices are structured by the drawings themselves. Kirby is the *ur-example* of that process—whereby the restless mind and the tireless hand work in perfect tandem, pursuing dreams, inscribing them against the teasing, empty whiteness of the page, and making imaginative fire.

# APPENDIX

## Kirby and Kirbyana in Print and in Fandom

Though Kirby's active career tapered off years before his death in 1994, his publication history remains an open book. Kirby publishing is an ongoing affair: the publication record of even his most popular and most studied work remains volatile, with new or revised reprint volumes appearing frequently. During his active career Kirby often competed with reprints of his own work, particularly at Marvel, and since his death a library's worth of reprints has appeared (especially since 2004). Both Marvel and DC Comics have reprinted Kirby extensively in the course of larger ongoing projects of legacy maintenance, nostalgia marketing, and self-reinvention. These projects consist of a range of publications, from comparatively affordable trade paperbacks through costly hardbound editions to very costly, even grandiose, bumper-sized "omnibus" editions. For example, Marvel's touted "Masterworks" series, which dates from 1987, consists of deluxe yet slender hardcover (and more recently softcover) compilations of vintage comics, mainly from the sixties and seventies. The series has been through multiple phases and printings and boasts well over 100 volumes to date, many penciled in whole or in part by Kirby. As an alternative, Marvel offers the budget-priced "Essentials" line, which consists of black-and-white reprints on newsprint in volumes of 500-plus pages each that make the same "masterworks" available at less cost. This line, launched in 1997, likewise boasts well more than 100 volumes to date, including a vast store of Kirby, and repeat printings are common. Finally, Marvel offers the so-called Omnibuses: ultra-thick, sometimes more than 800-page, hardcovers, each collating an entire series (or a very long run from a series) in one monumental, frankly unwieldy tome. The first of these was the Kirby-drawn *Fantastic Four Omnibus, Vol. 1* (2005), which collects the first three years' worth of *Fantastic Four* material. Other Kirby-centered Omnibuses have followed, including, unexpectedly, *The Eternals* (2006) and *Devil Dinosaur* (2007), both reprinting series that had never been reprinted before in any form—a sign, presumably, of Kirby's marketability to affluent hardcore fans. Between 2004 and 2008 Marvel also issued a spate of paperbacks reprinting Kirby's once-reviled mid-seventies run: *Captain America, The Black Panther*, and later *The Eternals*. As a result, the bulk of Kirby's work for Marvel in the sixties and seventies is now readily available.

DC has taken a similar multitrack approach to legacy maintenance, with a line of deluxe hardback reprints known as the "Archives" (since 1989) and a more cost-conscious series of fat black-and-white softbacks titled "Showcase Presents" (since 2005). Both of these series contain some Kirby: the late-fifties *Challengers of the Unknown* is available in both formats, while a portion of the early-seventies *Kamandi* is available in the Archives (also, *The All Star Comics Archives* and *The Shazam! Archives* Vol. 2 include some Simon & Kirby work). More recently DC has created its own so-called omnibus format, at first used exclusively for Kirby's work, particularly work from the seventies: the four-volume *Fourth World Omnibus* (2007–08) and then *OMAC* (2008), *The Demon* (2008), and even the comparatively obscure *The Losers* (2009). These volumes, striking a compromise between the glossy stock and bright colors of the Archives and the comparative coarseness of the black-and-white Showcase books, adopt a Pop Art aesthetic, with design motifs and paratexts that invoke artifacts of old-fashioned comics publishing such as Benday-dot coloring (shades of Lichtenstein) and vintage logotypes. Price-wise, however, they are closer to the Archives. As of this writing, the bulk of Kirby's work for DC in the seventies is in print (*Kamandi* is due in the fall of 2011). Also, DC has recently released Omnibuses of Simon & Kirby material, including a *Sandman* volume, comprising their run from *Adventure Comics* (1942–1946) and their reunion on *Sandman* #1 (1974); a *Newsboy Legion* volume, reprinting their run from *Star Spangled Comics* (1942–1944); and a *Boy Commandos* collection reprinting stories from *Detective Comics, World's Finest Comics*, and *Boy Commandos* (1942–1943).

The upshot is that most of the work spotlighted in this book—Kirby's output of the sixties and seventies—is currently available in hard and/or softcover form. Some of it can be found in anthologies like the two-volume *Marvel Visionaries: Jack Kirby* (2004–2006), but most is in series collections designed to cover entire comic book runs, either cheap newsprint collections to introduce readers to series continuity or lavish gift books for diehards. What's more, some of the comics have been made available digitally. From 2005 to 2007, Marvel issued DVD-ROMS of vintage comics, each including decades' worth of material (that series is now out of print); then, in 2007, the company established Marvel Digital Comics Unlimited, an online subscription service that includes a great many vintage comics from the sixties, including entire runs by Kirby (like most paper reprints, these have been touched up and recolored).

In other words, if republications of Kirby have long been a staple of Marvel and DC publishing, then the years since 2004 have been especially liberal. The signature works we've studied here, including *The Fantastic Four*, *Thor*, the Fourth World mythos, and *The Eternals*, are more readily available now than they have been at any time since their original comic book publication. Some, such as *The Fantastic Four*, are available in multiple formats, of varying quality and fidelity to the originals.

Unfortunately, much of Kirby's earlier, pre-Marvel, pre-*Challengers* work is now unavailable except in the original, ephemeral, and highly sought-after comic books in which it first appeared. Not that there haven't been multiple attempts to republish Simon & Kirby (and, as noted, some recent ones); it's just that these attempts have been sporadic and most have lapsed out of print. Until very recently, the most readily available mementos of the S&K years have been reprintings of the first ten issues of *Captain America Comics* (1941–42), published and republished by Marvel between 1990 and 2000 (and again starting in 2005). Marvel also published hardcovers, now out of print, of S&K's non-Marvel series *Fighting American* (1989) and *Boys' Ranch* (1991). Since original art board or film for most of the pages in these comics no longer exists, the art restoration required to produce these reprints usually entailed the physical bleaching-out of color from, hence destruction of, actual printed comic books, followed by delicate touchups and corrections on the resulting black-and-white line art—a technique pioneered by artist Greg Theakston, a longtime Kirby associate and biographer and the publisher of many volumes of reprinted comic art. Theakston mounted his own ambitious attempt to reprint early Kirby—not only S&K comics but also work before and after Kirby's partnership with Simon—with a handful of black-and-white paperbacks published under the Pure Imagination imprint. That series comprises *Sky Masters of the Space Force* (1991, rev. ed. 2000); the five volumes of the optimistically titled *Complete Jack Kirby* (1997–2007), which in fact cover only three areas: very early Kirby, early S&K to 1941, and a portion of S&K's work in 1947; the two-volume *Jack Kirby Reader* (2003–04), which is an eclectic sampler spanning various genres and titles pre-1960; and *The Comic Strip Jack Kirby* (2006), covering Kirby's embryonic newspaper strip and panel cartoon work from 1936 to 1940. These specialized volumes, some now scarce, were made with devotees in mind and are most readily found online.[1] Special mention should be made of another now out-of-print volume with production art partly prepared by Theakston, the Richard Howell-edited *Real Love: The Best of the Simon and Kirby Romance Comics: 1940s–1950s* (from the long-defunct

Eclipse Books), which was the first and to date is still the only book-length compilation of S&K's work in that genre. *Real Love* gathers together, in black-and-white, a baker's dozen of romance stories produced by the S&K shop for Crestwood/Prize between 1949 and 1953 (including stories penciled by Bruno Premiani, Leonard Starr, and Mort Meskin). Few contemporary comic book readers were aware of Kirby's substantial contribution to romance comics when Howell's book appeared in 1988.

Suffice to say that reprints of Simon & Kirby are spotty and scattered through various obscure publications, most of them exclusive to the direct market. Most such publications can be found now only with difficulty, primarily online or in the bins of especially well-stocked shops. In the early to mid-seventies, DC reprinted a spate of forties-era S&K stories (featuring the Sandman, Manhunter, and the Boy Commandos), mostly in the back pages of Kirby's Fourth World titles (1971–72), as well as a nine-issue reprint of the Crestwood/Prize *Black Magic* (1973–75). Most other S&K reprints are from small presses. Original S&K publications can of course be found in abundance through dealers in rare comics—such as are found at any large-scale comics convention—but at a price. Academic library holdings could make such vintage comic books available to researchers at little or no cost, but when it comes to early Kirby such holdings appear to be scant (though the Comic Art Collection at the Michigan State University Libraries houses a number of S&K publications, findable through their online catalog). In short, the bulk of Kirby's vast body of work prior to 1957 remains inaccessible to all but a handful of high-end collectors.

But this may change. The most impressive reprintings of S&K are new as of this writing: two coffee table art books from the British publisher Titan, authorized by Simon and the Kirby estate, overseen by Simon himself, edited by Steve Saffel, and with sumptuous digital art restoration by Harry Mendryk. The first of these, *The Best of Simon and Kirby* (2009), spans the years 1940 to 1955 and contains more than a score of S&K collaborations in diverse genres: superheroes, SF, romance, crime, horror, western, war, and humor. Brief essays by Mark Evanier serve to contextualize the stories, and a partial checklist of S&K comics appears as an appendix. The book's design is stylized in a nostalgic way, echoing that of the DC Kirby omnibuses in that it clings to the idea of four-color newsprint despite being a luxury art book. Mendryk's color restorations evoke the texture of history, capturing the Benday-dot look of old, pulpy, four-color comics but without their inevitable yellowing and wear. The book's style owes much to the Pop Art aesthetic of designer Chip Kidd's comics-related work (e.g., *Batman Collected* or *Peanuts: The Art of Charles M. Schulz*), which reflects a desire to find elegance and pathos in the detritus of popular culture. Instead of hiding the work's pulpy comic-book origins, as has been the strategy of so many garish, high-gloss reprintings of old comics, *The Best of Simon and Kirby* seeks to highlight those very origins, as if to invoke a larger pop-cultural archaeology. In other words, aesthetically, *The Best of Simon and Kirby* and DC's omnibus editions are brothers.[2] The book has been touted as the first in an extensive "Official Simon and Kirby Library" to be published by Titan, and indeed the second volume, *The Simon and Kirby Superheroes*, has also been released (a third volume, on crime, is pending). If this project continues, it will be a landmark. In any case, these books are a great gift to Kirby scholars and fans.

Fandom is an important yet under-acknowledged source for Kirby scholarship and information. Devout but limited in scope during his lifetime, the fan culture peculiar to Kirby—as opposed to that for Marvel—has mushroomed over the past fifteen years, spurred by fansites, blogs, fanzines, and prozines, most notably TwoMorrows Publishing's *The Jack Kirby Collector*. Launched in 1994 in the immediate wake of Kirby's death, the *Collector* has thrived in both regular magazine-sized (1994–2000) and deluxe oversized (2000 to present) formats, yielding some fifty-six issues to date as well as seven compilations, some in multiple printings. Though begun as a low-circulation labor of love, the *Collector* eventually became the kernel of a much larger publishing line that now includes various comics- and fandom-related magazines, books, and digital products. The compilations and recent oversized issues of the magazine are stuffed to overflowing with Kirbyana, including: nostalgic remembrances; interpretations of Kirby's stories and characters; interviews not only with Kirby but with other comics professionals, protégés, friends, and acquaintances; and, of greatest scholarly interest, bountiful samples of his original pencil art and informed analyses of the production processes behind his comics. Of special value is Mike Gartland's series "A Failure to Communicate" (spread over issues 21–24, 26, 28–29, and 36), which analyzes key differences between Kirby's original pencils for vintage Marvel comics, including his marginal plot notes, and the final published comics scripted by Stan Lee. The overall tone of *The Jack Kirby Collector* is one of affectionate indulgence and remarkable equanimity, considering the various contrasting and sometimes contesting voices within it. (My list of Works Cited reveals my considerable debt to the magazine, in particular contributions by Amash, Cooke, and Gartland.)

*Collector* editor John Morrow has benefited from and in turn benefits the Kirby estate by running art and articles that bear the estate's imprimatur and by co-founding, with Randolph Hoppe and Kirby's daughter Lisa Kirby, the online Jack Kirby Museum and Research Center (www.kirbymuseum.org, since 2005). Via the Kirby estate, Morrow has access to a huge and historically important archive of photocopied Kirby pencil art from the sixties and seventies amounting to a reported 5,000-plus pages, of which he has become de facto conservator and archivist, scanning and cataloging the artwork for posterity. Thus it is that the *Collector* can routinely feature never-before-published Kirby pages (in keeping with the emphasis on art collecting implied by its title). The Museum, whose larger ambitions have yet to be fulfilled, at this point serves as an online hub for Kirbyana. As of this writing, it also includes the Original Art Digital Archive (a project whereby collectors can donate scans of original Kirby art to the Museum) and hosts well-regarded blogs such as Bob Heer's *Jack Kirby Comics Weblog* and Harry Mendryk's *Simon and Kirby*.

On the other end of the spectrum, Chrissie Harper's harder-to-find U.K.-based magazine *The Jack Kirby Quarterly* (sporadic between 1993 and 2008) has given freer rein to quirkier and sometimes bombastic writing about Kirby, all of it loving of course. Both *Quarterly* and *Collector* have a yen for biographical interpretations of Kirby's work that are hagiographic in tone (virtually a subgenre of Kirby studies). Meanwhile, Kirby-centered articles and features have appeared intermittently in other prozines and fanzines, and, predictably, the Internet has incited rapid and decentered growth of another kind. Comic-Con International: San Diego, at which Kirby and his wife Roz were practically annual guests from 1970 to 1993, has done much to promote his legend over the years, including hosting an annual tribute panel almost every year since 1995.

Beyond the fraternal warmth of *The Jack Kirby Collector* and Comic-Con, etc., Kirby has inspired much commentary in the comics press. This writer recommends *The Comics Journal*'s gutsy coverage of and advocacy for Kirby during the controversies of the late eighties, in fact up to his death in 1994, the cream of which is collected in the essential *Comics Journal Library, Volume One: Jack Kirby*, edited by Milo George (2002). The *Journal*'s critical hip-shooting comes as a relief from the chummy, ingratiating tone of so many comics prozines. Just as *The Jack Kirby Collector* today works with the Kirby estate, so *The Comics Journal* in the eighties and nineties was not simply a source for Kirbyana but also an active intervener in Kirby's career, arguing Kirby's side in his dispute with Marvel management and shaping the way a generation of fans would come to understand his life story.

Kirby fans and collectors are the people who best understand Kirby's confusing publication record, which is not only long and twisty but also prone to doubling back on itself. By this I mean that much of Kirby's work for Marvel and DC, and some for other publishers, has been repeatedly reprinted, at times reformatted and/or cannibalized, with confusing results. Not only was Kirby prolific, he was and is eminently reusable: his byline and his drawings continue to appear in new comics, a practice that has radically blurred history. The list of what Kirby published, or rather has published to date—and what remains in print and out of print—is a slippery, vaporous thing, like smoke. That said, the best bibliographic resource for Kirby continues to be the *Jack Kirby Checklist* (TwoMorrows, 2008). Said *Checklist*, a distillation of Kirby fandom, reflects a massive collaborative effort that took as its departure point the list compiled by Catherine Hohlfeld, Ray Wyman, Jr., and Robert C. Crane for the now out-of-print *The Art of Jack Kirby* (Blue Rose Press, 1992). That effort, taken up by the *Collector's* readership, branched out to include Kirby's unpublished drawings, his animation and media-related work, and a bibliography of Kirbyana including fanzines (even the most obscure), books, and electronic media. This new, expanded list, compiled by Richard Kolkman, was first published at comic book size (1998) but has since been revised and greatly expanded in the "Gold" edition (2008), available in both paperback and downloadable PDF form. Further revisions and corrections will no doubt follow. Cross-referenced to link original publications with reprints, and therefore a godsend to cost-conscious collectors, the *Checklist* is a remarkable thing, a testament to the kind of dedication—obsession, really—required to chase down the wayward evidences of Kirby's career.

Much of what I know about that career would fall under the heading of fan lore, meaning that it is known to many fans but hard to document. I have been reading about Kirby for most of my life, and have had countless conversations about him with comics enthusiasts, to the point that it is sometimes tough to remember exactly where I learned certain things. Of course it is vital to separate confirmable fact from the swampiness of misinformation and assumption. The job is made harder by the very profuseness of Kirbyana. There exists to date no thorough and definitive biography of Kirby, but rather a vast lore of varying usefulness and reliability. More than one biography is said to be in the works as of this writing. To date the most generous, and closest, source for information about Kirby's life is the writing of Mark Evanier, Kirby's long-time friend and sometime assistant. Evanier writes regularly about Kirby for *The Jack Kirby Collector* and moderates the annual Kirby tribute at Comic-Con; moreover, he has produced one book about Kirby, the recent coffee table art book *Kirby: King of Comics* (Abrams, 2008). That book combines a wealth of terrific illustrations (many from surviving original artwork) with a personable and affectionate account of Kirby's life that is less a complete biography than an overview. Kirby appears here as he does so often in the fan press, as the honest, self-deprecating, and self-sacrificing family man, friend, and mentor that he must surely have been; yet the account, though at times tellingly detailed in ways that only an authorized biographer could manage, does not much extend or deepen the ample biographical writing, by Evanier and others, already published in the *Collector* and other zines. It serves as a convenient compilation of Evanier's efforts to date, but the approach taken is perhaps too cozy. The account minimizes controversy and—oddly enough, given the book's spectacular emphasis on Kirby's art—doesn't say much regarding his development as an artist. What it does is present Kirby to a general audience in a lavishly designed package: once again a tribute in a Pop Art style owing something to Lichtenstein, and again a presentation that, far from effacing, actually reinforces the aged and evocative qualities of old comic books and art boards as historic artifacts. *Kirby: King of Comics* is, in short, an uncritical but very enticing gift book. Reportedly Evanier plans a fuller, more in-depth biography of Kirby in due course.

Outside of pamphlets produced for the direct market, one other book to date offers a serious biography of Kirby. Ronin Ro's *Tales to Astonish* (2004) centers on the Marvel explosion of the sixties, as announced by its subtitle, *Jack Kirby, Stan Lee, and the American Comic Book Revolution.* Essentially, the book is a story about Kirby intertwined with the story of Marvel and the story of Stan Lee. It strikes me as a fair-minded and useful account, but it is thinly documented (the claims in the text are entirely unsourced) and un-indexed. Happily, Ro avoids the kind of hagiographic excess and partisanship too often found in the fan press; he depicts Kirby and Lee as interdependent talents and flawed but compelling characters. Unfortunately, his account suffers from a lack of historical context and detail regarding the very period he is most interested in. The latter half of the book is richer in dialogue and anecdote, testifying perhaps to Ro's reliance on original interviews with Kirby's surviving acquaintances, but the earlier and formative phases of Kirby's life, presumably less evocable or accessible via recent interviews, are only thinly sketched. *Tales to Astonish* has some of the immediacy and savor of an oral history—Ro has a thing for novelistic exchanges of dialogue—but at the cost of historical perspective-taking. Key parts of the book that delve into the Golden and Silver Age are more reliant on potted histories, less on anecdote, and so are less vividly realized and less accurate. Ro's chronology is unsure and the book contains factual errors that cast a shadow over the reliability of his account. That said, *Tales to Astonish* remains the most in-depth single treatment of Kirby's life to date, and may benefit from a certain distance from its subject, in contrast to Evanier's personally involved and openly invested take.

Other sources of biographical and historical information specific to Kirby I have found useful include: Joe Simon's memoir *The Comic Book Makers*, co-written with Jim Simon (rev. ed., 2003); the aforementioned *The Art of Jack Kirby* by Ray Wyman, Jr. et al. (1992); *Stan Lee and the Rise and Fall of the American Comic Book* by Jordan Raphael and Tom Spurgeon (2003); Theakston's *The Jack Kirby Treasury*, Vol. 1 (1982) and Vol. 2 (1991); Will Eisner's *Shop Talk* (2001); and, in my boyhood, Jim Steranko's *The Steranko History of Comics*, Vol. 1 (1970). These are in addition to the many books on comics history in general that I've read across the decades. Among the myriad magazines I consulted—*FOOM, Comics Scene, Comics Interview, Comic Book Artist*, etc., and of course *The Comics Journal* and *The Jack Kirby Collector*—I should make special mention of *Amazing Heroes* #100 (Aug. 1986), a themed issue on Kirby that I pored over like a Bible when it first came out so many years ago, and several issues of Roy Thomas's latter-day revival of *Alter Ego*, in particular the Timely/Marvel-themed issues (#57 includes an index of Marvel superheroes from 1939–57) and most particularly the Joe Simon special, #76 (March 2008). Many of the above sources are direct market publications that now serve me as artifacts of my years in the hobby. All have been useful signposts on the way to writing this book. Finally, I would be remiss if I did not acknowledge the helpfulness of the online Grand Comics Database (www .comics.org), an ongoing volunteer project that, heroically, aims to index every comic book ever published, and which I have found very useful for its historical reach, corroborative value, and sheer convenience. Its goal may be quixotic, but it truly is grand.

The above, I hope, situates this study by indicating how Kirby has been received among collectors, fans, critics, and historians, and by showing the extent to which his work is continually being recycled and recontextualized within today's comic book culture. It may seem strange to say it, but the career of Jack Kirby remains a live and unpredictable thing. Long after his passing, Kirby has become the household god of comic books, and the invocation of his name will serve many and sometimes competing purposes in the years ahead. May this book prove a useful addition to that conversation.

# NOTES

## INTRODUCTION

1. In the larger context of comic book history, the fan-coined terms "Golden Age" and "Silver Age" are misleading insofar as they privilege the changing fortunes of the superhero genre and the nostalgic focus of collectors. Too often these terms are used to tell the entire history of American comic books, as if that history could be collapsed into or summed up by the status of the costumed hero. In fact as larger historical categories these "Ages" are slippery, untrustworthy, and mystifying. Despite this, I have sometimes used them here, strictly in the contexts of superhero comics and superhero fandom, which are crucial contexts for understanding Kirby. Use of the Age terms is practically unavoidable when discussing the genre. Still, I refer readers to Benjamin Woo's cogent critique of the "Age" concept.

2. Marvel Entertainment, LLC, formerly Marvel Enterprises, is rooted in Marvel Comics and hence can claim a corporate history dating back to what collectors call Timely, that is, Martin Goodman's comic book publishing outfit launched in 1939 (if not further back to Goodman's pulp publishing venture, launched c. 1932–33). Note that Marvel officially observed its "70th Anniversary" in 2009, an observance that amounts to a claim of continuous and integrated history. In fact, however, the corporation's history is discontinuous and bewilderingly complex, the more so since Marvel went public in 1991. Suffice to say that today's Marvel, though related by name and of course intellectual property, is a distinctly different company from its pulp forebears, or even from the Marvel of the early nineties. The current Marvel Entertainment—the entity acquired by Disney—stems from the 1998 merger of Marvel Entertainment Group, Inc., and its partner Toy Biz, Inc., a merger that effectively redeemed Marvel from Chapter 11 bankruptcy and ended a bitter struggle among investors for control of the company. Officially, today's Marvel comics are published by Marvel Worldwide, Inc., a subsidiary of Marvel Entertainment; note, however, that the company licenses its intellectual properties through a wholly owned subsidiary called Marvel Characters, which can make the fine print on Marvel products confusing. Past Marvel owners, besides founder Goodman, include the Perfect Film and Chemical Corporation (later Cadence Industries), to whom Goodman sold the company in 1968, followed by New World Enterprises, then financier Ron Perelman's MacAndrews & Forbes Holdings,

Inc. During the nineties, Marvel's shifts in management, aggressive business practices, and eventual bankruptcy wrought havoc in the relatively fragile comic book market.

For background on the company, sources are legion but many are untrustworthy. I refer readers to Daniels' "official" history; Raphael and Spurgeon's biography of Stan Lee; and, for more recent financial history, Raviv (and the corporate information available at Marvel .com). Lee's autobiography *Excelsior!* (with George Mair, 2002) gives Lee's preferred version of his history at the company. Regarding Disney's buyout of Marvel, the deal, reportedly worth more than $4.2 billion, was announced in August 2009 and completed by year's end.

3. In September 2009 Kirby's four children notified Marvel, Disney, and various licensees of their intent to regain copyrights to a great many properties Kirby co-created for the company. In January 2010 Marvel filed suit to block this move, seeking to have the Kirbys' claims rendered invalid by judicial declaration. In March 2010 the Kirbys countersued, requesting a jury trial (*Kirby v. Marvel Entertainment, Inc.*). The upshot of all this hangs in the air, unresolved as of this writing. For context, see Barnes and Cieply; Goldberg.

4. I should note some habits in my handling of citations and quoted material. First, when citing passages or details from Kirby comics, I give the page numbering of the original comic book editions whenever possible. Because Kirby reprints are many and varied, and because I cannot predict which editions my readers will consult, I have tried to minimize confusion simply by giving the page numbers as they were originally inscribed on the comic book pages. That original numbering is typically retained in the various reprints (though reprint editions often include their own continuous page numbering as well). Second, given the lack of reliable release dates for so many old comic books, I have generally given the "cover dates," that is, the dates printed on the covers and/or in the indicia of the comics, knowing full well that comic books were typically released two to three months ahead of their cover dates and sometimes more. So, for example, *The Fantastic Four* #1 is generally dated November 1961, its cover date, though it is known that it actually came out some three months prior. This quirk of comic book publishing does not pose a serious problem in what follows, since my observations about chronology typically concern extended periods of activity and development (say, Kirby's workload during a lengthy interval or era, or the time from one major project to the next) rather than precise street dates. Third, at the risk of confusion and/or of seeming to shout at my readers, I have usually tried to honor the idiosyncratic punctuation and other forms of emphasis found in the original comic book texts. In the case of words that are doubly stressed with italics and bolding—a practice typical of Kirby's and other vintage comics—I have used italics. I have not, however, followed the comics' common practice of CAPITALIZING EVERY-THING. Such questions matter because the lettering in comics is emphatically *marked* text, in Johanna Drucker's sense, as opposed to the putatively neutral, unmarked text that dominates in most typeset books (*The Visible Word* 94–95), and in my opinion should be observed by the critic even though it does not read the same once transplanted to the academic page. (See Kannenberg, "Graphic Text, Graphic Context," on the matter of marked hands and fonts in comics lettering.) Unless otherwise noted, the emphases in quoted comics material come from the original. Also, since comics scripting often uses ellipses, I have had to note my own insertions of ellipses within square brackets.

5. During late revisions of this book, I learned of a recent French study that analyzes Kirby's work in terms of the apocalyptic, Harry Morgan and Manuel Hirtz's *Les Apocalypses de Jack Kirby* (Lyon: les moutons électriques, 2009). My copy arrived during my final edits, so I have not yet had a chance to absorb this study.

## CHAPTER 0

1. To say that the indicia of Marvel comics can be bewildering is an understatement. The company's history is made especially confusing by founder Martin Goodman's long-time practice, from the forties onward, of doing business under dozens of company names (ostensibly part of an elaborate financial shell game). For convenience's sake, collectors generally refer to Goodman's comics output prior to 1951 as "Timely" and his output from 1951 to 1961 as "Atlas" (in fact the name of Goodman's distribution company during much of that period).

Note that Goodman did use the Marvel brand name early on, if only fitfully: his first comic book title was the series *Marvel Mystery Comics*, at first titled simply *Marvel Comics* (1939), and small "Marvel" logos appeared intermittently on the company's covers in the late mid-forties up to 1950. In fact several Goodman titles of the forties and early fifties featured characters bearing "Marvel" in their names, including The Black Marvel (1940–41) and Marvel Boy (launched by Simon & Kirby in 1940, later revived). Only much later, though, would the company become known clearly and officially as Marvel. In fact, it was but part of Goodman's larger magazine business, which at some point by the early fifties had become known as "Magazine Management Company" (about which, see the memoir by Bruce Jay Friedman, "Even the Rhinos Were Nymphos"). When Perfect Film and Chemical acquired Marvel in 1968, what they actually acquired was Magazine Management.

Whatever the name(s) of the comic book line and its parent company, Stan Lee served as its editorial director throughout most of those years. Kirby, as argued herein, was Lee's powerhouse, and crucial to the transformation of the erstwhile Atlas into the more familiar Marvel brand of today. See Raphael and Spurgeon; Daniels, *Marvel*. The volume of interviews, *Stan Lee: Conversations* (ed. McLaughlin, 2007) is also helpful for context, though its earliest interviews are from 1968.

2. Like its rival Marvel, DC Comics has had a complex history. Founded in 1934 by Malcolm Wheeler-Nicholson as National Allied Publications (other similar names were used too), the company barely survived its early years. By 1936 Wheeler-Nicholson was dependent on the support of his major creditor, the distributor Independent News, owned by Harry Donenfeld and Paul Sampliner and managed by the team of Donenfeld and Jack Liebowitz. By late 1937 or early 1938, Donenfeld and Liebowitz, using the name Detective Comics Inc., had bought out the bankrupt Wheeler-Nicholson; by 1940 their comic books bore the "DC" logo. In 1944 Detective absorbed its sister company, All-American Comics, of which Liebowitz had been part owner (in later years the company would become known for buying up and revamping properties from defunct companies such as Quality, Fawcett, and Charlton). Then the company officially took the name National Comics, which began appearing in its magazines circa early 1947. Later Liebowitz arranged for National Comics, Independent News, and their affiliates to join into one larger corporation, National

Periodical Publications, Inc., which, crucially, cemented the long-term relationship between DC and its distribution. Independent was a highly successful distributor, handling a huge volume of not only comics but also magazines, such as *Playboy*, and paperbacks, such as the Signet line.

In 1961 National Periodical went public. By then its comics line had been familiarly known as DC for some two decades (in contrast to Marvel, which did not definitively settle on its Marvel brand name until the early sixties). In 1967 National Periodical was sold to Kinney National Services, which soon also acquired Warner Bros.-Seven Arts and would later become Warner Communications (1972), then Time Warner (1990). In 1976, under new publisher Jenette Kahn, the comic book line's name was officially changed to DC Comics, which was, after all, simply a tardy surrender to custom. In September 2009 Warner Bros. Entertainment announced that DC Comics would henceforth be part of a newly created division called DC Entertainment, Inc., the purpose of which is "to fully realize [. . .] the DC Comics brand and characters across all media and platforms" (Hyde n. pag.), a move generally seen as an attempt to compete with Marvel Entertainment, Inc. (and its new owner, Disney). For background, readers are referred to Jones, *Men of Tomorrow*; Gabilliet; Daniels, *DC*; and Goulart, *Over 50 Years*.

## CHAPTER 1

1. I myself heard Eisner declare this, that "style is a result of our failure to achieve perfection." It was a favorite line of his, though I have not been able to trace it back to a definitive written source. Jerry Stratton's online report on the 1993 Comic Arts Conference (which Eisner attended) quotes the remark, and I was to hear it, multiple times I believe, at later conferences. Colleagues of mine remember the line too.

2. To be precise, drawings are constellations of signs that join together to constitute larger-scale meta-signs. Some semioticians ignore the smaller constitutive marks that make up a drawing—say, strokes of the pencil, pen, or brush—or treat these only glancingly insofar as they may be subsumed into larger, catchall terms such as facture or "rendering." Others have attempted to discuss the details of cartoon drawings in terms of the smallest divisible or reducible units: the least elements that can be isolated and "read" for their semiotic function. (In this connection, Mark Newgarden's comic "Love's Savage Fury," a deconstruction of Ernie Bushmiller's *Nancy* in which the few marks that define Nancy's face are scrambled, is particularly interesting; see Newgarden's *We All Die Alone* 162–66.) I would argue that both these positions—that which entirely ignores mark-marking in favor of overall forms, and that which seeks to atomize drawings down to discrete elements—are inadequate to the study of comic art. See Elkins 3–6; Groensteen, *System* 3–6.

3. The career and ideas of Charles Sanders Peirce (1839–1914), who among other things was the initiator of philosophic pragmatism, add up to a vast and imposing field of study, even when one aims to focus only on his semeiotic. The most authoritative collection of his works, and most thorough record of the development of his thought, is the *Writings of Charles S. Peirce: A Chronological Edition*, a project launched in 1975 under the direction of Edward C. Moore and Max H. Fisch that has resulted in seven volumes to date (Indiana UP, 1982–2010). That edition is the ongoing work of the Peirce Edition Project, housed

since 1983 at Indiana University-Purdue University Indianapolis. Vol. 2, which spans 1867 to 1871, includes Peirce's first exposition of the icon-index-symbol trichotomy ("On a New List of Categories," 1867), while Vols. 5 and 6, 1884 to 1890, demonstrate both the triad's further elaboration and its roots in Peirce's habitually triadic thinking. It is also helpful to consult smaller anthologies of Peirce, and secondary works in semiotics, in order to get an overview of his thought and stature. I found the following most helpful: *The Essential Peirce*, Vols. 1 and 2, ed. Houser, Kloesel, and the Peirce Edition Project; *Peirce on Signs*, ed. Hoopes; Clarke, *Sources of Semiotic*; Pharies; Merrell, both *Peirce, Signs, and Meaning* and *Semiosis in the Postmodern Age*; and Misak et al., *The Cambridge Companion to Peirce*. Also useful is the Peirce Edition Project's website at IUPUI.

4. The difficulty of Peirce's theory of signs is proverbial. See for example Clarke's remarks in *Sources of Semiotic* (63), or Houser's in his Introduction to *The Essential Peirce*, Vol. 1 (xxxvii-xxxviii). To make matters more difficult, Peirce revised the theory substantially over years and decades, often in uncompleted manuscripts, so that, as T. L. Short has observed, what we are left with is "a sequence of contradictions, a series of ambitious yet unfinished sketches of elaborate but mutually incompatible structures" (214).

5. For background on the naturalist-conventionalist debate, see for example Gombrich's shifting arguments as reflected in *Art and Illusion*, Ch. II, and the seemingly contrary "Image and Code"; Mitchell, *Iconology*, Ch. 3; and Carroll, *Philosophy of Art*, Ch. 1. Goodman's *Languages of Art* famously sets forth the extreme conventionalist position.

6. For studies of Kirby's technique, see especially the Gallery section (titled "The Evolution of Kirby's Style") in *The Jack Kirby Collector* No. 37 (Winter 2003), as well as the following articles in *Collector* No. 38 (Spring 2003): Alexander, "The Cosmic Squiggle" and "The Kirby Burst"; Apeldoorn; Reinders. Also, Norris Burroughs' blog, "Kirby Kinetics," launched in May 2009, is insightful. Finally, see Brayshaw for an admirable analysis of Kirby's late style.

7. Dovetailing with Groensteen, Harry Morgan too observes that comic art is anthropocentric, meaning that the "graphic world becom[es] an extension of the character" and that therefore the distinction between character and world is unstable ("Graphic Shorthand" 39). "It is the character," Morgan says, "that gives the image sequence its semantic cohesion and it is around the character that the storytelling is organized." Indeed Morgan describes comics storytelling as, in essence, *caricature as spread over frame sequence* (35).

## CHAPTER 2

1. The name "Atlas" may also have been meant to identify Goodman's comic book publishing outfit itself, not just his Atlas News distribution company, since the appearance of the Atlas logo (a globe) on comic book covers predated and postdated Goodman's shifts in distribution (Lammers 47–51). That is, the Atlas logo appeared on covers seemingly months before Goodman began self-distributing via Atlas News (c. 1951–52), and it continued to appear for a while even after Goodman shut Atlas News down (1956–57). In fact the name Atlas appeared on a few covers even as early as 1943, as if that name were simply one of the many fictive entities in Goodman's portfolio. The issue remains hard to grasp—a testament

to Goodman's evasiveness—but Lammers makes the case that Atlas was supposed to be a comic book brand as well as distributor.

2. Famously, when profit-sharing on *Captain America Comics*, allegedly promised by Goodman, did not come as expected, Simon and Kirby booked a hotel room near the Timely offices and starting moonlighting there during lunches and on weekends—the discovery of which led to their summary dismissal by Goodman. By this time they were already doing work for DC, Goodman's chief rival and the originator of the costumed hero genre. Later, after WWII, S&K would move to Harvey, to Crestwood, and to other publishers as opportunities arose (even if those opportunities sometimes turned to sand and sifted through their fingers). One has the impression, from various accounts, that Kirby followed Simon's lead in business, trusting to the other's experience. Simon's own account (*Makers* 40–41) depicts Kirby as shy of risk, anxious to keep a solid if unspectacular gig for the sake of supporting his parents, and comically self-conscious about his height (Simon towered a full head above him). The causes probably went deeper than that, for Simon, Kirby would later reflect, "came from a middle-class background, and I'd never met a middle-class person." In fact Kirby came to consider Simon his "role model for learning how to acquire a different type of character" (Eisner, *Shop Talk* 197, 205).

3. Some of Marvel's non-superhero titles lasted well into the superhero era. For instance, *Patsy Walker* lasted until 1965, *Patsy and Hedy* until 1967, and *Millie the Model* until 1973. Obviously, and unfortunately, the rise of the superhero accompanied if not accelerated the abandonment of girl readers (or, alternately, girls' abandonment of comic books). Attempts to create feminist superheroes would follow in the seventies.

4. Actually, it is not quite accurate to say that the Marvel crossovers began in March 1963. The *superhero* crossovers began then, but Stan Lee clearly recognized the promotional value of crossovers before then, as evidenced by team-ups between Linda Carter and Patsy Walker (*Patsy Walker* #99, Feb. 1962) and Linda Carter and Millie the Model (*Linda Carter, Student Nurse* #9, Jan. 1963). Incidentally, these characters are now tied to the Marvel Universe: for example, the superheroine Hellcat, introduced in 1976, is supposed to be the same Patsy Walker (a character introduced in 1944).

5. If 1967 was a peak for Kirby, the period 1968–1970 was in some ways like coming down the other side of the mountain. It should be noted that in late 1967 Marvel downsized its original art boards in order to save money on engraving; thus Kirby's originals shrank from 12 1/2 by 18 1/2 inches a page, which was almost twice-up (that is, twice the dimensions of the printed comic book page), down to 10 by 15 inches. An economizing move, this enabled the makers of the printing plates to photograph four pages at once rather than two. Unfortunately, this change bemused Kirby and had a dampening effect on his art, starting with the Marvel titles cover-dated fall 1967. Kirby biographer Mark Evanier discusses the debilitating effects of this shrinkage in *The Jack Kirby Collector* #37. This is one reason why Kirby's artwork for Marvel in the sixties hits its peak prior to 1968 (my thanks to Craig Fischer for reminding me of this). Coupled with Kirby's contractual uncertainty and increasing frustration with Marvel, this cramping of his style contributed to Marvel's wilting near the decade's end.

# CHAPTER 3

1. Gruenwald's role as Marvel's "continuity cop" was jokingly acknowledged in the comics themselves. Walter Simonson's run on *The Fantastic Four* climaxes with a story (#352–354, May–July 1991) in which the team runs afoul of an other-dimensional continuity maintenance organization called the Time Variance Authority: in essence a cosmic office consisting of infinite desks hovering in empty space, presided over by a Gruenwald-like authority called Mr. Mobius (many of whose colleagues look just like him, that is, like Gruenwald). The TVA's mission is to see to it that "time in the Omniverse is measured, charted, recorded . . . and ultimately *judged*"—in a nutshell, to police continuity. The result is "a self-replicating bureaucracy of infinite dimension" (#353, pages 16–17). Having saved a "timeline" slated for termination, the FF are brought before the TVA on charges of "illegal time use" and "continuity theft." This story references several other complicated time-travel and alternate-timeline story arcs within the Marvel Universe.

# CHAPTER 4

1. The seeming disconnect, and yet perhaps underlying agreement, between Burke's aesthetic and political philosophy is beyond my scope. Extending the study of Kirby into the political realm, though, remains tempting and even important. I am convinced that Kirby shared certain aspects of Burke's conservative thinking—aspects highlighted by Byrne—including the sense of a higher order, a humbling awareness of human limitations, a respect for mystery, and an anti-intellectual side that valued intuitive responses and strong feelings. Also, both Burke's and Kirby's aesthetics are shaped by starkly gendered contrasts (beauty as feminine, sublimity as masculine), another issue I have bypassed here and that needs treatment. On the other hand, Kirby, an ardent American, was much more of a populist than Burke, and this helps relieve the chilly, alienating qualities of his more apocalyptic tales. Also, ever the futurist, Kirby was less resistant to social change (though his imagined futures are sometimes nightmarish).

In approaching these issues, I've found most helpful Byrne's "Burke's Higher Romanticism" (2006), White's *Edmund Burke: Modernity, Politics, and Aesthetics* (1994), Eagleton's *The Ideology of the Aesthetic* (1990), and, although it doesn't deal with Burke, Steiner's *Venus in Exile* (2001). Thanks to Jonathan Gray for the nudge.

2. It must be admitted that Kirby's depiction of scientists is often critical and antiintellectual. Note that the egghead, i.e., the super-smart character with an oversized or disembodied head, was a fallback device of his (used as early as 1940) and that he usually casts such characters as villains. Indeed Egghead is the name of an evil scientist Kirby cocreated for the "Ant-Man" series in *Tales to Astonish*. More revealing is the hyper-cephalic Modok (from "Captain America"), probably the best-loved example of the trope, who, like Metron, is dependent on a chair. Kirby often used the combination of overgrown head and small or atrophied body to render an implicit critique of an emotionless scientism. On the other hand, we have the example of Marvel's wheelchair-bound, bald-pated, hyper-intelligent Professor X, who, though rather Metron-like, is a science hero. Kirby's most bizarre example would be the bodiless, machine-driven Master Mind in *Captain Victory and the Galactic Rangers*.

3. *Journey into Mystery* was the first of Marvel's long-running anthology series post 1962 to make the nominal switch to a solo superhero title, though by then (1966) all the anthologies had been spotlighting superheroes for some time. In early 1968 the remaining anthology titles followed suit, part of a sudden expansion ostensibly enabled by Marvel's renegotiation of its distribution contract with Independent News (a switch to new distributor Curtis would follow in 1969). As part of this expansion, new series were launched and old series retitled. For instance, *Tales of Suspense*, which for years had been featuring Iron Man and Captain America, split into two new titles, *Iron Man* (starting with #1, May 1968) and *Captain America* (continuing the *Suspense* numbering with #100, April 1968). This hasty growth presaged Marvel's change in ownership a few months later, in the fall of 1968, when Martin Goodman sold the operation to Perfect Film and Chemical (see Daniels, *Marvel* 139). The fact that *Journey into Mystery* was retitled *Thor* so far ahead of the curve, coupled with the remarkable artistic development of both "Thor" and "Tales of Asgard," confirms that *Journey* was the anthology in which Kirby had the greatest personal investment.

4. Note that the Ray Harryhausen fantasy/effects film *Jason and the Argonauts*, produced by Charles Schneer and directed by Don Chaffey, had come out in mid-1963, about two years before Kirby and Lee's "argonauts" storyline began. "Tales of Asgard" would have made a terrific Harryhausen movie.

## CHAPTER 5

1. Prior to the *Fourth World Omnibus* volumes, DC put out paperback reprints of the Fourth World, beginning with black-and-white volumes mimicking Marvel's low-cost "Essentials" series. Released between 1998 and 2001, these collected *New Gods*, *Mister Miracle*, and *Forever People* respectively. Color paperbacks of *Jimmy Olsen* followed in 2003–04.

2. The matter of Colletta's inking is a source of continual hullabaloo in the fan press (see for example Bryant, *Line*). Personally, I agree with the many who detest his work, but recognize that Kirby's reliance on inkers raises a larger issue: it's an awkward reminder that he was not an autonomous artist-hero independently painting his masterpiece, but rather a worker who sometimes accepted less than optimal conditions for his work. It could be argued that the vilification of Colletta within Kirby fandom represents a displacement of anxiety over the inconsistency of Kirby's own output: by placing blame on Colletta, fans can talk about the inconsistency of the work without risk of maligning Kirby himself or of questioning the widespread belief that sheer speed and prolificacy equal quality and importance. I note that Colletta's work-for-hire ethic often comes up for criticism while Kirby's own (Kirby being perhaps the quintessential comic book artist for hire) is ignored, with the effect that Kirby appears a Romantic victim of or rebel against comics industry practice whereas Colletta appears merely a routine exploiter of same. This inconsistency is telling. The truth is that Kirby was responsible for accepting the terms under which he worked, and for years those terms included Colletta, a situation that, given Kirby's exalted and Colletta's less-than-exalted status, poses a conundrum. Perhaps the real sore point here is not the work or work ethic of Colletta himself, but the way Colletta reminds fans of the brute realities of work-for-hire, realities to which Kirby adapted but which often adversely affected the appearance of his published work. In this context Colletta would appear to be a scapegoat. That said, Kirby's personal investment in the work was clearly on a whole

other level from Colletta's, which helps explain why it is so painful to so many fans to think about the two artists being yoked together. In any case, the Fourth World's status as masterpiece is diluted a bit by the inconsistency of the finished art.

3. Criticisms of the superhero genre as inherently fascistic emerged in the forties and fifties, with notable contributions from Walter Ong ("Comics and the Superstate," 1945), Ong's mentor Marshall McLuhan (*The Mechanical Bride*, 1951), Gershon Legman (*Love and Death*, 1949), and Fredric Wertham, whose notorious *Seduction of the Innocent* (1954), the culmination of his anti-comics work, briefly addresses the issue. There were other voices too (see Beaty 115). Even contemporary cartoonists have joined this ideological critique; for instance, Art Spiegelman has suggested that there is a fascist sensibility behind Kirby's work (Interview 106–108). Certainly fascist iconography has had a role in the so-called revisionist superhero trend, beginning in the eighties. Regarding Spiegelman's critique of Kirby, and the larger question of fascism in superheroes, see Fischer, "Fantastic Fascism?".

## CHAPTER 6

1. Himon's name is curious, relaying as it does a homophonic pun that bears connotations Kirby presumably did not intend. Kirby had a penchant for such puns (Darkseid being the crowning example), but this one is particularly ripe. Besides physiological, sexual, and conjugal implications—from the hymen and its namesake, the Greek god of marriage—the name alludes, potentially, to the idea of a skin being sloughed off (Himon's successive bodies), to the principle of joining (as in marriage), and, via rhyme, to Simon Peter and various other Biblical Simons: apostles, cross-bearers, magicians. What Kirby intended by the name's suggestiveness is anyone's guess—it's a credit to his handling of the character that the name ceases to be a distraction. Intriguingly, Himon's appearance was based at least in part on Kirby's friend Shel Dorf, founder of what we now know as the San Diego Comic-Con (Evanier, "Dorf" n. pag.).

## CHAPTER 7

1. Jim Shooter, a controversial, even polarizing figure, began work at Marvel as an associate editor in 1977 and assumed the editor-in-chief's role in 1978, during the closing months of Kirby's last run there. He transformed Marvel, centralizing editorial power and placing more and more stress on continuity as a sales tactic. In the eighties, he ushered Marvel from the traditional (and fading) newsstand market to reliance on the emergent direct market. Often portrayed as a stubborn autocrat, Shooter seems a bridge between the Marvel over which Stan Lee presided and the later, more nakedly "corporate" Marvel that has played such an imperious role in said market. (He was the reigning editor, and James Galton the president, during Kirby's struggle with Marvel over his original art.)

## APPENDIX

1. The comics in the Pure Imagination collections are painstaking facsimiles, owed to Greg Theakston's unique production method. Reprints produced by other means may look different, and certainly the absence of color affects the flavor of the work (consider by way

of contrast the reprints in *The Best of Simon and Kirby*). Theakston has sought to copyright his facsimiles, on the grounds that, though the comics in these collections are ostensibly in the public domain, each image has been "slightly altered" in order to "fingerprint" the new version (see the indicia of several of his volumes).

2. In general, recent high-end reprints of vintage comics have turned away from the glossy Marvel Masterworks or DC Archives approach, favoring instead coloring that keeps close to that of vintage four-color comics and a design aesthetic that evokes the history and datedness of the work. See for example Greg Sadowski, ed., *Supermen! The First Wave of Comic Book Heroes 1936–1941* (Fantagraphics, 2009), the Fletcher Hanks anthologies assembled by Paul Karasik (Fantagraphics, 2007–2009), or Dan Nadel, ed., *Art Out of Time: Unknown Comics Visionaries, 1900–1969* (Abrams, 2006).

# WORKS CITED

As noted in our Appendix, most of the comics studied in this book have been reprinted multiple times, with the result that Kirby's bibliographic trail looks more like a frantic and constantly expanding scribble than a neat line. Giving concise, usable publication information for these comics would be near impossible. For this reason, the comics I have discussed are sourced by date and publisher as they come up in the main text. I refer readers to Chapter 0 for a chronological synopsis including key works, and to Richard Kolkman et al.'s *Jack Kirby Checklist* (TwoMorrows, 2008) for more detailed publication information.

Important examples of Kirby studies and Kirbyana are described in the Appendix. Many are listed in the following, which comprises the texts and art works—besides Kirby's comics—that directly informed this study, as well as certain non-Kirby comics I've compared to his.

"2005 Kirby Tribute Panel." With Mark Evanier et al. *The Jack Kirby Collector* 45 (Winter 2006): 64–75. Print.

Alexander, Mark. "The Cosmic Squiggle." *The Jack Kirby Collector* 38 (Spring 2003): 62–63. Print.

———. "The Kirby Burst!" *The Jack Kirby Collector* 38 (Spring 2003): 70–71. Print.

———. "The Quest!" *The Jack Kirby Collector* 36 (Summer 2002): 52–63. Print.

Amash, Jim. "A *Fine* Influence: Notes on Lou Fine's Style and His Importance to the Comic Book Field." *Alter Ego* Vol. 3, No. 17 (Sept. 2002): 9–12. Print.

*Amazing Heroes* #100. Spec. iss. on Kirby. Agoura, CA: Fantagraphics, Aug. 1986. Print.

Anderson, Murphy. *The Life and Art of Murphy Anderson*. With R. C. Harvey. Raleigh, NC: TwoMorrows, 2003. Print.

Apeldoorn, Ger. "More Krackle!" *The Jack Kirby Collector* 38 (Spring 2003): 66–67. Print.

———. "When Jacob Met Stanley." *The Jack Kirby Collector* 53 (Summer 2009): 6–10. Print.

Arnheim, Rudolf. *Visual Thinking*. Berkeley: U of California P, 1969. Print.

Ashwin, Clive. "Drawing, Design and Semiotics." *Design Discourse: History, Theory, Criticism*. Ed. Victor Margolin. Chicago: U of Chicago P, 1989. 199–209. Print.

Baetens, Jan. "Revealing Traces: A New Theory of Graphic Enunciation." *The Language of Comics: Word and Image*. Ed. Robin Varnum and Christina T. Gibbons. Jackson: UP of Mississippi, 2001. 145–55. Print.

Bal, Mieke. *Reading "Rembrandt": Beyond the Word-Image Opposition.* Cambridge: Cambridge UP, 1991. Print.

Barnes, Brooks, and Michael Cieply. "A Supersized Custody Battle Over Marvel Superheroes." *New York Times.* 20 Mar. 2010. Web. 15 Nov. 2010.

Barthes, Roland. "The Photographic Message." *Image-Music-Text.* Trans. Stephen Heath. New York: Hill and Wang, 1977. 15–31. Print.

Beaty, Bart. *Fredric Wertham and the Critique of Mass Culture.* Jackson: UP of Mississippi, 2005. Print.

Beerbohm, Robert Lee. "The Mainline Comics Story: An Initial Examination." *The Jack Kirby Collector* 25 (Aug. 1999): 86–95. Print.

Bourdieu, Pierre. "The Field of Cultural Production, or: The Economic World Reversed." Trans. Richard Nice. *The Field of Cultural Production: Essays on Art and Literature.* Ed. and intro. Randal Johnson. New York: Columbia UP, 1993. 29–73. Print.

———. *The Rules of Art: Genesis and Structure of the Literary Field.* Trans. Susan Emanuel. Stanford: Stanford UP, 1995. Print.

Brayshaw, Christopher. "The Monument Carver's Store." George 50–59. Print.

Broderick, Damien. "New Wave and backwash: 1960–1980." *The Cambridge Companion to Science Fiction.* Ed. Edward James and Farah Mendlesohn. Cambridge: Cambridge UP, 2003. 48–63. Print.

Brooker, Will. *Batman Unmasked: Analyzing a Cultural Icon.* London: Continuum, 2000. Print.

Bryant, Robert L., Jr. "Cut & Paste." *The Jack Kirby Collector* 48 (Spring 2007): 10–12. Print.

———. *The Thin Black Line: Perspectives on Vince Colletta, Comics' Most Controversial Inker.* Raleigh, NC: TwoMorrows, 2010. Print.

Bukatman, Scott. *Matters of Gravity: Special Effects and Supermen in the 20th Century.* Durham, NC: Duke UP, 2003. Print.

Burke, Edmund. *A Philosophical Enquiry into the Origin of Our Ideas of the Sublime and Beautiful.* 1757. Ed. and intro. James T. Boulton. Oxford: Basil Blackwell, 1987. Print.

Burroughs, Norris. *Kirby Kinetics.* Blog. The Jack Kirby Museum and Research Center. May 2009–. Web. 29 July 2010.

———. "Fine Development." *Kirby Kinetics.* 10 July 2009. Web. 29 July 2010.

Busiek, Kurt. Introduction. *Astro City: Life in the Big City.* By Kurt Busiek, Brent E. Anderson, Alex Ross, et al. La Jolla, CA: Homage Comics, 1996. 7–11. Print.

Byrne, William F. "Burke's Higher Romanticism: Politics and the Sublime." *Humanitas* 19.1–2 (2006): 14–34. *Expanded Academic ASAP.* Web. 12 Jan. 2011.

Carlin, John, Paul Karasik, and Brian Walker, eds. *Masters of American Comics.* Exhibition catalogue. Los Angeles: Hammer Museum and Museum of Contemporary Art; New Haven: Yale UP, 2005. Print.

Carroll, Noël. "Horror and Humor." *Journal of Aesthetics and Art Criticism* 57.2 (Spring 1999): 145–60. Print.

———. *Philosophy of Art: A Contemporary Introduction.* London: Routledge, 1999. Print.

———. *The Philosophy of Horror, or, Paradoxes of the Heart.* New York: Routledge, 1990. Print.

Casey, Joe, and Tom Scioli. *Gødland.* 34 issues to date. 2005–. Rpt. in 5 vols. Berkeley, CA: Image Comics, 2006–2010. Print.

Castle, Terry. *Masquerade and Civilization: The Carnivalesque in Eighteenth-Century English Culture and Fiction.* Stanford: Stanford UP, 1986. Print.

Cawelti, John G. *Adventure, Mystery, and Romance: Formula Stories as Art and Popular Culture.* Chicago: U of Chicago P, 1976. Print.

Chabon, Michael. *The Amazing Adventures of Kavalier & Clay.* New York: Random, 2000. Print.

———. "Secret Skin: An Essay in Unitard Theory." *New Yorker* 10 Mar. 2008: 64–69. Rpt. in *Superheroes: Fashion and Fantasy.* Andrew Bolton et al. New York: Metropolitan Museum of Art; New Haven: Yale UP, 2008. 11–23. Print.

"Change or Die!" Roundtable discussion by Neil Gaiman, Stephen Bissette, and Tom Veitch. Afterword. *The One.* By Rick Veitch. West Townshend, VT: King Hell, 1989. 188–209. Print.

Clarke, Arthur C. *Profiles of the Future: An Inquiry into the Limits of the Possible.* Rev. ed. New York: Holt, 1984. Print.

Clarke, D. S., Jr. *Sources of Semiotic: Readings with Commentary from Antiquity to the Present.* Carbondale, IL: Southern Illinois UP, 1990. Print.

Clowes, Daniel. *Modern Cartoonist: The Naked Truth.* Seattle: Fantagraphics, 1997. Pamphlet originally bound into *Eightball* #18 by Clowes. Available on the Fantagraphics website. 29 July 2010.

Collins, John J. *The Apocalyptic Imagination: An Introduction to Jewish Apocalyptic Literature.* Rev. 2nd ed. Grand Rapids, MI: Wm. B. Eerdmans, 1998. Print.

Coogan, Peter M. *The Secret Origin of the Superhero: The Origin and Evolution of the Superhero Genre in America.* Diss. Michigan State U., 2002. Ann Arbor: UMI, 2003. 3092128. Print.

———. *Superhero: The Secret Origin of a Genre.* Austin, TX: MonkeyBrain Books, 2006. Print.

Cooke, Jon B. "Jack Kirby's X-Files" [chronology of Kirby's work at DC, 1970–76, based on production numbers]. *The Jack Kirby Collector* 17 (Nov. 1997): 48–52. Print.

———. "The Story Behind Sky Masters." *The Jack Kirby Collector* 15 (Apr. 1997): 21–25. Print.

Crippen, Tom. "The Post-Human Review." *The Comics Journal* 281 (Feb. 2007): 132–34. Print.

Daniels, Les. *DC Comics: Sixty Years of the World's Favorite Comic Book Heroes.* Boston: Little, Brown, 1995. Print.

———. *Marvel: Five Fabulous Decades of the World's Greatest Comics.* New York: Abrams, 1991. Print.

Däniken, Erich von. *Chariots of the Gods?: Unsolved Mysteries of the Past.* 1968. Trans. Michael Heron. New York: Putnam, 1970. Print.

De Haven, Tom. *Our Hero: Superman on Earth.* New Haven: Yale UP, 2010. Print.

Dean, Michael. "Kirby and Goliath: The Fight for Jack Kirby's Marvel Artwork: An Overview." George 88–95. Print.

DeFalco, Tom, ed. *Comics Creators on Fantastic Four.* London: Titan Books, 2005. Print.

DeMatteis, J. M., and Paris Cullins, et al. *Forever People.* 4 issues. New York: DC Comics, 1988. Print.

Derrida, Jacques. "Differance." *Speech and Phenomena, and Other Essays on Husserl's Theory of Signs.* Trans. and intro. David B. Allison. Evanston, IL: Northwestern UP, 1973. 129–160. Print.

Devitt, Amy J. "Integrating Rhetorical and Literary Theories of Genre." *College English* 62.6 (July 2000): 696–718. Print.

Drucker, Johanna. *The Visible Word: Experimental Typography and Modern Art, 1909–1923.* Chicago: U of Chicago P, 1994. Print.

Eagleton, Terry. *The Ideology of the Aesthetic.* Oxford: Blackwell, 1990. Print.

Eco, Umberto. *The Limits of Interpretation.* Bloomington, IN: Indiana UP, 1990. Print.

———. "The Myth of Superman" ["Il mito di Superman e la dissoluzione del tempo"]. 1962. Rev. version trans. Natalie Chilton. *Diacritics* 2.1 (1972): 14–22. Print.

Eisner, Will, ed. *Will Eisner's Shop Talk.* Ed. Diana Schutz with Denis Kitchen. Milwaukie, OR: Dark Horse Comics, 2001. Print.

Ekstrom, Steve. "Jim Starlin: Ferryman of the New Gods." *Newsarama.com.* 11 July 2007. Web. 29 July 2010.

Elkins, James. *On Pictures and the Words That Fail Them.* Cambridge: Cambridge UP, 1998. Print.

Ellis, Warren, and John Cassaday. *Planetary.* With Laura (DePuy) Martin. 27 issues. 1999–2009. Rpt. in 4 vols. La Jolla, CA: WildStorm, 2000–2010. Print.

Evanier, Mark. Afterword. *Jack Kirby's Fourth World Omnibus Volume One.* By Jack Kirby et al. New York: DC Comics, 2007. 388–96. Print.

———. Introduction. *Jack Kirby's The Demon.* By Jack Kirby and Mike Royer. New York: DC Comics, 2008. 3–5. Print.

———. "Jack F.A.Q.s." *The Jack Kirby Collector* 37 (Winter 2003): 44–49. Print.

———. *Kirby: King of Comics.* New York: Abrams, 2008. Print.

———. "Shel Dorf, R.I.P." *NEWS from me.* Blog. 3 Nov. 2009. Web. 30 July 2010.

———. "The Unknown Kirby." Interview by Jon B. Cooke. *Comic Book Artist Special Edition* 1 (1999): 2–17. Print.

"The Evolution of Kirby's Style." *The Jack Kirby Collector* 37 (Winter 2003): 6–23. Print.

Ferguson, Frances. *Solitude and the Sublime: Romanticism and the Aesthetics of Individuation.* New York: Routledge, 1992. Print.

Feyerabend, Paul. *Against Method: Outline of an Anarchistic Theory of Knowledge.* 3rd ed. London: Verso, 1993. Print.

Fischer, Craig. "Fantastic Fascism? Jack Kirby, Nazi Aesthetics, and Klaus Theweleit's *Male Fantasies.*" *International Journal of Comic Art* 5.1 (Spring 2003): 334–54. Print.

———. "Serialism and the Single Superhero: Story, Plot and Soap Opera Aesthetics in the Silver Age Lee-Kirby *Captain America* Stories." *The Narrative Art of Jack Kirby* [panel]. Comic Arts Conference, Comic-Con International 2003. San Diego, CA. 19 July 2003.

———. "Unmasking the Villain: Notes on Ditko, Kirby and Marvel-Style Plotting." *The Comics Journal* #258 (Feb. 2004): 97–100. Print.

Freedland, Nat. "Super-Heroes with Super Problems." *New York Herald Tribune* 9 Jan. 1966, Sunday Magazine section. Rpt. in *The Jack Kirby Collector* 18 (Jan. 1998): 26–29. Print.

Fresnault-Deruelle, Pierre. "Semiotic Approaches to Figurative Narration." *The Semiotic Web 1989*. Ed. Thomas A. Sebeok, Donna Jean Umiker-Sebeok, and Evan P. Young. Berlin: Mouton de Gruyter, 1990. 587–603. Print.

Friedman, Bruce Jay. "Even the Rhinos Were Nymphos." *Even the Rhinos Were Nymphos: Best Nonfiction*. Chicago: U of Chicago P, 2000. 15–26. Print.

Fyfe, W. Hamilton, trans., revised by Donald Russell. *On the Sublime*. By Longinus. In Aristotle, *Poetics*. Loeb Classical Library 199. Cambridge, MA: Harvard UP, 1995. 143–307. Print.

Gabilliet, Jean-Paul. *Of Comics and Men: A Cultural History of American Comic Books*. Trans. Bart Beaty and Nick Nguyen. Jackson: UP of Mississippi, 2010. Print. Trans. of *Des Comics et des hommes: Histoire culturelle des comic books aux Éstats-Unis*. Nantes, Fr: Editions du Temps, 2005.

Gaiman, Neil, and John Romita, Jr., et al. *The Eternals*. 7 issues. 2006–2007. Rpt. New York: Marvel, 2008. Print.

Gartland, Mike. "A Failure to Communicate: Part One." *The Jack Kirby Collector* 21 (Oct. 1998): 36–39. Print.

———. "A Failure to Communicate: Part Two." *The Jack Kirby Collector* 22 (Dec. 1998): 36–43. Print.

———. "A Failure to Communicate: Part Three: Rough Surfing." *The Jack Kirby Collector* 23 (Feb. 1999): 36–41. Print.

———. "A Failure to Communicate: Part Four: The Last Straw?" *The Jack Kirby Collector* 24 (Apr. 1999): 12–17. Print.

———. "A Failure to Communicate: Part Six: The Best Laid (Out) Plans . . ." *The Jack Kirby Collector* 29 (Aug. 2000): 55–62. Print.

George, Milo, ed. *The Comics Journal Library, Volume One: Jack Kirby*. Seattle: Fantagraphics, 2002. Print.

Gerber, Steve. "The Other Duck Man." Interview by John Morrow. *The Jack Kirby Collector* 10 (Apr. 1996): 38–41. Print.

Gilbert, James. *A Cycle of Outrage: America's Reaction to the Juvenile Delinquent in the 1950s*. New York: Oxford UP, 1986. Print.

Gillis, Peter, Sal Buscema, and Walter Simonson, et al. *The Eternals*. 12 issues. New York: Marvel, 1985–86. Print.

Goldberg, Jay. "King Kirby and the Amazin' Terminatin' Copyrights: Who Will Prevail?!?". *American University Intellectual Property Brief* 2.1 (Summer 2010): 10–16. PDF edition. Web. 15 Nov. 2010.

Gombrich, E. H. *Art and Illusion: A Study in the Psychology of Pictorial Representation*. 1960. 4th ed. London: Phaidon, 1972. Print.

———. "Image and Code: Scope and Limits of Conventionalism in Pictorial Representation." *Image and Code*. Ed. Wendy Steiner. Ann Arbor: U of Michigan, 1981. 10–42. Print.

Goodman, Nelson. *Languages of Art: An Approach to a Theory of Symbols*. 2nd ed. Indianapolis: Hackett, 1976.

Goulart, Ron. *The Adventurous Decade: Comic Strips in the Thirties*. Rev. ed. Neshannock, PA: Hermes, 2005. Print.

————. *Over 50 Years of American Comic Books.* Lincolnwood, IL: Mallard, 1991. Print.

Groensteen, Thierry. "A Few Words about *The System of Comics* and More . . ." *European Comic Art* 1.1 (Spring 2008): 87–93. Print.

————. *The System of Comics.* Trans. Bart Beaty and Nick Nguyen. Jackson: UP of Mississippi, 2007. Trans. of *Système de la bande dessinée.* Paris: Presses universitaires de France, 1999. Print.

Gruenwald, Mark. "Mark's Remarks" [column]. *Marvel Age* #71. New York: Marvel, Feb. 1989. 10–11. Print.

Gruenwald, Mark, and Ralph Machio, et al. *Thor* #300. New York: Marvel, Oct. 1980. Print.

Hajdu, David. *The Ten-Cent Plague: The Great Comic-Book Scare and How It Changed America.* New York: Farrar, 2008. Print.

Harrigan, Pat, and Noah Wardrip-Fruin, eds. *Third Person: Authoring and Exploring Vast Narratives.* Cambridge, MA: MIT, 2009. Print.

Harryhausen, Ray, assoc. prod. and effects creator. *Jason and the Argonauts.* Dir. Don Chaffey. Prod. Charles H. Schneer. Columbia, 1963.

Harvey, Doug. "Skipping Formalities: *POW!* Et al." *Art Issues* 61 (Jan.–Feb. 2000): 16–19. Print.

Harvey, R. C. *The Art of the Comic Book: An Aesthetic History.* Jackson: UP of Mississippi, 1996. Print.

————. *The Art of the Funnies: An Aesthetic History.* Jackson: UP of Mississippi, 1994. Print.

Haspiel, Dean. "Jack Kirby Makes Me Stupid." *Graphic NYC: Graphic Novel and Comic Book Creators in New York City.* Blog. 9 Feb. 2010. Web. 29 July 2010.

Hatfield, Charles. *Alternative Comics: An Emerging Literature.* Jackson: UP of Mississippi, 2005. Print.

Heer, Jeet. "Comics and Class: Labour Day Notes." *Comics Comics.* Blog. 1 Sept. 2010. Web. 8 Nov. 2010.

Heintjes, Tom. "Newswatch: Where did all the art go? Marvel staffer reveals: in 1980, Marvel had over 35,000 pages of original art in its vaults." *The Comics Journal* 105 (Feb. 1986): 16–22. Print.

"Held Hostage: The Art That Changed the Face of Comics." Special section devoted to Kirby's dispute with Marvel [much is rpt. in George]. *The Comics Journal* 105 (Feb. 1986): 51–74. Print.

Hogarth, Burne. Interview by Gary Groth. Part I. *The Comics Journal* 166 (Feb. 1994): 60–104. Print.

Hyde, David. "Warner Bros. Creates DC Entertainment." *DC Universe: The Source.* 9 Sept. 2009. Web. 29 July 2010.

Infantino, Carmine. "Director Comments." Interview by Jon B. Cooke. *Comic Book Artist* 1 (Spring 1998): 6–14. Print.

————. "The Incredible Infantino Interview." Interview by Jim Amash. *The Jack Kirby Collector* 34 (March 2002): 16–20. Print.

Jones, Gerard. *Men of Tomorrow: Geeks, Gangsters, and the Birth of the Comic Book.* New York: Basic Books, 2004. Print.

Kane, Gil. "Gil Kane on Kirby." *The Jack Kirby Collector* 19 (Apr. 1998): 4a–5a. Print. Rpt. of excerpts from "Bypassing the Real for the Ideal." *The Harvard Journal of Pictorial Fiction* (Spring 1974): 16–23.

———. "Gil Kane: Reflections on 50 Years in Comics by the Outspoken Critic, Zestful Raconteur, and Legendary Artist." Interview by Gary Groth, Part I. *The Comics Journal* 186 (Apr. 1996): 46–109. Print.

———. Interview by Jon B. Cooke. *The Jack Kirby Collector* 21 (Oct. 1998): 40–47.

———. Interview by Will Eisner. Eisner, 180–91. Print.

———. "Kane on Savage." Interview by Gary Groth and Mike Catron. *Gil Kane's Savage*. Stamford, CT: Fantagraphics, 1982. 48–54. Print.

Kane, Gil, Wendy Pini, and Kenneth Smith. "Peer Pressure." Panel moderated by Gary Groth. Dallas Fantasy Fair. 6 July 1985. In "Held Hostage" 69–74. Rpt. in George 109–14. Print.

Kannenberg, Gene, Jr. "Graphic Text, Graphic Context: Interpreting Custom Fonts and Hands in Contemporary Comics." *Illuminating Letters: Typography and Literary Interpretation*. Ed. Paul C. Gutjahr and Megan L. Benton. Amherst: U of Massachusetts P, 2001. 165–92. Print.

Kant, Immanuel. *Critique of the Power of Judgment*. Ed. Paul Guyer. Trans. Paul Guyer and Eric Matthews. The Cambridge Edition of the Works of Immanuel Kant. Cambridge: Cambridge UP, 2000. Print.

Kasson, John. *Civilizing the Machine: Technology and Republican Values in America, 1776–1900*. New York: Grossman, 1976. Print.

Kelly, Benjamin. "Deviant ancient histories: Dan Brown, Erich von Däniken and the sociology of historical polemic." *Rethinking History* 12.3 (Sept. 2008): 361–82. Print.

Kidd, Kenneth B. *Making American Boys: Boyology and the Feral Tale*. Minneapolis: U of Minnesota P, 2004. Print.

Kirby, Jack. "Kirby Speaks!" Interview. *FOOM Magazine* 11 (Sept. 1975): 4–7. Print.

———. Interview by Will Eisner. Eisner, 192–223. Print.

Kirby, Jack, and Roz Kirby. Interview by Gary Groth. *The Comics Journal* 134 (Feb. 1990): 57–99. Rpt. in George 18–49. Print.

———. Interview by Juanie Lane and Britt Wisenbaker for Pepperdine University's student magazine *Oasis*. 1984. Rpt. in *The Jack Kirby Collector* 16 (July 1997): 16–23. Print.

Kolkman, Richard, comp. *Jack Kirby Checklist, Gold Edition*. Rev. ed. Raleigh, NC: TwoMorrows, 2008. Print.

Krentz, Jayne Ann. "Trying to Tame the Romance: Critics and Correctness." *Dangerous Men and Adventurous Women: Romance Writers on the Appeal of the Romance*. Ed. Jayne Ann Krentz. Philadelphia: U of Pennsylvania P, 1992. 107–114. Print.

Kubrick, Stanley, dir. *2001: A Space Odyssey*. Screenplay by Stanley Kubrick and Arthur C. Clarke. MGM, 1968.

Lammers, Thomas G. "Atlas Shrugged: A Detailed Look at the 1957 'Atlas Implosion' and Its Effects on Comics." *Alter Ego* Vol. 3, No. 49 (June 2005): 45–67. Print.

Lee, Stan. *Son of Origins of Marvel Comics*. New York: Simon and Schuster, 1975. Print.

Lee, Stan, and George Mair. *Excelsior!: The Amazing Life of Stan Lee*. New York: Fireside, 2002. Print.

Legman, Gershon. *Love and Death*. New York: Breaking Point, 1949. Print.

Lethem, Jonathan. "The Return of the King, or, Identifying with Your Parents." *Give Our Regards to the Atomsmashers!: Writers on Comics*. Ed. Sean Howe. New York, Pantheon: 2004. 2–22. Print.

Levin, Bob. "*The Someday Funnies*: How Michel Choquette (Almost) Assembled the Most Stupendous Comic Book in the World." *The Comics Journal* 299 (Aug. 2009): 30–81. Print.

Levitz, Paul. "Earth After Disaster!: Chapter Two in the Continuing Guide to Confusing Continuity." *The Amazing World of DC Comics* 12 (July 1976): 8–13. Print.

Levitz, Paul, and Keith Giffen, et al. *The Legion of Super-Heroes: The Great Darkness Saga*. 5 issues. 1982. Rpt. New York: DC Comics, 1989. Print.

Lovecraft, H. P. "Supernatural Horror in Literature." 1927. Rpt. in *At the Mountains of Madness: The Definitive Edition*. By H. P. Lovecraft. New York: Modern Library, 2005. Print.

Madden, Matt. *99 Ways to Tell a Story: Exercises in Style*. New York: Chamberlain Bros., 2005. Print.

Marion, Philipe. *Traces en cases: Travail graphique, figuration narrative et participation du lecteur: essai sur la bande dessinée*. Louvain-la-Neuve, Belg.: Académia, 1993. Print.

Marx, Leo. *The Machine in the Garden: Technology and the Pastoral Ideal in America*. 1964. 35th anniversary ed. New York: Oxford UP, 2000. Print.

McCloskey, Mary A. *Kant's Aesthetic*. Albany: State U of New York P, 1987. Print.

McCloud, Scott. *Understanding Comics*. Northampton, MA: Tundra, 1993. Print.

———. "I Didn't Say That." Reply to letter of Jeff Miller. *The Comics Journal* 207 (Sept. 1998): 8. Print.

McLaughlin, Jeff, ed. *Stan Lee: Conversations*. Jackson: UP of Mississippi, 2007. Print.

McLuhan, Marshall. *The Mechanical Bride: Folklore of Industrial Man*. New York: Vanguard, 1951. Print.

Medhurst, Andy. "Batman, Deviance and Camp." Pearson and Uricchio 149–63. Print.

Mendryk, Harry. *Simon and Kirby*. Blog. The Jack Kirby Museum and Research Center. Mar. 2006–. Web. 29 July 2010.

———. "A Final Transition." *Simon and Kirby*. 21 Aug. 2010. Web. 8 Nov. 2010.

———. "Inking Glossary." *Simon and Kirby*. [June 2007.] Web. 29 July 2010.

———. "Now for a Not So Little Romance." *Simon and Kirby*. 19 Mar. 2006. Web. 29 July 2010.

Merrell, Floyd. *Peirce, Signs, and Meaning*. Toronto: U of Toronto, 1997. Print.

———. *Semiosis in the Postmodern Age*. West Lafayette, IN: Purdue UP, 1995. Print.

Miller, Jeff. "Hardly Bullshit." Letter. *The Comics Journal* 206 (Aug. 1998): 5+. Print.

Miller, Perry. *The Life of the Mind in America, from the Revolution to the Civil War*. New York: Harcourt, 1965. Print.

Misak, Cheryl, ed. *The Cambridge Companion to Peirce*. Cambridge: Cambridge UP, 2004. Print.

Mitchell, W. J. T. *Iconology: Image, Text, Ideology*. Chicago: U of Chicago P, 1986. Print.

Morgan, Harry. "Graphic Shorthand: From Caricature to Narratology in Twentieth-Century *Bande dessinée* and Comics." Trans. Laurence Grove. *European Comic Art* 2.1 (Spring 2009): 21–39. Print.

Morgan, Harry, and Manuel Hirtz. *Les Apocalypses de Jack Kirby*. Lyon, France: les moutons électriques, 2009. Print.

Morrison, Grant. Introduction. *Jack Kirby's Fourth World Omnibus Volume One*. By Jack Kirby et al. New York: DC Comics, 2007. 7–8. Print.

Morrison, Grant, and J. G. Jones, et al. *Final Crisis.* 7 issues. 2008–09. Rpt. New York: DC Comics, 2009. Print.

Morrow, John. "Art vs. Commerce." *The Jack Kirby Collector* 24 (Apr. 1999): 28–31. Print.

———. "The Captain Victory Connection." *The Jack Kirby Collector* 6 (July 1995): 15. Print.

———, ed. *The Collected Jack Kirby Collector.* 7 vols. Raleigh, NC: TwoMorrows, 1997–2009. Print.

———. "Kirby on Film." *The Jack Kirby Collector* 44 (Fall 2005): 2. Print.

———, comp. "A Major Production." *The Jack Kirby Collector* 46 (Summer 2006): 39–47. Print.

Murray, Chris. "*Pop*aganda: Superhero Comics and Propaganda in World War Two." *Comics & Culture: Analytical and Theoretical Approaches to Comics.* Ed. Anne Magnussen and Hans-Christian Christiansen. Copenhagen: Museum Tusculanum / U of Copenhagen, 2000. 141–55. Print.

Murray, Will. "A Visit to the Fantastic 4 Set." *The Jack Kirby Collector* 42 (Spring 2005): 31–33. Print.

Nama, Adilifu. "Brave black worlds: black superheroes as science fiction ciphers." *African Identities* 7.2 (May 2009): 133–44. Print.

Nevins, Mark David. "Mythology and Superheroes." Rev. of Reynolds. *Inks: Cartoon and Comic Art Studies* 3.3 (Nov. 1996): 24–30. Print.

Newgarden, Mark. "Love's Savage Fury." *We All Die Alone: A Collection of Cartoons and Jokes.* Ed. Dan Nadel. Seattle: Fantagraphics, 2006. 162-66. Print.

Nyberg, Amy Kiste. *Seal of Approval: The History of the Comics Code.* Jackson: UP of Mississippi, 1998. Print.

Nye, David. *American Technological Sublime.* Cambridge, MA: MIT, 1994. Print.

Ong, Walter. "Comics and the Superstate: Glimpses Down the Back Alleys of the Mind." *Arizona Quarterly* 1.3 (1945): 34–48. Print.

Parsons, Patrick. "Batman and His Audience: The Dialectic of Culture." Pearson and Uricchio 66–89. Print.

Pearson, Roberta E., and William Uricchio, eds. *The Many Lives of the Batman: Critical Approaches to a Superhero and His Media.* New York: Routledge; London: BFI, 1991. Print.

Peeters, Benoît. "Four Conceptions of the Page." Trans. Jesse Cohn. *ImageTexT: Interdisciplinary Comics Studies* 3.3 (2007). Web. 29 July 2010. Trans. excerpt from *Case, planche, récit: lire la bande dessinée.* Paris: Casterman, 1998.

Peirce, Charles Sanders. *The Essential Peirce: Selected Philosophical Writings.* Vol. 1 (1867–1893). Ed. Nathan Houser and Christian Kloesel. Bloomington, IN: Indiana UP, 1992. Print.

———. *The Essential Peirce: Selected Philosophical Writings.* Vol. 2 (1893–1913). Ed. The Peirce Edition Project. Bloomington: Indiana UP, 1998. Print.

———. *Peirce on Signs: Writings on Semiotic.* Ed. James Hoopes. Chapel Hill: U of North Carolina P, 1991. Print.

———. *Writings of Charles S. Peirce: A Chronological Edition.* 7 vols. to date. Bloomington: Indiana UP, 1982–. Print.

The Peirce Edition Project. Indiana University-Purdue University Indianapolis. 6 Jan. 2011. Web. 12 Jan. 2011.

Pharies, David A. *Charles S. Peirce and the Linguistic Sign*. Amsterdam; Philadelphia: John Benjamins Pub. Co., 1985. Print.

Phelps, Donald. *Reading the Funnies: Essays on Comic Strips*. Seattle: Fantagraphics, 2001. Print.

Raphael, Jordan, and Tom Spurgeon. *Stan Lee and the Rise and Fall of the American Comic Book*. Chicago: Chicago Review P, 2003. Print.

Raviv, Dan. *Comic Wars: How Two Tycoons Battled over the Marvel Comics Empire—And Both Lost*. New York: Broadway, 2002. Print.

Reinders, Eric. "Kirbytech!" *The Jack Kirby Collector* 38 (Spring 2003): 65. Print.

Reinl, Harald, dir. *Erinnerungen an die Zukunft* [*Chariots of the Gods*]. Terra-Filmkunst, 1970.

Reynolds, Richard. *Superheroes: A Modern Mythology*. London: B. T. Batsford, 1992. Rpt. Jackson: UP of Mississippi, 1994. Print.

Ro, Ronin. *Tales to Astonish: Jack Kirby, Stan Lee, and the American Comic Book Revolution*. New York: Bloomsbury, 2004. Print.

Roberson, Chris. "Mark Gruenwald, the father of modern superhero comics." *The Myriad Worlds of Chris Roberson*. Blog. 2 July 2007. Web. 29 July 2010.

Roberts, Adam. *The History of Science Fiction*. Basingstoke, UK: Palgrave Macmillan, 2007. Print.

Rogers, Mark C. "Beyond Bang! Pow! Zap!: Genre and the Evolution of the American Comic Book Industry." Diss. U of Michigan, 1997. Ann Arbor: UMI, 1997. 9732173. Print.

Ross, Alex, Jim Krueger, John Paul Leon, and Bill Reinhold, et al. *Earth X*. 14 issues. 1999–2000. Rpt. New York: Marvel, 2000. Print.

Royer, Mike. "A Brush with Mike Royer—Part 1." Interview by John Morrow. *The Jack Kirby Collector* 4 (Mar. 1995): 10–12. Print.

———. "A Brush with Mike Royer—Part 2." Interview by John Morrow. *The Jack Kirby Collector* 6 (July 1995): 12–14. Print.

———. "Fastest Inker in the West: Mike Royer." Interview by Jim Amash. *The Jack Kirby Collector* 37 (Winter 2003): 24–43. Print.

Savage, William W., Jr. *Commies, Cowboys, and Jungle Queens: Comic Books and America, 1945–1954*. Rev. ed. Hanover, NH: Wesleyan UP, 1998. Print.

Schumer, Arlen. *The Silver Age of Comic Book Art*. Portland, OR: Collectors P, 2003. Print.

Schwartz, Julius. *Man of Two Worlds: My Life in Science Fiction and Comics*. With Brian M. Thomsen. New York: Harper, 2000. Print.

Short, T. L. "The Development of Peirce's Theory of Signs." Misak 214–240. Print.

Simon, Joe. "More Than Your Average Joe." Panel moderated by Mark Evanier. Comic-Con International 1998. San Diego, CA. *The Jack Kirby Collector* 25 (Aug. 1999): 33–49. Print.

———. "Simon Says!" Interview by Jim Amash. *Alter Ego* Vol. 3, No. 76 (Mar. 2008): 5–52. Print.

Simon, Joe, with Jim Simon. *The Comic Book Makers*. Rev. ed. Lebanon, NJ: Vanguard, 2003. Print.

Simon, Joe, and Jack Kirby, et al. *Real Love: The Best of the Simon and Kirby Romance Comics: 1940s-1950s.* Ed. and intro. Richard Howell. Forestville, CA: Eclipse Books, 1988. Print.

———. *The Best of Simon and Kirby.* Ed. Steve Saffel. Art restoration by Harry Mendryk. London: Titan Books, 2009. Print.

Simonson, Walter. *Fantastic Four #352–354.* New York: Marvel, May–July 1991. Print.

———. Introduction. *Jack Kirby's Fourth World Omnibus Volume Two.* By Jack Kirby et al. New York: DC Comics, 2007. 7–11. Print.

Sinnott, Joe. "No Ordinary Joe: Mr. Sinnott Speaks." Interview by Jim Amash. *The Jack Kirby Collector* 38 (Spring 2003): 6–21. Print.

———. Interview by John Morrow. *The Jack Kirby Collector* 9 (Feb. 1996): 24–33. Print.

Spiegelman, Art. Interview by Gary Groth, Part II. *The Comics Journal* 181 (Oct. 1995): 97–139. Print.

Spurgeon, Tom. "The Eternals #4." *The Comics Reporter.* Blog. 13 Jan. 2009. Web. 30 July 2010.

Starlin, Jim. *The Death of the New Gods.* With Matt Banning et al. 8 issues. 2007–08. Rpt. New York: DC Comics, 2008. Print.

Starlin, Jim, and Mike Mignola, et al. *Cosmic Odyssey.* 4 issues. 1988–89. Rpt. New York: DC Comics, 1992. Print.

Steiner, Wendy. *Venus in Exile: The Rejection of Beauty in Twentieth-Century Art.* New York: Free Press, 2001. Print.

Steranko, Jim. "Inking the King!" *The Jack Kirby Collector* 11 (July 1996): 3–4. Print.

———. "The Man Who Was the King." *Hogan's Alley* 1 (Fall 1994). Rpt. in *The Jack Kirby Collector* 8 (Jan. 1996): 4–7. Print.

———. *The Steranko History of Comics*, Vol. 1. Reading, PA: Supergraphics, 1970. Print.

Story, Ronald. *The Space-Gods Revealed: A Close Look at the Theories of Erich von Däniken.* New York: Harper, 1976. Print.

Stratton, Jerry. "San Diego Report: The Comic Arts Conference." rec.art.comics.misc. [Usenet newsgroup]. 24 Aug. 1993. Web. Accessed through Google Groups, 10 January 2011.

Sturm, James, and Guy Davis, et al. *The Fantastic Four: Unstable Molecules.* New York: Marvel, 2003. Print.

*Superman: The Amazing Transformations of Jimmy Olsen.* New York: DC Comics, 2007. Print.

*Superman: The Animated Series.* Warner, 1996–2000.

Theakston, Greg. "The Birth of Spiderman [*sic*]." *Pure Images* Vol. 3, No. 1. New York: Pure Imagination, 1990. N. pag. Print.

———, ed. *The Complete Jack Kirby, Volume One: 1917–1940.* By Jack Kirby. Historical text by Theakston. New York: Pure Imagination, 1997. Print.

———, ed. *The Complete Jack Kirby, 1940–1941.* By Jack Kirby. Historical text by Theakston. New York: Pure Imagination, 1997. Print.

———, comp. *The Jack Kirby Treasury, Vol. 1: 1917–1948.* New York: Pure Imagination, 1982. Print.

———, comp. *The Jack Kirby Treasury, Vol. 2: 1948–1960*. Forestville, CA: Eclipse, 1991. Print.

Thomas, Roy. "A Fantastic First! The Creation of the Fantastic Four—and Beyond!" *Alter Ego* Vol. 2, No. 2 (Summer 1998): 4–9. Published inverted with *Comic Book Artist #2*. Print.

———. Interview by Jim Amash. *The Jack Kirby Collector* 18 (Jan. 1998): 17–25. Print.

———, et al. *Thor #283–91*. 1979–80. Rpt. in *The Eternals Saga*. New York: Marvel, 2006. Print.

Toole, Douglas. "Post-Kirby Kirby." *The Jack Kirby Collector* 46 (Summer 2006): 67–75. Print.

*Ultimate Fantastic Four.* 60 issues. 2004–09. Rpt. in 12 vols. New York: Marvel, 2004–09.

Vadeboncoeur, Jim. "The Great Atlas Implosion." Based on research by Brad Elliott. *The Jack Kirby Collector* 18 (Jan. 1998): 4–7. Print.

Vassallo, Michael J. "What If . . . Joe Maneely Had Lived and Drawn in the Marvel Age of Comics?" *Alter Ego* Vol. 3, No. 28 (Sept. 2003): 3–41. Print.

Wells, Earl. "Once and for All, Who Was the Author of Marvel?" *The Comics Journal* 181 (Oct. 1995): 70–78. Rpt. in George 74–87. Print.

Wertham, Fredric. *Seduction of the Innocent*. New York: Rinehart, 1954. Print.

White, Stephen K. *Edmund Burke: Modernity, Politics, and Aesthetics*. Thousand Oaks, CA: Sage, 1994. Print.

Williamson, Catherine. "'Draped Crusaders': Disrobing Gender in *The Mark of Zorro*." *Cinema Studies* 36.2 (Winter 1997): 3–16. Print.

Witek, Joseph. "The Arrow and the Grid." *A Comics Studies Reader*. Ed. Jeet Heer and Kent Worcester. Jackson: UP of Mississippi, 2009. 149–56. Print.

Woo, Benjamin. "An Age-Old Problem: Problematics of Comic Book Historiography." *International Journal of Comic Art* 10.1 (Spring 2008): 268–79. Print.

Worcester, Kent. "Superman, Philip Wylie & the New Deal." *Comics Forum* 1.6 (Spring/ Summer 1994): 26–31. Print.

Wright, Bradford. "From Social Consciousness to Cosmic Awareness: Superhero Comic Books and the Culture of Self-Interrogation, 1968–1975." *English Language Notes* 46.2 (Fall/Winter 2008): 155–74. Print.

Wylie, Philip. *Gladiator*. New York: Knopf, 1930. Print.

Wyman, Ray, Jr. *The Art of Jack Kirby*. With Catherine Hohlfeld and Robert C. Crane. Orange, CA: Blue Rose Press, 1992. Print.

Zelazny, Roger. *Creatures of Light and Darkness*. New York: Avon, 1969. Print.

———. *Lord of Light*. New York: Avon, 1967. Print.

# INDEX

Except as noted, the "series" listed here are periodical comic books. Kirby's signature works are listed under his name, except for a few major works that are indexed separately: *The Eternals*, *The Fantastic Four*, *The Fourth World*, *Thor*, and the short stories "The Pact" and "Himon." Cross-references are given as needed. Very few Kirby characters are indexed on their own, though Kirby created legions (indeed too many to count here). Regarding Marvel characters, references to which are scattered like confetti over this book, only passages that have something substantive to say about the characters or about Kirby's work are indexed.